WORK, MOBILITY, AND PARTICIPATION

ROBERT E. COLE

WORK, MOBILITY, AND PARTICIPATION

A COMPARATIVE STUDY OF
AMERICAN AND JAPANESE
INDUSTRY

University of California Press
Berkeley · Los Angeles · London

UNIVERSITY OF CALIFORNIA PRESS
BERKELEY AND LOS ANGELES, CALIFORNIA
UNIVERSITY OF CALIFORNIA PRESS, LTD.
LONDON, ENGLAND
COPYRIGHT © 1979 BY
THE REGENTS OF THE UNIVERSITY OF CALIFORNIA
FIRST PAPERBACK PRINTING 1980
ISBN 0-520-04204-2 PAPER
    0-520-03542-9 CLOTH
LIBRARY OF CONGRESS CATALOG CARD NUMBER: 77-80468
PRINTED IN THE UNITED STATES OF AMERICA

 2 3 4 5 6 7 8 9

To Kaite Shingo—
a very rare individual in any society

CONTENTS

ACKNOWLEDGMENTS

The research reported in this book has been supported by various sponsors, as noted in the respective chapters. I would be remiss however not to express my deep indebtedness to the Ford Foundation for awarding Gary Saxonhouse and myself a grant to support an Interdisciplinary (economics/sociology) Seminar on Japanese Economic Organizations (Grant No. 740-0124). The grant proved invaluable in providing the resources necessary to bring this book to fruition. In particular, the research seminar attended by sociology and economics graduate students served as a critical sounding board which greatly contributed to the revision process by which drafts were converted into final products.

I would also like to thank Joseph Gusfield, Hugh Patrick and Irwin Scheiner who served as reviewers for the University of California Press and in that capacity made many useful suggestions. The Center for Japanese Studies and the Horace Rackham School of Graduate Studies of the University of Michigan provided financial support for manuscript preparation.

Finally I would like to thank Cathy Hayashi who endured typing the manuscript not once but twice and the professional staff of the Center for Japanese Studies at the University of Michigan who endured my tenure as director. In order of irascibility they were: Lawrence Hjort, Mitzi Hu, Nancy Eisenbeiser, Elsie Orb, Harry Wilkinson and Marianne Rudnicki.

INTRODUCTION

As a consequence of my earlier research on Japanese industrial relations practices, I became convinced that a more systematic analysis of labor market behavior within a comparative framework was necessary. Only in this way would we be able to disentangle the complicated web spun of ideology, myth, and actual industrial relations practices, which characterized descriptions of Japanese labor market behavior. The assumptions, often only implicit, which American scholars bring to the study of Japanese practices, distort our descriptions and interpretations of both American and Japanese behavior.

Western scholarly research on the social organization of work in Japan has taken several directions in the postwar period. James Abegglen initiated the discussion with a strongly culturalist interpretation of the distinctiveness of Japanese values and forms of social organization. In his case study of selected large firms, Abegglen focused on the lifelong commitment of employees to the same firms based on a system of obligations shared with management and the *nenkō* system of reward by age and length of service. He assumed historical continuity in these practices (Abegglen 1958). Abegglen's research captured the attention of Western social scientists and was often cited as an example of the impact of culture on organizational behavior. Rohlen's (1974) carefully crafted study of a Japanese bank provides more finely grained evidence in support of Abegglen's thesis. He stresses the persistence of culturally infused meaning in the daily behavior patterns of bank employees.

A second thrust of postwar Western scholarship may be characterized as the convergence hypothesis. Here it was envisioned that the imperatives of an advanced industrial society would increasingly reduce the differences in social organization between Japan and the United States. It was commonly assumed that Japan, as it gradually achieved the status of an advanced industrial nation, would alter its organizational behavior in the direction of Western practices as characterized by social organization in the United States (e.g., Bennett 1967). The unique Japanese national identity was expected to fade as common solutions to problems of social organization came to prevail in all industrial societies.

The motor for these changes was generally thought to be the complex technological organization characteristic of societies achieving high levels of economic development. Marsh and Mannari (1976), using cross-sectional data, examine the organizational characteristics of three Japanese firms. They find considerable evidence to support the thesis that the organizational determinants of employee behavior are quite similar to what we would expect to find in the United States and thus they infer convergence.

Ronald Dore (1973) has now given a new twist to the convergence thesis in his book *British Factory–Japanese Factory*. Based on its late industrialization and some peculiar aspects of its national heritage, Japan is viewed as the model toward which British industrial relations practices are moving. In short there is convergence toward Japanese practices.

Finally there are those who would "split the differences" between the convergence and culturalist positions. In *Japanese Blue-Collar* (Cole 1971), I argued for using the concept of functional alternatives to allow the possibility that the Japanese have often evolved different structural arrangements to solve many of the common problems faced by all industrial societies.

All these approaches can be criticized on empirical grounds. We would note here, however, three basic methodological problems which flaw the research results upon which the various formulations are based. Some of the research reflects just one of these problems but much of it is flawed on all three dimensions. First, although most of the researchers make inferences about change over time, these are largely cross-sectional studies. We cannot assume convergence over time from similarity at one point in time. The tendency to make inferences about social change from data collected at one point in time is hardly unique to students of Japanese organizations. Indeed it has been a common practice among social scientists. Yet we are increasingly aware of the enormous pitfalls in making inferences over time from cross-sectional data. To take just one of the more serious problems, we are unable, using such procedures, to differentiate between the life-cycle effect and social change. Secondly, most of these theoretical positions rest ultimately on case studies of Japanese organizations. Although the best of these case studies are extremely important for elaborating the cultural meanings of specific organizational behavior and ferreting out data otherwise inaccessible to survey researchers, they are commonly carried out in a way that makes it difficult to generalize the findings. In addition, problems of replication make it difficult to have confidence in their validity.

A third problem in assessing the studies that have laid the basis for our understanding of Japanese organizational behavior is that although they make inferences about differences and similarities between the West and Japan, they are not commonly explicitly comparative. Worse still, they are often implicitly comparative, which is to say that they contain many unstated assumptions about the state of affairs in the nation being compared with Japan. Practices thought to exist in the United States are labelled as modern while practices in Japan are conceptualized as non-modern, with the process of change always operating toward the idealized Western pattern. For example, Marsh and Mannari (1976, p. 138) define as traditional the situation in which pay is determined by seniority;

pay determined predominantly by job classification (and performance) is defined as modern. The problem with such a conceptualization, however, is first that it idealizes the American pattern, ignoring the significant role of seniority in wage determination in the United States. Indeed, Rees and Schultz found seniority to be the most important single determinant of individual earnings in their study of the Chicago labor market. They conclude, "firms that pay high wages and advance wages substantially with length of service will have fewer quits and hence less need to train new workers" (Rees and Schultz 1970, p. 219). Moreover, to label wage determination by seniority in Japan as traditional is hard to justify. To be sure the seniority principle is consistent with the importance the Japanese attribute to age. Yet seniority reward systems are not necessarily inconsistent with economic rationality, assuming that an employer and/or employee invest in training and that rewarding seniority enables the employer and/or employee to collect the returns on their investment. The Japanese situation, in which the risk of the employee leaving the firm is minimized, serves as both cause and effect of the important role assigned to seniority in wage determination.

This study attempts to minimize these three methodological flaws, but not by reliance on one particular method. The data and analysis introduced represent an eclectic approach. The reader will be exposed to survey research, case study design, macro- and micro-historical analysis, cross-national comparisons, a theoretical essay, and policy prescriptions. The possibility of inconsistent and disconnected findings is the danger we run in using several research methodologies. I would suggest, however, that the benefits of the multi-method approach outweigh the costs. By checking the existence and consequences of labor market practices through a variety of data sources, we gain greatly increased leverage for our analysis. The deficiencies of any one of the strategies adopted are often compensated for by the efficiencies of others. The result is that the validity of the research is enhanced and the power of the generalizations strengthened. The multi-method approach is a sounder methodological principle than the mechanical reliance on one method that so often characterizes sociological analysis (see Jagdeo 1975, p. 136).

One last methodological problem needs to be mentioned and it is one that characterizes this study as well. Most studies by Western scholars have focused on male employees in large firms. For purposes of examining the alleged unique characteristics of the Japanese employment system this is understandable, since it is the male regular employees in major firms that experience the benefits of this system and typify unique Japanese practices. Yet it must be kept in mind that about 40 percent of the labor force is composed of females. Insofar as the benefits of the privileged male worker aristocrats come at the expense of female employees, temporary workers and those working in small firms, the experience of the latter is very much part of the Japanese employment system. Indeed evidence supporting the existence of a relationship will be presented. This study is a step forward in the sense that we do not confine our attention to male employees in large firms but also examine the experience of male employees in smaller firms. Yet in the case of the Detroit-Yokohama comparative survey, we were unable to sample female labor force participants because of the large costs associated with increasing sample size. With respect to the investigation of job re-design in the auto industry, females were not intentionally excluded from the sample. Management chooses not to employ female workers in production-line operations because of the prohibition on night work for females. It is our hope that the Detroit-Yokohama survey and the study of borrowing and job redesign will serve as benchmarks for future research involving female employees and other disadvantaged members of the Japanese labor force.

4

Quite apart from the methodological issues discussed above, evaluation of the historical evolution of the social organization of work and labor market behavior in Japan has focused on tradition. For Abegglen the system he described reflected the persistence of tradition, though in his first book he made no attempt to seriously investigate the matter. In his subsequent work he has downplayed the historical uniqueness of such practices as the permanent employment system (Abegglen 1973). Critics such as Marsh and Mannari (1976) reject assigning a special role to tradition and argue that an examination of contemporary practices reveals either an absence of traditional Japanese elements or a transition away from them. Their analysis is, however, subject to a number of weaknesses. Consider the previous example of categorizing pay by seniority as traditional and pay by job classification and performance as modern. This formulation simplistically dichotomizes a very complicated phenomenon, thereby losing sight of the subtle process of change. Perhaps the "real" distinction is between a job-based wage system and a potential-ability-based wage system. The one may be no less efficient than the other in allocating labor. Had Marsh and Mannari adopted this more "tolerant" framework, they might not have been so surprised by their "curious finding" that workers who favor the seniority system do not conceive of themselves as denying the importance of the "modern" criterion of ability as a determinant of pay (Marsh and Mannari 1976, p. 54). The Marsh and Mannari formulation is typical of that class of modernization theories dominant in the 1960s which assumed a bipolar characterization of the development process and which were based on ideal-typical categorizations of social organizational forms. Such formulations increasingly appear sterile and evidence little understanding of the dynamics of non-Western nations (Portes 1976, pp. 55–85).[1]

The problem of tradition is of general concern for those seeking to understand the dynamics of economic development and social change. For even were there a tendency toward convergence in economic and institutional forms, there is still the possibility that there are many paths leading to this outcome (cf. Kerr et al. 1960; Verba et al. 1970). One way to understand the different trajectories followed by nations in the course of industrialization is to see traditional values and practices as providing a resource base which constrains original and subsequent choices and solutions.

In the first chapter we examine the emergence of the permanent employment practice and attempt to account for its evolution as an interplay between the pragmatic decisions made by government, management, and workers, and the

1. For the general critique, see Armer and Schnaiberg (1972), Berger et al. (1975), Frank (1967), Gusfield (1966), Portes (1973; 1976), and Tipps (1973). For the Japan-specific critique see White (1974) and Dower (1975).

cultural and structural environment. This environment provided the "traditional" resources for the conscious institution-building involved in the formation of the Japanese employment system. A comparison with England and Germany is designed to clarify the extent to which tradition operated as a resource at the disposal of management. We find that whereas Japanese management had a more exclusive monopoly on the deployment of traditional values and practices, the English employers had to compete more evenly with employees, while the German case represents a middle position. Throughout the analysis we continually ask the question, who is in a position to mobilize tradition and for what purposes? The results of this analysis lead us to reject the position taken by Immanuel Wallerstein (1974, p. 356) that tradition "represents primarily the conservative instincts of some group threatened with declining social status." This is simply too narrow an approach to accommodate the empirical reality and, in particular, it does not allow for the integral relationship between tradition and institution building. The limitations that acceptance of Wallerstein's views would impose should be apparent in our own analysis. Finally we examine the claims made for the late-development hypothesis in explaining paths of economic development and social change. We conclude that its explanatory power is more limited than its proponents would suggest.

Chapters II and III examine the nature of the contemporary employment structure through a unique dataset of Detroit and Yokohama male respondents in the labor force in 1970–71. We gathered systematic and detailed information on jobs and job changes experienced by respondents in both cities using a survey research design. This procedure allowed us to use retrospective life history data to make inferences over time; the data are explicitly comparative and have the advantage of providing us with a relatively representative sample of labor force experiences. In addition to data on inter-firm job changing, we have also gathered information on intra-firm job changing. Although many scholars make inferences about the nature of intra-firm job changing, especially with regard to Japan, this is to our knowledge the first serious attempt to measure the incidence and character of such mobility across a broad segment of the labor force. Our analysis reveals striking similarities in the pattern of job change among the labor forces in the two cities. The determinants of job changing also appear to be similar. This is reassuring for those of us who seek to develop generalizations about job mobility and labor market behavior. Although the *pattern* of job changing seems to be quite similar in the two cities, the *volume* of inter-firm and intra-firm job changing among Yokohama respondents is only about half that of Detroit respondents. These differences persist after controlling for the relevant variables.

In Chapter IV we attempt to account for the differences in volume of inter-firm and intra-firm mobility among respondents in the two cities. Our account involves an examination of the historical development of job structures in Japan and the United States in the context of the scientific management movement in the two countries. This leads us to question the conventional wisdom that jobs and job structures are simply a response to technological imperatives. Rather, differing historical experiences exert a continuing impact on the evolution of job structures. This historical analysis should contribute to a demystification of the job creation process. To phrase the matter in these terms brings us back to the issue of tradition. The analysis of most American social scientists studying Japan seems to assume implicitly that Americans have no traditions—only the Japanese seem to have traditions, which will or will not be shed depending on the position of the analyst. Yet it is apparent from our analysis that the job structures which have evolved in the United States reflect the historical characteristics of American society during the early twentieth century and the particular form of capitalistic development America experienced. In the course of any nation's economic development, new traditions are created. National development produces tradition! (See Portes 1976, p. 73). To use the Japanese experience to more clearly understand the unique quality of American economic development and social change, and the role of tradition in these events, is a major goal of this book.

Chapter V introduces the following two chapters. Taken as a whole, these three chapters allow us to attack the issue of convergence from quite a different perspective. One of the commonly unspoken issues in the study of convergence involves its source. It is generally assumed that the complex technological organization characteristic of advanced industrial societies produces similar outcomes. But there is another explanation. Levy (1966, p. 744) stresses the importance of the diffusion resulting from cultural contact between relatively modernized and relatively unmodernized societies. Despite the many studies of Japanese development, we have remarkably little information on the process of borrowing either technological hardware or organizational software, and of the consequences of such borrowing. Nor do we know much about the interaction between technological determinants of convergence and diffusion of ideas and practices. Chapter V explores the postwar process of borrowing in personnel management practices, incentives for borrowing and the process of adapting foreign innovations to indigenous needs. The global movement for work redesign provides an excellent vehicle for the examination of international information flow relating to the borrowing and adaptation of this "organizational software." We pay particular attention to issues of quality control in industry and Japanese innovation in establishing quality-control circles within production workgroups as a means of solving quality-control problems. The Japanese appear very much attuned to the output of Western social science and quite innovative in adapting Western ideas and practices to their own needs. These chapters permit us to explore the nature and sources of convergence, but once again reveal not only convergence but continuing differences as the Japanese adapt Western ideas and practices to their own needs.

This issue of borrowing and diffusion is important from still another point of view. The reverse convergence thesis argued by Ronald Dore implies that we ought to learn from the Japanese. No longer is Japan to be a model for third world nations; now it is to serve as a model for other industrialized nations. The intellectual moorings of this reverse convergence position lie in the failure of the British economy in the postwar period. The use of Japan as a model of future development is based, however, more on wishful thinking than on solid analysis of evolutionary trends (Cole 1974). Nevertheless there are now a large number of writers in America advocating that we should learn from the Japanese. It has become a popular sport among American management specialists and journalists (e.g., Drucker 1971; Johnson and Ouchi 1974; Kraar 1975). Just as the difficulties of the British economy inspired Dore's analysis, so were the American views inspired by the sluggishness of the American economy and its persistent balance-of-payments problems in the early 1970s. The American version focused specifically on the potential for borrowing Japanese practices in eclectic fashion rather than on the analysis of evolutionary developments which informs Dore's study. Yet if borrowing from Japan is to produce similar outcomes in the West, we presumably require a much more systematic understanding of the social, economic, and political bases of Japanese practices and values than we now have. Our goal is to contribute to this understanding. Once we have such an understanding, it will clarify what we can learn from the Japanese. One way to illustrate this is to examine Japanese borrowing of American personnel management practices and the transformations which took place as they adapted these practices to their own environment.

Chapter VI deals with the practices of work design at Toyota Auto Body. The movement for worker participation in decision making has gained great momentum in Western Europe; it is also a subject of considerable discussion in the United States. Japanese practices are quite innovative in this area, yet not very well-known in the United States. The Japanese approach is characterized by management-initiated worker participation in shop floor decision making.

Chapter VII discusses the work-redesign movement in Japan and compares it with American, Yugoslavian, and Chinese practices and ideas on the subject. Particularly notable is the Japanese emphasis on career development even for industrial workers; such programs are commonly limited to management in the United States. Secondly, unlike the United States, the Japanese emphasize moving away from reliance on segregated units composed of university-trained experts to initiate and execute small-scale innovations and adjustments of work organization and technology. Instead Japanese management is exploring ways of harnessing worker initiatives to introduce changes in work and productive organization. The study of work redesign in Japan also provides an excellent opportunity to "test" conclusions arrived at from analysis of the Detroit-Yokohama data. A specific set of predictions are derived about Japanese job-redesign practices that should hold if the analysis of the survey data in Chapter IV is valid. By and large these predictions find support in the data presented in Chapter VII.

In Chapter VIII I examine the possible meanings of the Japanese work ethic viewed in comparative perspective. We do find evidence to suggest that there is a distinctive Japanese work ethic, though the differences lie along very specific dimensions. An analysis of the structural bases of dependency relationships is designed to clarify the authority relationships underlying the Japanese work ethic. The final chapter examines the potential for borrowing from the Japanese. The case of the Japanese work ethic shows the limitations of the borrowing process. Yet this is not to say that we cannot learn from the Japanese. Policies which unite personal and organizational goals, while recognizing the legitimacy of the former, seem to be a promising area for exploration. Finally I propose specific policies adapted from Japanese practices that might fruitfully be applied in an American context. These center on career enlargement and job security.

The problems dealt with in the various chapters can be summarized in some major themes. This book is about the similarities and differences in social structure and values between Japan and other nations—particularly the United States—and the changes these structures and values undergo over time. It is about the problematic issue of convergence. The approach taken here is quite critical of that class of modernization theories that concerns itself with the impact of economic change on social organization. The question is an important one and deserves continued attention, but a satisfactory answer requires that we go beyond ideal-type categorizations and examine the process of change over time in comparative perspective. We must do so, moreover, using categories that do not blind us to empirical processes.

It is not only American scholars who are rethinking the utility of past formulations based on what is loosely called modernization theory. Many Japanese scholars are reexamining their ideas on the potential for change in the Japanese system. Indeed, the thinking of Japanese and American intellectuals on this subject represents an interesting case of convergence in itself. In the post-World War II period, Japanese intellectuals generally condemned existing industrial relations practices as undemocratic and destined to change—generally in the direction of the West. Historically the Western model of industrial relations was held up as supplying that which was needed to make Japan a modern nation.

Recently, a subtle shift has taken place, whereby many Japanese intellectuals increasingly question the relevance of foreign models. Despite rapid industrialization the Japanese see that their practices continue to retain their distinctive character. In many respects they believe themselves to be no closer to Western practices than they were twenty years ago. They have come to understand that Western models as presented to the Japanese were often quite abstract and idealized and not necessarily suited to Japanese conditions, while the negative aspects of Western practices were often ignored. Koshiro (1975, pp. 80–86), for example, strongly criticizes those advocates of worker participation in management who talk glibly about importing Western European practices into Japan without considering Japanese conditions (see, for example, Tsuda 1975, pp. 4–17).

On another level, Japanese practices thought to be holdovers from the past, destined to disappear with further economic development, have suddenly been "discovered" in the West. A good example is that of the dual labor market, which deals with discrepancies between wages and working conditions experienced by employees in large-scale firms in the modern or primary sector and the inferior conditions experienced by employees in the secondary sector. As the wage gap between large and small firms in Japan diminished in the 1960s, many Japanese scholars predicted the demise of the dual labor market. In recent years, however, the situation seems to have stabilized with the relative wage gap holding constant (Japan Productivity Center 1976, p. 52). At the same time, Japanese scholars were mildly amused to learn that many American scholars had just discovered the applicability to the American situation of "dual labor market theory" and "segmented labor markets" (e.g., J. Cain 1976; Doeringer and Piore 1971).

Nakayama (1974, pp. 66–67; 1975, p. 197) maintains that Japan is entering a new era in which models no longer exist. Without such models to provide inspiration, Japanese management and labor must cautiously plot their own course. The potential danger he sees in such a situation is that it will encourage a narrow-minded parochialism, as management concentrates on the benefits of traditional values and practices. With labor going in a different direction, this might lead to a renewed cycle of labor-management conflict. Nakayama (1975, p. 201) points out that the Western European model for labor has largely been realized in terms of achieving equality in wage levels. In order to achieve this equality militant unions have argued for years that all traditionally Japanese elements, starting with the enterprise union, should be removed. The intense struggle for "democratization" focused on such matters. Yet somehow the unions have managed to achieve parity with the West without doing away with Japanese practices.

It is striking to see the shift in the intellectual positions of many Japanese scholars in response to the new situation in which Japan finds itself. Tsuda, who once (1959) predicted the dissolution of "feudal practices" such as permanent employment and the length-of-service reward system (*nenkō*), now writes books with titles like *Protecting Japanese-Style Management* (1976). At present he is adamantly opposed to the abandonment of permanent employment, citing such reasons as the aging of the Japanese population, the need to use older employees more efficiently, the lack of a national welfare system in Japan, and the contribution of permanent employment to management objectives, including low absenteeism and tardiness. The shifts in the positions of still other scholars are more subtle. Sumiya Mikio states that he never believed that *nenkō* and permanent employment would disappear. Although he did see them as characteristic of backward economies (*okureta kuni*), he thought that further economic development would change, though not destroy them.[2] In his more recent writings, however, Sumiya (1974) is more likely to emphasize that these practices have quite modern elements and are characteristics of late-developers. This reflects a considerably more "upbeat" view.[3] These shifts in academic positions coincide more recently with management's increasingly critical posture toward permanent employment and *nenkō* in an era of reduced economic growth rates and an aging labor force. It is not surprising to see Japanese scholars take the position that if management is against it, then it must be worth preserving.

The background for the emergence of these new world views both among American and Japanese scholars lies, of course, in the tremendous advances made by the Japanese economy in the postwar period. Japan now ranks among the major industrial powers of the world, and it is recognized that Japanese indus-

2. Personal interview, February 1976.
3. The Ministry of Labor has also reversed its longstanding position of urging greater labor mobility. The Labor White Paper published in 1976 urged maintenance of the lifetime employment practice, emphasizing its stabilizing effect particularly in the light of the growing share of older workers in the labor force (Ministry of Labor 1976).

trial relations practices are not incompatible with such progress. Indeed, the more enthusiastic interpretations by Western scholars see practices such as permanent employment and the lack of sharp job jurisdictions as directly contributing to Japan's economic success. This, however, has never been demonstrated other than by pointing to the coexistence of the two phenomena (Abegglen 1973). Again we return to the question of what can we learn from the Japanese.

At a minimum our goal is to develop a better understanding of Japanese labor market practices and work organization and in so doing develop a more enlightened vision of American practices. We will greatly enhance our ability to achieve both these goals by arriving at a better understanding of the comparative experience of the two nations over time. We can no longer afford the delusion that what exists in the United States reflects the characteristics of industrial society in its most advanced form. Yet to follow current fashion in simply denying that the United States is the very model of a modern society, while advocating that we imitate the Japanese, is to take a course filled with its own pitfalls. Perhaps it is time we accepted the fact that the social scientist's intense commitment to generalization cannot be allowed to obscure the fundamental observation that nations develop along their own paths, based on their own political, cultural, economic and social histories. As nations industrialize there is undoubtedly convergence in important institutional spheres, such as the expansion of education, the adoption of common technologies and determinants of labor mobility. Certainly nations can learn from one another, and indeed some nations impose their will on other nations. Yet there are also unique solutions to common problems.

CHAPTER I

PERMANENT EMPLOYMENT AND TRADITION IN JAPAN: THE THEORY OF INSTITUTIONALIZATION

The practice of permanent employment has come to be seen as a striking symbol of a unique industrial relations system in Japan. Permanent employment refers to the practice whereby an employee enters a company after school graduation, receives in-company training, and remains an employee of the same company until the retirement age of fifty-five. Such a practice is commonly seen by Western social scientists as inconsistent with the requirements of labor mobility in an advanced industrial society. We will elaborate on the character as well as costs and benefits of the contemporary permanent employment practice in Chapters II, III, and the final chapter.

Our purpose in this chapter is to examine the meaning of the permanent employment practice in historical and comparative perspective. It is a subject about which Japanese and American scholars have written a great deal. Some, like Abegglen (1958), see the practice growing out of traditional social relations. In recent years, however, a growing number of scholars, particularly Japanese scholars, have come to the conclusion that it was institutionalized only during and after World War I (Taira 1962; Sumiya 1948 and 1966; Ōkochi 1965; Odaka 1961). They suggest that its adoption resulted from the desire of employers to stabilize labor relations in large firms by cutting high labor turnover, especially among skilled workers and technicians.

This chapter represents a substantially revised version of my essay "The Theory of Institutionalization: Permanent Employment and Tradition in Japan," *Economic Development and Cultural Change* 20 (October 1971): 47–70.

Notwithstanding these developments, the practice of permanent employment only applied to a minority of employees, even in the major firms, until the labor-mobilization programs of the late 1930s and the tumultuous events of the immediate postwar period. The labor-mobilization programs inhibited labor mobility and encouraged enterprises to give on-the-job training to new employees. These developments were given legal impetus by the Ordinance Prohibiting Changes in Place of Employment (1940). It was not until the post-World War II period that the permanent employment practice was extended to the majority of semiskilled blue-collar workers in large-scale industry. Its emergence at this time may be attributed to the demands of workers as expressed in the policy of Japanese enterprise unions; the unions sought to protect their members during the chaos and drop in employment following the end of the war. Whenever employers tried to curtail employment, the workers responded with long-term strikes, and labor-management relations worsened. With management prestige at an all-time low, firms developed a very cautious attitude regarding layoffs and discharges. The right of the firm to discharge employees was in effect limited, and it remains so today. Concentrating on this period, some scholars have gone so far as to insist that the permanent employment practice should not be seen as a World War I phenomenon, but rather as a product of the wartime mobilization (Magota 1965). Still others assert that it is essentially a postwar development (Takahashi 1965, pp. 117–23). Marxist scholars focus on the closed character of an emergent monopolistic industry, which in the process of development produced a balkanization of the labor market by individual firms (Kishimoto 1962).

Taira (1962, p. 160) showed some time ago that interfirm mobility has not been "traditionally" low. Rather, he suggests, it was above 10 percent per month at the beginning of the twentieth century, fluctuated around 5 percent per month during the interwar period, and fell to 2 percent and below only during the 1950s. Given this rather well-documented criticism, is there any sense in referring to the practice of permanent employment as traditional? Is there any way of reconciling the view of permanent employment as traditional with the view of permanent employment as a pragmatic response to the labor market problems of the World War I and World War II periods? In his critique of Abegglen, Taira implies that a sociological explanation of permanent employment and the economic explanation are mutually exclusive, and he clearly opts for the latter. Vogel (1975, p. xix) concludes flatly that the system of permanent employment results not from traditional Japanese practices but from a combination of labor-market conditions, managerial decisions and union pressures (see also Marsh and Mannari 1976, p. 308).

This chapter is, however, an attempt to seek a reconciliation between the economic and sociological explanations of permanent employment. It is also designed to clarify, in the process, the use and misuses of the concept of tradition. We will adopt here the definition of tradition proposed by S. N. Eisenstadt (1973, p. 139), developed to a large extent in response to the various criticisms of the concept as used in the past.

Tradition can perhaps best be envisaged as the routinized symbolization of the models of social order and of the constellation of the codes, the guidelines, which delineate the limits of the binding social order, of membership in it, and of the boundaries, which prescribe the "proper" choices of goals and patterns of behavior; it can also be seen as the modes of evaluation as well as of the sanctioning and legitimation of the "totality" of the cultural and social order, or of any of its parts.

We will conclude this chapter with a comparative analysis through which we seek to make explicit the relative contributions of Japan's historical experience, and its status as a late-developer, to the formation of the permanent employment system.

All industrializing countries confront the problem of allocation and supply of labor skills. Many countries have experienced labor scarcity and the need to train and commit skilled workers to the firm during the early stages of industrialization. Similarly, many countries have experienced labor surplus and the desire by workers and their unions to protect employment status, such as occurred in Japan after World War II. It should be pointed out that the postwar expansion of permanent employment occurred at a time when the Japanese people, at least on the surface, were rejecting traditional values as having carried the seeds of a disastrous war. Hence, at this time, the spread of permanent employment should be seen primarily as a response to market conditions. Yet with the passage of this crisis period permanent employment did not disappear. The practice has not emerged in another economy over as long a period in a manner closely resembling Japanese company practices.[1] This suggests the possibility that when Japanese employers, workers, and unions were faced with the day-to-day problems, the solutions to which they were directed were based on traditional values and behavior patterns.

What does it mean, however, to say that the solutions are based on traditional values and behavior patterns? First it is necessary to examine the role of ideology in legitimating a new practice such as permanent employment. At the very least the adoption of permanent employment in the World War I period was supported by and cloaked in traditional family values, unity of the social group, and emphasis on place (membership in the firm) rather than the specific qualifica-

---

1. The conditions for the emergence of such a structural pattern may be increasingly present in many of the industrially underdeveloped countries today. The increasing scale of industrial enterprises in such countries, the desire to take advantage of the latest technologies, the reliance upon on-the-job training, and the desire to secure a return on training costs are important in this respect. Nationalist sentiment in such countries often involves a rejection of colonial practices of discharging employees whenever it seems economically advisable. Still such structural conditions are no guarantee that the Japanese pattern will be reproduced. For example, such countries might turn to state-inaugurated social policy or other state regulatory measures, such as have characterized many European countries in early industrialization, in order to cut labor turnover or protect employment security. The impetus for the development of permanent employment systems seems more likely to flow from the impact of democratic ideology upon these societies, along with early trade-union development. This contrasts with the post-World War I period in Japan, where management interests in cutting labor turnover and building workers' morale were paramount (see Dore 1974).

tions possessed by individuals. That is, the new practice was cloaked in the rhetoric of traditional values and practices, stressing the importance of the corporate group, to help insure its acceptance.[2] Workers, after all, would have had a number of reasons for being reluctant to accept this new arrangement. Above all, the practice of permanent employment reduced the advantages of bargaining among different employers for better wages and working conditions, not to speak of limiting those workers who preferred to drift in and out of wage employment.

As industrial development proceeded in the Meiji period, the new industrial workers grew restless; their participation in industrial life increasingly separated them from traditional behavior and sanctions. Urbanization and the increasing scale of business firms diminished the closeness of the bond between employers and employees. On the other hand, management came to emphasize the importance of systematizing existing labor-market arrangements, as a consequence of an expanding economy. The selection and emergence of the innovative practice of permanent employment and a legitimating ideology stressing traditional values sought to resolve both these issues. As a new practice in large firms, employees faced something unfamiliar in management's attempt to limit their inter-firm mobility. The invoking of traditional symbols was an attempt to render it familiar, to map the behavior that employees were now expected to display. As Geertz (1964, p. 62) observes, symbols systems are "extrinsic sources of information in terms of which human life can be patterned—extrapersonal mechanisms for the perception, understanding, judgment, and manipulation of the world." Prior to the adoption of the permanent employment practice, the dominant cultural symbols emphasized the individual employee's relationship to his work superior, who was commonly a master craftsman, a labor contractor, or a subcontractor. Such relationships were highly authoritarian and drew on those symbols associated with the superior-subordinate relationships of the feudal period. The period of industrialization during which these symbols prevailed, however, coincided with considerable labor mobility. Under permanent employment company officials applied a remolded version of these traditional symbols to relate the employee to the firm. Thus the major shift in the cultural symbols was one from a particularism of individual status relationships to the particularism of company loyalty.

We can examine in greater detail the core of these cultural symbols as reflected in the emergent management ideology that was used to legitimate permanent employment. What has come to be called management familism (*Keiei kazoku-shugi*) had been, prior to the Russo-Japanese War (1904–5), more of an autocratic ideology emphasizing a master-servant relationship between employer and employee. This proved unsatisfactory as the government and management tried to deal with the turmoil in labor relations that arose after the war. Numerous spontaneous worker uprisings broke out, as workers protested against management actions and rules that seemed devoid of traditional legitimacy. The lowered standard of living for workers that resulted from the Russo-Japanese War pro-

2. For discussions of the important role that the corporate group has played in Japanese history see John Hall (1962) and Ezra Vogel (1967).

TABLE 1
Composition of Employees in the Manufacturing Sector in 1909

	Male	Female	Total
	%	%	%
Textile	72,231 (14.8)	414,277 (85.2)	486,508 (100.0)
Machinery	60,721 (95.1)	3,100 (4.9)	63,821 (100.0)
Chemical	51,805 (66.5)	26,078 (33.5)	77,883 (100.0)
Food and beverage	64,320 (72.4)	24,420 (27.6)	88,740 (100.0)
Other manufacturing	54,197 (68.0)	25,576 (32.0)	79,773 (100.0)
Total	303,274 (38.0)	493,451 (62.0)	796,725 (100.0)

SOURCE: The Ministry of Agriculture and Commerce, Kōjō Tōkei Hyō (Table of Factory Statistics). In the original table workers in electricity and gas were included as workers of "special factories," but they are excluded here because we are limiting our focus to manufacturing industries with factory operations.

vided further incentive for worker unrest. Between 1903 and 1907 some 107 spontaneous strikes were recorded, involving 20,789 workers. In 1907 alone fifty-seven cases were reported, involving 9,855 workers. If we keep in mind that the uprisings occurred primarily among male workers and that there were only some 300,000 male factory workers in manufacturing in 1909, this is an impressive figure and one that was bound to have disturbed managers and government (see Table 1). Indeed, the Saionji cabinet ordered the immediate disbanding of the Socialist party, as the socialists sought to take advantage of these events (see Totten 1966, pp. 29–30).

The government and management solution at the level of the firm, apart from their action on the political front, was a revitalized familial ideology which created the image of the sympathetic father. It stressed the employer's warm feeling toward the employee and the intimacy of the family (Sumiya 1955, 1966; Matsushima 1962).[3] The persistence of family ownership in new and existing industry during the Meiji and Taisho periods and the relative slowness with which ownership was separated from control added to the credibility of these claims (Hirschmeier and Yui 1975, pp. 186–89). The practice of permanent employment coincided with and was legitimated by this conscious remolding of tradition by government and management.

It was ironically the textile industry, with its large female labor force, that supplied much of this revitalized ideology (Hazama 1964; Dore 1973). Females constituted 62 percent of all factory workers in manufacturing, but as may be seen from Table 1 more than 85 percent of workers in the textile industry were women. Textile workers constituted 61 percent of all factory workers in manufacturing. Thus the textile industry was in a commanding position in the economy. The model set by such firms as Kanegafuchi Spinning Company and

3. For other English-language treatments of Japanese managerial ideologies and practices see Byron Marshall (1967) and M. Y. Yoshino (1968). Professor Yoshino's discussion of the rise of prewar industrial paternalism draws heavily on the work of Hazama (see below); it closely parallels our own discussion of permanent employment.

its well-known spokesman, President Muto Sanji, was to have far-reaching consequences (see Muto 1963). This involved the establishment of a wide range of welfare benefits on the model of the paternalistic employer. Some of these, as Hazama notes, were based on the experience of Western companies. The welfare benefits included pension and welfare funds, improved recreational facilities, subsidized consumer cooperatives for those living in the company dormitories, and improved company housing arrangements for married employees (see Dore 1973, p. 395, for a fuller account). Interestingly enough, recent scholarship suggests that the textile industry reforms in this period were far less successful in reducing labor turnover than has been commonly thought (Saxonhouse 1976). Yet, insofar as they gradually spread to other industries, they were to have a profound effect on subsequent personnel practices.

On another level, the prevalent ideology of the family as perpetuating itself through the generations reflected the actual social household structure of pre-Meiji Japan. At this time most occupations were businesses that could be passed on from generation to generation. As late as 1872, 81 percent of the total gainfully employed population were in agricultural occupations and only a minority experienced regular wage employment. The economic basis of this family-based system was gradually weakened in the Meiji period, especially by geographical mobility. The traditional *ie* (household) system persisted as ideology, however. It was also the corporate basis of countless small family firms in commerce and traditional manufacturing, not to speak of farm units. In the Tokugawa period, membership in the *ie* and *dōzoku* (a kin-linked confederation of households), particularly in merchant houses, included both kin and non-kin members. Toward the end of the Tokugawa period, however, both the *ie* and *dōzoku* gradually began to exclude non-kin members from normal *ie* membership. These changes were accelerated by the new Meiji Civil Code, which equated the *ie* with the modern concept of family. With the turn of the century there was a growing attempt made by the *ie* and *dōzoku* leadership in merchant houses to treat non-kin individuals as "familial employees," in a fictive sense.

With both the *ie* and *dōzoku* system, the normal situation was one of permanent tenure for which male members were rewarded. A common procedure established among merchant firms in the Tokugawa period was the so-called branch house system. Outstanding employees, who had served long apprenticeships and accumulated long-term service, were given a sum of money to start a separate business. Clients of the main firm were sometimes made available to the new firm to get it started. This new business remained under the tutelage of the main firm and served to insure the continued prosperity of the *ie* as an ongoing entity. Horie (1966, pp. 80–84) suggests that this process of starting separate houses was a means of awarding retirement allowances for devoted employees of long tenure. Although a number of great merchant houses failed to make the transition to the Meiji era, some did, including such well-known houses as Mitsui and Sumitomo. In summary, the *ie* system could serve as a model, ideologically and structurally, for the practice of permanent employment, and experienced changes parallel to those in the more modern sector.

Ultimately it was the principles that regulated family life which were crucial. Such principles, emphasizing the closed and particularistic nature of the corporate group, appear to have been uppermost in the Japanese value system. They were thus resources available for regulating and limiting the shape of newly emergent behavior. Eisenstadt (1956, p. 43) suggests that when the main integrative principles of the social structure harmonize with those of the family, there is a relatively smooth transfer of identification and extension of solidarity as the individual moves from family to civic or other kinds of corporate solidarity.[4] We may note that in Japan one of the main integrative principles of the social structure—the importance of the corporate group—has to a great extent harmonized with the principles regulating the family during the course of industrialization. Here, then, is one way of understanding how Japanese industrialization could proceed without giving rise to major protest movements on the scale of the Western European experience.

Historically it was not only a matter of the large firms being able to draw upon general cultural symbols as well as upon the practices of small traditional units of economic production. Permanent employment developed as a solution to problems experienced by the large firms themselves. In many large firms in the machine, metal-working, and shipbuilding industries, there was initially a carry-over among male workers into the Meiji period of traditional master-apprentice (*oyakata-kokata*) relations as practiced by Tokugawa artisans. Master craftsmen (patrons) rewarded their retinue of apprentices (clients), if qualified, according to age and length of service. These masters were essentially subcontractors, who were hired by firms for specific jobs and were responsible for all aspects of recruitment, training, supervision, and payment of the labor force. Although it was the custom of many apprentices, once they had learned the essentials of their trade, to move around to different firms learning new skills, they often ended up by returning to their original master.

From the Russo-Japanese War through World War I and a short time thereafter, employers displayed an increasing desire to systematize and standardize recruitment, training, and supervision of workers; this contributed to the establishment of the permanent tenure practice. Employers wanted direct control over the work process and were dissatisfied with the *oyakata*. A crucial management decision in many companies involved co-opting the *oyakata-kokata* system rather than simply doing away with it. *Oyakata* were given special consideration, such as permanent tenure in the firm. Their retinue of apprentices "were slotted into wage positions in line with the preexisting status hierarchy and were guaranteed tenure" (Levine 1965, p. 647). They were gradually shorn of their special privileges to set wages and the like. In short, in the period under question, the traditional work relationships were gradually modified and finally dissolved, as management achieved direct control over the worker (Hyōdō 1971, p. 100). This allowed them to shift to a policy of recruiting new school graduates, for whom they could provide their own training. An essential aspect of this process, however, was that it maintained continuity with existing authority patterns and labor

4. Takeyoshi Kawashima (1964) deals with the familial system as the ideal for the entire society in pre-World War II Japan.

►skills. Shimada (1968–69), in a case study of Yahata Steel Corporation, concludes that, contrary to various scholarly hypotheses, older experienced workers were not driven out in the late 1920s but were rather "warmly retained."[5]

In short, we see how a given structure undergoes changes without losing its distinguishing characteristics. This contrasts with English experience, where the formal basis of traditional authority was laid bare in the space of some ten years (1803–13) with the sweeping away of the entire paternalistic code and, in particular, the apprenticeship codes. Here the coercive nature of the new laissez-faire manifested itself immediately in wage cutting and labor dilution (Thompson 1963, p. 517–18, 526–29, 544–45).

Additional precedents available to Japanese management included the practices of government arsenals and shipyards; they provided an avenue through which past practices could penetrate new forms of organization (Fujita 1961; Hazama 1964). These government enterprises adopted a variety of practices that could be traced to Tokugawa merchant practices and the feudal and Meiji bureaucracies. Dore (1973, pp. 380–85), drawing upon Hazama's investigation of records from the Yokosuka Shipyards, summarizes these influences as follows: minute specification of personnel administration, sharp status distinctions, collective responsibility system among workers, foreman responsibility for extramural behavior of subordinates, compulsory savings system, and use of Tokugawa job titles. Combining other innovations such as company training and the distinction between permanent and temporary workers, the government arsenals and shipyards of the early Meiji period served as prototypes for emergent employment practices in Japanese industry, including the permanent employment system.

Our discussion thus far has focused on the values and practices capable of serving as precedents for crystallization of the new pattern of permanent employment. In addition we have examined some of the motivations of management and government, the most notable being the desire to reduce turnover among skilled workers. The process by which workers came to accept these new practices has been dealt with far less satisfactorily in the scholarly literature. We tend to emphasize the pragmatic character of management decision making rather than power relationships. Neither ideology, structural precedents nor the simple desire of those in strategic positions is sufficient to guarantee the acceptance of a new pattern such as permanent employment. To say so would be to adopt a simplified interest theory of ideology which sees those in strategic positions of power using this power in an unlimited way to deceive the uninformed (see Geertz, 1964, p. 58).

To grasp the process of institutionalization involved in a practice such as permanent employment, one must examine the exchange relations that come to operate among the affected parties. Here it is apparent that employers were compelled to offer various material inducements, along with instituting a number of

5. Dore (1973, p. 387), drawing upon the research of Hyodo, reports the contrary experience of Shibaura, in which some of the *oyakata* bosses were finally fired. The issue fuels considerable dispute among Japanese scholars, which is centered on the extent to which feudal practices such as the *oyakata* system survived into the modern period.

negative sanctions, in order to get workers to accept the new practice. Now workers were to be rewarded according to age and length of service; thus they would be penalized for entering the firm midway in their work cycle. This was the origin of the *nenkō* system of reward by age and length of service. Labor would be hired at fixed periods and wages increased at regular intervals. The new pattern of payment according to age and length of service was often from the worker's point of view a great improvement over the arbitrary wage setting practiced by foremen and contractors. Finally the permanent employment practice provided security in a strange urban environment and a guarantee that one would not be returned to an overpopulated countryside. It gave the regular male worker in the large firms an advantage compared to those in smaller business enterprises with lower wages (wage-differentials by firm size are clearly present by the late 1920s), poorer working conditions and less job security. A similar advantage existed over temporary workers and female workers in large firms. Insofar as the "worker aristocrats" could be made to look upon these disadvantaged categories as their comparison groups, they would have good reason to accept the new arrangements of permanent employment and reward by age and length of service. Permanent employment came packaged in a traditional ideology which was consonant with the rural value system of recent migrants. In short, it was a map whose contours and gradations were easily grasped by the participants and whose contents proved quite attractive. Such acceptance, however, should always be viewed against the background of management and government power. Government officials were quite committed to the new arrangements, as witnessed by the formation of the Conciliation Society in 1925 (see Dore 1973, p. 397). The society was committed to diffusing the new ideology of management familism, welfare benefits and workers' councils. Moreover, according to the recent and as yet unpublished research of Hazama, the Industrial Training Association (Kōgyō Kyōikukai), under the leadership of Uno Riemon, played a vital role in diffusing the new ideas of increasing length of service; this eventually crystallized into the permanent employment system. The association, sponsored originally by the spinning and weaving industry, was especially active after the Russo-Japanese War. Uno, who started out as an apprentice himself, saw the association's task as that of providing a reconciliation between worker needs and management concerns. Through extending length of service, the provision of welfare benefits and increased training, he thought that the class conflict of the West could be avoided and worker efficiency raised.

The government also took a variety of direct measures throughout the Meiji and Taisho periods designed to restrict the growth of unions. Article 17 of the Peace Policy Law of 1900 prohibited, in effect, unions and strike behavior. It was not repealed until 1925, and no explicit legislation recognizing the right of workers to organize and bargain collectively was enacted in Japan until the postwar period. The almost continual repression and suppression under which fledgling unions operated—not to speak of the proletarian parties—must be counted as a major factor contributing to worker acquiescence in permanent employment. Other avenues were simply closed off to them. Large (1976, p. 55) emphasizes that practices such as permanent employment "sapped the vigor of the labor

19

movement by catering to aspirations for security and status that could not be met by most trade unions in inter-war Japan."

We may also ask, however, what we mean by worker acceptance of permanent employment. Insofar as managers were committed not to fire regular male employees in selected occupational categories, this policy hardly required a worker initiative. The heart of the matter concerns the willingness of workers to quit for alternative work opportunities. But if the wages and working conditions were much poorer in smaller firms, and larger firms were unwilling to hire the products of another large company, then we might better speak of worker acquiescence than worker acceptance of permanent employment. We cannot simply assume that workers internalized the ideology of management familism. In any case we must speak of the degree of internalization; it is not an all-or-nothing proposition. Until the age of attitude surveys, history has left few records of how ordinary people felt about institutions. We are thus forced to rely on records of employee behavior such as turnover, but this is obviously inadequate for assessing worker motivations and the nature of their commitments. Examination of postwar data heightens the significance of the questions raised here. Attitude surveys (Marsh and Mannari 1976) and participant observation studies (Cole 1971) indicate that workers may be far less accepting of permanent employment than commonly thought. They often conform to the practice not because of any strongly held commitment to the firm but because of economic reasons, desire for security, lack of alternatives, age, and family ties. Marsh and Mannari (1976, p. 253) conclude:

> Insofar as Japanese employees in large firms do remain in one firm, this is due mainly to factors other than loyalty to the company as such. Japanese employees' motives for staying in one firm are essentially the same reasons that tie Western employees to a firm.

These postwar data also coincide, however, with management's abandonment of the familism model, and do not necessarily cast light on prewar worker behavior. Nonetheless they suggest that the degree of worker acceptance of permanent employment in the prewar period should be left an open question. Whatever the extent of worker benefits under the new arrangements, it is quite clear that the new practices worked against worker interests as well. In particular they deprived workers—primarily skilled male workers—of the advantages of moving from job to job, thereby heightening management control. Skilled male workers were not unhappy with their ability to bargain among employers. It was the employers, unhappy at having to cope continually with quits by their skilled workers, who sought to develop seniority rewards and other means of retaining their labor.

The process of implementing the permanent employment practice, along with the related emphasis on reward by age and length of service, covered a number of years. It was interrupted by World War I, with the rapid expansion of the economy and resultant labor shortages. Price inflation, the rationalization of work, the Russian revolution, and the 1918 Rice Riots all contributed to the heightening of labor demands. Labor union organization and disputes increased rapidly. In 1918, 417 labor disputes occurred, involving some 66,500 workers; the following year disputes rose to 497, involving 63,000 workers. The number of labor unions increased from 40 in 1911 to 187 in 1919 and 273 by 1920 (see Totten 1966, p. 32). These events, along with increasing efforts to organize workers politically and the drive for factory legislation, greatly accelerated management efforts to develop familism as an alternative model for incorporating workers into the developing business enterprises. By the middle of the 1920s, management had made considerable progress in instituting the new recruitment, training and reward systems. Labor turnover of male employees in the large firms declined significantly as the length of continuous service increased and industrial relations gradually became more stabilized (see Hyodo 1971, p. 405). This was in sharp contrast to the preceding periods of high labor mobility.

One last point needs to be considered. How is it that permanent employment historically in the case of the manufacturing sector, as well as today, seems least relevant to the small-scale enterprise? After all, it is in these firms that we would expect both management and employees to be most subject to traditional constraints. Does it make any sense to see traditional ideology and practice as more dominant in large-scale firms than in small-scale ones? Under certain market conditions, the answer is yes. There are market situations which do not allow traditional practices and ideology to operate. Such is the case in many small-scale firms where high rates of employee inter-firm mobility are based on high bankruptcy rates, low wages, failure of wages to increase with seniority, unstable product demand and a shortage of capital funds.

This does not mean that all long-term employment commitments are impossible under such circumstances. On a psychological level, De Vos and Wagatsuma (1973, pp. 209–216) suggest that the Japanese small-scale entrepreneur tends not to think about his potential failure in a competitive market. Rather, he is hopeful, if not confident, that his diligence will somehow be rewarded in the long run. Historically De Vos and Wagatsuma find evidence of long-term employment commitments on the part of these small-scale paternalistic employers. That is, such entrepreneurs sought to abide by traditional ideology despite the objectively high risk of failure. In addition the high rate of mobility in small enterprises is somewhat misleading. Employers may be offering employment security as long as the company lasts, but workers may still choose to move on in search of better wages and working conditions. Moreover, those small firms in the past which survived, and increased their share of the market despite strong competitive pressures, could have been expected to adopt some form of long-term employment guarantee.

It is important here not to juxtapose market situations with traditional Japanese practices and ideology. Economic historians have demonstrated the considerable diffusion of market relationships in the late Tokugawa period, though these activities still met with moral disapproval in the official ideology (Hauser 1974). Finally, Western scholars analyzing the permanent employment practice as part of Japanese industrial paternalism often fail to distinguish between the personalized paternalism of the small-scale employer and the administrative paternalism of the large firm. They make predictions for large firms based on the personalized paternalism of small firms, and conclude erroneously that paternalism does not exist in large Japanese firms. The research of Marsh and Mannari (1976) provides one such example. There is nothing logically inconsistent in the process whereby large firms borrowed practices and values from small firms and adapted them to their own needs while at the same time the original practices were gradually dying out in many smaller firms.

Analysis

In the cultural and structural context of World War I and its aftermath, large-scale firms made the decision to adopt permanent employment. This context limited the options and controlled the directions of the solution. This is not surprising. No matter how innovative new institutions may appear, they do not develop in a cultural and structural vacuum. This is the insight of Ogburn, who pointed out that culture provides not only the sources but also some of the adaptive criteria of social invention and innovation (Duncan 1964). In the rejection of the view that permanent employment is traditional, many of the critics see institutionalization as an *event*. But institutionalization is a *process* composed of many events. As Eisenstadt (1965, p. 32) notes, it is a process that consists of "continuous crystallization of different types of norms and frameworks regulating the processes of exchange." We have seen earlier that there has been considerable scholarly debate concerning the dating of the permanent employment practice. Such attempts at dating miss the mark. What is important is the process of institutionalization of the practice, which drew upon traditional resources and satisfied market requirements at the different historical stages of development. To be sure the Japanese scholars involved in this debate have been aware of the way the permanent employment system evolved by integrating traditional elements with more universal requirements. This comes through clearly in their Japanese publications. In their English contributions, however, they have been so concerned with correcting the distortions created by the work of Abegglen that they have tended to downplay these traditional elements.

The crystallization of permanent employment was based on the limited number of possible patterns of labor market arrangements and the requisite elements of all such patterns. To be successful and persist, for example, all labor market arrangements must allocate labor skills to meet minimum efficiency norms of output, as well as commit to the firm key persons upon whom the enterprise is dependent and in whom extensive training investments have been made, such as skilled workers and management executives. Some devices must exist which penalize movement out of the system, or training and other related costs will prove unmanageable. On the other hand, labor market arrangements must guarantee some degree of employment tenure if they are to successfully motivate workers, who develop psychological as well as economic stakes in their employment. Thus the basic core of the permanent employment practice is present in any industrial society; Japan is not unique. The task, however, is to understand how and why it crystallized in the way that it did in Japan. For this we must examine the nature of the cultural and structural universe in which the actors operated. In this connection we are particularly interested in the predispositions of those actors in positions of power, such as employers, managers, contractors, and government officials.

We may speak of those resources whose availability creates a potential for a wide—though not unlimited—range of emergent patterns, while their absence imposes constraints which limit options. As general categories, we may list technological resources, organizational resources, demographic resources, and environmental resources, including degree of exposure to and acceptability of foreign models. Finally there is a resource which interpenetrates all others and may be labeled cultural resources. By cultural resources we mean the stock and strength of native cultural symbols available to a society. These may all be seen as resources which may potentially be mobilized for institutionalizing a new pattern, such as permanent employment, insofar as they can be freed from the demands of other structures or be made to do double duty. It is the availability of these resources and possible combinations among them which determines the mix in the emerging process of institutionalization.

Sometimes foreign models will not be compatible with existing cultural symbols. The colonial experience often makes it difficult for nationals to evaluate foreign models in a dispassionate fashion. At other times existing cultural symbols will operate to set organizational efficiency norms so low as to severely limit the options of key actors. Again, the cultural symbols may be so fragmented in an ethnically diverse population as to preclude their effective utilization for social mobilization. There may not be enough people available to be mobilized, because of lack of training and the commitment of people to existing statuses. The above-noted possibilities are those that we commonly associate with the difficulties of many of the industrially underdeveloped societies in the present-day world. In retrospect Japan appears to have been remarkably free of such constraints. Yet her very freedom was based on the adaptability of the traditional culture. This plasticity acted paradoxically as a constraint which both enabled and compelled Japanese leaders to frame piecemeal solutions to emergent problems to a great extent in terms of past experiences. Combined with a high rate of literacy, this tendency enabled the population to understand such innovative activities.

This strategy is, of course, not the only path to industrial success. Writing on the meaning of revolutionary breakthroughs, Kirchheimer (1965, p. 967) states, "The social and economic frame of the particular society, then, lays down a conditioning perimeter within which the original choice has to be made and solutions have to be sought." Kirchheimer's problem is the extent to which we can speak of an expansion of this perimeter, an expansion by which the original confining conditions have been changed by a decisive breakthrough. He then suggests that we can measure revolutionary change by the new system's ability to extricate itself from the confining conditions of the previous period. The conversion of Russia by its leaders into a major industrial power would be one example of such revolutionary change. The Japanese case may be described as one of nonrevolutionary change in the light of the strength of its confining perimeter. This is not to deny the critical nature of many of the reforms of the early Meiji period, but they were just that—reforms.

We can see this Japanese pattern of development clearly in the case of permanent employment. A new practice became institutionalized in which the innovators were both able and constrained to draw heavily from the stock of traditional values and practices. Indeed, the borrowing and use of native cultural resources is so pronounced in the case of permanent employment, at both a structural and symbolic level, that its emergence may be seen as a recrystallization of similar norms and structures that had been operative earlier in Japanese society. It is in these terms that the practice of permanent employment may be described as having traditional elements. It is not a matter of permanent employment being a pure embodiment of tradition. To describe an innovation as traditional is a contradiction in terms. What we are dealing with is an amalgam; and in the case of permanent employment, the amalgam was heavily loaded with traditional elements. The solutions arrived at, however, were not traditional in the sense of being irrational or antithetical to further industrialization. What strikes the observer in reading an historical account of the development of permanent employment is the way in which it changed in accordance with economic needs (see Taira 1964).

This interpretation does not deny that the emergence of permanent employment was a pragmatic response of employers to problems of labor control and turnover in the context of existing social, economic and political conditions or, later in the post-World War II period, to employee problems of job scarcity. Pragmatism in this context always involves taking into consideration the existence of what may seem to the uninitiated to be nonrational or irrational elements. To ignore such factors would itself be irrational and nonadaptive. Moreover, employee acceptance of permanent employment was pragmatic in the context of the overwhelming power wielded by management in concert with the government during the pre-World War II period and with union power in the immediate postwar period.

The preceding discussion illustrates the care that is required in using the concept of tradition. One must specify the uses (by whom) and the meaning of tradition in an industrializing society. Tradition based on a carry-over of habitual attitudes and behavior from preindustrial society is quite different in content and consequences from tradition based on the conscious manipulation of the past to devise new solutions to emergent problems. This is roughly the distinction that Bert Hoselitz (1966) makes between tradition-oriented social action and traditionalism. Although there are some aspects of an unconscious persistence of custom in the evolution of permanent employment, for the most part it represents a conscious act of institution-building. As Dore (1973, p. 392) notes, the Japanese had to learn, both by borrowing and innovating, how to apply traditional principles to large-scale organizations. It was by no means self-evident. It is this "creative" use of tradition, in combination with the core elements of the economic structure, that has characterized Japanese success in industrialization. In particular, Japanese leaders have been adept, on both a conscious and an unconscious level, at using traditional symbols to secure the legitimation of new practices and the motivation of new kinds of performances. The ultimate goal of Japanese leaders, however, was not simply to control labor or to use tradition to industrialize. Rather, it was to use industrialization to ward off the perceived military threat from the West and maintain a unique Japanese identity in both values and social structure. In this sense tradition was both a means and an end.

The Comparative Experience

The Japanese experience contrasts with English industrial development, where tradition was more a weapon in the hands of the emergent working class in its struggle against other classes. Employers saw their own demand for an end to state interference as a liberating influence. Hence they were not in a clear position to invoke tradition in legitimating their activities. Similarly the aristocrats and Anglican church leaders never allied themselves with the industrialization effort, as occurred in Japan. To be sure, Methodism did operate to mediate the work discipline of English industrialism, but the generalization still stands. Deference by workers to traditional authority as exercised by employers is not a major theme in the development of English capitalism. Instead, it was the working-class movement which often invoked the imagined and remolded tradition of the "free-born Englishman" to advance its claims to new social and political rights (Thompson 1963, p. 761). Dore (1973, p. 409) notes that by 1830 the British already had formal political organizations representative of the different social classes. Consequently the search for solutions to poverty and security were sought on the national level rather than among individual employers. This analysis suggests the importance of knowing which social groups are in a position to use tradition and for what purposes.

A more interesting comparison in many respects is of the role of tradition during early industrialization in Japan and Germany.[6] This assumes that comparison is more interesting when there are a large enough number of similarities to highlight the dissimilarities. At first glance the similarities are indeed impressive. Both Japan and Germany were late developers; both industrialized with ruling elites and governing bureaucracies composed of traditional leadership. In Germany the ruling elite consisted of a small group of upper Prussian aristocracy around the emperor. The Junkers, frequently not very wealthy, working poor soil, and dependent on protective tariffs and government subsidies, made a major contribution to the governing bureaucracy. In Japan the ruling elite from the Meiji period to World War I was composed of individuals from Satsuma and

6. This comparison has been of long-standing interest to social scientists. Thorsten Veblen, in the same year that he wrote *Imperial Germany and the Industrial Revolution* (1915), turned to a similar theme with his article on Japan entitled "The Opportunity of Japan." In recent years two well-known scholars of European industrial history have turned their attention to Japan-Germany comparisons. They are Reinhard Bendix (1967) and David Landes (1965). These publications have served as source materials for the comparisons in this section. I am indebted to Professor Adolf Sturmthal for his critical comments on my presentation of the German case.

Choshu—two of the leading domains that helped topple the Tokugawa Shogunate. As in Germany the lower-ranking aristocracy (i.e., lower samurai) contributed heavily to the formation of the governing bureaucracy. The Junkers also provided many of the officers in the new German army, as did the samurai in Japan.

In both countries the new bourgeoisie, composed of diverse social strata, failed to develop as a self-reliant social class. In its place strong-willed government officials played a major role in the political sphere and, to a great extent compared with England, in the economic sphere as well. In Germany leading industrialists aligned themselves with the Junker government; a corresponding development took place in Japan.

At the level of the emerging industrial enterprises one may point to the persistence and utilization of traditional social relations of superordination and subordination.[7] The ruling oligarchies and industrial entrepreneurs of both countries practiced policies which were a mixture of repression and benevolence, based on an authoritarian political model. The patriarchal family model was transposed into the political, social, and economic realms. Furthermore the leaders of both countries found the military experience useful for inculcating appropriate habits of work discipline and diligence upon the new industrial recruits. Not uncommonly early factories were modeled on military procedure and discipline.

Finally, ideologies of social harmony and national community expressed in traditional terms were paramount in the two countries from the time of initial industrial expansion. An ideology of nationalism based on a state of national emergency persisted with few interludes until the end of World War II. The military interests of the state provided the engine for economic growth. The governing oligarchies in Japan and Germany sought to restructure the old power of tradition in order to develop and use the new power of industry. Not incidentally, this served to maintain their own positions of leadership, based as they were on a legitimation in traditional terms.

As impressive as these similarities may be, there are also important differences. First, the content of German tradition was less clear. Throughout her history, Germany has been constantly exposed to outside forces, and this has greatly intensified her cultural and political heterogeneity. Military might was the foundation of German unity in a hostile environment; indeed, German unity was achieved only in 1870 with the Franco-Prussian War. In this respect, Japan has much more in common with England. In Japan an unbroken tradition persisted of the emperor as the single source of legitimacy; there were 250 years of unified rule under the Tokugawa Shogunate just prior to the industrial revolution. The continuity of the imperial tradition served as a major focus and provided significant content for the new national identity that was forged during the Meiji period.

The difficulty in clarifying the content of German tradition no doubt made it harder to mobilize it in the service of industrialization. To the extent that a unified tradition existed, it was a Prussian tradition imposed on the rest of the

7. For the German case see Hartmann (1959, p. 270).

newly unified country. Until Prussian influence became predominant after 1870–71, it was not at all certain whether Prussia or Austria or southwest Germany would set the tone. Because of the consequent difficulties in remolding tradition as an instrument of control over the emergent working class, employers and the government were more dependent on social welfare benefits, manipulation of national sentiment based on fear of foreign invasion, and coercive measures. An alternative course would have been to carry out a thoroughgoing reform involving a sharing or relinquishing of power, but the ruling oligarchs were unwilling to move in this direction. A different way of expressing this interpretation is that coercion was a stronger element in the German tradition than it was in the Japanese. In this sense the content of the tradition provided an internal legitimation for the behavior of the German business and political elite but was of less help in securing the willing compliance of the emergent working class.

The role of coercion in the German case appears particularly in the extensive modeling of industrial organization after military patterns. The noted German sociologist and economic historian Gotz Briefs writes: "The model of the military quite palpably formed business leadership. . . . The strongly liberal concept of private property often joined with the military ideology of leadership and command to a company militarism" (quoted in Hartmann 1949, p. 80). Employers often hired only those with prior military experience. In the Japanese case the military model was also important in the early heavy industries which were initiated, often by the government, to equip a modern army. This military model, however, appears as an initial passing phase in Japanese industrial development; it was fairly quickly replaced in most industries by less coercive motivational incentives—in particular by familial models. Although the familial model has currency in the German experience as well, it was far less pervasive and important.

One explanation for the importance of familial models in Japan and the relatively greater reliance on military models in Germany may lie in different craft guild traditions. In Germany the craft guild tradition was well developed and offered an alternative base for worker attachments. For employers to establish their unchallenged authority, it was necessary to use more coercive measures to pry workers loose from these commitments. Their lack of total success is apparent in the way that the craft tradition served as a strong basis for the early development of the socialist movement (Feldman 1966, p. 20). Thus the German employer class was forced to share and compete with workers for the use of traditional symbols and practices. In Japan the craft guild tradition was relatively weak and consequently the employer class did not have to deal with a competing tradition. Japanese employers could more easily mobilize workers through the use of familial models and the specific manipulation of *oyakata-kokata* relations.[8]

The split between ideologies of tradition and modernity was much sharper in the German case. Dahrendorf (1967, pp. 9, 50) refers to the "cultural pes-

8. I am indebted to discussions with Professor Okamoto Hideaki on this point.

simism" of the Germans, a pessimism with which the German populace were dutifully indoctrinated. It involved the glorification of the country and the denigration of the city as the root of all evil, as well as the resentment of everything Western (and therefore modern) and an effort to develop in a way peculiarly suited to the unique German people. Finally there was present a melancholy nostalgia for security which denied the modern world the ability to make people happy. No doubt each of these individual elements appeared at various times in the Japanese case as well. The radical right of the 1930s, particularly in the military, drew much of its ideology from a belief in the corrupting influence of the city and the simple, healthy, and natural values of rural life (Duus 1976, p. 188). In the German experience, however, these ideas were part of a long-term systematic ideology, whereby it was felt that the concession of any single element would jeopardize the entire system. In Japan this split between tradition and modernity was less sharply defined and never became a matter of high principle. It was possible, therefore, to have a constant reformulation of tradition to suit industrial needs, legitimate new activities, and motivate performance.

A number of important structural differences between the two societies help explain these ideological differences. In Germany the split between tradition and modernity was heightened by the resistance of the lower aristocracy to industrialization. Many of the Junkers correctly saw industrialization and urbanization as a threat to their own privileges. In overcoming this resistance, class consciousness was heightened; this made it difficult for the industrializing elite to use tradition to legitimate its privileges and motivate new activities among workers. One indication of the heightened class consciousness lies in the strong appeal that the doctrine of class struggle and internationalism had to the socialist labor movement of nineteenth-century Germany. These developments gathered force with the events of 1848 and 1918 demonstrating to all the sharpness of class conflict and the wide chasm of class differences within the society. Secondly, Prussian tradition was less viable because of the presence of a strong regional Catholic tradition. The Catholic church and the Center party encouraged the labor movement; class cleavage was particularly severe in those areas where workers were predominantly Catholic and managers were Protestant, as in Upper Silesia (Roth 1963, pp. 66–67).

The situation was quite different in Japan, where the samurai had long been separated from the land and turned into government bureaucrats. No landed aristocracy existed to oppose industrialization; no major revolutionary struggle had to be made against feudal inequality. The rising peasant landlords of the Meiji period quickly became allies of the ruling elite. The Japanese labor movement is notable for its weakness relative to the Western experience, and for the attempts of workers to demonstrate their nationalism and desire for social harmony, especially by the 1930s. Unlike the Junkers, the samurai played an important role in the formation of the new industrial entrepreneur class. They contributed both to its membership and ideology. In the Meiji era many non-Satsuma and Choshu samurai who had difficulty securing positions in the governing bureaucracy turned to entrepreneurial activities.

These structural differences point to the greater difficulty the German industrializing elite had in mobilizing tradition as compared with the Japanese. The German case seems to represent a middle position between the English and Japanese ones. The English workers often drew upon the remolded tradition of the "free-born Englishman"; Japanese employers, with their more exclusive monopoly on tradition, instituted familial ideologies. By contrast the respective parties in Germany competed more evenly in their attempt to mobilize traditional symbols and practices. This is one way of explaining the great need to use coercion in the German case. Industrialization creates the problem of the political and social integration of the emergent industrial work force. The above analysis emphasizes not simply the inherent dynamics which universally create labor protest, but the way that cultural, political, and economic heritages influence outcomes.

The Late-Developer Hypothesis

The preceding comparative analysis of two late developers—Germany and Japan—raises some interesting questions in the light of the alternative conceptualization offered by the late-developer hypothesis.[9] Despite relatively similar time frames for their industrial development and some significant similarities in the process of development, we have nevertheless identified some rather fundamental dissimilarities.[10] This leads us to question the ability of the late-developer hypothesis to give a comprehensive accounting of the development process. We were able to discern some of the factors which enabled the Japanese to mobilize traditional values and practices to initiate the permanent employment practice, but which were unavailable to the Germans. We have the opportunity to pursue the matter in further detail in view of Dore's (1973, pp. 404–20) use of the late-developer hypothesis to explain the emergence of the permanent employment practice in Japan and its failure to germinate in England. Instead he sees the market principle as triumphant in England.

The time frames under consideration are Japan from 1880 to 1930 and Britain from 1800 to 1875. Dore (1973, pp. 408–15) lists some thirteen dif-

9. The late-developer hypothesis and its variants have had considerable currency in the social sciences in recent years (see Sahlins and Service 1960; Gerschenkron 1962; Eckstein 1966; Matossian 1966; Rosovsky 1966; Barby 1969). Its origins can be traced to the observations of such students of social organizations as Thorsten Veblen ("penalty of taking the lead") and Leon Trotsky ("privileges of backwardness"). Alexander Gerschenkron (1962, pp. 353–54) crystallized a number of these observations in a specific set of propositions based on his comparisons between England and the successively later developers of Western Europe and Russia.

10. Actually German industrialization may be dated somewhat earlier than Japan's. The initial period may be dated as 1860–69, compared to 1878–87 in Japan. Moreover Germany started at higher levels of per capita income and lower proportions of population located in agricultural occupations. Domestic steel production in Germany reached 690,000 tons in 1880, while it was less than 60,000 tons in Japan as late as 1903. That Japan saw Germany as one of the major countries from which she might learn and borrow reflects Germany's more advanced status. Nevertheless the kinds of differences elaborated in the preceding section do not seem to derive from this lag in timing. For a treatment of the state of the Japanese economy relative to other industrializers at the initiation of modern economic growth in Japan, see Henry Rosovsky (1966, pp. 110–12).

ferences between Britain and Japan, which he maintains can be generalized as differences between early developers and later developers. We shall not examine each of these differences in detail here, but rather seek to provide a generalized critique. First, the methodology of Dore's analysis often results in collapsing the time periods under consideration. To be sure his analysis covers some very long time periods. This does not, however, justify the arbitrary selection of such data within the broad time frame as are convenient for supporting the late-developer hypothesis. To do so is to destroy historical sequence and provide a misleading understanding of the processes involved. Two examples will suffice. Dore argues that because of the nature of the capital-intensive machinery adopted by late-developers such as Japan, there was a need to stabilize employment of even semiskilled operatives. Yet male semiskilled operatives did not get a meaningful guarantee of permanent employment until the post-World War II period and semiskilled female operatives have yet to receive one. Consequently such stabilization could not possibly have been a response to the nature of the capital-intensive machinery adopted by the Japanese in the pre-1930 period. Secondly, Dore maintains that the adoption of capital-intensive industries with high skill requirements led to an unusual need for in-company training. Yet at the time of World War I there was a core of trained technical workers for whom turnover was not an unusual event and a set of employers for whom recourse to the market to recruit labor was commonplace. The need for in-company training to provide new skills not present in the labor force, as argued by Dore, seems most relevant to an earlier period of industrialization. Indeed, based on available evidence, one could argue that labor market institutions in Japan in the period around World War I resembled those of nineteenth-century England more than they did post-World War II institutional arrangements in Japan. Another methodological problem faced by Dore in making the comparison between early and late developers is that in principle he has no basis for distinguishing the causal strength of historical as opposed to late-developer effects.

On a substantive level a number of points need to be made. First, Dore downplays the availability of market models in the late Tokugawa and early Meiji periods in order to explain the Japanese rejection of the market principle for employment relationships. Yet if one evaluates the strength of the market principle in Japan through examination of the prevalence of the putting-out system, the commercialization of agriculture, and the spread of capitalist wage relationships in the late Tokugawa period, there seems to be no dearth of market models. These practices were rather widely diffused throughout the population (Ranis 1957; Smith 1963, 1969; Crawcour 1965; Hauser 1974, p. 136, 1974a). Dore chooses to ignore what is perhaps the major thrust of post-war Western revisionist scholarship in Japanese economic history. Thus he underplays the significance of the market forces operative in the late Tokugawa and early Meiji periods. David Landes (1965, pp. 114–15) concludes to the contrary that the commercialization and industrialization of the Japanese countryside, at least in the more advanced areas, bore a striking resemblance to pre-industrial Britain, despite the fact that it did not proceed as far in Japan. What Dore does is to confuse what is most *distinctive* in the comparison between Japan and Britain (market practices undoubtedly had less currency in Japan) with what was *important* in Japan (market practices were well-diffused). Marsh and Mannari (1976, p. 336) note that this is a common failure of comparative theorists.

Lastly, Dore adopts the position of Gerschenkron (1962) in emphasizing the early role of highly capitalized heavy industry in the industrialization of late developers. This allegedly leads to an inability to rely on the market in Japan because of the large technological gap between traditional and new industry, which in turn requires the development of entirely new occupational skills and a reliance on in-company training. Heavily capitalized industry is also said to lead to a need to reduce the costs of turnover and absenteeism because the costs of leaving machinery idle are greater.

Yet economists stress that the major industries of the Meiji period were not those of the late developers envisioned by Gerschenkron, involving the most advanced techniques and therefore requiring high-level technical skills. Rather, they were the typical first-generation industries of the classic industrial revolution: textiles, shipbuilding, railroads, and mining, smelting and refining. The labor-intensive production functions represented in these choices tended either toward the use of unskilled labor, as in the textile industry, and/or toward the use of traditional skills (Ranis 1957; Rosovsky 1961). Such industries rested heavily upon on-the-job training and intelligent empiricism (Landes 1965, p. 110). In particular Dore downplays the important role of the textile industry in Japanese industrialization; light industries of this nature do not require the kind of heavy capital investment in new equipment leading to a quantum leap in new kinds of occupational skills. Yet it was the textile industry that took the lead in publicly expressing the greatest concern with absenteeism and turnover, developing extensive welfare facilities, and contributing the ideology of management familism, particularly for its minority core of skilled male workers. Dore, sensing the difficulty created for his explanation by the textile industry, argues for its relative unimportance in Japan. He notes that textile workers made up 24 percent of the total British labor force in 1856 but never reached 10 percent in Japan (Dore 1973, p. 407). The more relevant comparison, however, is the proportion of the non-agricultural labor force or factory workers made up of textile workers, and here we have seen that they constituted a dominant force in the Japanese economy. In summary, Japan's industrial history is marked by the dominance of the typical first-generation industries. It is difficult under these circumstances to argue for the distinctive impact of large-scale heavy industry.

The point of the preceding critique is not that the late-development effect is non-existent. It does seem apparent that the increased role of government, technological discontinuity, and the rapid growth of universal education are characteristic of late developers. Such factors are, however, insufficient to explain emergent institutional arrangements such as permanent employment. The partial explanation they offer must be interwoven with the universal characteristics of the development process and the unique historical experience of nations.

To put it differently, the interaction of the period effect with historical factors and basic economic constraints is so great as to make predictions based exclusively on the period effect (late development) extremely hazardous.

Dore is not unaware of the importance of historical factors—indeed he has made major scholarly contributions in elucidating them—but in trying to provide a comprehensive explanation of employment practices based on the late-development effect, he stretches the evidence beyond tolerable limits. It may be that Smith (1963, p. 160) is correct in saying that the introduction of historical and cultural factors reduces the late-developer theorist to the statement that "backward nations are different in many ways and hence the modes of industrialization are also many."

CHAPTER II

PATTERNS OF JOB MOBILITY: A COMPARATIVE STUDY OF DETROIT AND YOKOHAMA
An Introduction
with the collaboration of PAUL MATHEW SIEGEL

In the first chapter we traced the historical evolution of permanent employment in Japan with a particular effort to put the practice in comparative and analytical perspective. In this second chapter we provide an introduction to post-World War II Japanese job-mobility behavior. Again a comparative framework will provide the vehicle through which we attempt to come to grips with describing and interpreting these practices, though this time the chosen research instrument is the social survey and the focus is our comparison of Japan and the United States. Our intent is to better understand Japanese and American job-mobility patterns through detailed comparisons of work history experiences. In the first part of the chapter we examine recent sociological and labor market theory and research as it relates to our study; in the second section we describe the nature of our sample and the appropriateness of a Detroit-Yokohama comparison. In the last part of the chapter we outline the kinds of conceptual distinctions necessary to pursue the analysis.

Data collection in Detroit supported by Detroit Area Study, University of Michigan; in Japan by Horace H. Rackham School of Graduate Studies, University of Michigan. Data analysis funded by NSF Grant GS-35308 as well as Ford Foundation Grant 740-0124. Overall research design and implementation in Japan involved collaboration with Professors Naomichi Funahashi of Hosei University and Yasumitsu Nihei of Keio University. In addition, interpretation of findings benefitted greatly from the critical comments and suggestions of the Japanese collaborators. The following individuals partici-

Sociological research on stratification originated in concern with how social inequality is reproduced through time. This focus was translated to a concern with the correlation between the statuses of fathers and sons, and in turn this was translated to a focus on the "achievement process," i.e., how fathers' status and other ascribed characteristics of sons affect the sons' socioeconomic achievement. While much of the original problem has been lost in the translation—e.g., the effort to link societal inequality at one point in time with societal inequality at another and the effort to deal with the effects of "structural changes"—the concern with status achievement has brought job changing and job tenure into heightened interest, under the heading "intra-generational mobility." Blau and Duncan's original model (1967) contained very simple relations between the statuses of first and current occupation, and elsewhere in that work they speculated about relations between the statuses of occupations spaced evenly in time across the interval from first job to the interview. Somewhat later Featherman (1971) introduced empirical results which seemed to require that occupational status at one point in time depend not only on status at an immediately prior measurement, as Blau and Duncan had tentatively urged, but also and simultaneously upon occupational statuses more remote in time. Kelly (1973) soon showed that these puzzling effects could be made to disappear by making appropriate adjustments for hypothetical random measurement errors. In all these discussions, jobs and the organizations which give rise to them are quite noticeable in the argument, and notable by their absence from the empirical materials. These models concern, instead, the status of an individual's occupation at regular points in time.

Recent work by Sørenson (1974, 1975, 1975a) has explicitly shifted concern from a focus on the statuses of occupations held at fixed points in time or age to a focus on the statuses of occupations held with successive employers, with some innovative attention devoted to modelling when employees change occupations. The contribution of this approach lies in its characterization of careers in jobs, but it has two weaknesses from our standpoint. First, the characterization of careers reduces to two properties—an ultimate destination level defined by the individuals' educational attainment and other background characteristics, and the rapidity with which the individual reaches that level, which is determined by observation and held to define the "openness" of the society. Second, in this model individuals are allowed to have careers only through experiencing inter-employer mobility, i.e., they achieve their careers by moves between successive employers.

The first property of the model strikes us as a weakness in that it does not permit investigation of the effects of individual or employer action on careers. It is characteristic of a great deal of stratification research, dictated in part by currently fashionable measurement techniques. That is to say, measurements are commonly too gross to capture the detailed individual sequences as they evolve

pated at one time or another in preparing and/or analyzing the data: Andrea Foote, Carol Yorkievitz, Rex Leghorn, Leonard Lynn, David Thompson, and Terry Williams. I thank Michael Flynn for contributing this last sentence.

out of the interaction between employee and employer strategies. In a related observation, Harrison White (1970, p. 6) notes that "the overall impact of . . . small successive changes and the amount of conscious thought and planning devoted to them may well be the bulk of the total effects of mobility." Yet such changes commonly evade existing measurement techniques, which typically examine individuals' movements in gross categories of occupational prestige or classes of jobs. More generally, aggregate analysis destroys individual sequences and diverts attention from process. In making this same point, Norman Ryder (1965, p. 859) advocates cohort analysis as a means of avoiding some of the problems.

The second property of the Sørenson model—allowing individuals to have careers only by moving between successive employers—is clearly overly restrictive in the context of the Japanese setting, where the achievement of careers without change of employers is held to be a common pattern.

It is not, however, a matter of this second property being applicable in the United States and inapplicable in Japan. In the sociological literature on the "achievement process" there has been remarkably little consideration given to separating out two fundamentally different patterns of socioeconomic achievement. In the first, socioeconomic achievement for employees proceeds through **upgrading or downgrading within a specific firm, hereafter referred to as intra-firm mobility. Sets of related jobs lead to a clustering of job-mobility patterns within an organizational context. In the second, socioeconomic achievement occurs through changing employers (inter-firm mobility). The conceptualization and measurements of these distinctive patterns will be considered below. At best the extant sociological literature has failed to differentiate between the two patterns; at worst it has hopelessly confused them.[1] Yet to ignore intra-firm job changing is to ignore a great many of the small successive job changes that may, as Harrison White suggests, constitute the bulk of mobility effects. Since the existing literature on intra-generational occupational mobility focuses on inter-firm mobility, it puts the analyst in the absurd position of insisting that occupational mobility only occurs when there is an employer change; occupational mobility that results when firms fill jobs by upgrading is commonly ignored by sociologists.[2] Indeed, there do not appear to be any reliable estimates of its incidence.**

1. Apart from Sørenson, a notable example is the work of Harold Wilensky (1961) who writes about occupational mobility, although the data seem to refer only to inter-firm mobility.

2. Harrison White's (1970) research is an exception and represents an innovative approach to intra-firm mobility. It builds on a vacancy-chain model in which the natural subject of prediction at the individual level is not the careers of men or jobs, but vacancies. This means that opportunities for advancement arise not from individual preferences but from the flow of vacancies. Because of the data analyzed and the model employed, however, a number of limitations are present in White's analysis. They are:
a) White's case study data utilized members of the Episcopal, Methodist and Presbyterian clergy. Yet compared to most members of the labor force the clergy are unusually committed to careers within a particular organization—once in, they seldom exit (p. 49). In short, his analysis applies more to professional and managerial categories than to the bulk of labor force participants. Application of the White model is particu-

Not surprisingly, then, we know very little about the relationship between intra- and inter-firm job changing. Byrne (1975, p. 54) reports that only 9.5 percent of the men changing occupations in 1972 did so in the same company, compared to a figure of 19.1 percent reported for 1965. This raises the question, however, of what we mean by occupational change.

36   To take a case in point, let us consider the work of Ornstein (1976, p. 104). Using a national sample of noninstitutionalized males between the ages of thirty and thirty-nine, he reports that only 11.7 percent of white respondents and 5.8 percent of black respondents attained their second job, after entering the labor force, by promotion. Since the overwhelming bulk of respondents changed firms to register their second job change, he concludes that this "shows that the impact of movement within firms is limited." Upon closer examination we find that respondents were allowed to register an intra-firm job change only if they changed occupations as recorded in the three-digit classification of the U.S. Bureau of the Census. This means that an individual must change from one of the 296 census codes to another to register an intra-firm job change (U.S. Bureau of the Census 1971). The problem is, of course, that we can increase the amount of intra-firm job changing simply by increasing the detail of the occupational codes. As will be noted in Chapter IV, we found that 25 percent of all intra-firm job changes reported by our Detroit respondents and 28 percent of those reported by our Yokohama respondents were within the census occupation categories. Nor, as we shall discuss below, do these self-reported changes necessarily ex- haust the number of intra-firm changes. If we had used Ornstein's method, we would have ignored a quarter of the intra-firm job changes reported by our respondents. When we do not gather and analyze such information, we cannot conclude with any confidence, as does Ornstein, that the "impact of movement within firms is limited" (even for the limited time span he considers). Using

----

larly fitting in the case of formalized hierarchical promotion systems. Recruitment for vacancies is also notably limited by the requirement that occupants of positions be ordained clergy. Protestant churches are also unusual organizations in that there are few fixed jobs that are not 1–1 jobs (p. 184). By fixed jobs that are 1–1, White means jobs defined as being for a single incumbent, which can therefore be uniquely identi- fied in the mobility process. White's use of the clergy also leads him to limit his con- sideration to a case in which men move at most once a year (p. 27).

b) To apply his model White must assume that movers are representative of the structure into which they move (p. 40). This means that movers do not have any distinctive characteristics.

c) Exit from organizations but not destinations are considered. This makes it impossible for White to consider the relation between intra-firm and inter-firm mobility. Further- more, it leads him to overemphasize the organizational constraints imposed by vacan- cies on individual mobility. If we consider the possible change of employment to another organization as an alternative (notwithstanding that these also are ultimately dependent on different organizational vacancies), then the individual has more initia- tive to choose than if he were limited to moving into vacancies within one orga- nization.

d) There is no analysis of the causes of different mobility-rate parameters across orga- nizations (Grove 1975, p. 19).

These comments also apply for the most part to others who have analyzed internal labor market systems using Markov chain models (cf. Stewman 1975; Forbes 1971).

his methods—a not uncommon practice when sociologists do decide to investigate intra-firm job changing—perpetuates the conventional wisdom that the prime concern of analysts of job changing lies with employer changing. On the other hand, Ornstein fails to tell us the proportion of employer changes that involve a change in census occupational categories; the assumption seems to be that such changes are important in themselves, while the importance of intra-firm job changes has to be demonstrated.

It is our contention that the failure to gather systematic data on intra-firm mobility marks a major omission in sociological research on intra-generational mobility. Both from a descriptive and an analytical perspective, we need to know how these strikingly different patterns of movement operate, how they interact and whether they have similar or different outcomes. The research presented here is designed to take us the first few steps in this direction.

The general characteristics of the stratification research described above set it in direct contrast with another sociological tradition. This tradition deals with careers and, though more qualitative and impressionistic, is just as venerable as the stratification literature.

Following Max Weber (1947), career is seen in this literature as one of the core elements in bureaucratic organizations (see Glaser 1968). Stinchcombe (1959), in listing these core elements, emphasizes the organization of work statuses into some sort of career in which future rights and duties depend upon present performance according to specified standards. Wilensky (1964) defines a career structurally as a succession of related occupations, through which individuals move in an orderly, predictable sequence within the firm. Mannheim (1940) suggests that this element of predictability enables, indeed compels, the formation by the individual of a "life plan" in which the stages are specified in advance. It is the probability that individuals will experience continuous predictable advancement on some ascending scale that distinguishes "career" from more generalized notions of socioeconomic achievement. Wilensky argues that careers are a major source of stability for industrial societies, even though they may apply only to a minority of the labor force. He maintains that careers serve to recruit, commit, and motivate role occupants in organizations, organizational groups, and societies. The importance to individuals of maintaining careers with firms is suggested by the title of Palmer's (1963) study of individuals "forced" to change firms—*The Reluctant Job Changer*—in which it was discovered that aside from pecuniary considerations and uncertainty, job changers had some commitment to a career with a particular firm. It is the importance to the individual of having a career—i.e., both stable employment and probable advancement with adequate performance—which allows firms to utilize the promise of careers as part of their recruitment, retention, and motivation strategy, according to at least some theorists of organizational behavior (see Thompson 1967; Dubin 1958). Thus careers take on an importance for both employers and workers. A specific account of how employers and employees derive their interest in careers may be found in variants of human capital theory and dual labor market theory.

Expressed differently these two theories constitute the theoretical bases for assuming that intra-firm mobility is a process distinct from inter-firm mobility.

Internal labor markets have been labelled the heretofore missing dimension in studies of labor mobility (Hunter and Reid 1968, p. 80). The literature focuses on the factors underlying employer decisions to recruit for vacancies from within the firms as opposed to going outside to the external labor market (Doeringer and Piore 1971). In brief, the internal labor market of a productive unit (e.g., the firm) is connected to the external labor market by certain job classifications which constitute ports of entry and exit to and from the internal labor market. The remaining jobs in the firm are shielded from the direct influence of competitive forces in the external market and are filled by the promotion and transfer of workers who have already gained entry. From this perspective, the firm, as an organization of differentiated jobs, provides an important source of careers for its members, which inter-firm mobility would necessarily disrupt.

This approach has been generalized by Piore (1975) to explain what he sees as a fundamental split in the labor market. According to this formulation, there are primary and secondary labor markets. The participants in these markets do not compete with one another. The primary section is composed of jobs in large firms, commonly unionized, in which the internal labor market plays a dominant role. In this market, wages and working conditions are good, career progressions exist, employment security is high, and the rules for treatment of workers are objective and public. By contrast, in the secondary sector the situs for the bulk of jobs is small firms. It is here that the lowest-paying jobs are located, working conditions are poor, employment tenure is short, with workers having little employment security, and personalized relationships between workers and supervisors encourage favoritism and arbitrary treatment of workers. In this secondary tier the external labor market plays a far greater role in determining working conditions than does the internal labor market. Dual labor market theory in the United States developed as a response to the perceived inability of neoclassical theory to explain continuing poverty and unemployment as well as race and sex discrimination (see Cain 1976; Montagna 1977).

The constraints imposed by the structure of the internal labor market focus our attention on the opportunity structure, the demand side of the labor market. A complementary approach—though many scholars see it as a conflicting approach—involves a consideration of the personal attributes of those who enter the labor market. This turns our attention to the supply side of the labor market and theories of human capital. They provide the basis for a set of inferences on how employers derive an interest in employee careers and how workers and employers structure their decision making as it relates to sustaining the employment relationship. The particular human capital theories of relevance here are those which focus on the role of education, occupational experience and on-the-job training. Becker (1964) estimated the rate of return to training at higher levels of education. In the course of his analysis he introduced the important distinction between specific training and general training, a distinction that has been central to much subsequent theorizing in this area. Mincer (1962, 1970) extended Becker's analysis with systematic examination of the amount of investment in on-the-job training and the role of experience.

The essence of human capital theory is that investments in the human capital of a worker increase his future marginal productivity, thereby generating rising earnings (Becker 1964; Mincer 1962). Becker, by distinguishing between general and specific training, introduces a basis for differentiating the earnings profile as well as influencing employer-changing probabilities. Specific training is training which increases the recipient's productivity more within the firm providing the training than in other firms. Since such training is useful primarily within the firm that provides it, the firm may be willing to finance its cost. The assumption is that the employer will collect returns after training by paying wages lower than the worker's post-training productivity. The employer is presumably able to do so because the risk of losing the employee to another firm is minimized. This is true as long as the wages being paid in the post-training period are still superior to those the worker would receive in a competitive market for his skill and experience level prior to having received specific training. If a worker is fired or quits soon after the firm has paid for his specific training, its investment is partly wasted, with the firm being unable to collect any further return. Moreover, a replacement who had not received such training would have a lower marginal productivity than the old employee. If a worker is fired or quits after receiving specific training, he will find it difficult to collect any further return at a different firm. On this basis Becker (1964, p. 21) concludes that "the willingness of workers or firms to pay for specific training should, therefore, closely depend on the likelihood of labor turnover." To insure that workers who have received specific training do not quit, the employer has an incentive to offer them higher wages after training than could be received elsewhere (in effect, sharing some of the returns with employees). In short, specific training of employees provides an employer with an incentive to establish policies that lengthen expected periods of employment. These policies include not only wage premiums but also establishing or extending pension plans or profit-sharing plans, improving working conditions, guaranteeing promotion from within and so on (see Oi, 1962, p. 545).

General training is useful for firms other than those providing it; that is, it increases the employee's marginal product in other firms as well as in the one providing the training. Employers generally seek to have workers bear the costs of general training, since they have little assurance that the employee will not leave after securing such training. This means that employees undergoing general training would receive wages equal to their opportunity marginal productivity minus their current (opportunity) productivity (Becker 1964, p. 13). Persons receiving general training may be willing to pay these costs on the assumption that the training will increase their wages in the future (see Becker 1964). To the extent that the worker perceives uncertainty in future rewards, however, he tends to be less willing to bear the costs of training and thereby accept lower than marginal productivity wages during the first years of employment. An increase in employer willingness to guarantee employment security and a routinized wage increase formula will lead an employee to be more inclined to share the costs of training in a competitive labor market. Such guarantees reduce uncertainty concerning future rewards (Shimada 1974, p. 15). Similarly the existence of some kind of long-term employment contract or understanding leads employers to be more willing to share the costs of even general training. Such a contract in effect converts all training into completely specific training (Becker 1964, p. 27).

This brief treatment of human capital theory should be sufficient to establish that the interaction between wages, benefits and training appears to be an important variable determining worker propensity to change employers and employer propensity to retain workers. The practical effect of an increased employer propensity to retain workers is to provide them with a sense of career through a rising earnings and benefits profile. In particular, employees who have received specific training have less incentive to quit and employers have less incentive to fire them than is the case with employees who have received general training.

We shall use the theories of internal labor markets and human capital to explain our findings and where possible evaluate their utility. The data to be reported compare the patterns, volumes, and outcomes of inter- and intra-firm job mobility among individual male respondents in Detroit and Yokohama.

The Japanese comparison seems especially apt because of the distinct characteristics of male job mobility reported for Japan (Abegglen 1973; Cole 1971; Dore 1973). Other critical facts about the Japanese case deserve mention here: first, Japan sustained a high rate of rapid technological innovation at least since 1954, with the real economic growth rate averaging over 10 percent through 1970. This remarkable rate of change has been accompanied by drastic transformations in occupational structure; for example, the category of craftsmen, production process workers and laborers increased from 22 percent of total employment in 1950 to 32 percent in 1970, while clerical and related employees went from 8 percent in 1950 to 14 percent in 1970. At the same time, in a seeming paradox, the practice of permanent employment has been institutionalized in large firms. The appearance of paradox may arise from the failure to recognize the dual impact of rapid growth under conditions of labor surplus. Under rapid growth most growing firms had no need to engage in large-scale discharges. Yet if there was minimal need for discharges, workers also were reluctant to engage in voluntary job changing under conditions of labor surplus. Simply put, the incentives for large-scale job changing were not available in the aggregate. A wage system which put a heavy premium on age and length of service reinforced this tendency. This hardly does justice to the complexities of the subject. Yet quite apart from this explanation it seems clear that recruitment from external labor markets seems to have been minimized in postwar Japan relative to other industrial nations (Organization for Economic Cooperation and Development 1973).

Based upon these established facts is the unsubstantiated but commonly accepted view that intra-firm mobility takes on particular importance in Japan where the opportunity for external recruitment is limited (OECD 1973). Because of the high cost of having to guarantee employment to individuals until retirement, it is thought to be critical that the firm use its employees in the most efficient manner, transferring, upgrading, and downgrading them to avoid surpluses and shortages (Ono 1973, p. 4).

These suppositions fit with the reported company career consciousness of Japanese employees, whereby normally qualified regular male employees, especially in large firms, have reason to expect a step-by-step progression in rank, responsibility, and rewards. In this framework, advancement up the occupational ladder is contingent on length of service. The underlying assumption is that the employee accumulates experience and knowledge which make him valuable to his firm, but which commonly have less value to another employer. This situation is generally associated with selected white-collar mobility patterns in Western industrial societies (Hunter and Reid 1968, p. 90). In Japan, however, it seems to apply not only to an unusually high proportion of male white-collar employees, but to selected blue-collar workers as well (Cole 1971; Dore 1973, pp. 109–10). The rapid expansion of Japanese firms since 1955 involved the construction of new factories and establishment of related companies, and occurred in the context of a relatively youthful labor force. This provided promotion opportunities for large numbers of employees and thus gave substance to this structure (see Ono 1973, pp. 14–15). To express the matter differently, internal labor markets constituted the major arena within which individual socioeconomic achievement has been played out for large numbers of employees in the postwar period. We do not yet know the relative importance of internal versus external labor markets for individual socioeconomic achievement in the United States. However important internal labor markets turn out to be, there is prima facie evidence that they will prove to be a weaker determinant than is the case in Japan.

All things being equal, employers face a lower risk of losing their investment in specific as opposed to general training. The Japanese employer is willing and able to invest heavily in specific training, and even in what is usually thought of as general training, because the high rewards that he pays for seniority lead individual employees to develop a strong sense of loyalty to the firm. As a consequence the male employee of a large firm is highly conscious of the costs involved in his leaving the firm (see Nakane 1970). As we have seen earlier, there is an alternative model which separates the creation of this investment in human capital from its use. Large-scale Japanese employers seem to have been able to shift the burden of investment onto male employees in return for providing employment security and a regularized wage increase schedule. Youthful Japanese employees by their low wages (less than marginal productivity) bear the investment costs in both the specific and general training that is provided by Japanese employers. The training benefits employers in ways described above, as well as employees, for whom the uncertainty of future rewards is reduced. The practice of permanent employment in Japan tends to produce a long-term employee commitment among male employees in large firms so that in principle all general training becomes, in effect, employer-specific training. In a fundamental sense we see here the basis for the formation of careers as Stinchcombe, Wilensky, and Mannheim describe it. That is, it is the element of predictability that is central to the concept of career and it appears to be a condition of employment that large-scale Japanese employers have been willing to make available to regular male employees in the postwar period.

Numerous scholars suggest that the Japanese firm makes an unusually heavy investment in specific training (e.g., Dore 1973, pp. 71–73; Drucker 1971;

Organization for Economic Cooperation and Development 1973, pp. 137–39; Umetani 1968). Yet the evidence is often quite indirect. For example, these scholars point to the weakness of vocational training in postwar Japan (see also Reubens 1973). In our own questionnaire each respondent was asked to report on vocational, technical and apprenticeship courses and programs (both within and outside the company) taken in addition to formal education and informal on-the-job training.[3] Forty-nine percent of the 638 Detroit respondents reported such training, compared to only 22 percent of the 583 Yokohama respondents. The number of courses averaged 0.75 per respondent in Detroit compared to 0.25 per respondent in Yokohama. We also asked the respondents whether they used any of their coursework on their jobs. Thirty percent of the Detroit sample reported using material from one of their courses on their current job compared to only 12 percent in Yokohama.[4] These differences generally hold up by occupational and educational categories as well as by number of jobs previously held by respondent.

Not only do Detroit respondents take more courses (though it is still a minority of the total number of respondents) and use them more on their jobs, but the courses taken by Yokohama respondents are more company oriented. Of the 463 courses reported by Detroit respondents, 55 were apprenticeships and 336 were used on at least one of their jobs. In Yokohama, of the 145 courses listed, 135 were apprenticeships and 123 were used on at least one of their jobs. Thus a significantly higher proportion of the courses reported by Yokohama respondents were, by definition, in-company training programs. This is at best, however, only suggestive with regard to the alleged heavy investment made by Japanese management in specific training. Even though the Japanese may rely more heavily on in-house training, we would assume that most on-the-job training, at least for blue collar workers, takes place informally. How much of this training constitutes specific as opposed to general training is not immediately obvious.

Logically we would expect that the more necessary preentry or specialized training becomes, the less probable career mobility is once into an occupation (see Hunter and Reid 1968, p. 89). Increased investment prior to employment

3. The specific question asked was: "Aside from the regular education that people receive in grade school, high school, and college, and the informal on-the-job training they get, some people have had other courses such as technical, vocational training and apprenticeship programs. Have you ever had such training? Please include company schools where full-time study lasted *at least six weeks*. (Also include any vocational or technical training you may have received in the military service.)"

4. The U.S. Department of Labor (1964) carried out a similar survey in 1963 on a national sample. They examined the vocational training background of workers between the ages of twenty-two and sixty-four. The results are not directly comparable because the Department of Labor survey focused on those with less than three years of college, and included vocational, business, and commercial programs in high school. Forty-four percent of the males report having taken such training; 57 percent of those with such training report that they were using at least one skill learned through this training on their current job. Thurow (1975, p. 78) argues that most cognitive job skills in the United States, general or specific, are acquired either formally or informally through on-the-job training after a worker takes an entry job and participates in its promotion line.

narrows employee job options, though not necessarily employer options. In this sense the relatively unspecialized nature of Japanese public education dovetails well with the strength of the internal labor market. In the case of higher education Michio Nagai (1971, pp. 77–79, 84, 89) concludes that relative to the United States the Japanese university system serves more to grant credentials than to provide occupational specialists for society. Professional education in Japan, he believes, lacks the scope of such training in the United States and the rigor of Soviet practices. Dyck (1975, p. 91) discusses the failure of Japanese universities to produce professional engineers in the following implicitly comparative terms:

> Because of the lack of facilities and staff, universities impart only the basic knowledge necessary for future practical competence. It is up to the company to turn the graduate student into an engineer.

Peck and Tamura (1976, pp. 578–79) also emphasize the extensive investment in the training of engineers made by Japanese firms relative to American and British firms.[5] In the case of graduates of technical colleges, once employed the need for resuming their education to keep pace with rapid technological change and innovation is met primarily by in-service training. Universities, and particularly the national universities, have kept their doors closed to the graduates of technical colleges (Japanese National Commission for UNESCO 1972, p. 7). Doeringer and Piore (1971, p. 6) associate the importance of the internal labor market relative to the external labor market with investment in enterprise-specific human capital, on-the-job training, and the role of labor as a quasi-fixed factor of production. These characteristics are said to loom especially large in Japan (Somers and Tsuda 1966, pp. 195–337, esp. p. 207), though they are by no means absent in the United States (Kerr 1964; Doeringer and Piore 1971). It should be repeated, however, that we have no systematic and accepted measure of specific training in either Japan or the United States. The utility of the concept still remains to be demonstrated.

Japanese scholars have themselves increasingly come to accept the concept of the internal labor market as a useful mode of characterizing and rethinking the basis of the reward by age and length of service system (nenkō) in Japan (Koike 1962; Sumiya 1974; Sumiya 1974a). As early as 1962, Koike was struck by the universality of certain Japanese practices. He theorized that the introduction of mass production systems led to increasing specialization of tasks, on-the-job training and an internal wage structure. With a closed labor market the need to match wages precisely with particular jobs is reduced and the firm can pay salaries more in accord with length of service. Some Japanese scholars, however, are critical of the applicability of the concept of internal labor markets to

5. The Conference Board (New York Times 1977) conducted a study of in-house education by major U.S. corporations in 1975. In the course of the study they examined executive satisfaction with the occupational preparation of school graduates. The responding executives of 610 companies reported considerable dissatisfaction with the occupational preparation of graduates from liberal arts colleges (by a three-to-one ratio). These same executives believed (by a ten-to-one ratio) that four-year engineering science colleges did a good job in preparing employees, as did vocational schools.

Japan. Funahashi (1975), in criticizing Sumiya's usage, argues that the concept leads to an underestimation of the extent to which the external labor market works to determine wage rates, that the original exposition by Piore and Doeringer was not built on a firm data base, and that the concept minimizes the fundamental differences between Japanese and American practices. With regard to the latter, Funahashi argues specifically that the degree of built-in automatic wage increases associated with merit ratings in the United States is quite moderate and cannot be equated with the *nenkō* practice. Most of his criticisms, however, can be interpreted to mean not that the concept of the internal labor market itself is inapplicable, but rather that we must devise a more comprehensive modelling of the wage determination process (so that the impact of the external labor market is represented). Similarly we must allow for international variations in the strength, historical origins, and bases of the internal labor markets (cf. Shimada 1975). The distinctive origins and structural characteristics of the internal labor markets in Japan and the United States will be dealt with in Chapter IV.

Finally, as public ideology, inter-firm mobility in the United States is associated with success; the image is of self-reliant individuals seeking out their own destiny. Suttles (1973, pp. 173–76) details the existence of an indigenous laissez faire ideology which makes an ideal of everyone's full ability to bargain in the labor market. To recognize that many workers are company men would be to question the ubiquity of the laissez faire model in America and be disruptive of it. Suttles concludes that a modern industrial society cannot function if it is fragmented into territorial groups of such a small scale as the firm because of the recurrent need to reconstitute work groups irrespective of current loyalties. Consequently he believes that industrial society cannot tolerate a dissident ideology which recognizes the legitimacy of territoriality in work.

In making this latter argument, Suttles seems to have become a prisoner of this very ideology himself. He shares this distinction with many in the modernization field and especially with the popularizers of the idea of a distinctive "post-industrial" society (e.g., Toffler 1970; Bennis and Slater 1968). Yet in Japan, an advanced industrial society, there is a sharply contrasting public ideology as advocated by managerial and government officials. The latter identifies inter-firm mobility with failure; the image portrays those who leave employment in large firms as having been found wanting in quality, and for that matter those who work in smaller firms are presumed never to have had the qualifications necessary to secure entrance into a large modern firm (Tsuda 1968; Koike 1975, p. 14). Quite naturally, in this world view, the company man appears as a culture hero and "territoriality" is put on the highest pedestal. In the words of a government publication, "In Western countries changing employers is designed to increase the workers' income but in our country (because of the permanent employment and reward by age and length of service systems), changing employers can be thought of as a response to *defective* [italics added] human relations" (Office of the Prime Minister 1973, p. 27).

We can not assume that these contrasting ideologies reflect actual behavioral patterns. In Japan the strong interests of ruling elites underlie the territoriality ideology. In the United States employers, the government, and econo-mists are by no means unaware of the costs of high levels of turnover, yet the laissez faire ideology prevails. The ideology obviously has still other benefits from the viewpoint of the ruling elites, insofar as it serves to convince the mass of Americans that everyone can climb the ladder of success by bargaining in the open market to the best of his or her ability. In view of the strong class interests that underlie the contrasting ideologies, a detailed analysis of job-changing patterns and their associated rewards is required. Groves (1975) pro-vides some initial insights into the U.S. situation, using national data, with his findings that inter-firm job changers tend to increase their wages proportionately over their peers who remain with the same firm. Inter-firm job changers are, however, predominantly first-year workers at lower wage levels. Controlling for length of service, the differences in wage gains diminish, with wage changes for those experiencing inter-firm mobility becoming more erratic relative to those experiencing intra-firm job changes.

Notwithstanding the seeming importance of intra-firm mobility in Japan, apart from selected case studies by Japanese scholars there has been no syste-matic investigation of intra-firm mobility, much less systematic comparative research on the subject.[6] Our research should permit a partial assessment of the above interpretations. We will present and evaluate evidence on the purported differences in labor force experiences in the two cities in the course of describing the respective job-changing patterns.

Sample

The data were collected in a 1970 sample of 638 residents of the Detroit metropolitan area. Dwelling units within the metropolitan area were chosen by means of a multi-stage probability sampling plan devised and supervised by the sampling section of the Institute for Social Research of the University of Michi-gan. Within dwelling units respondents were picked at random from among those eligible. To be eligible an individual had to be male, between the ages of sixteen and sixty, have worked for pay for a period of at least six months at

6. The closest the Ministry of Labor comes to measuring intra-firm mobility is in the Survey of Employment Trends (Koyō Dōkō Chosa Hokoku). This is an establish-ment-based survey which reports the number of individuals transferred from one plant in a company to another plant. In 1971 this number totalled 753,800, or some 17 percent of all separated employees. However this not inconsiderable total is not broken down into those whose job is actually changed and those who continue to do the same job. Moreover it does not include those within a given plant who experience job transfers (Ministry of Labor 1972a, p. 34). The usual translation of job transfer in Japanese is *haichi tenkan*, but conversations with numerous management and union officials indicate that this term commonly refers to changes between sections or departments, and may include cases in which the individual is doing the same job but in a different department or section. It is not unusual for Japanese unions to become involved in such matters. Job changes taking place within the small work unit are, however, often left to the discretion of the foreman. Depending on the company a variety of different terminologies are used, such as *jōbu rōtēshon* (job rotation) and *shokushu henka* (change in type-of-work). The absence of union involvement in internal job changes contrasts with the relatively higher involve-ment of many U.S. unions in these matters.

some time in his life, and be in the labor force, i.e., either employed or looking for work, at the time of the interview. The 638 completed interviews represent approximately 70 percent of the estimated number of eligible individuals in the sample. The remaining 30 percent is accounted for by 15 percent refusals and another 15 percent of the respondents whom we were unable to locate for a variety of reasons. The sample of 638 contained 536 white males and 102 black males.

In Japan 583 interviews, nearly parallel to those administered in Detroit, were conducted in 1971 on the basis of a multi-stage probability sample of members of the labor force of the city of Yokohama.[7] The 583 interviews represent approximately 80 percent of the eligible sample. The representative character of the two samples will be discussed below in the context of our analysis of specific variables.

The data to be presented rest on the compilation of the complete work histories of respondents by interviewers. The one exception involves pre-1945 work experience; for respondents with such experience, only the first full-time job prior to 1945 was collected. Thus for those with pre-1945 experiences of more than one job, the data are incomplete (we refer to incomplete states hereafter as "gap states"). Six percent of the total person years between start of first job and interview fall into the gap state in Detroit and 1.6 percent in Yokohama. The discrepancy between the two cities is partially explained by the mode of calculation interacting with the lower mobility of the Japanese respondents. Specifically, time in the gap state spent in jobs which terminated after 1945 was excluded from the above calculations. The point to emphasize, however, is that the proportion of person-years spent in the gap state represents a significant blank in our knowledge, at least in the case of Detroit. The particular strategy that led to this outcome was dictated by time constraints. Respondents were requested to supply detailed job descriptions for each job experience (labelled a job state). Information was also collected on interrupted job states, including periods of unemployment and withdrawals from the labor force resulting from health problems, a return to school, military service, etc. The longitudinal data and inter-cohort comparisons to be discussed thus rest on retrospective data; the inherent limitations of such data are significant. For the present, however, we have one of the few data sets which permit examination and comparison of intra- and inter-firm mobility.

Job-change data are less subject to distortion than attitude data, but if we examine different types of job-change data, there are likely to be differences in recall abilities and amount of distortion. In particular, respondents will have more difficulty in recalling intra-firm job changes than inter-firm ones. The latter often involve residential and geographic changes, new commuting patterns, and adjustments to new sets of workmates and managers. We will have the opportunity to discuss this matter again in the context of specific hypotheses.

A related problem is that the data represent work experience of a cross-

7. The sample design was devised and interviewing supervised by Komai Hiroshi, then of the Population Problems Institute of the Ministry of Public Welfare, and Nihei Yasumitsu of Keio University.

section, consequently leaving us with empty cells for the incomplete work experiences of the younger respondents. This severely limits the types of possible inter-cohort comparisons. It is also true that we have at best a representative sample of the male labor force for Detroit only in 1970 and for Yokohama only in 1971. Thus when we talk about the earlier labor force experiences of this sample, we cannot assume that these experiences are representative of labor force experiences say in 1950. This is because many of the people in the labor force in 1950 may have since left the labor force or moved away from the Detroit or Yokohama area. Again, we will have the opportunity to point to this problem in the context of specific hypotheses.

We have gathered data for the purpose of examining work history patterns. Consequently the most suitable unit of analysis for us is individual behavior. Nevertheless we are handicapped in answering certain questions about intra-firm mobility patterns as a result of not having available the firm as a unit of analysis. For example, we cannot utilize the vacancy-chain model elaborated by White (1970). The ideal dataset would include a probability sample of employed individuals and their employers; resources for this purpose were not, however, available to us. Notwithstanding, we have collected data on firm size and industry for each job change as reported by individual respondents; this does give us some leverage in assessing the impact of organizational characteristics.

A brief discussion of the selection of the two cities, Detroit and Yokohama, is in order. The selection process involved a mixture of fortuitous events, constraints imposed by limited resources, and attempts to match characteristics. The Detroit Standard Metropolitan Statistical Area (SMSA) became the target as a result of the author having been selected as the chief investigator for the Detroit Area Study, an annual project of the Department of Sociology of the University of Michigan. The counterpart Japanese city (not metropolitan area) was selected to provide a rough match of the characteristics of Detroit, particularly in terms of its industrial structure. Yokohama was selected in the final analysis because its industrial structure was comparable to that of Detroit and its location was convenient for my Japanese collaborators, who were based in Tokyo. A profile of the two cities reveals both significant differences and similarities, and is broadly suggestive of the patterns and volume of job mobility we report below.

The city of Detroit, located in southern Michigan on the Detroit River, between Lakes St. Clair and Erie, had its origins in the late eighteenth century as a trading post. The French fort and settlement community were taken over by the British in 1760, with American control being established in 1796. The city began to develop rapidly after 1830 as a consequence of improved land and water transportation. Connected to New York by the Erie Canal, it became a major link in the emerging national transportation system. By the middle of the nineteenth century its shipbuilding, shipping, and manufacturing activities brought the city to national prominence. It was conveniently situated to receive shipments of iron ore and copper from the North, convert Michigan's own forests to lumber and other consumer goods, transport immigrants to the West, and agricultural products from the West to the East. The development of the railroads in the latter quarter of the nineteenth century spurred these developments, and the city's population increased rapidly. The foundation laid by the railroad and carriage industries became the basis for the emergence of Detroit as the center of the world's automobile industry and the largest city in the state of Michigan. Other notable manufacturing industries include steel mills, food processing, chemical machinery, and metal products. Detroit is a port of entry and a major Great Lakes shipping and rail center. In 1970 it was the fifth largest city in the nation, with 1.5 million inhabitants.

Beginning in the 1950s, economic decline became noticeable. Business enterprises increasingly relocated to the suburbs, and the city itself lost about 340,000 in population between 1950 and 1970. At the same time the racial composition of the city began to change rapidly. Blacks made up 16 percent of the city population in 1950, 29 percent in 1960 and 45 percent just ten years later. A white exodus to the suburbs ensued, while the black population more than doubled between 1950 and 1970. Although the city itself lost population, the overall metropolitan area continued to grow, increasing from three million to four million in this same period. By using the Detroit Standard Metropolitan Statistical Area as the universe for our sample, we include both the expanding and declining parts of the area. In 1970 the city of Detroit constituted approximately 35 percent of the total population of the Detroit SMSA (Holli 1976).

The city of Yokohama in central Honshu island is located on the western shore of Tokyo Bay just twenty miles south of Tokyo; it is the capital of Kanagawa prefecture. Yokohama had its origin as a small fishing village; it was the Meiji Restoration in 1867, and subsequent opening up of Japan to foreign trade, that led to its rapid growth. Indeed, it was among the most rapidly growing cities in Japan in the latter part of the nineteenth century, with silk and canned fish being two of the exports associated with its growth as a port city. By 1891 it was the sixth largest city in the nation.

From 1920 to 1940 heavy industries began to develop in the area of Tokyo, Yokohama, and the surrounding prefectures of Saitama and Chiba; iron and steel, chemicals, and engineering industries were the most notable. Population growth followed; twenty of the 124 new cities incorporated in the period from 1920 to 1940 were within this area (Wilkinson 1965, pp. 66–67). This gave added impetus to the growth of Yokohama. By 1920 its population had risen to over 400,000.

Yokohama was heavily bombed during World War II, but resumed its growth after the end of the war. It continued to build on its transport industries and developed important electrical machinery and transportation equipment industries, including shipbuilding and auto. Steel, machine tool, and chemical industries also developed in importance. As the capital of Kanagawa prefecture, Yokohama developed a service-administration sector as well. In 1970 it was the fifth largest city in Japan, with a population of 2.2 million.

After 1950 population and industry began to concentrate in unprecedented numbers in the area of Tokyo and its surrounding prefectures. Administrative prefectural and city boundaries were crossed to produce a large-scale integrated economic system of production and consumption. At present the population of Tokyo and the prefectures of Chiba, Saitama and Kanagawa represents a concentrated urban agglomeration of twenty-five million. This constitutes 24 percent of Japan's total population. Twenty-one percent of the total number of businesses are located here, in a region comprising only 3.6 percent of Japan's total land area. Yokohama is an integral part of the metropolitan Tokyo area.

In 1970 the population of the Detroit SMSA was approximately double that of Yokohama City (4,199,931 to 2,238,264). The Detroit population is dis- tributed over a much larger geographical area; the Detroit SMSA (1,952 square miles) is more than ten times the size of that of Yokohama City (161 square miles). As noted, however, Yokohama City is an integral part of an industrial belt that also includes nearby Tokyo. Many employment sites outside the city are easily accessible to people living in Yokohama as a consequence of the efficient Japanese commuter rail and bus systems. Indeed, about one-third of the over-fifteen work force living in Yokohama worked outside the city in 1970—approximately two-thirds of them were employed in Tokyo. Two lines of the national railroad and two private rail lines carry some 780,000 people each day into Tokyo from the Yokohama area. On the other hand, 19 percent of the total employed in Yokohama City commuted from outside the city, with almost one-quarter of them coming from Tokyo. In the city of Detroit 33 percent of the employed sixteen years and older were working outside the city in 1970. This is strikingly similar to Yokohama City. Our sample is not drawn from the city of Detroit, however, but from the Detroit SMSA. Only 2 percent of workers living in the Detroit SMSA work outside the SMSA. Thus the Detroit sample is drawn from a quite inclusive labor market, and we would not be amiss to assume that the inferences we draw from the data are descriptive of this labor market (see U.S. Bureau of the Census 1973). Such is not the case in Yokohama, since our sample captures only a piece of a larger labor market (see Office of the Prime Minister 1972). Consequently we cannot assume that our inferences are descriptive of this broader labor market. This should be kept in mind in evaluating our results. Our sample data are suggestive in this regard: 35 percent of our Yokohama respondents reported that it took them an hour or more to get to work from home, compared to only 4 percent of the Detroit sample. Roughly comparable aggregate data for Yokohama suggest the representative character of our sample: 36.1 percent of Yokohama residents who were the main earners of the household commuted more than one hour to work in 1973 (Office of the Prime Minister 1976, pp. 222–23).

An examination of population changes in Detroit and Yokohama since 1930, when the oldest respondents entered the work force, is instructive. From 1930 to 1970 the population of the Detroit SMSA did not quite double, while the population of Yokohama City nearly quadrupled. With only minor land annexations, the population of Yokohama increased by more than 60 percent in the 1960s. During this same period, the population of the Detroit SMSA increased only some 12 percent and was concentrated in a land area just slightly smaller than the 1,978 square miles which constituted the SMSA in 1930. The expansion of industry reflected by the growth of Yokohama's population suggests a dynamic labor market with large-scale opportunities for both inter- and intra-firm mobility. Nevertheless, we cannot attribute these opportunities to specific individuals, since the individual opportunity structure is the outcome of a complex equation reflecting the capital individuals bring to the market (including age, education, and work skills) and the actual internal and external employment opportunities represented by the practices of specific firms. Notwithstanding these qualifications, the rapid growth of Yokohama, based on the increased demand for employees, would seem in the aggregate to have been conducive to high (voluntary) inter-firm and intra-firm job changing relative to Detroit. In terms of the arguments to be presented in Chapter III, this situation reinforces the interpretations proposed in Chapter IV.

Our sample data reflect the important role of immigration in Yokohama. Fifty percent of our Detroit respondents were born and raised in Detroit, and an additional 20 percent had lived in Detroit for twenty-five years or more. This compares to only 28 percent of the Yokohama sample born and raised in the city, and an additional 10 percent who had lived there for more than twenty-five years. It is possible that some of these differences are accounted for by the smaller size of the Yokohama unit, which excludes the outside ring of population. If we had a sample of the more inclusive labor market, we might expect the rate of immigration into Yokohama to drop. When we examine the age at which migration to the respective cities took place, it is clear that most of the moves occurred during the prime working-force ages. Some 63.6 percent of the Detroit migrants moved to the area between the ages of fifteen and thirty-seven and an even larger 76.9 percent of Yokohama migrants moved during this interval. The impression that the Yokohama migrants' decision was more work-related than that of the Detroit migrants is supported by the observation that 28.5 percent of the Detroit migrants moved between the ages of one and fourteen; we may presume they had dependent status at this age. However, only 9.1 percent of the Yokohama migrants reported moving to Yokohama between the ages of one and fourteen.

An examination of the educational achievement of migrants and non-migrants in the two cities is quite suggestive. There is no difference in the educational attainment of migrants and non-migrants in the case of Yokohama, while for Detroit wide differences in the expected direction appear (i.e., migrants have lower levels of educational attainment). Specifically, 44.6 percent of the migrants to Detroit had less than twelve years of education, compared to only 24.1 percent of the non-migrants. The image of city growth suggested by the data is that Detroit has been slow to turn from its traditional role of providing employment for less educated workers who staff semiskilled jobs in manufacturing and low level jobs in the service sector. The lack of difference in educational achievement for migrants and non-migrants in Yokohama suggests a city which, in its rapid growth, has provided a range of employment opportunities sufficient to draw migrants in all education categories. The similarity of migrants and non-migrants in level of educational attainment must also be understood in the context of the Tokyo-Yokohama region being the center of higher education in Japan. There is a ready surplus of more highly educated persons in the area, many having migrated to enter universities. The difficulty of securing adequate

TABLE 2
Percentage Distribution of Total Employed
Persons (Both Sexes) by Industry: Detroit and Yokohama, 1970[a]

	Yokohama	Detroit
Agriculture	1.5	—
Construction	8.9	4.3
Manufacturing	35.5	37.4
Wholesale and retail	20.6	19.8
Finance, insurance, real estate	3.7	4.7
Transport, communication, electricity, gas and water	11.2	5.6
Services	15.4	22.8
Government	2.9	4.0
Non-classified	1.8	1.3
Total	101.5[b]	99.9[b]
Base for percentages	1,058,905	1,570,953

[a] In Yokohama data include persons fifteen years of age and over; in Detroit, sixteen years of age and over.

[b] Total differs from 100.0% because of rounding error.

SOURCE: Yokohama (Office of the Prime Minister 1970:Table 14). Detroit (U.S. Bureau of the Census 1973:Table 186).

housing in Tokyo contributes to a "spillover" of those living in Yokohama and commuting to the Tokyo area.

Although I reported earlier that the population of the Detroit SMSA was almost twice that of Yokohama City, the difference in size of employed labor force (both sexes) is much smaller. The employed labor force living in Yokohama City totalled 1,073,000, compared to some 1,570,000 in the Detroit SMSA. Two-thirds of this narrowing in size differentials is accounted for by the higher proportion of the population in Yokohama which falls into the productive working ages. An additional one-third of the narrowing is accounted for by the higher labor force participation rate in Yokohama: 63 percent compared to 59 percent in the Detroit SMSA. An examination of the industrial profile of the two cities in 1970 (see Table 2) via census data reveals some notable similarities. In particular the proportion of total employment in the manufacturing, wholesale and retail trade, and finance, insurance and real estate categories is almost identical in the two cities. The major differences lie in the higher proportion located in the construction and transport categories in Yokohama, and the higher proportion employed in services in Detroit. The prominence of Yokohama as a port and entrepôt for the Tokyo metropolitan area helps explain the large numbers in the transportation category, and probably influences the construction category as well. The larger proportion employed in services in Detroit reflects differences in the health and educational services subcategories. Although the Detroit SMSA has 50 percent more employed persons, it has 325 percent more employed in health and educational services. Apart from the impact of differing coding assignments, the cities' different demographic profiles would seem particularly relevant to explaining these differences.

The overall similarity in the distribution of employment by industry must be understood not simply as the author's attempt to match cities. Rather, in any city on the scale of Yokohama and Detroit, a common set of core activities must go on for the city to function; this alone may constitute 35 percent of labor force activities (Morrisset 1958).

A further concern of many readers, no doubt, is the role of the automobile industry in Detroit and how it might influence our subsequent comparisons. The Detroit auto industry is currently much less dominant in Detroit SMSA employment than is popularly thought. The early postwar period was marked by the failure of a number of long-time Detroit automobile manufacturers such as Packard and Hudson. In the past twenty-five years, the remaining Big Three have diversified their facilities to move closer to regional and international markets, and many of the parts suppliers followed suit. As a consequence the relative position of automobile-related employment in the Detroit SMSA has declined significantly. In 1950 those employed in the motor vehicle and motor vehicle equipment category accounted for 28 percent of the total employed in the Detroit SMSA. By 1970 the percentage had dropped to only 17 percent (U.S. Bureau of the Census 1952, 1973). This represented an absolute as well as a relative decline. For males only the decline was from 33 percent in 1950 to 23 percent in 1970.

An examination of our sample reveals that 23.3 percent of the total number of job states reported by Detroit respondents originated in the motor vehicle and motor vehicle equipment category. This compares to 4 percent of the job states in the Yokohama sample.[8] In short, although automobile employment in Detroit remains a most significant feature of the sample's labor force experience, it does not dominate, at least in a direct sense. Finally, the image of a regimented assembly line worker as the typical auto worker is a gross caricature. Only a small proportion of auto workers work in assembly plants. To be sure, there are assembly line operations in manufacturing plants, but then it is also true that in a typical assembly plant perhaps 20 percent of the hourly rated may not be working directly on the assembly line. About 30 percent of all hourly rated employees at General Motors are classified at the level of the model production wage (though not all of these are assemblers). General Motors management officials estimate that about 16 percent of its hourly rated employees are classified as skilled workers, another 16 percent as semiskilled (e.g., job setter, spray painter, welder), with the rest essentially unskilled laborers in that only minimum training time is required before they are producing at normal levels. This is quite different from the distributions suggested by sociologists. For example, Blauner (1964) estimated that in 1950 the automobile industry was composed of 29 percent skilled craftsmen and foremen, 64 percent semiskilled operatives, and 7 percent unskilled laborers. It is not that the situation has changed so much between now and 1950, but rather that Blauner took literally the occupational categories and classifications of workers reported by the Bureau of the Census.

8. These numbers reflect the fact that the auto industry, by its higher turnover compared to many other industries, "creates" a larger number of job states.

TABLE 3
**Percentage Distribution of Employed
Persons (Both Sexes) in Non-Agricultural
Labor Force by Occupation: Detroit and Yokohama, 1970[a]**

	Yokohama	Detroit
Professional, technical and kindred	9.4	14.4
Managers and administrators	9.1	7.1
Clerical and kindred	21.4	19.2
Sales	9.6	7.2
Craftsmen, foremen and kindred; operatives		
except transport; laborers except farm	37.5	36.0
Transport equipment operatives	4.8	3.8
Service workers	8.2	12.4
Non-classified	—	—
Total	100.0	100.1[b]
Base for percentages	1,038,607	1,567,158

[a] In Yokohama data include persons fifteen years of age and over; in Detroit, sixteen years of age and over.

[b] Total differs from 100.0% because of rounding error.

SOURCE: Yokohama (Office of the Prime Minister 1972:Table 21). Detroit (U.S. Bureau of the Census 1973:Table 171).

NOTE: To produce more comparable categories we collapsed and split some of the conventional categories used in both nations. For Detroit the craftsmen, foremen and kindred worker category was combined with operatives and laborers to make it comparable to the standard blue-collar category in Japan. Personnel and labor relations workers were removed from the professional and technical category to make it more comparable to Yokohama, where such workers are with few exceptions classified as clerical. In the case of Yokohama the communications occupations were split from transport occupations and entered into the general blue-collar category to make it consistent with U.S. assignments. In addition retail dealers and restaurant operators were moved from the sales-worker category and added to managers and officials to increase comparability with U.S. categories. Members of the self-defense forces entered in the service occupations were removed entirely from the sample to limit our consideration to the civilian labor force.

As Braverman (1974, p. 424–47) shows, these categories and classifications grossly distort the level of skill required. For our purposes the classification of machine operatives as semiskilled workers as opposed to non-farm laborers is of particular import. The upgrading implied in this classification is little more than a sleight of hand in view of the minimum training time required by these jobs. In summary, the estimates of General Motors management officials bring us closer to the real skill distributions of the industry, allowing for differences between the firm and industry, than do reliance on census categories and classifications.

An examination of the occupational structure of the two cities is also in order. As is the case with industry, we find striking similarities in the occupational distributions within the two cities (see Table 3) and for some of the same reasons discussed earlier. The often arbitrary coding assignments in use by the censuses of both nations should lead us to interpret these similarities and differences with some caution. The most significant difference between the two cities, and one that bears some discussion, lies in the professional and technical category. These differences are apparent at the national level as well; Japan is notable for the low proportion of professional and technical workers compared to other advanced industrial societies as reported in the *Yearbook of Labour Statistics* (International Labour Office 1975). Some of these differences are real, in the sense that specialization of function and training for certain economic activities has not proceeded as far in Japan. For example, there are only 925 lawyers, judges and prosecutors in Yokohama, compared to 5,481 in the Detroit SMSA. In other cases the matter is more complicated. There are, for example, 16,187 accountants in Detroit, compared to only 845 registered accountants in Yokohama. This reflects, in part, differing legal requirements. We find coded under clerical workers in Yokohama an additional 52,000 accounting clerks; moreover, company auditors are coded under managerial employees as company directors. In the case of accounting clerks, there is no comparable category in the United States, but accounting clerks are coded as clerical workers under the titles of bookkeepers and bookkeeping and billing machine operators. Undoubtedly some of these personnel are performing similar functions to those accountants classified as professionals in the United States. This discussion should illustrate some of the difficulties of developing comparable categories as well as of interpreting differences (see U.S. Bureau of the Census 1971; Office of the Prime Minister 1970). More generally, 72 percent of the difference in the size of the professional and technical categories between the two cities is accounted for by only three categories: engineers and technicians, health-related occupations, and professors and teachers. Some portion of these differences may be explained by the assignments of individuals performing such functions to clerical, managerial, and crafts categories in Yokohama. For example, craftsmen are classified as technicians in the U.S., but are placed in the crafts category in Japan.

Yet the magnitude of the differences is too great to be explained by differing assignments. The differences are consistent with the relatively low investment the Japanese make in education and health services (though they insure a more egalitarian distribution of the benefits derived from these investments). One reason for these smaller investments is that there are fewer individuals attending schools and far fewer older people; older individuals have a higher demand for health services than the general population. With respect to education, there are 3.3 times more individuals in school in the Detroit SMSA than there are in Yokohama, although the population is not quite twice as large. Thus it is not surprising that there should be fewer teachers in Yokohama.

In part because of the above-mentioned difficulties in insuring comparable categories—differences could be elaborated for each of the occupational categories—we have used formal education instead of occupation as a major analytic distinction in our subsequent Detroit-Yokohama analysis. It is more directly comparable between individuals and cities and, unlike occupation, has the virtue of being relatively unchanging over an individual's worklife. Yet we note for informational purposes that the occupational distribution of the two samples by current job is relatively comparable to the 1970 census reports for males in both cities. In Yokohama, however, we oversampled the sales category (14.2% compared to the census report of 10.4%) and undersampled the blue-collar craftsmen, foremen, and operative category, including transportation and communication (41.0% compared to the census report of 48.3%). On the other hand, the Detroit sample contains a higher proportion of managers and administrators than this category accounts for in the census data (16.5% compared to the census report of 9.3%) and a correspondingly lower proportion of both sales and service workers than reported by the census. We have reason to believe that the variance between sample data and census reports enumerated here stems more from coding problems in the case of Yokohama than is the case in Detroit.

We now examine the size and number of employing establishments in the Detroit SMSA and Yokohama City, keeping in mind that many of those living in Yokohama City work outside the city. Unfortunately it is only in the case of manufacturing that the concept of establishment is similarly defined in the two locations (i.e., a branch of a firm is counted as a separate establishment). In 1970 there were 6,788 manufacturing establishments in Detroit out of a total of 56,921 establishments. In Yokohama, at the same time, there were 7,408 manufacturing establishments out of a total of 72,443 (despite the fact that the number employed in Yokohama was only 67 percent that of the Detroit SMSA). The mean number of employees per manufacturing establishment in Detroit was 83.2, well over twice the 35.6 recorded for Yokohama. For non-manufacturing concerns, the data show Detroit establishments recording a mean number of employees of 15, twice the 7.5 registered for Yokohama. Because of differing definitions of establishment referred to above, however, the number of establishments in Detroit relative to Yokohama in non-manufacturing units is underestimated.

Were size of firm and number of discrete units the sole determinants of intra- and inter-firm job-changing possibilities, these figures would suggest a favoring of inter-firm changing in Yokohama and intra-firm changing in Detroit. As will be discussed below, however, the causal connections are a good deal more complicated. In any case, controls for firm size and industry should minimize, though not eliminate, the likelihood that such differences significantly distort our findings.

A final consideration in this presentation of city profiles concerns our ability to generalize about entire nations from the findings in these two cities. Undoubtedly labor market practices vary by city and region within the two societies, and are influenced by such factors as rate of industrial growth and mix of industrial and occupational characteristics (see Fuchs 1967). One must, therefore, exercise extreme caution before making such generalizations. As a rough check we may compare the distribution of employees by industry in the two cities to the relevant national figures for non-agricultural employees. These comparisons reveal that the Yokohama distributions are remarkably similar to the national totals, but that some marked differences appear when we compare the Detroit distributions to the national ones and to the average for the eleven largest cities in 1970. The major difference lies in the more prominent role of manufacturing (37.4 percent in Detroit compared to 27.4 percent nationally and 27.5 percent for the SMSA's of the eleven largest cities). Correspondingly, with the exception of government employment, the Detroit SMSA scores slightly lower in each of the other major industry categories compared to the averages for the eleven largest cities. The major discrepancy occurs in the service sector, which accounts for 14.8 percent of Detroit SMSA employment; the average for the SMSA's of the eleven largest cities is 18.3 (Holli 1976, p. 280). These differences should be kept in mind in evaluating the subsequent analysis. Nonetheless, one must start somewhere, and Detroit seems no poorer a choice than many other major cities.

Conceptualizations

The basic unit of analysis is individually recorded job changes. By job we mean a bundle of tasks that individuals are assigned to perform as part of their employment contract. Occupational categories are groupings of related jobs. Our concern is with a specific aspect of what labor economists commonly refer to as labor mobility. To the labor economist, labor mobility is a means of achieving an improved distribution of labor resources to bring about more efficient production. For the sociologist, job mobility is primarily a means of or threat to individual socioeconomic achievement and security. Job change or job mobility, as we use the terms, refer to both intra- and inter-firm mobility. Unlike intra-firm job changing, a change in employer (inter-firm job changing) does not by definition result in a change in the job tasks being performed.[9] Nevertheless, we follow convention in referring to a change of employer as a type of job changing.

It is tempting to look at inter-firm job changing as a model of employee decision making and intra-firm job changing in terms of employer decision making. Although this may be useful as a rough characterization for some purposes, it represents a gross oversimplification. Employee decision making with regard to inter-firm job changing is conditional upon the hiring decisions of new employers as well as involuntary discharges or threatened discharges. Intra-firm job changing, on the other hand, is influenced by employee support for seniority and other provisions regulating intra-firm movement; these arrangements may be formalized at the insistence of unions. Moreover, employee threats to change employers often have an impact on employers' job transfer policies.[10]

Intra-firm job changes derive either from change in the job being performed within the organization or from the transfer of the employee to a new job within the same firm. In either case the job change may or may not register as occupational change as measured by the various occupational classification schemes in use. As we have seen, this reveals the arbitrary character of attempts to define and measure occupational mobility that has so bedeviled researchers. Simply increasing the detail of the occupational codes (i.e., increasing the number of categories used) increases the amount of occupational mobility, independent of any behavioral change (cf. Groves 1975, pp. 124–39). Since we are engaged in a comparative study, these problems are even more severe.

With respect to intra-firm job changes, some of the problems of conceptual-

9. An employee shift from one department or section to another without a change in job duties is not defined as an intra-firm job change.

10. Note the difference between our position and Harrison White's insistence that the major constraint on volume of intra-firm job changing is the number of vacancies created by termination of occupants and creation of new jobs. We are more concerned with who makes decisions than with how the amount of job changing is determined.

ization become evident if we consider the possibility not only of workers changing jobs but also of the jobs themselves changing. The most common form of labor mobility, suggest Hunter and Reid (1968, p. 28), involves small innovations in job duties, which in turn require some degree of flexibility on the part of labor. Looked at in this light, job mobility becomes a pervasive phenomenon. It should also be clear that problems of identification, measurement, and comparison become insurmountable when the concept is defined in this broad fashion. In order to tap mobility of this sort, we would require more detailed characterizations of job duties over time than we could possibly obtain. What we do have instead are data on the changes in job duties reported by respondents; these necessarily become the basis of our operational definition. Although this constitutes a narrowing of the concept of intra-firm job changing, it does tap an important dimension—that of individual perception of change. It focuses on that aspect of intra-firm job changing that may be characterized as a social process. This approach also allows the aggregation of data so that broad comparisons can be made. A particular danger, however, is that cultural and structural differences in the two societies may lead respondents in the two cities to differential perception of intra-firm job changes. There is, in fact, reason to think that this is the case and the matter will be discussed in Chapter IV.

One final problem with the concept of intra-job change, as we have operationalized it, derives from the source of data being a retrospective cross-section. Job content changes over time in terms of additions or subtractions of duties, responsibilities and rewards (though job titles may remain the same). But individual respondents will, we believe, often average out these changes or just report the most recent or perhaps the beginning job duties, rather than report changes over time. Consequently we lose the job mobility that arises from job enlargement or job shrinkage (see White 1970, pp. 171–79). Not having access to individuals over time so that we can ask them the nature of their job duties at different points in time, we are at the mercy of their subjective "frozen" descriptions.

Clearly many of the conceptual and measurement problems heretofore discussed with respect to intra-firm job changing are minimal in the case of inter-firm job changing. Nevertheless, they are by no means absent. A rapid succession of employer changes in a short period, particularly at an early stage in the work history, presents difficult problems of recall. Because we would question the validity and reliability of such information even if reported, and in response to the time constraints on our interview schedule, we elected not to request detailed information for jobs lasting less than six months, though we did solicit a report of every job held, no matter what its duration. Thus for these "short" jobs we know when they happened, but nothing about the employer or the occupation involved, and we do not even know how many different employers are involved if an individual experienced a consecutive series of these short jobs with different employers. Of the "states" which record experience in the labor force (1948 in Yokohama and 3598 in Detroit) about 1 percent of those in Yokohama and 8 percent of those in Detroit refer to these short jobs and are lost to detailed analysis by our interview design. In terms of time spent, 0.4

percent of the person-years of labor force experience of our Yokohama sample and 1.4 percent of those of our Detroit sample were in these short jobs. The distribution of short jobs by age is similar to what one would expect, with a rather heavy concentration at the younger ages. Thus if we compare time spent in short jobs to person-years of experience in the labor force (i.e., time spent either employed or "looking for work"), about 3 percent of the experience between ages sixteen and twenty-five, 1 percent of the experience between ages twenty-six and thirty-five, 0.5 percent of the experience between ages thirty-six and forty-five, and almost none of the experience at older ages is gained in jobs of less than six months' duration in Detroit. The corresponding percentages for Yokohama are about 0.8 percent, less than 0.5 percent, almost none and almost none. In much of the analysis which follows we have excluded all of these short jobs, largely because we know so little about the conditions which they entail. While this exclusion does not offer much distortion in the case of Yokohama— there are only nineteen short-job states in the entire Yokohama sample—we may well be glossing over a significant, albeit minor, influence on careers in Detroit. While we cannot perforce offer much analysis of their brief duration, we should remain alert to the possible influence of these short jobs on later experiences in the individual's career.

Conceptually the distinction between intra- and inter-firm job changing is not as obvious as one might initially think. In the case of Japan, in particular, with its characteristically large numbers of small affiliates and subcontract firms which maintain close ties of dependence to the "parent" firm, movement to related firms is commonly excluded from government turnover statistics (movement between firms from employers' perspective). Ono Tsuneo, a labor economist, emphasizes that this leads to underestimating inter-firm mobility. He initiated studies, along with other scholars in the Industrial Relations System Research Committee, to examine this dimension (Ono 1973; Nihon Rōdō Kyōkai 1975). In the present study such job changing will be classified as inter-firm, assuming that individual respondents perceive that they have shifted their employment to a new firm; this meets the recent objections of Ono. It should be clear, however, that the institutional mechanisms governing job mobility between related firms and the consequent outcomes for socioeconomic achievement are likely to be quite different than is the case for job mobility between unrelated firms. For example, transfer to a related firm may not represent an interruption of career development but may be central to it. Unable to discriminate between these two types of inter-firm mobility, we lose what may be an important distinction.

Work histories of individuals do not come in neatly packed bundles that clearly separate those with intra-firm job trajectories from those with inter-firm ones. Instead, individuals often experience both forms of job mobility in the course of their work histories as well as temporary withdrawals from the labor force and movement into self-employed and unemployed statuses. If in the name of such conceptual and measurement difficulties, however, we continue to ignore the relation between these fundamentally different patterns of socioeconomic achievement, we continue to seriously distort the process of intra-generational mobility. Without gainsaying the above-mentioned problems, it is our belief that longitudinal studies of occupational achievement can and should make an effort to identify intra-firm job changing and its relation to inter-firm job changing; we hope to demonstrate that meaningful analysis of the two patterns, their outcomes, and their relationships is both possible and revealing from a sociological perspective.

CHAPTER III

PATTERNS OF JOB MOBILITY:
A COMPARATIVE STUDY OF
DETROIT AND YOKOHAMA
The Survey Evidence
with the collaboration of PAUL MATHEW SIEGEL

The purpose of this chapter is to describe the patterns and volume of intra- and inter-firm job changing among Detroit and Yokohama respondents. Our analysis begins with an introduction of the meaning and scope of the permanent employment practice in contemporary Japan. This leads us to consider the differences in the two cities between those who have never changed their employer and those who have. After pursuing this analysis, we move toward a broader consideration of the probability of job mobility in the two samples. In this connection we examine the impact of age, education, firm size and industry upon these probabilities. Finally, we discuss the reasons for inter-firm job changing in the two samples and the degree of difference and similarity.

Since most discussion of the Japanese labor market focuses on the practice of permanent employment, it is appropriate to begin our analysis with data that examine this practice and compare it with experiences of our Detroit respondents. Despite the extensive historical and contemporary scholarship that exists on the subject, the serious analyst immediately discovers a number of measurement difficulties. This is apparent in the attempts to estimate the scope of the present-day permanent employment practice. Taira (1962, p. 167) estimated that in the early 1960s permanent employment covered about one-fifth of all wage earners in Japanese manufacturing. More recent estimates by Dore (1973, pp. 304–5), using 1970 data, suggest that at least ten million workers—half of the total number of employees or about one-third of all those gainfully employed—

are involved in a full version of the "Japanese system" of which permanent employment is a central element. Dore delimits the loci of these practices in terms of: (a) government employment, (b) firms with more than 500 employees, and (c) a fair proportion of enterprises with 1 to 500 employees, especially in the white-collar industries and in those manufacturing firms with trade unions. Using Dore's own criteria and figures, however, produces a discrepancy in the results. Apparently his estimate that half of the total number of employees benefit from permanent employment is calculated as a proportion of total male employees. Similarly his estimate that one-third of those gainfully employed benefit from the system is calculated as a proportion of total males gainfully employed. If one accepts, as seems reasonable, that females are almost totally excluded from the experience of permanent employment, then one ought to use the total labor force (not just males) as the denominator to determine the scope of permanent employment in the Japanese economy. When one does so, the proportion of all employees experiencing permanent employment drops from 50 percent to 32 percent, and the proportion of all those gainfully employed experiencing permanent employment drops from 33 to 20 percent. In short, using these measures the practice seems far less pervasive than suggested by Dore. Permanent employment is presumed to be least applicable to the small-scale private sector, where working conditions are poor, product demand unstable, and capital funds often in short supply. In any given case white-collar employees and management officials are more likely to be convinced of the guarantees of permanent employment than are regular blue-collar employees. Moreover, as indicated above, regular male employees are more likely to believe that they have some guarantee of employment security than do female and temporary employees. The estimates developed by Dore and Taira adopt the strategy of using firm size and government employment as the criteria for defining who has permanent employment. This is obviously a very indirect procedure, which leaves a good deal to be desired.

The grossness of the estimating procedure and the amount of disagreement over the accuracy of the estimates indicate that severe measurement problems exist. The reasons for these difficulties need to be enumerated before we go on to suggest our own indicators. In this way the reader can better assess the validity of the alternatives.

Above all the difficulty of determining who has permanent employment derives from the practice not being a formally guaranteed right. This is another way of saying that the practice is not fully institutionalized. Building on Blau (1964, p. 276), we can list three conditions for determining the degree of institutionalization of a social practice:

> Patterns of organized community life must become formalized and part of the historical conditions that persist through time, the social values that legitimate these patterns must be transmitted in the process of socialization, and the society's dominant groups must be especially interested in the survival of these patterns.

We have seen in Chapter I how these conditions evolved and were perpetuated. The point to emphasize here is that the first condition, the degree of formalization, is relatively weakly developed, and as a consequence the analyst faces significant problems. The simplest way to demonstrate this conclusively is to point out that there is no widely used term among workers that refers to their rights in this area. If one asks workers whether they have *shūshin kōyō*, a relatively new term popularized through the translation of James Abegglen's book into Japanese, or *shōgai kōyō*, the historical term for the practice, they will often register confusion as to what you mean. This alone should tell us a great deal about the degree of formalization of the practice. During the 1975 recession, scholars, government, and management officials engaged in intense discussions as to the advisability of adopting formal guarantees for the practice along the lines legislated in many Western European nations (e.g., Fujita 1976).

Government statistics do not give us a great deal of leverage in delimiting the number of workers covered by the practice of permanent employment because they use the rather nebulous category of regular workers. Labor contracts between unions and employers in Japan tend to be general and abstract, without specifying the rights and obligations of either party. With the exception of such special categories as temporary workers, Japanese labor contracts generally bind the contracting parties together for an indefinite period of time. Permanent employment has been established as a company practice and employee behavioral pattern that is reinforced by the distribution of rewards according to age and length of service and strengthened by social and judicial pressures. For example, fellow employees are reluctant to accept as social equals those individuals hired with prior job experience. Employers commonly pay lower wages and give lower yearly wage increments to such employees. These distinctions were gradually reduced during the late 1960s and early 1970s as a reaction to the growing labor shortage.

Under the postwar Civil Code, workers do not receive significant protection from the disciplinary and discharge powers of employers. Article 627 of the Civil Code focuses primarily on giving employees proper notice according to the nature of their employment contract. Japanese postwar labor legislation provides somewhat greater protection for workers, but does not fundamentally alter management rights. Article 19 of the Labor Standards Act restricts the discharge of workers during periods of recuperation from injuries or sickness and during maternity leave as well as thirty days thereafter. Article 7 of the Labor Union Act prohibits the discharge of workers for participating in legitimate union activity, and Article 20 of the Labor Standards Act requires employers to give thirty days' advance notice before discharge or thirty days of pay. This is the extent of legal limitations on the discharge of employees in Japan (Fujita 1976).

Additional restrictions based on office or shop rules (Labor Standards Act) and labor agreements (Article 16 of the Labor Union Act) have a quasi-legal status (Fujita 1976). The standard clause relating to discharge in most labor agreements states only that:

> The company shall do everything in its power to avoid personnel cutbacks and will strive to maintain employment. If layoffs should become necessary, discussion will be held with the union beforehand at the labor management conference.

The courts, however, influenced by the practice of lifetime permanent employment, have developed extensive legal rules which restrict management rights to some extent. The fundamental principle here is that it is an abuse of the employer's right to discharge his employees if the discharge is not based on "just cause." The employer bears the burden of proof, and if he cannot establish it the discharge is void. In that event the employee is reinstated with back pay. The courts have also operated under the "limit of the abuse of rights" school, under which it is held that layoffs violate workers' rights by denying them the right to subsistence and public welfare. Using these basic principles, the courts have been adjudicating cases quite favorably for employees. An examination of dismissal cases acted upon by the civil courts and Central Labor Relations Commission shows, however, that they tend not to be ordinary dismissal cases but rather involve employee claims that they were dismissed for their political and/or union activities. The limited nature of these court cases suggests that "ordinary" employer attempts to rid themselves of workers because of worker incompetence and malfeasance are generally handled by mechanisms other than dismissal, except in extreme cases. Apart from maintaining such employees on the payroll, there are a variety of informal "back door" equivalents to discharge (Cole 1971, pp. 119–29).

This leaves the matter of the position taken by the courts on the dismissal or layoff of workers resulting from poor economic conditions. There are numerous precedents recognizing employer obligations to consult with the union when discharge or layoffs are contemplated. Many court decisions recognize the court's right to examine the necessity for and conditions of the layoff, including the measures taken prior to the layoff, and to evaluate whether proper procedure was followed in providing advance notification to employees. The courts also recognize the importance of persuading employees that there are sufficient causes for the dismissals or layoffs (Tōyō Seiki Case, Nagoya District Court, 30 September 1974). Yet in no case have the courts ruled that discharges or layoffs are not a legitimate response of firms experiencing economic difficulty during a recession (Fujita 1976).

The rapid economic growth in postwar Japan further clouds the issue of whether employees have permanent employment or whether employers are simply in a better position to guarantee continuous employment. In the context of present-day Japanese values, de facto continuous employment among regular male employees lends itself to being interpreted by management and workers alike as evidence of permanent employment. Moreover, workers and management do not always make the same evaluations with respect to the presence or absence of permanent employment. Workers in large firms are likely to emphasize their loyalty to their firm and management's obligation to keep them employed until retirement age. In medium-sized firms, employees are more likely to emphasize only management's obligation not to lay them off when business is slack. At the same time, however, they may assert their right to quit should alternative job offers seem promising. In the case of management, the smaller the firm, the more likely it is to simply assert that it makes great efforts to retain employees even in times of downturns in the economic cycle.

TABLE 4

Percent Never Changing Employers, by Year of
First Full-time Employment, Yokohama and Detroit, 1970

	Total	Year of First Full-time Employment									
City	All Workers	1966–70	1961–65	1956–60	1951–55	1946–50	1941–45	1936–40	1931–35	Before 1931
Yokohama	34.9	76.5	50.6	36.0	38.3	31.3	23.6	6.5	5.1	9.1
Detroit	13.5	36.8	16.8	11.0	15.2	12.2	8.8	5.6	11.4	0.0
		Number of Workers[a]									
Yokohama	561	51	77	89	94	99	55	46	39	11
Detroit	630	57	95	82	79	98	68	71	44	36

[a] Twenty-two respondents in Yokohama and eight in Detroit excluded because they do not report education or firm size, or both.

NOTE: The hypothesis that there is no difference in the percent never changing employers between cities within cohorts (while the distribution of respondents over cohorts may differ between cities, and the percent never changing employers may vary from cohort to cohort) can be rejected at the 0.001 level (chi-square = 88 with 9 degrees of freedom).

Changers and Non-changers

In the light of this discussion, it is clear that any single indicator of "permanent employment" will be subject to controversy. In our initial inquiry we have chosen a naively literal distinction—between those who have and those who have never changed employers during their career in the labor force—to represent workers without and with permanent employment. Clearly those whose worklife has been spent with a single employer have had de facto permanent employment, whether or not under the aura of a peculiar cultural norm or set of expectations about mutual commitments between employer and employee. Only those workers who have had but a single employer manifest the full ideal-typical pattern of "permanent employment"—though others may have had the expectations without their actualization. The data we are about to examine are irrelevant if permanent employment is solely a matter of attitudes and expectations, and they are not the best data to look at if permanent employment refers merely to a relatively low probability of leaving any employer. While we may come to entertain these interpretations, for the present we focus on remaining with one's first employer for the duration of one's worklife as the crucial test of permanent employment.

Table 4 shows the percentages of workers in Detroit and Yokohama still employed by their first employer at the date of interview by the year in which they were first employed. In the total column, it can be seen that about 35 percent of the workers in our Yokohama sample have never left their first employer after school leaving, while in Detroit about fourteen percent of the sample display this permanence. While somewhat more of our Detroit respondents entered the labor force in the years before 1945 (as can be seen in the lower panel of the table), and might bias the total figure for that city downwards because of their lower level of permanence, the ratio of the percentage of permanent employees in Yokohama to that in Detroit is about two and one-half to one for each of the cohorts entering the labor force after 1940.

Those cohorts entering the labor force in 1940 or earlier would have been approaching or have passed the "customary" Japanese retirement age of fifty-five at the interview date, while only the oldest cohort shown would have approached the corresponding socially significant age (sixty-five) in the United States. This may account for the dramatically lowered incidence of permanence among the older cohorts in Yokohama, where the practice of "retiring" to another (smaller) firm is prevalent. Members of these early cohorts would also have had to remain with the same employer through the dislocations of the war years —or return to the same employer directly after military service—in order to be counted as permanently employed, and this may also account for some of the dramatic decline for these cohorts in Yokohama. Nevertheless, the impression that permanent employment is more prevalent among our Yokohama respondents than among those in Detroit cannot be gainsaid on the basis of Table 4.

The important and incontrovertible observation to be made in Table 4 is that among individuals entering the labor force in different periods over the last forty years, different proportions remained with their original employers at the time of our interview, and the proportions also differ between cities. Our analytic strategy will be to attempt to understand the temporal pattern in itself, and to introduce two further variables with which perhaps to isolate, if not explain, the inter-city differences.

In pursuing our analysis of the data in Table 4, the two variables we introduce in an attempt to extract some evidence on permanent employment are educational attainment and size of firm.[1] Abegglen's seminal observations on permanent employment in Japan emphasized its prevalence among the employees of large firms, and education is a property of individuals likely to differentiate their value to employers and their own perceptions of career opportunity, and thus influence their likelihood of inter-firm mobility.

Our exploration of the impact of these two variables leads us to a single model, which we employ to describe the relations among size of firm, education, year of labor force entry, city, and the odds of remaining with one's first employer at the time of our interview.[2] (The details of our explorations can be found in Siegel and Cole 1976.) In our best-fitting model, education has no effect on the odds of remaining with one's first employer. There is, however, a strong effect associated with labor force cohort, and there is a strong and significant interaction between firm size and city, indicating that the effects of firm size are markedly different in Yokohama and Detroit. Yet in both cities the odds of remaining with one's first employer increase as the firm gets larger, with a particularly marked increase in the largest size class. This general pattern is what discussions of lifetime employment in Japan would lead us to expect there, but it is surprising to find that the relation is even stronger in Detroit. Thus while in Yokohama the odds of remaining with an employer of 1000 or more is four times the average odds for that city, for employees of these largest firms in Detroit the odds are almost six (5.7) times that city's average odds. Similarly, for employees of the smallest firms, the odds are half the average in Yokohama, but three-eighths the average in Detroit.[3] Insofar as the notion of permanent

1. Firm size was recorded in five size categories: 1 to 9 employees, 10 to 99, 100 to 499, 500 to 999, and 1,000 or more. Educational attainment was recorded in years of formal schooling at the time of entry to the labor force; the variable is trichotomized at less than twelve years completed, twelve years completed, and more than twelve years completed. For further discussion of the construction of these variables and their rationale see detailed discussion in the following section.

2. The analysis involved two stages: first we fit various logit models to the data, employing an iterative fitting procedure to provide estimated frequencies for the table under the hypothesis of each model, utilizing chi-squared as a means of evaluating the fit of actual and expected frequencies and of statistically assessing the advantage of one model over another (see Goodman 1971; Bishop, Feinberg, and Holland 1975). In the second stage we extracted a regression-like equation from the "best-fitting" model in stage one in order to examine and discuss the nature and magnitude of the effects present, and what they imply about the nature of permanent employment in Yokohama and Detroit.

3. Since odds are a relatively unfamiliar way to measure likelihood it is well to contrast their behavior with that of proportions. Thus if a percentage increases by two points, say from 20 to 22 percent, that represents a 10 percent increase, while an increase of the same absolute magnitude from say 78 to 80 percent represents only a 2.6 percent increase. With respect to odds, however, the increase in the first case is from 0.250 to 0.282, a

employment as a unique Japanese phenomenon requires the effect of firm size to exist only in Japan, or to be stronger there, these data offer no support for it. Instead, we see much the same pattern in the two cities with, if anything, a stronger effect of firm size on the odds of remaining with one's first employer in Detroit than in Yokohama. These data provide some support for the American dual labor market theorists who emphasize the distinctive labor markets operative in large and small firms.

Finally, within each birth cohort and firm size class, the odds of remaining with one's first employer in Yokohama are at least four and one-half times as great as in Detroit. In a sense the fact that this city differential remains so large indicates our failure to explain the elevated chances of remaining with one's first employer in Yokohama relative to Detroit by reference to differences in the age, education and firm size composition of the two cities, and our only partial success in attributing this difference to inter-city differences in the effects of age, education, and firm size.

Our model estimates that the odds of remaining with one's first employer in Yokohama are four and one-half times the Detroit odds in the largest size class, six times the Detroit odds in the intermediate size class, and ten times the Detroit odds in the smallest size class. Yet if we assume that the proportion of "permanent employees" (i.e., employees who will never leave) increases with firm size, as the literature so strongly suggests, we would have expected the Yokohama/ Detroit ratio to decrease from larger to smaller firms. Given these results, it is difficult to accept the view that permanent employment is concentrated among the employees of large firms. This conclusion is based on the assumption of the naively literal view that the world is divided into the permanently employed who are not exposed to the probability of leaving, in the sense that they never consider the possibility of changing employment, and the impermanently employed, all of whom are exposed to the risk of leaving though some may never move. While one might construct reasons to expect that for those without permanent employment, firm loyalty would be weaker in Japan in large firms than in small (relative to the U.S.), it is not obviously necessary that these explanations deal with permanent employment at all. For even if one assumes that there is no permanent employment, one must account for the fact that relative to their counterparts in Detroit, workers in large firms in Yokohama are less immobile than workers in small firms. Thus rather than attempt to continue to maintain that there are two kinds of employees in Yokohama—those who can and those who cannot change employers—and to seek to explain their incidence, we prefer to take as our task for the rest of this chapter the isolation of subgroups of individuals which vary in the probability of mobility between and within employers.

Our exploration of the data and the model which best fits them have shown us that education does not appear to be a characteristic of individuals which in-

---

12.8 percent increase. In the second case the odds increase from 3.545 to 4.0, also a 12.8 percent increase. One must not think that the effects of various variables on the odds of remaining with one's first employer are stronger in Detroit than in Yokohama simply because the overall probability is much lower in Detroit.

fluences that probability, and that firm size has strikingly similar effects in the two cities—though these effects are different enough to lead us to abandon concern with a naively literal version of permanent employment. While our analysis was not particularly sensitive to temporal-historical patterns of change in economic and social conditions, the vastly different postwar economic and social histories of Yokohama and Detroit led us to expect marked inter-city differences in the association between remaining with one's first employer and time. Since we could find none, we are inclined to attribute the bulk of the strong effect associated with cohort to the continuous exposure of individuals to relatively stable or gradually declining probabilities of mobility as they age. Finally, our explorations have left us with an across-the-board effect of city, which makes the odds on remaining with one's first employer in Yokohama at least four and one-half times as great as the odds in Detroit.

The Probability of Mobility

Our previous discussion suggests that an examination of labor market practices in the two cities, exclusively in terms of a comparison between those who have never changed employers and those who have, is based on a rather restrictive characterization of labor market experience. This limited characterization implies that if we omit the behavior of those never having changed employers, the behavior of the changers in both Yokohama and Detroit would be quite similar. For a simple examination of this thesis, we computed the rate of employer changing in both cities among those who had experienced at least one employer change in their work history and who had no "gap states." Among these changers, we found that the mean number of employer changes, adjusting for amount of labor force exposure, was higher in Detroit than in Yokohama for each of the exposure groups listed in Table 4 except one. The total mean number of employer changes was 2.16 among Yokohama changers and 3.26 for the Detroit changers. This makes it clear that the labor market experiences of respondents in the two samples is very different, independent of the effects of the experience and size of the non-changer group. For this reason, as well as those outlined above, rather than elaborate on the line of analysis heretofore developed, the subsequent analysis will involve a less restrictive categorization of the respondents in order to capture labor market experiences in the two cities more fully.

To provide this greater coverage, we display a more detailed breakdown of job changing in Tables 5 and 6. These tables show as annual rates intra- and inter-firm job changing, in particular age intervals for the members of the various cohorts actually at risk of such movement. Thus the upper left-hand entry of Table 5 indicates that for Yokohama, individuals born between 1915 and 1924 experienced 0.04 intra-firm job changes per year of employment and 0.11 inter-firm job changes per year of employment between the ages of sixteen and twenty-five. An examination of the totals for all birth cohorts and age groups reveals, not surprisingly, that the rate of inter-firm job changing is twice as high in Detroit (0.16) as compared to Yokohama (0.08). It is striking to discover, however, that the rate of intra-firm job changing is also twice as high in Detroit (0.10) as compared to Yokohama (0.05). The within-city comparison of respondents is also revealing. The ratio of intra- to inter-firm job changing in both Detroit and Yokohama is 0.63. These latter two results suggest, rather surprisingly, the seemingly equal role of intra-firm job changes in Detroit; this finding runs counter to our initial discussion of the centrality of the internal labor market in Japan. Consequently a good part of our remaining efforts will be devoted to clarifying and explaining this discrepancy between predicted relationships and empirical results.

Further examination of Tables 5 and 6 reveals first that, in both the Detroit and Yokohama samples, the mean number of inter-firm job changes is at its highest in the sixteen to twenty-five age groups and falls off fairly rapidly thereafter. A still finer analysis showed that the mean was even higher for the sixteen to twenty age group than for the twenty-one to twenty-five age group in both samples with only one exception. In both cities the respondents' experiences square with prior research results that inter-firm job changing is at its height for young people. Youthful employment has a "shopping-around" character, based as it is on incomplete information and the minimal investment young people have in a stock of training and experience; thus, the costs of inter-firm job changing are rather small.

The corresponding life-cycle data for intra-firm job changing is less clear cut. This is especially the case with the Yokohama data, in which there is minimal variation by age. There does appear to be a decline in mean intra-firm job changing in the older age groups for the Detroit respondents, a pattern which is barely discernible for Yokohama. This would fit a model of employer and employee decision making which is based on minimizing investment in new job training; with retirement nearing, management and employees conclude that they are unlikely to collect returns on their investment. That such a reduction would already begin as young as the late thirties for Detroit respondents may reflect management's view (which may be incorrect) that the employee has found his proper niche in the company or is incapable of upgrading or both. Insofar as the opportunity structure for given bundles of job skills can be conceptualized as a pyramid, it is reasonable to expect a narrowing of opportunities as the individual ages, having scaled some of the heights of the hierarchy. That this pattern is less observable in the Yokohama data may reflect more optimistic conceptions of employee growth potential, a subject to be explored in the final chapters.

To avoid the possibility that the important role of the auto industry in Detroit was influencing our results in some special fashion, we constructed Tables 5 and 6 for non-automobile employees (excluding family workers and the self-employed). There were no appreciable differences from the results reported here. We also constructed the tables using five-year intervals for our age groups instead of ten years. This retention of age information allowed us to compare more cells that were unaffected by missing data (e.g., the gap state for older workers). There were no appreciable differences in the results reported here. Finally we constructed these same tables using only job states in which the respondent was employed by others (excluding family workers and the self-employed). The only significant difference from those results reported here is that the proportion of intra-firm to inter-firm mobility in both samples increases slightly when we exclude the self-employed and family workers (who almost by definition cannot experience intra-firm job changes as we have conceptualized this category).[1]

TABLE 5
(Yokohama)
Distribution of Mean Number of Intra- and Inter-firm
Job Changes per Person-Year of Exposure by Year of
Birth and Age at Each Job Change

Year of Birth		Age at Each Job Change					
		16–25	26–35	36–45	46–55	Total	N
1915–24	intra	0.04[a]	0.04[a]	0.05	0.04	0.05	105
	inter	0.11	0.07	0.04	0.04	0.06	
1925–34	intra	0.04[a]	0.05	0.05	—	0.05	188
	inter	0.10	0.08	0.03	—	0.07	
1935–44	intra	0.03	0.05	—	—	0.04	188
	inter	0.13	0.07	—	—	0.10	
1945–54	intra	0.03	—	—	—	0.03	70
	inter	0.10	—	—	—	0.10	
Total	intra	0.04	0.05	0.05	0.04	0.05	551
	inter	0.11	0.07	0.03	0.04	0.08	

[a] Rates in these cells are based on job changes and labor force exposure which exclude pre-1945 jobs and job changes except for respondent's first job. This applies to Tables 5–10, 12, 13.

NOTE: By dividing the total number of changes of a specific type occurring in a given interval of age by the total number of person-years of employment experienced by a cohort in that interval, the reported rates correct for the fact that individuals could enter the labor force at ages beyond the lower bound of the interval; could leave the labor force before attaining the upper bound of the interval; could be unemployed, and thus removed from the possibility of changing jobs for some portion of the interval; or, because of the structure of our data, could have been out of our scrutiny—in the "gap state"—for part of the interval. The exposure data were created by assigning to each state a starting and ending month and year, based on their reported duration and cumulating backwards from the interview date. These calculations also furnish a precise attributed age at which changes occur. Once the durations of employment states have been distributed over the age intervals they span, it is a simple matter to obtain the denominator—person-months of exposure—of the fraction shown in each cell. The same technique underlies every other table showing rates of mobility. The individual events have been treated as independent across individuals and within individuals over time, so the rates presented are not, strictly speaking, instantaneous probabilities.

Rates are based on a total of 446 intra-firm job changes and 750 inter-firm changes. Fifty-three intra-firm job changes and eighty-five inter-firm job changes are excluded primarily because the respondent was older than fifty-five by the time the job state was completed. These exclusions arise in the case of thirty-two respondents. Thus the total sample N is 583.

Entries in this table and subsequent ones include changes from both less than six-month single job states and those of more than six months. Multiple job states with several employers occurring within a six-month period are excluded from all tables. Those respondents who have never changed jobs or employers are included in Tables 5–13.

TABLE 6

(Detroit)

**Distribution of Mean Number of Intra- and Inter-firm
Job Changes per Person-Year of Exposure by Year of
Birth and Age at Each Job Change**

Year of Birth		Age at Each Job Change					
		16–25	*26–35*	*36–45*	*46–55*	*Total*	*N*
1915–24	intra	0.06[a]	0.09[a]	0.07	0.05	0.07	135
	inter	0.16	0.12	0.08	0.05	0.10	
1925–34	intra	0.12[a]	0.11	0.06	—	0.10	169
	inter	0.28	0.14	0.08	—	0.16	
1935–44	intra	0.16	0.12	—	—	0.14	180
	inter	0.29	0.17	—	—	0.23	
1945–54	intra	0.16	—	—	—	0.16	86
	inter	0.36	—	—	—	0.36	
Total	intra	0.13	0.10	0.07	0.05	0.10	570
	inter	0.27	0.14	0.08	0.05	0.16	

[a] See notes to Table 5.

NOTE: Rates are based on a total of 969 intra-firm job changes and 1568 inter-firm job changes. Eighty-one intra-firm job changes and 159 inter-firm job changes are excluded primarily because the respondent was older than fifty-five by the time the job state was completed. These exclusions arise in the case of sixty-eight respondents. Thus the total sample N is 638.

These data may be displayed in still different fashion to demonstrate the relationship between intra- and inter-firm mobility. Tables 7 and 8 present the ratio of mean intra- to inter-firm job changing per person year of exposure by year of birth and age at each job change. The data for both cities suggest an almost steady increase in the ratio of intra- to inter-firm job changes by age group. Although both intra- and inter-firm job changing tends to fall off for the oldest age groups, apparently the decline is much sharper for inter-firm job changing.

We can also examine the birth cohort data presented in Tables 7 and 8 with an eye to evaluating two competing hypotheses, both of which assert that the relationship between intra- and inter-firm job changing is not fixed over time. In the first hypothesis, Hunter and Reid (1968, pp. 12, 80, 133) maintain that the importance of intra-firm mobility relative to total job mobility has grown in recent years in industrial societies as a consequence of the prevailing high levels of employment, growing industrial concentration, new programs of personnel management oriented to internal labor mobility and the insistence of trade unions on greater personal security for employees (see also Dore 1973, pp. 12, 355). This perspective is also consistent with Mincer's findings (1962, p. 73) that aggregate and per capita investments in on-the-job training increased in the United States between 1939 and 1958, though at a slower rate than investments in

TABLE 7
(Yokohama)
**Ratio of Intra- to Inter-firm Job Changes per Person-
Year of Exposure by Year of Birth and Age at Each Job Change**

Year of Birth	Age at Each Job Change				
	16–25	26–35	36–45	46–55	Total
1915–24	0.36[a]	0.57[a]	1.25	1.00	0.83
1925–34	0.40[a]	0.63	1.67	—	0.71
1935–44	0.23	0.71	—	—	0.40
1945–54	0.30	—	—	—	0.30

[a] See notes to Table 5.

NOTE: This table was created by dividing the mean intra-firm job changes for each cell in Table 5 by the mean inter-firm job changes in the same cell.

formal education. To the extent this involved increases in specific training, this would put an increased emphasis on intra- rather than inter-firm job changing. The large-scale shift of Japanese employees to larger firms, especially pronounced in early postwar Japan, would also fit with this interpretation, insofar as the shift allowed for greater opportunities for internal adjustments of the labor force. In short, the hypothesis should apply to both the Detroit and the Yokohama data.

The alternative hypothesis presented for Japan suggests that intra-firm job changing is beginning to play a diminished role relative to inter-firm job changing as a result of the growing labor shortage and the new work ethic manifested by young militant workers (Organization for Economic Cooperation and Development 1973, pp. 121–23; Kobayashi 1974, pp. 13–28). Umetani (1968, pp. 95–96) maintains that the reliance on internal labor markets and the associated enterprise training is threatened by the disruption caused by the increasing pace of technological innovation and the failure of firms to meet the demand for an adequately trained labor force. More recently, however, some Japanese scholars have come to argue that there is no reason for the importance of intra-firm mobility to decline (Sumiya 1974, 1974a).

Our ability to test these hypotheses is severely limited by the presence of a number of empty cells representing the incomplete work experiences of the younger birth cohorts. Moreover, since our data are only representative of the Detroit and Yokohama male labor forces in 1970 and 1971 respectively, we cannot presume that the earlier experiences of the older birth cohorts are representative of some earlier historical period. Yet the Yokohama data provide no support for the hypothesis that intra-firm mobility is declining in importance in Japan; indeed there is some indication that the more recent birth cohorts in the twenty-six to thirty-five and thirty-six to forty-five age categories are experiencing more intra-firm relative to inter-firm job changing (i.e., consistent with the Hunter-Reid hypothesis). A more detailed breakdown into five-year age group intervals shows that the more recent birth cohorts experience increases in the ratio of intra- to inter-firm job changing for the twenty-one to twenty-five,

TABLE 8
(Detroit)
Ratio of Intra-to Inter-firm Job Changes per Person-
Year of Exposure by Year of Birth and Age at Each Job Change

Year of Birth	Age at Each Job Change				
	16–25	*26–35*	*36–45*	*46–55*	*Total*
1915–24	0.38[a]	0.75[a]	0.88	1.00	0.70
1925–34	0.43[a]	0.79	0.75	—	0.63
1935–44	0.55	0.71	—	—	0.61
1945–54	0.44	—	—	—	0.44

[a] See notes to Table 5.

NOTE: This table was created by dividing the mean intra-firm job changes for each cell in Table 6 by the mean inter-firm job changes in the same cell.

twenty-six to thirty, and thirty-six to forty age groups; earlier birth cohorts' experience declines in their ratios. The Detroit data displayed in Table 8 show little support for the Hunter-Reid view that intra-firm mobility is growing in importance relative to inter-firm job changes. This conclusion is further confirmed by a breakdown of the age groups into five-year intervals, in which case only one group, those sixteen to twenty, experience an increase in the proportion of intra- to inter-firm job changing for the more recent birth cohorts. Since there is missing data from the older birth cohorts resulting from the gap state, even this conclusion cannot be taken that seriously. We also constructed Tables 7 and 8 excluding changes from six-month jobs, and in that case both Yokohama and Detroit data showed somewhat more support for the Hunter-Reid hypothesis. These conclusions are at best tentative and are intended only to suggest that further investigation of the hypothesis using panel studies seems warranted. Examination of the ratio of intra- to inter-firm job changing by size of firm later in the chapter will shed further light on this matter.

One of the first observations we reported was a lower volume of both inter- and intra-firm mobility in Yokohama. We will now consider whether these results, in particular the surprisingly low volume of intra-firm mobility in Yokohama, arise from spurious associations. If the distributions of four critical variables that we have identified—age, education, firm size, and industry—differ in our respective samples, this may explain the low volume of intra-firm mobility in the Yokohama sample (or conversely, the unusually high volume of intra-firm mobility in the Detroit sample). It is generally accepted that inter-firm turnover varies inversely with age, education, and firm size (see Hunter and Reid 1968). It is also reasonable to suggest that intra-firm mobility varies directly with these three variables. If, for example, our Yokohama sample was drawn primarily from those with low educational achievement, this would result in minimizing intra-firm job changing and maximizing inter-firm job changing. Insofar as the samples are representative of the respective labor forces, this is not simply a statistical artifact but permits us to identify significant differences in labor force experiences.

Secondly, quite apart from the matter of the distribution of the samples, we want to know whether in fact the variables we have mentioned—age, education, firm size, and industry—do operate in the same fashion in the two samples. Is the Japanese labor market so unique that the generalizations we draw from observing empirical regularities in the West do not apply? In particular we want to know whether the introduction of these four variables will provide us with an explanation for the surprisingly low volume of intra-firm mobility recorded in the Japanese case.

Our previous discussion has already elaborated on the impact of age. All that needs to be mentioned here is, first, that age does act in the same fashion in both samples, and second, that the age distribution of the two samples is quite similar. Taking age thirty-six to be the median age of respondents reported in our tables, 53.3 percent of both samples between ages sixteen and fifty-five were between the ages of thirty-six and fifty-five, with the remainder below. Using grouped interval data, the median age of the Detroit sample was 36.1 and the mean age was 37; the comparable totals for Yokohama are 36 and 36.5. In view of this remarkable similarity, we can dismiss the possibility that age accounts for the differences in volume we have reported.

The Impact of Education

Next we turn to education. With the adoption of the American 6–3–3–4 educational system by the Japanese in the postwar period, the twelve-year cutting point has relatively comparable meaning in the two societies, i.e., the completion of high school. In Japan compulsory education extends to nine years; 64 percent of those graduating from middle school went on to high school in 1926 with the proportion rising to 92 percent by 1976.

Education will be used as a proxy for occupation. Just how valid a proxy may be gleaned, in part, from an examination of 1970 census data. For employed American males age twenty-five or above, if you guessed white-collar for everyone with thirteen or more years of education and blue-collar for everyone else, you would be right 76 percent of the time. Comparable data from the 1970 Japanese national census reveal a quite similar outcome; if you guessed white-collar for everyone with thirteen or more years of education, and blue-collar for everyone else, you would be right 74 percent of the time. If we change the cutting point and guess white-collar for everyone with twelve or more years of education and blue-collar for everyone else, the percentage of correct guesses declines to 69 percent in America but holds at 74 percent in Japan. It would seem that the high school diploma in Japan still gives the recipient a slight edge over his American counterpart with respect to obtaining a white-collar job. These respective situations are not, of course, unvarying characteristics of the two societies, but rather are subject to historical change. In both societies those graduating from high school in an earlier era represented more of an elite, thereby having access to more desirable white-collar jobs. This situation has simply persisted later in Japan. Many of our older Japanese respondents received their education in the prewar period; the prewar school system was quite elitist, based as it was on a "graduated" school system of the European type. It is estimated that in 1935, although almost 100 percent of the relevant age groups received the six-year compulsory education, only 40 percent received some form of secondary education and only 3 percent were exposed to higher education. By contrast some 29 percent of the American population seventeen years old were high school graduates by 1930 with the proportion rising to 62 percent by 1956.

Quite apart from the issue of how good a proxy education is for occupation, it should be noted as a substantive issue that since an individual's formal education rarely changes over his lifetime, the "tighter" the fit between an individual's education and his occupation, the less room there is for intra-generational mobility. As suggested above, the fit was undoubtedly far "tighter" in the past in both societies.

Tables 9 and 10 report the mean number of intra- and inter-firm job changes per person-year of exposure in the male civilian labor force by age at each job change and educational level. Because of the small number of cases in many of the cells, however, inter-cohort comparison was not possible. Consequently we elected to limit ourselves to examining the relationship between age and education by collapsing the birth cohort experiences for each educational category and age group.

Examining the marginals in Tables 9 and 10, we see first that the Detroit sample is a notably more educated one, with 69 percent of our sample having twelve or more years of education; the comparable total for Yokohama is fifty-five percent. The U.S. Census for 1970 and the 1970 Population Census of Japan (U.S. Bureau of the Census 1972a, pp. 24, 709–10; Office of the Prime Minister 1972, p. 127) show 47.3 percent of males in the Detroit SMSA who are fourteen years and over with twelve or more years of education, and fifty-four percent for males in Yokohama fifteen years and over. Thus the Yokohama sample is much more representative of the city than our highly educated Detroit sample is of the Detroit SMSA. This reflects both the difficulty of locating lower income, less educated respondents in Detroit as well as interviewer bias in not strongly pursuing interviewing opportunities in the inner city.[4] Insofar as our highly educated sample in Detroit results in the data exaggerating the amount of intra-firm mobility relative to Yokohama, it is important to examine job changing within each educational category to see the extent to which the initial differences reported are maintained.

First, we reported in our discussion of Tables 5 and 6 that the rate of inter-firm job changing in Detroit was twice as high as in Yokohama. Tables 9 and 10 allow us to examine whether this pattern holds for all educational levels. The ratio of the mean number of inter-firm job changes per person-year of exposure in Yokohama to that of Detroit is 0.47 for the less than twelve years' education category, 0.53 for the twelve years' education group and 0.44 for those with more than twelve years of education. In short, the ratio of per capita inter-firm

4. It may be that our sample is more representative of suburban counties in the Detroit SMSA, such as Oakland and McComb, than it is of Wayne County, which includes the inner city. It should be noted that this problem of developing a representative sample in major metropolitan areas was characteristic of the 1970 national census as well (see Parsons 1972).

TABLE 9
(Yokohama)
Distribution of Mean Number of Intra- and Inter-firm Job
Changes per Person-Year of Exposure by Age at Each
Job Change and Educational Level

Educational Level		Age at Each Job Change					
		16–25	26–35	36–45	46–55	Total	N
Less than	intra	0.03[a]	0.03[a]	0.04	0.04	0.03	249
12 years	inter	0.12	0.07	0.03	0.03	0.08	
12 years	intra	0.05[a]	0.06[a]	0.07	0.11	0.06	152
	inter	0.10	0.08	0.04	0.00	0.08	
More than	intra	0.05[a]	0.08[a]	0.08	0.05	0.07	147
12 years	inter	0.10	0.07	0.03	0.05	0.07	
Total	intra	0.04[a]	0.05[a]	0.05	0.04	0.05	548
	inter	0.11	0.07	0.03	0.04	0.08	

[a] See notes to Table 5.

NOTE: Fourteen respondents are excluded because of missing educational data and an additional twenty-one are members of the excluded 1905–14 birth cohort.

job changing achieved by the Yokohama respondents relative to Detroit respondents shows no systematic pattern of variation by educational category, though it achieves its highest level for those with twelve years of education. When we examine the same data in more detail by age and education categories, the ratio of mean intra-firm job changing in Yokohama relative to Detroit shows no consistent pattern.

We also reported in Tables 5 and 6 that the rate of intra-firm job changing in Yokohama was only half that of Detroit. Again, Tables 9 and 10 permit us to break the data down by educational level. The ratio of the mean number of intra-firm job changes per person-year of exposure in Yokohama stands at 0.50 of that in Detroit for those with less than twelve years' education, rises to 0.60 for those with twelve years' education and falls again to 0.47 for those with more than twelve years' education. An examination of the same data in more detail by age and education categories shows that the ratio of mean intra-firm job changing in Yokohama to that in Detroit rises with age in all education categories—exceeding the figures for Detroit in the oldest age groups.

The differences between educational categories are too modest to account for the massive differences in the volume of intra- and inter-firm job changes per respondent registered in our initial comparisons of the Detroit and Yokohama samples. This discussion should not be allowed to obscure the fact that within each sample the mean number of intra-firm job changes generally rises for each more highly educated category in an age interval. Only in the oldest age group in both samples do we see some decline in the mean number of job changes between the twelve years' and more than twelve years' education categories.

In our discussion of Tables 5 and 6 we also reported that the ratio of intra-

TABLE 10
(Detroit)
Distribution of Mean Number of Intra- and Inter-firm Job
Changes per Person-Year of Exposure by Age at Each
Job Change and Educational Level

Educational Level		Age at Each Job Change					N
		16–25	*26–35*	*36–45*	*46–55*	*Total*	
Less than	intra	0.09[a]	0.06[a]	0.04	0.03	0.06	175
12 years	inter	0.27	0.16	0.10	0.05	0.17	
12 years	intra	0.14[a]	0.09[a]	0.08	0.09	0.10	199
	inter	0.27	0.12	0.06	0.04	0.15	
More than	intra	0.18[a]	0.16[a]	0.10	0.07	0.15	195
12 years	inter	0.27	0.14	0.07	0.06	0.16	
Total	intra	0.13[a]	0.10[a]	0.07	0.05	0.10	569
	inter	0.27	0.14	0.08	0.05	0.16	

[a] See notes to Table 5.
NOTE: Twenty-five respondents are excluded because of missing educational data and an additional forty-four are members of the excluded 1905–14 birth cohort.

to inter-firm job changing was 0.63 in both Yokohama and Detroit. By educational level, the proportion of total job changes accounted for by intra-firm job changes stands at 0.38 for Yokohama and 0.35 for Detroit for those with less than twelve years' education, rises to 0.75 and 0.67 respectively for those with twelve years' education, and to 1.0 and 0.94 for those with more than twelve years' education. In both samples we see that higher education and presumably better paid and more prestigious occupations result in sharp increases in the importance of intra-firm job changes in the individual's work history. This fits with the observations of a number of scholars, including the dual labor market theorists, that the better jobs are filled mainly through intra-firm promotion and that recruitment from outside the firm is generally through ports of entry that are best characterized as "small" jobs (see Reynolds 1951, p. 242; White 1970, pp. 113–14). Those with high levels of school education may be presumed to be recipients of greater investments in human capital. Mincer (1962, p. 59) found that on-the-job training becomes more important the higher the level of schooling. He sees this as a logical outcome of school education serving as a prerequisite or basis on which to build more specialized training. Consequently employers will be more willing to provide incentives to keep employees with higher levels of education, and to the extent that they receive more specific training than those with less schooling, these employees will be less willing to leave, lest they forfeit their investment. Thurow (1975) arrives at a rather similar outcome using a labor queue model of job competition.

Tables 9 and 10 show that for almost all educational categories in both samples, the mean number of inter-firm job changes per person-year of exposure reaches its peak in the sixteen to twenty-five age group and falls rapidly thereafter. The only exception is the more than twelve years' education category in the Yokohama sample, where the mean number of job changes rose slightly in the forty-six to fifty-five age group. In short, in each educational category for both samples, age operates in roughly similar fashion to that reported in Tables 5 and 6.

The life-cycle data for intra-firm job changes, reported in Tables 7 and 8, showed a pattern of decline for the oldest age group in Detroit with minimal variation by age in the Yokohama sample. This pattern is generally upheld for the Detroit sample at each educational level. The Yokohama pattern of no variation by age seems to hold primarily for the more than twelve years' education category with increases in the mean number of job changes by age being recorded for the twelve years' education group.

We may conclude from this treatment of education that it seems to have relatively similar effects on the volume and pattern of relationship between inter- and intra-firm job changing in both samples. The higher proportion of Detroit respondents in the highly educated categories operates to increase the amount of intra-firm job changing and minimize inter-firm mobility relative to the Yokohama sample. Yet within each of our three educational categories large differences persist in the amount of both inter- and intra-firm job changing between the two samples, though less so in the case of intra-firm job changing. Even if our respective samples had the same educational distributions, the volume of intra- and inter-firm job changing per respondent in Yokohama would have been not much more than half that of Detroit. Thus, the basic differences in volume of mobility between the two samples cannot be explained by education.

The Impact of Firm Size

Our next task is to analyze whether the differences in volume between the two samples can be accounted for by the variable of firm size. Japanese scholars commonly emphasize that the size of the firm is the single most important factor in labor market stratification (Odaka 1967; Ohkawa 1962). The dualistic labor market has been central to this analysis. This is in contrast to the United States, where until recently size of firm has been ignored for the most part as a major factor influencing the operation of labor markets (some early exceptions include Kerr 1964; Lester 1967; and Rees and Schultz 1970). Some American sociologists emphasize the importance of size in organizations but they neglect its significance for broader social and economic stratification. The U.S. government seldom collects and reports data by size of firm. It is only with the appearance of the dual labor market theorists that a reconsideration of the importance of firm size is taking place.

In Japan it is commonly pointed out that permanent employment with its corollary of highly developed internal labor markets, is confined to large firms. In small and medium-sized firms workers are disadvantaged with regard to wages and working conditions; there is a higher rate of turnover and employers rely more heavily on recruitment from the external labor market (e.g., Funahashi 1973, p. 390). On this basis we might expect that the differences in the volume

TABLE 11
Distribution of Current Firm Size by City

Firm Size	Detroit (in %)	Yokohama (in %)
1–9	10.0	22.0
10–99	15.4	19.0
100–499	8.5	12.7
500–999	4.7	5.1
1000+	56.7	39.1
NA Size	4.7	2.1
	100.0	100.0
	(N = 638)	(N = 583)

of inter-firm job changing would be minimized if we compared the inter-city differences among employees in small and medium-sized firms.

Alternatively, we might hypothesize that the differences between large firms and small and medium-sized firms in Japan are graduated; hence, we would expect that aspects of the permanent employment relationship would still be apparent and would distinguish mobility patterns in small and medium-sized firms in Japan from those of comparably sized firms in the U.S. Our earlier analysis of the impact of firm size on the odds of changing or not changing employers is suggestive in this regard. Moreover, as reported in Chapter I, small firms try to live up to the ideal norm of permanent employment. On this basis we predict that even when we hold firm size constant, the differences in the volume of job mobility will be maintained between the two samples.

The following analysis will bring evidence to bear on these hypotheses as they relate to job-mobility patterns, and will also provide treatment of the impact of firm size on job changing in the two cities. We begin with a presentation of the distribution of firm size for respondents at the time they were interviewed (i.e., current job state). The distributions reported in Table 11 conform to the expectations generated in our Chapter II discussion of city characteristics. The Yokohama sample is characterized by significantly larger numbers employed in smaller firms; 41 percent of the Yokohama respondents were employed in firms of under ninety-nine employees, compared to only 25.4 percent of Detroit respondents. Similarly, 56.7 percent of Detroit respondents were employed in firms of 1000 or more, compared to only 39.1 percent of Yokohama respondents. Notable is the relative absence in both cities of firms in the 500 to 999 category. This is consistent with an ecological perspective on organizational growth in which the emergence of large-sized organizations poses a competitive threat to medium-sized organizations but if anything increases the survival chances of small organizations by removing their immediate competitors from the environment (Hannan and Freeman 1977, p. 946).

There are two possible implications of the differing size distributions for our subsequent analysis. Insofar as availability of a firm of a given size may modify an individual's behavior, the inter-city differences in firm size will in-

TABLE 12
(Yokohama)
**Mean Number of Intra- and Inter-firm Job Changes by Age
at Each Job Change and Firm Size of Origin**

Firm Size of Origin		Age at Each Job Change				
		16–25	*26–35*	*36–45*	*46–55*	*Total*
1–9	intra	0.03[a]	0.01[a]	—	—	0.01
	inter	0.13	0.10	0.04	0.03	0.09
10–99	intra	0.03[a]	0.02[a]	0.01	0.01	0.02
	inter	0.16	0.12	0.06	0.05	0.12
100–999	intra	0.04[a]	0.04[a]	0.05	0.03	0.04
	inter	0.14	0.07	0.05	0.04	0.09
1000+	intra	0.07[a]	0.09[a]	0.09	0.10	0.08
	inter	0.06	0.03	0.01	0.03	0.04
Total	intra	0.04[a]	0.05[a]	0.05	0.05	0.05
	inter	0.11	0.07	0.03	0.03	0.07

[a] See notes to Table 5.

fluence our analysis results. To the extent that one's current firm size is the only firm size that has any impact on current behavior, the inter-city comparisons within firm-size groups to be presented will be unaffected by the firm-size distributions. Tables 12 and 13 present the distribution of inter- and intra-firm job changes by firm size of origin and age at each job change adjusted for person-years of exposure. Examining the raw numbers upon which Tables 12 and 13 are based, it is apparent first that the bulk of intra-firm job changes in both samples are accounted for by employees in firm sizes 1000+ (72.1 percent in Detroit and 74.9 percent in Yokohama); conversely those in firms of one to nineteen employees account for a mere 2 percent of all intra-firm job changes in Detroit and 3 percent in Yokohama. In short, there are striking similarities in the proportion of intra-firm job changes accounted for by the different firm-size categories. With respect to inter-firm job changing, there are some differences between the two samples. In the case of Yokohama, the larger the firm, the smaller the proportion of total inter-firm job changing accounted for; firms employing one to nine employees account for 30 percent of all inter-firm job changes, compared to 20 percent for firms employing 1000+. The behavior of Detroit respondents, however, shows no such inverse relationship. Indeed, with the exception of the 100–999 category (18 percent of all inter-firm job changes), the relationship tends to be positive, increasing from 21 percent of job changes originating in firms of one to nine to 25 percent in firms of ten to ninety-nine and 25 percent in firms of 1000 or more.

We may turn now to an examination of the actual patterns manifested in Tables 12 and 13. They show some striking similarities between the two cities. There is a marked tendency for the number of inter-firm changes per person-year

TABLE 13
(Detroit)
**Mean Number of Intra- and Inter-firm Job Changes by Age
at Each Job Change and Firm Size of Origin**

Firm Size of Origin		*Age at Each Job Change*				
		16–25	*26–35*	*36–45*	*46–55*	*Total*
1–9	intra	0.03[a]	0.01[a]	0.01	—	0.02
	inter	0.37	0.23	0.15	0.11	0.25
10–99	intra	0.10[a]	0.05[a]	0.03	0.04	0.06
	inter	0.32	0.20	0.14	0.08	0.21
100–999	intra	0.17[a]	0.10[a]	0.05	0.04	0.09
	inter	0.35	0.19	0.07	0.06	0.18
1000+	intra	0.18[a]	0.13[a]	0.09	0.06	0.12
	inter	0.19	0.09	0.05	0.02	0.09
Total	intra	0.13[a]	0.10[a]	0.06	0.05	0.09
	inter	0.27	0.13	0.07	0.05	0.14

[a] See notes to Table 5.

of exposure to decline with increasing firm size for each age category; this is particularly true in the Detroit sample. This fits with the expectation that large firms, with their generally higher human and physical capital investments in a worker, will reward employees at a level sufficient to minimize high turnover and its attendant costs. This being so we might also anticipate that intra-firm changes per person-year of exposure would rise with increasing firm size. This should be the case because large firms should be more committed to utilizing the skills of their existing labor force, and have the market power to allocate wages in a way that insures this outcome. Secondly, opportunities for internal job changing may be greater in larger firms, depending on skill and length of job ladders. One may expect that large organizations tend to be more functionally differentiated than small ones. To the extent that a larger number of different job skills are required among members of functionally differentiated organizations, this leads to a need for coordination, gradation of responsibility, and sharing of job-related information. Consequently there is greater interdependence among vertically organized jobs in a particular unit. This increases the probability that job skills have overlapping requirements, and are institutionally linked in a common promotion progression (Groves 1975, pp. 231–33; Pugh et al. 1968, pp. 306–7). We noted earlier Piore's (1975) stress on the importance of career progressions in the primary sector.

Yet we ought also to be careful in assuming that larger firms have a higher probability of vacancies that can be filled from within than small firms, just because of their larger size. This logic ignores the complex division of labor in the larger firms, which reduces the number of internal applicants eligible for any given vacancy because of the specificity of the skills required and the location of the vacancy in a given job progression. To take a non-industrial example, nurses do not become doctors. Clark Kerr (1964, pp. 96, 105) notes that institutional rules, more prevalent in larger firms, restrict worker competition within the internal labor market, because craft jobs are likely to be fairly standardized and industrial jobs are filled in accordance with seniority. Groves (1975, p. 301) found that only two of seven major occupational categories (skilled workers: 33 percent; management: 61 percent) recruit more than 30 percent of their personnel from one of the other major occupational groups within the firm. We will propose in the following chapter that the Japanese tend to have more diffuse job requirements and broader recruitment reservoirs for given job vacancies but this does not diminish our overall observations.

Thirdly, and probably more important than the logic of firm size per se, is the fact that large firms are more bureaucratized; the presence of systematic rules for job transfers and pressure to recruit from within would lend itself to increasing the number of intra-firm job changers per person-year of exposure in larger firms. Larger firms may simply define job boundaries more narrowly and therefore have more job categories. Here the impact of unions may be critical. That is, the institutional factors may be the most powerful ones inducing a reliance on intra-firm job changing in larger firms. Larger firms, then, not only have an interest in recruiting from within, and the market power to insure the outcome they desire, but are also under employee pressure to do so. Although it is not possible to sort out the causal strength of these various factors using our data, it is apparent from Tables 12 and 13 that the data strongly support the predicted outcome. In almost every age group for both samples increasing firm size results in a larger mean number of intra-firm job changes.

There is always the danger that firm size will be confounded with the industry variable. On the assumption that the important role of large auto firms in Detroit might have influenced our results in some special fashion, we constructed Tables 12 and 13 excluding job states originating in the auto industry. The results were not notably different from the patterns just discussed. As with previous tables, we also constructed Tables 12 and 13 using five-year intervals for the age groups and including only those respondents working for others. The resultant tables confirmed in more graphic detail the interpretations reported above, as well as those to be reported below.

In short, the Yokohama sample does not exhibit any unique behavior with regard to the pattern of job changing according to firm size. Despite the lengthy literature detailing the distinctiveness of the Japanese dual economic structure, we find strikingly similar patterns of job changing by firm size in both samples. The lesson to be learned is that American and Japanese social scientists seem to have underestimated the importance of firm size as a variable predicting job-changing behavior in the United States.

Our concern, however, is not only with patterns of job changing but with volume. We set out to determine whether controlling for firm size would result in a reduction of the differences in inter-firm and intra-firm mobility between the two samples as reported in Tables 5 and 6. In the cases of both intra- and inter-firm job changing, the number of changes per person-year of exposure for

TABLE 14
**Ratio of Mean Number of Intra- to Inter-firm Job
Changes by Firm Size and City[a]**

City	Firm Size of Origin			
	1–9	10–99	100–999	1000+
Detroit	0.08	0.29	0.50	1.33
Yokohama	0.11	0.17	0.44	2.00

[a] Calculated from total columns in Tables 12 and 13.

each firm size (see total columns) in Yokohama rises above 50 percent of the Detroit figure in only two cases (0.57 for inter-firm job changing in the 10 to 99 firm size and 0.67 for intra-firm job changing in the 1000+ firm size). If we examine changes per person-year of exposure for each firm size and age group cell, we find a notable tendency for such changes in Yokohama to approximate or even exceed equivalent ones in Detroit in the older age groups of the larger firm sizes. This is especially notable in the case of intra-firm job changing. This observation does fit better with the view that investment in intra-firm training is higher in large Japanese firms, and the internal labor market more developed. That was our original hypothesis, but the overall data provide only the faintest resemblance to the robust relationship that we predicted at the beginning of the essay. They certainly do not reveal any markedly different Japanese behavior related to highly developed internal labor markets. In the case of inter-firm job changing the data sustain our second hypothesis that differences between small firms in both samples would be maintained. We reject the first hypothesis that differences between the two samples in the number of inter-firm job changes per person-year of exposure disappear when we compare the experience of employees in smaller firms.

In summary, firm size appears to have similar effects on the volume and pattern of job-changing behavior in both samples. Significantly, the initial differences recorded in the volume of intra- and inter-firm job changing do not disappear when we control for firm size, except for the two oldest age groups in the two largest firm sizes.

We are also able in this section to pursue further our earlier discussion of whether intra-firm job changing becomes more significant relative to inter-firm mobility over time. Table 14 presents the ratio of the mean number of intra- to inter-firm job changes by size of firm. It is apparent that in both cities the mean number of intra-firm job changes grows rapidly relative to the mean number of inter-firm job changes with increasing firm size. It is notable that in the largest firm size the Yokohama ratio significantly exceeds that of Detroit, giving credence to the hypothesized more important role of internal labor markets in large firms in Yokohama. Insofar as this relationship of increased importance for intra- relative to inter-firm job changes in both cities holds over time (and our data do contain historical records), this is a significant, though not surprising, finding. It is significant because the size of employing units, at least in manufacturing, has increased over time in industrializing societies. In the United States, manufacturing firms with more than 1,000 employees accounted for about 18 percent of all wage earners in manufacturing in 1900 (calculated from Nelson 1975, pp. 4–8). Blau (1974, p. 630) estimates that those in firms of 1,000 or more increased their proportion of all industry employees from 15 to 33 percent between 1909 and 1967. The sharpest increases seem to have occurred during World War I and World War II. There are no continuous data series for prewar and postwar Japan, but those establishments employing 1,000 or more workers have rapidly increased their share of manufacturing employment (Asahi Shinbunsha 1930, p. 960; Naikaku Tōkei Kyoku 1935, pp. 28–33).[5] The number of workers in establishments of 1,000 or more workers increased from 111,279 in 1909 to 160,782 in 1914. As in the United States, a sharp increase occurred during World War I; by 1920 there were 339,101 workers recorded for establishments of more than 1,000 workers. The high point in the prewar period was reached in 1929, at which time those employed in establishments of more than 1,000 workers totalled 586,671 and accounted for 28 percent of all workers. With the onset of the depression the total number of workers employed in such firms declined, falling back to 365,854 by 1933, and accounting for only 18.2 percent of all workers. These data also cast some further doubt on the extent of permanent employment in the pre-World War II period. The data are poor or non-existent after 1933 until the postwar series begins. The sharpest rise in the postwar period came in the 1950s during the period of economic recovery. By 1974 manufacturing firms with more than 1,000 employees accounted for 30 percent of all manufacturing employees (Office of the Prime Minister 1969, pp. 234–35; 1975, pp. 122–23).

Insofar as employment shifted to larger employing units over time, we would expect that intra-firm mobility would increase in importance relative to inter-firm job changing, given the positive association between firm size and the importance of intra-firm job changing reported in Table 14 and our discussion of Tables 12 and 13.

We cannot, however, simply project the growing importance of intra-firm changing into the future. It may be that with the rapid increase of employment in the service sector, the size of the employing unit will decline, at least in the private sector. Indeed there are signs this is already occurring in Japan. This might well halt the growing importance of intra-firm job changing, insofar as it is dependent on growing firm size and everything size stands for.

Although the focus of the discussion in this section is on the impact of size of firm of origin upon job changing, it is useful to examine the relation between size of firms of origin and destination. Tables 15 and 16 present these data. By examining the diagonals in each table, we see a strong tendency for job changing to take place between firms of similar size in both samples. Among those originating in a given category, there is no case in which the proportion ending up in the same firm-size category drops below 28 percent in the Detroit sample and 31 percent in the Yokohama sample. This tendency for destinations to be in the

5. The prewar Japanese data are not strictly comparable to Blau's data, as they are for all factory workers and are based on the concept of gainful employment. The unit of analysis is the establishment rather than the firm.

TABLE 15
(Yokohama)
Distribution of Inter-firm Job Changes
by Size of Present and Previous Employer

Firm Size of Origin		Firm Size of Destination				
		1–9	10–99	100–999	1000+	Total
1–9		80	44	26	31	181
10–99		42	84	33	33	192
100–999		23	31	39	32	125
1000+		26	30	18	43	117
	Total	171	189	116	139	615

TABLE 16
(Detroit)
Distribution of Inter-firm Job Changes
by Size of Present and Previous Employer

Firm Size of Origin		Firm Size of Destination				
		1–9	10–99	100–999	1000+	Total
1–9		57	52	31	62	202
10–99		48	114	41	82	285
100–999		23	39	71	70	203
1000+		48	54	56	206	364
	Total	176	259	199	420	1054

same firm size appears to be somewhat stronger for the two smallest categories in Yokohama (44 percent) than for the comparable sizes in Detroit (28 and 40 percent). This difference is reversed for the largest firm-size category. Fifty-seven percent of those who leave the largest firm-size category of 1000+ end up in the same category in Detroit, as compared to 37 percent for Yokohama. These observations fit the standard observations about the distinctive characteristics of segmented labor markets in Japan. Those in the smaller disadvantaged firms have difficulty penetrating the largest firms paying the greatest benefits, because these employers prefer to hire new school graduates. Conversely, we see that the proportion leaving large firms who end up in large firms is much greater in Detroit than Yokohama. This fits with the notion that large-scale Japanese employers are more reluctant to hire those with prior experience in large firms, because they are believed to have been shaped by their past employer in such a way as to make them less useful to a new large employer. Furthermore it may be assumed that such employees must have some personality problem which made it difficult for them to stay with their last employer. Here we find some support for the view that inter-firm mobility in Japan reflects individual failure, insofar as access to large firms guarantees higher wages and benefits. Before rushing to exaggerated conclusions, however, we should note that even in the case of Yokohama, employers still hire disproportionately from among those whose last job was in the same size class (though the tendency declines with increasing size and reaches its lowest point in the 1000+ category, where only 31 percent of those hired in Yokohama originated in the same size category).

We can also compare the ratio of inflow to outflow for given firm-size categories. The ratio of those leaving the 1000+ category to those entering it is 0.87 in Detroit, while in Yokohama it is a comparable 0.84. In the smallest firm size, the ratio of those leaving the 1 to 9 firm size to those entering it is 1.15 in Detroit compared to 1.06 in Yokohama. Thus no great differences manifest themselves. Growth is suggested in the largest firm-size category in both samples, with more entering than leaving it, and a modest decline is suggested in the smallest firm size, with more respondents leaving than entering.[6]

This pattern, while perhaps reflective of past institutional arrangements, does not necessarily reflect the current situation. Notable among recent developments in Japan has been the growing trend for employees in small firms to be recruited to large firms in response to the labor shortage of the late 1960s and early 1970s. Of males changing jobs in all of Japan in 1974, for example, 48 percent shifted to larger firms (Ministry of Labor 1975, p. 35). In our samples, however, we find that 32 percent of each sample left smaller firms for larger ones. The difference between our findings for Yokohama and the Ministry of Labor report lies in their more detailed size classification scheme and the fact that we are aggregating changes over a long historical period in which only scant attention is given to experiences in the 1970s.

One of the problems with this analysis is that it does not take into consideration the impact of the differing number of job changes that originate in the various firm-size categories. To deal with this problem, we constructed expectancy tables for the two samples.[7] These tables are based on the assumption that if employment changes were random with respect to firm size—if firm size of current job were independent of firm size at prior job—then the percentage distributions would be identical from one column to the next. The ability to compare the two datasets also rests on the assumption that where an individual moves in a given year depends only on where he was the preceding year and not on previous job states. Tables 17 and 18 are constructed to compare the actual percentages reported in Tables 15 and 16 with what would be observed under the "random" (or independence) hypothesis. This is done for each cell by dividing expected into actual distributions. The resultant tables are reported as the ratio of observed to expected frequencies for the aggregated work experiences of the two city samples. These tables measure the extent to which inter-firm mobility in and out of each firm surpasses or falls short of chance; the value of 1.0 indicates that the observed mobility from one size firm to another size firm is equal to that expected on the assumption of statistical independence.

6. The sample does include those newly entering the labor force.
7. I previously carried out these same procedures using different samples (Cole 1972). The results reported here are relatively comparable.

TABLE 17
(Yokohama)
Ratio of Observed to Expected Inter-firm Mobility by Size of Firm

Firm Size of Origin	Firm Size of Destination			
	1–9	10–99	100–999	1000+
1–9	1.59	0.79	0.76	0.76
10–99	0.79	1.42	0.91	0.76
100–999	0.66	0.81	1.65	1.13
1000+	0.80	0.83	1.22	1.63

TABLE 18
(Detroit)
Ratio of Observed to Expected Inter-firm Mobility by Size of Firm

Firm Size of Origin	Firm Size of Destination			
	1–9	10–99	100–999	1000+
1–9	1.69	1.05	0.81	0.77
10–99	1.00	1.63	0.76	0.72
100–999	0.68	0.78	1.85	0.87
1000+	0.79	0.60	0.82	1.42

Examining Tables 17 and 18, it is apparent that in both cities most job changing takes place between firms of the same size, to a degree well above what would be expected on the assumption of statistical independence. The main diagonal cells all exceed one and have the highest values of any cells in their respective columns. Because of the arbitrary nature of our firm categories it is difficult to establish the meaning of "distances" travelled in terms of firm size. Nevertheless, the values of the cells do generally tend to decline the further one goes from the main diagonal. This suggests the short distance quality of most moves by size of firm. One additional similarity is that the greatest inheritance of firm size among job changers is found in the medium size category of 100–999; this may reflect in part that this size category has the largest range excluding the open-ended category of 1000+.

In terms of permanent employment in Japan, the disposition of those leaving firms of 1000+ is particularly interesting. Internal labor markets should be important in both cities in firms of this size, but the literature on Japan would suggest that it is still stronger there. In fact the inheritance of firm size does show up at a slightly higher level in Yokohama (1.63) than Detroit (1.42).

Notwithstanding this difference, there is not much in these tables to suggest that remarkably different patterns of inter-firm mobility are operative in the two cities. We may not interpret this data, however, to mean that the volume of mobility is similar in the two cities; the data say nothing about the probability of job changing by size of firm.

Reasons for Employer Changing

Before concluding this section, it is important for our discussion of differences in inter-firm mobility patterns to distinguish between various types. Commonly researchers and government statisticians categorize inter-firm job changing as voluntary or involuntary. This is not a particularly satisfying distinction in that it fails to capture a much more variegated reality. In Table 19 we attempt to summarize a more differentiated picture of the types of inter-firm mobility which respondents report they have experienced for each employer change. Such data are subject to considerable retrospective distortion, as well as to interpretation problems. Nevertheless they should give us a rough idea of whether we are talking about the same kinds of inter-firm mobility in our two samples and their orders of magnitude.

This is, of course, an important issue because it casts light on the meaning of the numbers we report. In the case of Yokohama they should tell us something about the operation of the permanent employment system. Do workers never get fired in Japan? Is the inter-firm mobility that does occur of an overwhelmingly voluntary kind? High rates of economic activity, such as Japan experienced in the late 1950s and 1960s, are generally associated with a high ratio of voluntary to involuntary mobility. On the other hand, since this economic growth occurred in the context of labor surplus for large categories of workers, would this not lead to low levels of voluntary job changing? Alternatively, with the significant role played in Detroit by the cyclical employment patterns induced by the automobile industry, can we assume that involuntary job changes characterize most inter-firm changes?

First we may examine whether there are any inter-city differences in the reasons respondents give for job changes. In Detroit the three major reasons for leaving—financial, involuntary dismissal, and job dissatisfaction—account for a total of two-thirds of all job changes. At first glance the situation seems quite different in Yokohama where of the above three reasons only the financial (16.4 percent) makes the list of the top three. Both mobility/self-fulfillment and per-

TABLE 19
Response to the Question: "What was your major reason for leaving?"

Reason	Detroit (in %)	Yokohama (in %)
Financial	25.2	16.4
Threat to job security	5.6	9.4
Job dissatisfaction	20.2	15.5
Mobility/self-fulfillment	16.1	20.7
Involuntary dismissal	21.4	15.3
Personal non-job-related	9.0	19.0
Other	2.5	3.7
	100.0%	100.0%
	(N = 1418)	(N = 695)

NOTE: This was an open-ended question for which we constructed response categories.

TABLE 20
Summary of Reasons for Leaving Past Employer

Reason	Detroit (in %)	Yokohama (in %)
Push away from old job	61.1	62.1
Pull toward new job	26.0	25.1
Combination of push and pull	3.4	0.7
Ambiguous	4.2	5.5
Non-job-related reason	5.3	6.5
	100.0%	99.9%[a]
	(N = 1418)	(N = 695)

[a] Totals differ from 100.0% because of rounding error.

sonal reasons account for a higher proportion of responses (20.7 and 19 percent respectively). The high ranking given to involuntary dismissal in Detroit (21.4 percent) conforms to our image of a more cyclical labor market, with employees subject to dismissal with the frequent ups and downs of the automobile industry. Involuntary dismissals account for 15.3 percent of inter-firm job changes in Yokohama. Although notably less than in Detroit, this is by no means a negligible proportion. Most significantly, however, if we add threat to job security to the involuntary dismissal response, the total for Yokohama rises to 24.9 percent (just a little below 27.0 percent for the combined response in Detroit).[8] In short, strong push factors account for a comparable proportion of total inter-firm job changes in both cities.

In terms of the image of people using inter-firm job change as a means of self-betterment, it is interesting to see a rather comparable proportion in both samples choosing mobility/self-fulfillment reasons (16.1 percent in Detroit and 20.7 percent in Yokohama). Some of the categories in Table 19 include both push and pull factors. For example, financial reasons include not getting enough money at the previous employer as well as getting better pay with the new employer. To distinguish more clearly between push and pull factors in job changing, we constructed Table 20. This should be regarded as "softer" data than that reported in Table 19, because it involves still finer discrimination by the coders. Nevertheless it is instructive that a marked similarity emerges in the proportion of job-change decisions accounted for by push and pull factors in the two samples. One-fourth of both samples appear to be pulled toward the new job, with some 60 percent pushed away from the old job.

We also tested Tables 19 and 20 for possible effects due to differences in education and firm size. The basic conclusion is that while education and firm size do make a difference in the reasons for leaving, these effects are minor compared to the basic patterns reported above. Some of these minor effects were similar in both samples, some were different. The following effects that we

8. This is a reasonable decision since the threat-to-job-security category includes people who quit their jobs in anticipation of involuntary dismissal. The category includes: firm moved elsewhere, firm in difficulty, firm reorganizing, working week cut, security, and other.

report were statistically significant at the 0.001 level (chi-square test). Mobility/ self-fulfillment reasons increase with education in both samples. Financial reasons for job changing declined with increasing education in Yokohama; no systematic variation with education is apparent for the Detroit respondents. Conversely, involuntary discharge reasons decline sharply with increasing education in Detroit, but show no systematic variation for the Yokohama respondents. An examination of Table 20 revealed that pull factors increased in importance in job-changing decisions with more education in both samples. As for firm-size effects, financial reasons for employer changing decline with increasing firm size in both samples (though in Yokohama this is apparent only with the sharp dropoff in the largest firm size of 500 or more employees). On the other hand, the Detroit sample shows a consistent increase in the importance of the mobility/ self-fulfillment reason with increasing firm size; no such effect is apparent among Yokohama respondents. Again, there are some areas where the "dualistic labor market" apparently operates more in Detroit than in Yokohama. Finally, despite the stereotype that firing in Japan is done almost solely by small firms, no such tendency was apparent. In fact the proportion of leavers giving involuntary discharge as their reason was highest in the largest firms and lowest in the smallest firms.

In conclusion, many of the minor effects produced by education and firm size are similar in both samples. The minor differences are overshadowed by the similar overall pattern that emerges when we examine the "soft" distinction between push and pull factors in the two samples in Table 20. On the "harder" distinction in Table 19, we find in both samples that the core push factors of involuntary dismissal and threat to job security account for a little over one-fourth of all inter-firm job changes. In summary, the types of inter-firm job change and their distribution seem rather similar in the two samples. They cannot, therefore, provide any clues toward understanding the different volume of inter-firm job changing in the two cities.

Although the high proportion of job changing in Japan accounted for by the push factor may come as a surprise to some Western observers, our findings are quite consistent with the aggregate data findings of the Japan Ministry of Labor (Ministry of Labor 1973, p. 59). The ministry reports that until the late 1950s more than 30 percent of all job changes were forced, as a result of company bankruptcy, rationalization of company operations, unsatisfactory work performance, and expiration of employment contract (for temporary and seasonal workers). With the rapid growth of the 1960s, the proportion of involuntary changes among job changers declined to less than 10 percent. Both figures probably underestimate the "true" proportion of involuntary job changes because of their more conservative definition.

Our initial investigation uncovered the not surprising fact that the volume of inter-firm job changing in Yokohama was only about half that of Detroit; it was surprising to find, however, that the intra-firm mobility recorded for Yokohama was also only about half that of Detroit. We controlled for age, education, firm size, and industry in an attempt to see if these initial differences in volume would hold up. They did for the most part, with the exception of the older age groups in the larger firm sizes (see Tables 12 and 13). Even here, however, there was scant evidence to support the commonplace view that internal labor markets operate with distinctive strength in Japanese firms. Table 14 is suggestive in this regard but hardly conclusive, given that it is based on a ratio of intra- and inter-firm changing. Indeed, our evidence suggests that American scholars should pay a good deal more attention to firm size as an analytic distinction and all that firm size entails. The nature of the reported mobility patterns associated with firm size adds creditability to the position taken by the labor market segmentation theorists.

What explanation can we offer for the overall persistently lower volume in both inter- and intra-firm job changing among Yokohama respondents? In the case of larger firms, what was responsible for the failure of Yokohama respondents to evidence the distinctive behavior that we would expect to be associated with the strong internal labor markets alleged to be operative in such firms? To answer this question is the task we set for ourselves in the following chapter.

CHAPTER IV

PATTERNS OF JOB MOBILITY:
A COMPARATIVE STUDY OF
DETROIT AND YOKOHAMA
Interpretation

To evaluate the significance of the lower rates of intra- and inter-firm mobility reported for Yokohama respondents, we need to consider the two forms of mobility from a broad sociological, economic, and political perspective. In this chapter we discuss the meaning of high and low rates of job changing, try to isolate the relevant causal variables, and bring comparative data to bear where possible. This leads us to examine the very meaning of the concept of job in Japan and America. Through an analysis of historical data we seek to lay bare the social, political and economic context of job definitions in the two societies. In so doing we will propose, in particular, an explanation for the low rate of intra-firm mobility reported by our Yokohama sample and attempt to reconcile these low rates with the allegedly strong internal labor markets operative in Japan. Finally, we will present survey data that give us added leverage on these questions.

Western social scientists have either implicitly or explicitly viewed the Japanese practice of low inter-firm job changing as less modern compared to practices in the United States. The basis for this view (or ideology) is that individuals, as resources to be used efficiently and rationally by work organizations, must be separable from these organizations under certain economic conditions. These conditions are said to be present in advanced industrial societies, characterized as they are by rapid technological innovation and the need continually to adjust and transfer factors of production (see Marsh and Mannari 1971).

This position may be attacked from two different perspectives. First, we can identify three different means to meet new and expanding occupational requirements (Hunter and Reid 1968, p. 75). They are (1) alternations in the directional flow of new labor force entrants, (2) internal recruitment of those already employed in the same firm (resulting in intra-firm job changing), and (3) recruitment of those already employed in other firms and statuses (resulting in inter-firm job changing). The size of the first category, new labor force entrants, may change with increases or decreases in labor force participation or changes (sometimes lagged) in fertility and mortality. In an advanced industrial society many of these entrants are channeled into the labor force directly from school and often have to migrate to take advantage of job opportunities. The size of the second category would seem to be a function of the level of economic advancement and firm and industry size distributions and the resultant skill mix. Union and government policies further influence the propensity of employers to recruit from within. The size of the third category is, in part, a function of the level and rate of economic advance. Insofar as decisions are economically rational, the process involves transfers from inefficient sectors and firms in the economy (such as agriculture and handicrafts) to more efficient ones. It may also involve shifts from unemployed, family-worker, and self-employed statuses to employee status. Of course, what is rational from the perspective of the economy is not necessarily rational from the individual point of view. Individuals change employers all the time without making the economy more efficient; they are motivated by personal goals such as desire to acquire a skill (which may not necessarily be the skills the economy needs most), desire to live in a certain geographical locality, and so on.

Finally, immigration has played a notable role in many societies as a source of labor elasticity, providing labor force entrants especially for the first and third categories. In postwar Japan immigration has been a negligible factor except for the repatriation of large numbers of Japanese citizens and military immediately after World War II.

In contemporary industrial societies there is good reason to think that the rate of technological innovation is too high to allow any one solution. Moreover, as suggested in the preceding discussion, there is no reason to assume that the mixes between these three alternative sources must be the same. Different historical experiences, levels and rates of economic advance, firm size and industry distributions, and labor market circumstances lead employers and employees in different nations to opt for different mixes; they may operate in rough fashion as functional alternatives in meeting new, expanding, or declining occupational requirements. On the other hand, some strategies may be more effective than others in producing economic growth. Kindleberger (1967) discusses some of the sources of national variation in labor force elasticity in Western Europe in his attempt to test the fit of W. Arthur Lewis's model of growth with unlimited supplies of labor.

The point of this extended discussion is that to focus only on inter-firm job changing—as many analysts of the Japanese labor market have done—without considering its relation to intra-firm mobility and to new entrants to the labor force, is a simplistic approach that ignores the possible mixes available. There is reason to think, for example, that the Japanese with their one-time-a-year national system of recruitment and sharply differentiated dual economic structure have more effectively channeled new entrants to the labor force (particularly new school graduates) to rapidly expanding industries with high productivity than has been the case in the United States. An examination of the composition of new hires in Japanese establishments with thirty or more employees on an annual basis reveals that an average of 48 percent of new hires between 1956 and 1972 were either new school graduates (32.6) or otherwise occupationally inexperienced (15.4); the definition of the latter category is that they entered the labor force after having been inactive for at least one year (Japan Institute of Labour 1974, pp. 68–69). By contrast, Groves (1975, pp. 60–62), using the Social Security Administration's Continuous Work History Sample for 1960–62 and 1967–72, estimates that only about 17 percent of new hires each year in the Detroit SMSA are new labor force members or those with intermittent employment. Moreover, if we assume that Japanese firms employing over 500 employees were responsible for a large part of the productivity increase during this period, we will want to examine these same totals for this size category. Such an examination reveals that an even higher proportion of new hires in these establishments (53 percent) were either new school graduates (40.2) or otherwise occupationally inexperienced (12.8). The educational quality of new school graduates is considerably higher than that of those new hires who are either job changers or occupationally inexperienced. The new school graduates have come to be overwhelmingly composed of high school graduates, while the job changers and occupationally inexperienced are rather evenly divided between middle school and high school graduates. Finally, the youthfulness of the age structure of rapidly growing Japanese firms suggests the importance of new school entrants to achieving increased productivity (Cole 1976). These data indicate just how important a component of labor adjustments is the efficient use of new entrants to the labor force relative to intra- and inter-firm mobility.

With the reduction in the birth rate and aging of the Japanese labor force now taking place, the importance of new school graduates in bringing about labor force adjustments is being drastically reduced. The proportion of new school graduate hires to total hires declined from 37.7 percent in 1965 to 25.7 percent in 1972. However, those otherwise occupationally inexperienced rose from 17.6 percent of all new hires in 1965 to 21.9 percent in 1972. This category has come to be composed overwhelmingly of females returning to the labor force after a prolonged period of absence; they constituted 76 percent of all otherwise occupationally inexperienced in 1972. The decline in the number of new school graduates available for employment will put increased pressure on intra- and inter-firm mobility to meet labor adjustment needs in the future.

An alternative tack is not to ask why inter-firm job changing is so low in Japan, as American social scientists are wont to do, but rather to ask why it is so high in the United States. Although cross-national comparisons are notoriously difficult, turnover in North America is said to be notably higher even than in Western Europe (OECD 1965). A survey of job separation rates in the early 1970s by the Japanese Ministry of Labor reports that they are highest in the

United States and France, with West German and English rates running about 80 percent of the American rates, and the Japanese recording 60 percent of the American rates (Ministry of Labor 1975). In a national sample of employed workers in America it was reported that in 1966, 25.9 percent of those interviewed had started their job less than one year before (Hamel 1967, p. 32).

In an eleven-nation survey commissioned by the Prime Minister's Office in Japan (1973) and carried out by Gallup International, 2,000 youths in each nation between the ages of eighteen and twenty-four were questioned about their job-changing (i.e., employer-changing) behavior. Excluding those youths without work experience, 60.4 percent of the Japanese sample had never changed employers, compared to 23.3 percent of the American respondents. The discrepancy is striking. However, the comparable percentages in Western European nations are: West Germany 52, France 51.2, Switzerland 48.2, Sweden 45.2, and England 37.2. In short, although Japan still scores higher in this respect than the Western Europeans, it is the Americans that appear more out of line than the Japanese. It may be added that less industrialized nations such as Yugoslavia (72.5 percent), India (85.5 percent), and the Philippines (63.8 percent) scored higher than the Japanese. The survey also asked the number of times the individual respondent had changed employers. Excluding those youths without work experience, the same differences appear. For example, those changing employers more than four times totalled 2.7 percent in Japan and a remarkable 27.6 in the United States. But the comparable figures for the Western Europeans are: West Germany 5.7, Sweden 10.8, Switzerland 10.5, England 14.3, and France 17.4.

Shimada (1976) finds a corresponding ordering in his examination of the relation between production decline and declines in labor input during the worldwide recession of the mid-1970s. His study analyzes the movement in these two variables in the period from November 1973 to December 1975 in Japan, the United States, Britain, West Germany, and France. The specific measure used is labor input elasticity, which measures the amount of decline in labor input with each 1 percent reduction of production. Labor input is defined as the product of the number of regular workers times the number of hours worked. Shimada found a significant decline in labor input for the first year (November 1973–December 1974) in Japan, but it is accounted for almost entirely by a reduction in working hours, not by a reduction of workers. By contrast the largest decline in labor input in the first year occurs in the United States and it is achieved primarily through a reduction of workers. The Western European nations fall between Japan and the United States in these movements.

In the second year (December 1974–December 1975) the decline in labor input in Japan continues, but in this period a significant reduction of workers takes place, at a level that makes the Japanese employment adjustment quite comparable to that of the Western European nations. What we see then is a lag in Japan in employment adjustment as measures other than layoffs are tried. When the economic situation proves too serious to handle in this fashion the reduction in working hours is followed by a reduction of workers that produces a decrease in labor input quite comparable to that which occurs in the Western European nations. The depth of adjustment in terms of reduction in numbers of workers per 1 percent of production decline is twice as high in the United States as it is in Japan and the Western European nations. Fujita (1976, pp. 28–29), using different measures of the same phenomenon, reports that during the 1974–76 period, West Germany and England had roughly double the employment elasticity of Japan, but that the United States' employment elasticity was four times higher than Japan's.

Perhaps we have in the United States not a marked case of modernity but rather excessive labor mobility. We may define this concept as rapid and costly labor turnover in some sectors without in the end securing a net redistribution of the labor force (Hunter and Reid 1968, p. 196). Lloyd Reynolds (1974, p. 514), responding to the fear that heavy emphasis on seniority reduces labor mobility and interferes with the market mechanism, writes:

> Moreover, labor mobility can be too high as well as too low. It is not desirable that everyone in the labor force shuttle about constantly from job to job. Efficient operation of the market requires only a mobile minority, which may be made up largely of new entrants to the labor force plus the unemployed. For the bulk of the labor force, stability has advantages in terms of productive efficiency as well as personal satisfaction.

After all, to say that individuals as resources must be separable from their work organizations in order to be efficiently and rationally used, cannot be interpreted to mean the more job changing the better. Purposeless reshuffling leads to the imposition of extra costs, which are borne by employers, workers, and the society at large (Hunter and Reid 1968, p. 99).

To take the ultimate cost for the individual—that of the probability of continued life—Caplan (1971) reports evidence that excessively rapid and continuous change in employment, which presumably gives rise to great stress and insecurity, is a significantly high risk factor producing heart disease in the United States. The occupationally mobile seem to have a greater likelihood of experiencing heart disease as a consequence of the new and complex demands made upon them (House 1974, p. 156). On the other hand, Matsumoto (1970) associates the unusually low risk of heart disease reported for Japanese workers with the stability, security, and supportive atmosphere characteristic of employment conditions in Japan. Brenner (1973; 1975), using U.S. data, demonstrates a clear link between mental and physical health, as well as aggression, and short-term changes in the national rate of unemployment and per capita personal income over the last seventy years. In periods of economic downturn, significant increases (often lagged) in heart attacks, cirrhosis, alcohol abuse, suicide, infant mortality, and mental illness occur. For example, the best predictor of short-term mental hospital admissions was found to be economic conditions; the relationship was strongest for men aged thirty-five to fifty-four. At the micro level, Kasl, Gore and Cobb (1975, pp. 106–22) examined the changes in health symptoms and illness behavior associated with the experience of losing a job in two American firms. They found that men experiencing a lot of job changes had an "average days complaint" notably higher than men experiencing few changes.

If we take suicide rates as our measure of stress and examine them cross-nationally, we find that the rates for males in age groups fifteen to twenty-four and twenty-five to thirty-four are slightly higher in Japan than the United States (Young 1974, pp. 560–61). However, they hold steady for Japan in age groups thirty-five to forty-four and forty-five to fifty-four, while they rise rapidly in the United States, substantially surpassing the Japanese levels for these two age categories. These are the peak years of employment, when men are most likely to be main providers of family and when unemployment is most likely to threaten security and self-esteem. It should be noted that the average Japanese blue-collar worker marries late—at twenty-eight—by U.S. standards. An examination of the rates for the forty-five to fifty-four age group shows that the U.S. suicide rate per 100,000 males is 27.2, compared to 18.8 in Japan. In an eight-nation comparison with Western industrial nations, Japan scores the third highest in suicide rates for males in the fifteen to twenty-four age group, falls to fourth in the twenty-five to thirty-four age group, and to the sixth rank in the thirty-five to forty-four, forty-five to fifty-four, and fifty-five to sixty-four age groups. Work-related stress is, to be sure, only one of the determinants of suicide rates; nevertheless the comparative rates and changes by age group are highly suggestive and conform to the inferences one would derive from our discussion above. It should be noted, however, that case studies of attempted or actual suicides have not succeeded in isolating the role of unemployment (Kasl 1974, p. 180).

Augustine (1972) examines the costs of turnover and recruitment and estimates that turnover costs American employers some eleven billion dollars a year. Leghorn (1976) estimates the "costs" of inter-firm mobility in terms of subsequent organizational attachment. Using the Detroit-Yokohama dataset, he found that the cost of inter-firm mobility in both Yokohama and Detroit was a 61 percent reduction in the strength of organizational attachment. Specifically, movers in a particular year were more than twice—2.56 times—as likely to move again the subsequent year as was a non-changer in that same first year. Moreover, whether the change was voluntary or involuntary seemed to make no great difference.

There is a striking dichotomy between how employers perceive turnover and how many sociologists conceptualize its significance. It is not our purpose to demonstrate conclusively that excessive labor mobility is descriptive of American patterns of job changing, yet it is instructive that this description does fit with those characterizations of the American labor market put forward by some economists (e.g., Lebergott 1968). This is not to deny that there are important advantages in the American practice of encouraging movement between firms, both from employee and employer perspectives.[1] Nevertheless, our

1. Perhaps the best way to note the limited nature of this perspective is to point out that even in the United States there are clearly industrial sectors and individual categories of workers that would benefit currently from an *increase* in inter-firm mobility. Most notably, declining industries would benefit from more rapid transfer of employees out of the industry and the economy would benefit from the transfer of such workers into more productive industrial sectors. On the individual level older workers who come to career dead ends, often because of occupational obsolescence, would benefit from the opportunity to voluntarily transfer to more promising occupations (HEW 1973, pp. 121–34).

discussion should establish that the use of the American labor market as a yardstick of modernity distorts our interpretations.

Whether a society has too much or too little job changing is a question of great complexity at best. Worker and employer interests are often not consistent on the matter and the character of job mobility sharply influences worker and employer evaluations. Involuntary job changing is by definition regarded less favorably by employees than by employers. There is no optimum ratio between the volume of intra- and inter-firm job changing. This is true because we have to consider the role of new entrants to the labor force as well as the rate of productivity increase. In addition, there are tradeoffs from both employer and employee perspectives and the value of these tradeoffs varies according to economic and social conditions.

Intra-firm Mobility

We turn now to a consideration of intra-firm mobility. In Chapter III, we found that intra-firm job changing not only did not compensate for the low level of inter-firm mobility in Yokohama, but that its volume per respondent was even lower than that reported for Detroit respondents. To phrase the matter in this fashion reflects the presumption that the "normal" volume of total job changing has been achieved in the United States and that therefore the combined total of intra- and inter-firm mobility in Japan should approximate the American total. There is no reason, however, to assume that two countries with quite different labor market traditions, degrees of industrial concentration, growth experiences, and occupational and industrial structure should have the same total requirements for job mobility. Moreover, we have already suggested the possibility that the volume of inter-firm mobility in the United States may be excessive, in which case the proposition becomes meaningless. Finally, we pointed to the important role in labor adjustments performed by new entrants to the labor force in Japan.

Yet, having said this, the volume of intra-firm job changing reported in the Yokohama sample still seems remarkably low, given the critical importance observers attach to internal labor markets in Japan as well as to Japan's rapid economic growth. There are a number of related explanations that we may offer for the low level of intra-firm job changing reported by Yokohama respondents. First, it is well accepted that occupational and job consciousness in a narrow sense is quite low in Japan compared to other industrial nations (Cole and Tominaga 1976a; OECD 1973, pp. 10–11). In place of occupational consciousness there tends to be a well-developed sense of company belongingness. One basis for this is that intra-firm job changes in Japan tend not to be associated with wage and salary adjustments, because the major explicit determinants of wages are age, length of service, and ability. The result is that consciousness of intra-firm job changes, especially in large firms, tends to be diminished. Shifting status (title) and section identification are strong in a situation in which the internal labor market is not based on job consciousness.

Culturally the explanation for this phenomenon in Japan is that the task is assigned to the group, not its individual members, and that the responsibility for performing these tasks is shared by the entire group. Moreover, this delegation takes place with general rather than specific work instructions. Yoshino (1968, pp. 202–3) maintains that individual members of the group are at the disposal of its leaders. This seems to overstate the case. It is not a matter of mindless robots at the service of their superiors as Western stereotypes suggest. Rather, individuals seek achievement of their goals in and through control of the group (see Marsh and Mannari 1976, pp. 210–13). This is different from the idealized individualism of the West. For our purposes here, it is only important to note that the achievement of collective goals, through which individual career goals evolve, takes precedence over developing individual occupational expertise. This situation becomes more understandable if we keep in mind institutional characteristics; Japanese foremen are not only first-line supervisors who regulate job assignments, they are also the senior members of the work group. Members of the work group share a common career ultimately, and this serves to produce a highly integrated and solidary work group (Koike 1975, p. 8).

These kinds of explanations suggest that intra-firm job changes are heavily underreported relative to their actual occurrence in the Yokohama sample.[2] To use the term underreported, however, avoids what is a more fundamental question. As a consequence of the various factors just mentioned, job descriptions in Japanese firms tend to be quite diffuse. Job descriptions, if they exist at all, tend to be extremely brief and general. The job a Japanese employee reports that he is performing may actually stand for a whole range of jobs that he is carrying out. That is, when a Japanese respondent reports that he is, say, a driller, he will be using it as a generic term to span a whole range of activities carried out by drillers in his section, activities which an American worker would be likely to perceive as separate jobs, and thus would be more likely to list in his job history report. In short, the relative lack of sharp jurisdictional definitions of job duties on the part of both management and workers tends to make Japanese workers less conscious of job changes.[3] Thus it is not simply a matter of underreporting, but rather that the very concept of job and job change seems to differ

2. We were quite sensitive to the difficulty of eliciting intra-firm job changing data from respondents, especially in Japan, at the time of questionnaire construction. The language used in the interview was: "Sometimes a person will be transferred, promoted or have changes in rank and responsibility. Now I would like you to think of *all the things* you did at (interviewer fill in employer's name). Did you hold any other jobs that you would say were different from the job you started with there?" Once a respondent identified other jobs he was asked to describe them in detail. The comparable Japanese question read as follows: "Yatowaretē iru baai shigoto no naiyō ya chii ga kawaru koto ga arimasu. Ima sono shigoto de keiken shita idō ya shōshin o zenbu omoidashite kudusai. Sono shigoto o hajimete kara shigoto no naiyō ya chii ga kawatta koto wa arimasu ka. ('Hai' no baai). Zenbu de ikutsu no shokushu o keiken shimashita ka." It is possible that, compared to the English question, the Japanese translation puts more emphasis on change of status as opposed to change of job.

3. In recent years many large firms have initiated job evaluation schemes which necessarily involve more definite job descriptions. Yet an examination of some of the systems in operation suggests that they are still remarkably vague compared to American standards (e.g., Funahashi 1973, pp. 375–79).

in the two societies. Were it simply a matter of underreporting, one might conclude that this research has been a futile exercise inasmuch as it failed to tap the large amount of intra-firm job changing in Yokohama. It has failed to tap such mobility, but in a very real organizational and subjective sense this mobility does not exist, at least not in the way conceptualized by American social scientists. To put the matter differently, the concept of an internal labor market assumes the existence of a set of rules for governing internal labor allocation and pricing which accord preferential rights and privileges to the presently employed. To say that a firm has a "strong" internal labor market is to say, first, that there are rigid rules which limit the ports of entry and define the requirements for admission. Secondly, strong internal labor markets are characterized by precise rules for allocating opportunity within the firm, that is, rules for governing the pricing and allocation of labor (see Kerr 1964, pp. 102–3).

Do large Japanese firms have strong internal labor markets? Certainly there are rigid rules which limit ports of entry to new male school graduates where possible. Yet if we take the term labor market to mean that there is an explicitly delineated supply and demand function for specified job skills, it would be difficult to argue that they have strong internal labor markets. It is not necessary, however, that the criteria for differentiating individual rights and obligations in strong internal labor markets be based on clearly delineated boundaries between explicitly elaborated job classifications, each with standard wage rates. Instead, individual characteristics such as age, education, seniority, ability and merit may play a dominant role in pricing and allocating labor within the firm. Such a set of rules exists in large Japanese firms, and together with high job security they may be even more effective than Western arrangements in defining the rights and privileges of those currently employed. Moreover, the internal labor market in Japan is not undercut by strongly developed occupational markets as in selected spheres in the United States. As Kerr (1964, pp. 96–98) notes, a tight relation to occupation generally forces a looser relation to employer. These conclusions are consistent with the position taken in Chapter II that internal labor markets may have quite different bases in different nations. One of the few detailed cross-national studies of the relation between technology and work which includes Japan is the eight-nation study of work relations in thermal power stations by Shiba (1973; 1973a). He concludes with some observations that bear quoting:

> Turning now to the grouping for promotion and wage determination criteria and in-grade wage differentials, we found that promotion in India, Pakistan, Malaysia, Singapore, Canada, and the U.S.A. is decided on the basis of company or national examinations directly geared to the particular job. In Japan and Thailand, however, promotion is based on the education, diligence, or age of the individual worker. This job-based/potential-ability-based criteria [sic] can also be seen in wage determination. In India, Pakistan, Malaysia, Singapore, Canada, and the U.S.A., the influence of the job factor on wage determination was shown to be almost total, whereas age is the decisive factor in Japan and education in Thailand. The use of job-based or potential-ability-based criteria affects wage structure, especially the in-grade wage range and rates of overlap. In those countries where job-based cri-

teria are employed, wage rates approximate to a single rate. Where latent-ability-based criteria are used, in-grade wage ranges and rates of overlap between adjacent grades are considerable. (Shiba 1973, pp. 146–47)

In summary, the large Japanese firm is characterized by strong internal labor markets, but the criteria for distinguishing rights and obligations are not those of explicit job classifications with standard wage rates.

The Concept of a Job in Historical Perspective

These observations and interpretations call into question facile assumptions about the invariant consequences of industrialization in producing a division of labor manifesting a high degree of job differentiation.[4] Sociologists influenced by functional theory see the core of modernization as a development toward greater specialization and differentiation. In this context a standard observation is to point out the "enormous proliferation of occupational specialties" that has accompanied the process of industrialization in the United States, and to assume that this growth operates in the same fashion and has the same consequences in all industrialized nations (Treiman 1970, pp. 215–17). In 1970 the *Dictionary of Occupational Titles* listed some 22,000 separate job titles. The interpretation of the causes of this growth in occupational specialization varies according to author. Some (e.g., Treiman 1970, p. 216) take their lead from Adam Smith, whereby an increasing division of labor increases the scale and efficiency of production. The fundamental proposition of the economist is that specialization of function permits each person, firm, and region to use to best advantage any peculiar differences in skills and resources. Other scholars such as Peter Blau (1974, p. 628) point out that historical trends and cross-national comparisons reveal that an increase in occupational differentiation is positively associated with a growth in the level of education and the proportion of the male labor force in professional and related occupations. Blau and Schoenherr (1971) see organizational size as a major factor in determining the degree of horizontal differentiation, defined as the number of positions and subunits in the organization. These views provide a rather mechanical explanation of the causal processes involved. Many draw their inspiration from the works of classical scholars such as Max Weber and Emile Durkheim. Weber's perspective on bureaucratic organization, for all the criticism it has received, still exercises a powerful influence on sociological thought. In the context of our discussion, the relevant propositions are: each bureaucratic office has a clearly defined sphere of competence; they are organized in a clearly defined hierarchy of offices; the salary scale is graded according to rank in the hierarchy; and the office is treated as the primary or sole occupation of the incumbent (Weber 1947, pp. 333–34). These, together with other elements of his model, are supposed to insure efficient operation. Those operating in the Weberian tradition emphasize the bureaucratization of work organizations associated with industrialization which, in the name of efficiency, requires increasing specificity of job definitions. In Durkheim's model it is increases in the size and density of a population which jointly bring about

4. I am indebted to Thomas Rawski for stimulating my thinking in this area.

an increasing division of labor (Durkheim 1947). Some human ecologists have seized upon this formulation to argue that the division of labor increases in almost automatic fashion in response to the size of the population (Gibbs and Martin 1962). We see an almost total absence of cultural and social norms in these explanations (Friedson 1977). Whichever model one adopts, we see that the division of labor increases almost automatically in response to the researcher's favorite independent variable. The increasing specificity of job definitions, in turn, makes possible and necessary the "free-floating" character of human resources manifested in high job mobility.

We would like to consider an alternative line of thought, to wit, that there may be an unusual set of historical circumstances that shaped American industrialization, which produced both an exceptional degree of occupational differentiation and a high valuation of this differentiation. Specialization is perceived to be a positive good in American society; Moore (1962, pp. 96–97) suggests that this view rests, in part, upon the doctrine of individualism. In short, the belief in the positive benefits of specialization may be deeply rooted in our culture. Other societies which place less value on individualism may be less inclined to value specialization. The notion that the division of labor is not a universal outcome but historically influenced is not novel. Many of the classical sociologists debated the point—Simmel, Durkheim, and Schmoller to name but a few (see Dahrendorf 1970, p. 13). The debate was, however, primarily between individual and social determinants. Marx's research focused on the relation between the division of labor and changes in the class structure. The problematic view of the character of the division of labor has given way to a conventional wisdom which sees it as fully determined by the level of industrialization or, more specifically, by the degree of bureaucratization, organizational size, character of industrial structure and level of technological development.

We have seen that sociologists are wont to interpret the 22,000 different job titles classified in the *Dictionary of Occupational Titles* simply as a reflection of the division of labor associated with advanced levels of industrialization. Yet knowledgeable government officials who work with the data report that the type and amount of differentiation reflect the influence of collective bargaining arrangements (e.g., Machinist I, II, III, IV, etc.) and, more generally, the impact of professional societies and unions. They also reflect the personnel policy of American corporations in constructing specific kinds of job ladders (Wolfbein 1971, p. 53). In short, occupational categories often are a response to administrative needs (Form 1968, p. 24). Nor does this exhaust the influences in constructing these categories (see Hodge and Siegel 1964, pp. 176–92). It does make clear that a simple-minded technological determinism will not suffice as an explanation for the degree of differentiation reflected in American occupational categorizations.

To pursue some of those specific characteristics of American industrialization, we may first examine briefly the salient features of American unionism (see Shimada 1974, p. 140). Those institutional labor economists who take their lead from Perlman (1928) maintain that one of the most notable features of American unionism has been its orientation toward control of job opportunities.

This can best be understood in the context of an industrialization process which occurred under conditions of labor shortage and the failure of workers to participate collectively in national politics. At a minimum, control of job opportunities involved standardizing and articulating rules of wage determination and job allocation. To conclude contracts that allow this assumes the determination of rates of earnings on the basis of sets of explicitly defined jobs. Moreover, the continuing pressures of potential interfirm mobility made it difficult for the rate to deviate from the value of the worker's productive contribution. With advancing industrialization, this union function decreased, as the scale of enterprises grew and internal labor markets developed in importance relative to external labor markets. However, the earlier patterns became institutionalized in both unionized and non-unionized firms in the form of job rates. In adapting to new pressures and conditions, there evolved a complex set of industrial relations rules whereby the equity principle—still predicated on the ability to identify and compare sets of clearly defined jobs—became a central basis for wage determination. In summary, the careful and detailed delineation of job duties and jurisdictions was particularly encouraged by this set of historical circumstances. Furthermore, these discrete jobs took on special importance with regard to wage payments and the rights and obligations of incumbents.

We may compare this outcome with the situation in Japan. First, the role of the state in determining industrial relations practices was more significant in Japan's case. The state is not as likely as private employers and unions to encourage the use of minute job distinctions as criteria for wage determination in the private sector. Among Japanese unions there was considerably less interest in crystallizing the rights, duties, and boundaries of jobs than in the U.S. In the pre-World War II period the unions had trouble simply establishing their legitimacy. Furthermore Japan experienced labor surplus rather than labor shortage throughout much of its industrialization. Consequently control over job opportunities, and the job specification that follows from this, was less feasible as a union strategy. Yet the unions were not uninterested in job security, as we saw in Chapter I. After World War II they played the major role in the diffusion and crystallization of the permanent employment practice. Finally, the history of economic development in Japan was such that they skipped the craft stage of union organization, precisely the stage at which the model of job specification was most carefully worked out in the American experience. Dore (1974) suggests that many of these characteristics can be generalized to the late developers.

Quite independently of union influence, one can consider the influence in the United States of scientific management ideas as synthesized by Frederick Taylor (1947). These became the dominant American personnel management ideology in the first quarter of the twentieth century and strongly influenced managerial practices as well. Although Taylorism gradually fell into disrepute and was replaced by new managerial ideologies, such as human relations, it has left an important legacy, with many of its ideas becoming interwoven with newer approaches. Herbert Simon, for example, with his characteristic focus on decision-making processes, stresses the benefits obtained from the division and specialization of the decision-making function (Simon 1965, p. 152, cited in

Men-Koy Wong 1973, p. 359). Taylor's intellectual legacy continues to strongly influence both managerial and social science perceptions of what is and what ought to be. During the period from about 1910 to the late 1920s Taylorism became firmly established as the dominant framework within which management acted to modify the organization of work. Taylor's ideas became the intellectual core of the new profession of industrial engineers (Men-Koy Wong 1973, p. 270). The work of Taylor and Gilbreth (1911) set a firm foundation for the field of engineering psychology, especially that branch known as time-and-motion study. Written job specifications based on the use of these techniques developed as an aid to the recruitment and selection of employees. In the post-World War I period job analysis became a standard feature of personnel practices in large American firms (Nelson 1975, p. 151). If scientific management has disappeared as a separate movement, it is because it has been thoroughly absorbed as the basic underlying assumption in the organization of work within American industry (Braverman 1974, pp. 86–88; Drucker 1954, p. 280).

104

Taylorism is relevant to our discussion because it was concerned with devising appropriate production norms by analysis of the individual job and rewarding workers accordingly. This involved developing the specific technology of job analysis and work measurement. To utilize these techniques required dividing the job into its simplest parts and measuring the time required for doing each component task. Taylor advocated extensive and systematic specialization of job tasks. Every worker was to be allotted specific, predetermined tasks and was responsible to superiors for performing them (Taylor 1911). All this presumes detailed management control over the work process and a contraction of worker discretion. The refinements of Taylor's successors led to a concentration on subdividing and apportioning human efforts to the most elementary tasks so as to increase reliability by encouraging machine-like motions (Bright 1958, p. 16–17). Gilbreth (1911), for example, added to time study the concept of motion study, which involved the classification of the basic motions of the body involved in the labor process.

Although Taylor himself saw his ideas as an alternative to collective bargaining, the unions, once established, learned to negotiate over rate setting for particular jobs, a process that was cemented during the cooperative eras of World War I and World War II (see Gomberg 1955, p. 249). Instead of the individualized incentive payment systems often preferred by management, the unions sought standard job rates. The outcome was a melding of union interest in control over job opportunities and management attempts to systematically rationalize work operations. The convergence contributed to the development of tight and narrowly defined job definitions. Put differently, it reinforced and deepened the division of labor that was dictated by the level of industrial development. The emergent unions had two basic options. They could struggle to increase the amount of worker discretion on the job, thereby "enlarging" the job, or even insist on a worker voice in job design. Alternatively the unions could accept the given framework of power and struggle to make quantitative improvements in worker rewards. The first option was clearly a radical one, which the unions eventually rejected in the face of management and government power and lack of worker support. They accepted the more limited second solution, whereby collective bargaining came to legitimate the existing extreme division of labor (cf., Fox 1974, pp. 201, 204–5). Piore (1974, p. 81) suggests that the unions' acceptance of industrial engineering derived from their efforts to institutionalize seniority as the basis for allocating jobs and income; the use of seniority as the ultimate arbiter depends on unambiguous job assignments. This is the basis for union interest in a rationalized job structure. Seniority also presupposes that job requirements are set small enough to insure that virtually any worker can perform the job, hence the union interest in job simplification.

Katherine Stone (1974, pp. 155–56) reports the experience of the steel industry in which the War Labor Board (World War II) responded to a union request for elimination of wage-rate inequities by directing the company and union to negotiate a simplification and rationalization of job classifications. The directive instructed the company and union to (1) describe simply and concisely the content of each job, (2) place the jobs in their proper relationship, and (3) reduce the number of job classifications to the smallest practical number by grouping those jobs having substantially equivalent content. As a result of the board's ruling, the steelworkers union and the steel companies began in 1945 to reclassify and reevaluate the entire industry's job and wage structure. Out of this effort, two years later, came a new job classification manual for the entire industry, including a procedure for classifying new jobs and a standard hourly wage scale on which all rates would be based. The steel manual became the model for job reevaluation in other industries and remains in effect in all major steel companies today. In U.S. Steel alone, the number of job titles prior to this effort was between 45,000 and 50,000. These were reduced in the manual by half and all were filed into thirty separate wage-rate classifications. Between each of them was a hierarchically ordered 3.5 cents-an-hour increment (the increment is now 12 cents an hour). The steelworkers unions never seriously questioned the existence of elaborately stratified wage and job structures, but worked to introduce equity among different categories of workers, including the use of seniority to control movement from one job to another. In the process they contributed to cementing the structure of a finely divided job hierarchy into the wage system.

The willingness of the unions to accept the existing framework of job differentiation must be traced back to the very evolution of the system. Similarly the strong impact of Taylorism must be understood in the cultural and economic context provided by late nineteenth-century capitalism, the drive toward internal rationalization of the capitalist factory system under conditions of labor shortages, and the desire to legitimate management authority in the face of an emergent union movement.

Again, the experience of the steel industry is instructive. Stone (1974, pp. 123–27) shows how a stream of technological innovations in the steel industry around the turn of the century transformed the tasks involved, with the result that a homogenization of worker skills occurred. In this process the semiskilled worker became the model worker. This levelling was accompanied by a similar compression of the wage structure. These technological innovations were made possible, in turn, by the breaking of the steel unions symbolized by the great Homestead Mill strike at the Carnegie Corporation in 1892. The steel companies struggled to wrest control of the work process from the craft unions. It was the inability of the once powerful Amalgamated Association to resist technological innovation, as the skilled workers lost their once strong control over work methods, that led to the transformation of worker skills.

Thompson (1967, pp. 108–9) characterizes the semiskilled job as requiring skills widely distributed in the population or quickly developed on the basis of these common skills, requiring little worker discretion, and having a highly determined quality. This combination of characteristics permits nearly complete knowledge of cause-and-effect relationships in job tasks, thereby allowing the organization to calculate standards of required behavior. In short, it was ideally suited to the techniques of scientific management. Most importantly, these characteristics minimize the gradations between entry-level and top jobs in the occupation, so that we may designate these jobs as early-ceiling occupations (i.e., the highest job to which one will be promoted is reached early in one's career).

Steel employers at the beginning of the twentieth century were quite prepared to draw all the advantage they could from these characteristics, but they were aware of two basic problems. The first was motivational. If employees were subject to early-ceiling occupations they would have little incentive to work hard to improve themselves. How could labor discipline be maintained under these circumstances? Secondly, a political problem was created, insofar as unified opposition by workers now became possible. Taylor, who began his career as a foreman in a steel plant, warned employers of this problem in 1905:

> When employers herd their men together in classes, pay them all of each class the same wages, and offer none of them inducements to work harder or do better than the average, the only remedy for the men comes in combination. (Cited in Stone 1974, pp. 127–28)

Stone documents the process by which the steel employers arrived, in fairly self-conscious fashion, at the solution to develop an elaborately stratified job structure, with concomitant wage rate distinctions, which would operate to fragment worker interests and serve as a motivational force. The job ladders were designed to give workers a sense of upward movement and serve as an incentive for them to work harder. By pitting workers against each other in a competitive fashion opportunities for worker unity were undercut.

These conclusions are reinforced by other researchers as well. Kerr and Siegel (1969, p. 142), in a classic article, observe that the iron and steel industry ranks relatively low on the scale of strike activity, and they attribute this in part to the high degree of job differentiation which marks the industry and "both separates one worker from another and creates a ladder for each worker to climb." These empirical observations and conclusions fit with Thompson's (1967, pp. 108–12) generalization that early-ceiling occupations encourage collective action as the characteristic worker strategy for career building (one tries to protect and enhance the occupation itself as distinct from enhancing the individual's status within it). On the other hand, late-ceiling occupations, which permit individuals to exercise discretion, lend themselves to individual bargaining strategies. Stone (1974, p. 136) summarizes her empirical argument as follows:

> In this way, the steel companies opened up lines of promotion in the early years of the century by creating job ladders. Employers claimed that each rung of the ladder provided the necessary training for the job above. But, the skilled jobs in the steel industry had been virtually eliminated and production jobs were becoming more homogeneous in their content. If . . . one could learn to be a melter in six weeks, then certainly the training required for most jobs was so minimal that no job ladder and only the minimum of job tenure were needed to acquire the necessary skills. At the same time, technological development made it possible to do away with distinctions between skilled and unskilled workers. Instead of following this trend, they introduced divisions to avoid the consequences of a uniform and homogeneous work force. Therefore, the minutely graded job ladders that developed were a solution to the "labor problem" rather than a necessary input for production itself.

The preceding historical analysis should establish that in the different historical periods under consideration there were strong union, worker, and management interests in developing and consolidating the process of job differentiation. Marxist analysis would simply attribute the fragmentation to superior management power and co-opted unions. Yet it was also a strategy reflecting worker interests in an industrialization process under conditions of labor shortage (the craft model) and the desire to institutionalize seniority as the primary criterion for allocating jobs and income in a situation in which employment security was tenuous (the industrial worker model).

We do not have comparable analyses of the automobile industry, which would have been helpful in view of the topics to be covered in subsequent chapters. It is possible, however, to make a few observations on the subject.[5] The auto industry never achieved the degree of standardization in job classifications developed in the steel industry as a consequence of the War Labor Board's activities. At General Motors, for example, current company-wide job classifications for their 400,000 hourly-rated personnel are based essentially on local job classifications. The great variation in these classifications belies the impact of technology, and suggests instead the enormous importance of the political process as unions, workers, and management negotiated solutions to particular problems at the divisional and plant levels. In some divisions, for example, assemblers are categorized into detailed job titles, reflecting the actual task of the individual in question, such as headlining installer; in other divisions, the broad title of general assembler is given to most line workers with some exceptions, such as spray painters, torch solderers and metal finishers. These local plant job titles are slotted into twenty-five to twenty-eight wage-rate levels, which unlike those in the steel industry are not determined contractually at the

5. I am indebted to John Mollica, assistant director of labor relations at the General Motors Corporation, for sharing his expertise on this subject with me.

national level, but are simply the effective categories that arose from custom and piecemeal attempts to standardize.

Company officials are aware that very detailed job titles allow for more mobility between classifications, while broader classifications limit this movement, but they claim to have no conscious strategy of using narrow classifications

to increase mobility or provide the illusion of mobility. Indeed they point out that they are moving toward broader classifications, because they create less administrative problems for both the union and management.

Ford and Chrysler have come further in the direction of standardization of job titles and codes, with a national list that is applied to each plant. Yet closer examination shows that even their job classifications are strongly influenced by local custom and practice. For example, some job titles on the national list appear at only one plant. This does not necessarily mean that the exact job does not exist elsewhere, only that at some point in the union-management negotiation process they needed to identify that job separately at that particular plant. In short, local plant politics influence the job classification system in a very direct fashion.

In the U.S. auto industry work measurement is the basis on which companies set direct labor costs for inclusion in price studies. It rests ultimately on direct observation of the time and procedures necessary to perform a given job. Some job tasks are "neutral" in the sense that they can be assigned to a variety of jobs. In other cases there is a "logical" clustering of job tasks to form a particular job. This logic, however, is based on practice and custom as well as on technological requirements. In the American auto industry when an industrial engineer and production supervisor decide to add a new task to a given job they have relative freedom to do so below the skilled trades. With the skilled trades their flexibility is limited, because the bundle of tasks associated with a given job is fixed by custom and contract. Below the skilled worker level management is continually adding and subtracting tasks to and from existing jobs, as well as creating new ones. A worker may protest, however, that the new task makes an existing job quite different from what it was and therefore requires a new wage rate. Instead of being classified as drilling general, for example, he wants to be classified as drilling special and heavy, which pays a higher rate. Should this occur, it becomes a matter of negotiation between union representatives and management. At an early stage of this procedure the time-study man may be called in to reexamine the operation in detail and work with the foreman and union committeeman. (At General Motors this has been specified in the national agreement with the UAW in paragraph 79, under production standards.)

A comparison with Japan on the fate of Taylorism heightens these contrasts.[6] Taylorism did indeed attract considerable attention among Japanese man-

6. My presentation of the course of scientific management in Japan relies heavily on the pioneering research of Okuda (1968–71). Contrary to popular notions, he has clearly established the quite significant impact of scientific management in Japan. Mr. Okuda, the director of education at Nippon Kokan, was kind enough to grant me personal interviews, in which he made available to me his recent observations based on further research in the area.

agement and government officials. Taylor's *Principles of Scientific Management*, published in 1911, was translated almost simultaneously into Japanese under the title *The Secret of Saving Lost Motion*. Published later in pamphlet form, it is said to have sold 1.5 million copies, with some employers giving free copies to their employees. As in the United States, a great deal of employer and government interest stemmed from the expectation that the introduction of scientific management would result in a reduction in intensity of the growing labor-management confrontation. The Kyōchōkai (Labor Management Cooperation Society) was established in 1919 with a government subsidy and preached a strong brand of familistic paternalism, but it also had a special section on scientific management, the Industrial Efficiency Institute. This institute played an important role in diffusing information about scientific management to industry. The interest in scientific management in prewar Japan can be represented as two waves with a subsidence in between. The first wave of enthusiasm focused primarily on the Navy arsenals, the National Railway, and the textile industry, with innovations in selected footwear and cosmetics companies. Many of these initial efforts were directed toward standardizing work procedures rather than toward undertaking thoroughgoing time-and-motion studies. For example, in the National Railways systematic time-and-motion studies were not introduced until 1929. The remarkable reductions in repair time for rolling stock achieved prior to this date came about chiefly through intensive open discussion and study within each work team, and the initiation of detailed work schedules based on a thorough analysis of each step of the operations, which involved the preparation of a standard process table for each repair item. It is significant that, with the exception of the textile industry, most wage systems for affected employees in all these industries were not geared to individual job achievement. The Taylor principle of high wages for high efficiency was simply ignored. In the case of the textile industry, where time-and-motion studies were applied early and were tied to piecework wages, the scope of application was limited primarily to young unskilled female laborers—a not insignificant proportion of the labor force, as shown in Chapter I. The wage determination of skilled male workers in the industry was based primarily on age and length of service rather than job-determined rates. In parts of the private sector, such as the mass production of cosmetics, tooth powder and footwear, time-and-motion studies, such as they were, were used in helping set piece rates, but the piece rates accounted for only a portion of the total wage. The generally accepted principle seems to have been the greater the skill of the workers, the smaller the proportion of wages accounted for by piecework.

A second wave of enthusiasm for scientific management began in the mid-1920s and lasted to the late 1930s. This second stage of interest was characterized in particular by the strong direction the government gave to efforts designed to introduce scientific management. The national drive for industrial rationalization was part of the government's efforts to overcome the worldwide depression. Specific government agencies, such as the Japan Industrial Association, which was established in 1931, were designed to disseminate scientific management practices. The industrial association took as two of its tasks, for example, the training of competent time-study experts and the activation of "mutual enlightenment" meetings among industry officials. The time-and-motion studies carried out under the efficiency promotion movement at the Railway Ministry factories were the first in Japan applied to actual large-scale operations in factories in a systematic fashion. The immediate objective of this program was to modernize the incentive pay system among railroad employees. Other pioneering efforts based on systematic time-study techniques were successfully introduced by Mitsubishi Electric and Tokyo Shibaura Electric. These scattered efforts were gradually abandoned after 1938. Many companies found the time, effort, and staff resources necessary to keep time-and-motion studies current (jobs have to be constantly retimed as new machines are introduced) to be excessive in view of the more pressing demands made for wartime mobilization. The legal ceiling on wage increases during the war effectively prohibited the wartime industrial rationalization movement from tying wage rates directly to individual work performance. In some cases, such as the textile industry, the piecework rates of female workers were changed so that they accounted for only about half their total earnings, with the rest being a fixed wage (*kotei chingin*).

As we look over Japan's prewar experience with scientific management we find that, in tandem with the rise of interest in scientific management, a growing emphasis on familialistic paternalism developed. Paternalism, especially in its post-World War I form, emphasized the principles of permanent employment and payment and promotion according to the seniority system. As these practices became institutionalized in large firms, the principles of scientific management were adapted so as to complement them. For our purposes the important point is that time-and-motion studies were used primarily to determine "correct" job procedures and played a minor role in wage determination. It should not be thought that scientific management and familialistic paternalism were simply incompatible. Okuda (1968–71) demonstrates how they were both concerned with producing disciplined workers and with motivating workers to look on cost reduction and other management goals as a personal challenge. Moreover paternalism, based as it is on the familial model, includes not only the element of cooperation among family members but also the element of competition among siblings. Thus scientific management, to the extent that it was used to stimulate competition between and within work sections and departments, was not incompatible with the model of paternalism. Japan had every opportunity to incorporate Western style scientific management into its repertoire of behavior. What prevented Japan's absorption of scientific management as it developed in the United States was not that its late-developer status provided more flexibility, but rather the interaction of ideas of scientific management with existing social practices, labor market characteristics, and values.

Japanese management's control of worker training in the absence of an organized labor movement led to an acceptance of management's prerogative to arbitrarily decide on work assignments, job demarcation, and the restructuring of job assignments to meet changing technology. In the steel industry, for example, there was no struggle for control over work methods comparable to that at Homestead. The modernizers of the Japanese steel industry were not faced with strong craft unions. There was consequently no domestic model of job control available, and that meant there was none to be resurrected at a later date as unions developed their strength. Even today the idea that management has a discretionary right to move its work force about without union interference is strongly entrenched (Okamoto 1975). In this context neither management nor labor saw many benefits to be derived from tying wage determination to the performance of specific jobs. The interplay of union interests and demands with management interests and demands that led to sharp job demarcation in the United States had exactly the opposite outcome in Japan! Furthermore, the pressure to rationalize the process of wage determination was simply far less in Japan, with its low wages and abundant labor force, than it was in the United States, characterized as it was by full employment and high wages (comparatively speaking). Whatever the economic realities, it was the belief in America during the early twentieth century that our comparative advantage lay in an industrial strategy based on high wages and low costs. This was based on the principle that as more efficient machinery substituted for labor, only labor of high quality and, presumably, commanding a high wage should be used, so as to increase productivity and maintain low unit costs. It was possible for the Americans to pay higher wages than their European competitors and still undercut their prices.[7] It was within this context that Taylor formulated his system of scientific management (Men-Koy Wong 1973, p. 260). Without such a background, it is hardly any wonder that the appeal of Taylorism in Japan was quickly diluted and adapted to indigenous circumstances.

These historical observations on union influence and management ideas and practices are preliminary at best. Nevertheless they do suggest that we reconsider the Japanese-American comparison. It is significant that recently a movement has emerged in America which recognizes the disadvantages of too precise and narrow job specialization and advocates instead job enrichment and enlargement, a practice that would blur jurisdictional boundaries of jobs (HEW 1973). This movement assumes that high job differentiation and specialization are not necessarily immutable consequences of advanced industrialization. Alternatively, we proposed that job diffuseness already characterizes the "typical" large Japanese firm. It is this situation that is responsible for Prof. Koike Kazuo being able to distinguish Japanese from U.S. workers by the high level and broad diffusion of skill formation patterns among the former. Since the job enlargement movement has spread to Japan as well, it will be useful in subsequent chapters to examine the approaches taken in both countries to provide further evidence for our analysis.

The significance of the line of reasoning adopted in the preceding analysis is not simply that perception of job boundaries may be different in different industrial societies. We readily grant that the level of industrialization and nature of technological constraints are variables determining the degree of occupational

7. This did not, of course, stop American industry officials from engaging in a variety of practices to hold down wages, including the encouragement of immigration and the breaking of unions.

differentiation. Yet the degree of their influence would seem to be mediated by a number of the historical factors we have outlined. Common industrial technologies do indeed dictate common job tasks. The issue, however, is the similarity in the degree and scope of functional differentiation, the extent to which distinct job tasks are performed by different organizational members and the range of their jurisdictions (see Hage and Aiken 1967). In short, common tasks are not universally tied in the same bundles to form the same discrete jobs as a consequence of industrialization. Sociologists seem to have moved too quickly from the fact of common job tasks to the assumption of common bundles of job tasks having similar consequences. More strongly put, the number and types of precise jobs into which one divides many of the operational tasks required in an industrial society may be dictated far less by the nature of technology than is commonly thought. These findings fit with studies of specific occupational groups. The research of Friedson (1977) and Stinchcombe (1959) suggests that certain crafts and professions are able to negotiate with the state to set stable occupational boundaries, and thereby reduce the number of occupational roles (and, we might add, competitors as well). Yet Johnson (1972) has shown that there is a great deal of variation among industrial nations in the ability of the professions and crafts to control and form their own occupational identities, and that this reflects different social and political processes. As reported in Chapter II, for example, Japan is a case in which the professions have not crystallized to the extent they have in the United States. What comes through most clearly in our analysis is that the job structure is an outcome of a process of social interaction. Sometimes the process may seem rather arbitrary, influenced, for example, by the practices of multi-national corporations, industrial engineers, or vendors of equipment. At other times we are dealing with a systematic process in which the outcome is a function of the relative power of management, labor, and government. Nor does it appear to be merely a zero-sum game in which the workers either win or lose, as implied by Marxist analysis. Finally, technology itself often becomes part of the strategy of the parties involved to cope with the ongoing conflict among them.

In addition, we tend to assume a one-to-one relationship between a worker and his job (White 1970). In a cross-section this is true by definition—only one person will be doing one set of job tasks. However, over time, some industrial structures, such as that of Japan, may be organized more around the principles of job rotation and career development than is the case in the United States (Cole 1971; Dore 1973; Koike 1975). That is, if we take a process perspective, the one-to-one relationship seems quite weakly developed in Japan compared to the United States. This difference seems to be based on the greater fluidity and permeability of jurisdictional boundaries among related job tasks. Although the need for specialization and standardization in modern industry is apparent to the Japanese, they also give great weight to the need for flexibility and the job re-design that becomes possible through extensive job rotation. In a similar fashion, Marsh and Mannari (1976, p. 91) are struck by the emphasis on job diversification rather than on narrow specialization, and by the limited number of job titles used to distinguish the job tasks of workers in the shipbuilding firm that they investigated. Osako (1973, p 122) comes to this same conclusion in her examination of the job structure of a major Japanese auto firm. She states that "there is no formal skill level differentiation among assembly line jobs in this plant. All non-supervisory production jobs were classified as 'production.'" There are no specialized relief-man and utility-man designations in the Japanese auto industry, as there are in the United States. Instead, the norm is that crew members will cover for the absence of a workmate. With lower absenteeism and tardiness rates, and fewer days lost to holidays and vacations, this works reasonably well (Tanaka 1977, pp. 37–38). Emphasis on the fluidity and permeability of jurisdictional boundaries in Japan among related job tasks should not be overdone. The nature of the technology, skill requirements, and physical location may all operate to crystallize certain related job tasks into a given job in Japan, no less than they do in other industrial nations. In addition, we have seen that U.S. auto companies, while constrained in their ability to add and subtract tasks to given jobs, have considerable flexibility below the level of the skilled trades. Notwithstanding, the differences outlined in this section suggest that the consequences for one's work career of having a particular job are different in Japan than in the U.S. The conclusions we have reached here are consistent with the recent observations of a number of scholars, who are questioning many of the assumptions of formal organizational theory and empirical research which uses cross-sectional analysis, as typified by many of the articles published in the *Administrative Science Quarterly*. The "new" perspective rejects the logic of economic rationality that automatically links organizational structure with technology and urges further recognition of the importance of power, status, conflict, and on-going organizational adjustments in determining organizational structure (Scott 1975; Bensen 1977). Rueschemeyer (1977, p. 19) concludes that prevailing sociological conceptions of occupational specialization have emphasized impersonal socioeconomic mechanisms which respond to changes in scope of markets, technology and environment at the expense of the part played by organized interests, power, regulation, and planning.

Some Additional Evidence

Our explanation for the low volume of intra-firm job changing focuses on the strength of internal labor markets in Japan and the associated low level of job consciousness. This encourages Japanese employees not to perceive themselves as filling a sequence of discrete jobs. To avoid tautology it is important that we adduce evidence for the strength of internal labor markets independently of asserting a low level of job consciousness as manifested in a low volume of intra-firm job changes.

One question in our survey that bears on this discussion was asked of all respondents whenever they reported a change of job within a firm. The question was: "On the whole, was your next job at [employer] something you tried to get or did it just happen?" In the Detroit sample, 54.4 percent reported that they tried to get the next job, and 45.3 percent stated that it just happened. In the Yokohama sample, however, only 29.4 percent reported that they tried to get the next job, compared to over 70.6 percent who stated that it just happened. Controlling for education seems to have no effect on the Yokohama distributions, but there is a moderate rise in the "tried to get" response with increasing education in the Detroit sample. These data suggest that intra-firm movement in Yokohama is much more of an escalator-type mobility based on seniority considerations; it is consistent with our image of intra-firm mobility as a "natural" process which does not get much attention called to it.[8] This contrasts with the emphasis on the "tried to get" approach as reported for over half the intra-firm job changes in Detroit, which suggests individuals aggressively seeking to control their futures and less willing to be dependent on company discretion. The differences between the two samples' experiences fit with the almost total absence of a posting and bidding system enforced by militant unions for jobs in Japan, in contrast to the prevalence of these systems in the United States in such industries as auto, basic steel and rubber (though union-enforced seniority provisions are still the primary determinant of selection in these industries). These results should not be interpreted to mean that Yokohama employees are more happy or satisfied because they can leave their future to their employers. On the contrary, the meeting of career expectations may lead to dissatisfaction. As Ishida (1971, p. 47) notes, an individual's future is so clearly calculable in terms of income and position by one's age and seniority that one's imagination, dreams and hopes seem futile. That is, dissatisfaction may be generated in the process of stifling individual initiative.

A second way to assess our interpretation is to examine the rankings respondents assign to job characteristics. Specifically, we asked respondents to choose from among six job characteristics the one they regarded as most important for them to have on a job. Table 21 reports the percentage distribution for the two samples. Some notable differences are apparent in the two sets of responses. Promotion is for all purposes irrelevant as a consideration for Yokohama respondents but is ranked as most important by 8.2 percent of the Detroit respondents.[9] It is, of course, ranked low by respondents in both samples, but the particularly low ranking assigned to this characteristic by Yokohama respondents might seem surprising, since we might expect that promotion would be more important in

8. The escalator process starts early in Japan, with a strong emphasis on directing youth to focus their energies on passing university entrance exams. Once accepted into a good university, little work is required during the next four years, relative to the effort required in the lower grades. Indeed a government white paper reports that primary school pupils spend twice as many hours in study outside of the classroom as do college students (Office of the Prime Minister 1974). Attendance at a good university puts one on the Japanese escalator of success and assures one of a secure livelihood in private or public employment, assuming poor economic conditions do not prevail at the time of graduation.

9. We also asked respondents how well these six characteristics described their job. This enabled us to calculate the correlation between the extent to which the respondent felt his job had good chances for promotion and his evaluation of the importance of this particular characteristic. The r^2 for the Yokohama data is 0.067 and for Detroit 0.045. This indicates that knowing the extent that respondents saw their job as one with good chances for promotion does not help us predict very accurately how important promotion is to the individual (or vice versa). Put differently, the respondent's evaluation in the abstract does not seem to be heavily influenced by his own perceived chances of promotion.

TABLE 21
Detroit and Yokohama
Job Characteristic Ranked Most Important

Job Characteristic	Detroit (in %)	Yokohama (in %)
A place where people are friendly and helpful	15.4	23.3
A job with good income	25.2	32.6
A job with good fringe benefits	5.7	1.9
A job that gives you the chance to use abilities	14.4	25.2
A job that has a secure future for you	31.2	16.8
A job with good chances for promotion	8.2	0.2
	100.1%[a]	100.0%[a]
	(N = 584)	(N = 481)

[a] Total differs from 100.0% because of rounding error.
NOTE: Self-employed are excluded from consideration.

labor markets where employees' future orientations are toward internal opportunities. More considered thought, however, suggests that the absence of a concern with promotion in the Yokohama sample fits both with the escalator quality of intra-firm job changing reported earlier as well as the absence of clearly differentiated jobs. Without clearly differentiated jobs, the concept of promotion has sharply diminished meaning (cf., Grinker et al. 1970, p. 12).[10]

We do find instead that a high proportion of the Yokohama responses are accounted for by the categories: good income, a chance to use your abilities, and a place where people are friendly and helpful (in that order). By contrast the first-ranking characteristic in Detroit is a job with a secure future (31.2 percent), a characteristic that ranks fourth (16.8 percent) for Yokohama respondents. This is prima facie evidence for the view that internal labor markets are more important in Yokohama, where job security is taken more for granted than in Detroit.[11]

10. In my earlier research (Cole 1971, p. 107) I interpreted the unwillingness of Japanese workers to admit aspirations for promotion as a sign of the extreme sensitivity of the subject and the great importance attached to promotion where workers are oriented toward internal markets. This interpretation now seems in error. The above, however, is not intended to deny the strong competition for supervisory positions, such as the oft-noted competitive struggle to become section chief in Japanese companies. What I do suggest is that for the vast number of functionally differentiated job tasks the promotion ladder is not obvious, for the job boundaries themselves are vague.

11. In the original questionnaire respondents were not only asked to rate the six characteristics of their jobs in terms of the one they regarded as most important for them to have. We also asked them to select the second and third most important characteristics. This creates the possibility that even if a characteristic is not rated as the most important by respondents its score on the second and third most important characteristics might be quite high. To summarize the information from all three rankings we created an additional score. A value of three was given for each time a characteristic was rated most important, a value of two for a rating of second most important and a value of one for a rating of third most important. The totals were then summed for each characteristic.

The one appreciable difference that we found requiring some modification of our conclusions drawn from Table 21 concerned the category of "a job that has a secure fu-

TABLE 22
Yokohama
Job Characteristic Ranked Most Important by Education (in %)

Job Characteristic	Less than 12 Years	12 Years	More than 12 Years
A place where people are friendly and helpful	24.4	23.5	21.2
A place with a good income	35.2	36.8	24.2
A job with good fringe benefits	1.4	2.2	2.3
A job that gives you the chance to use abilities	18.3	20.6	40.9
A job that has a secure future for you	20.7	16.2	11.3
A job with good chances for promotion	—	0.7	—
	100.0%	100.0%	99.9%[a]
	(N = 213)	(N = 136)	(N = 132)

[a] Total differs from 100.0% because of rounding error.
NOTE: Chi-square = 29.7 with ten degrees of freedom. Significant at 0.01 level.

TABLE 23
Detroit
Job Characteristic Ranked Most Important by Education (in %)

Job Characteristic	Less than 12 Years	12 Years	More than 12 Years
A place where people are friendly and helpful	17.6	18.4	9.8
A place with a good income	27.8	25.0	22.4
A job with good fringe benefits	9.3	4.1	3.3
A job that gives you the chance to use abilities	10.7	10.7	22.4
A job that has a secure future for you	29.8	36.2	27.3
A job with good chances for promotion	4.9	5.6	14.8
	100.1%[a]	100.0%	100.0%
	(N = 205)	(N = 196)	(N = 183)

[a] Total differs from 100.0% because of rounding error.
NOTE: Chi-square = 42.4 with ten degrees of freedom. Significant at 0.01 level.

Of general interest in Table 21 is the greater importance attached to a job with a good income in Yokohama (32.6 percent compared to 25.2 percent in Detroit) despite Western stereotypes of Japanese employees as willing to sacrifice their own economic security for the benefit of the company. In a related question we asked employees to indicate their preference in the hypothetical situation where they had to choose between receiving a higher rank or position with a small increase in pay or keeping the same rank or position and getting a somewhat larger pay increase. Large majorities in both samples chose higher pay. In Detroit 78 percent of the respondents chose higher pay, compared with 22 percent choosing higher rank. In Yokohama, however, the proportion choosing higher pay was even larger (85 percent), with only 15 percent selecting higher rank. This is consistent with the findings presented in Table 21 and raises some question about the alleged importance in Japan of worker desires to achieve promotion in rank, as emphasized by Western observers.

The Western image of Japanese employees being more concerned with work-group relations, however, is sustained in Table 21, with greater emphasis in Yokohama (23.3 percent) on a place where people are friendly and helpful as compared to Detroit (15.4 percent). Without entering into mystical explanations focusing on the primary importance of the group in Japan, we can attribute this difference to the longer length of service at the current employer in Yokohama. All things being equal, we would anticipate that the greater the duration of a social relationship, the greater the emotional investment. Consequently we would expect to find greater value placed on social relations at the workplace in a Japanese context.

We can also compare our two samples on the importance attributed to job characteristics by education. Tables 22 and 23 report these distributions for the two samples. Again, education may serve as a proxy for occupational differences. Notable similarities in the two distributions include the growing importance respondents assign to jobs that permit individuals to use their abilities as educational attainment increases, as well as the decline in the importance attributed to income with increasing education. This is to be expected, insofar as those with higher education tend to expect more from their jobs and to have jobs which pay higher incomes, so that income security is not as pressing a worry for them. Differences between the two samples are as follows: the importance attributed to a job with a secure future declines with increasing education in Yokohama but not in Detroit. This suggests that in Yokohama those with higher education have greater job security. On the other hand, the proportion choosing promotion rises

---

ture." It fell to second place in the Detroit rankings, with 25 percent of the combined scores falling into this category (compared to 32.2 in Table 21), while in Yokohama this category rose in importance, taking 22 percent of the combined scores (compared to 16.8 in Table 21). Thus the differences between the proportion of responses accounted for by this category are considerably narrowed when we look at the combined scores for the three most important characteristics of a job. This characteristic still ranked third in Yokohama, however, compared to second in Detroit. Moreover, even though the combined scores for the three most important characteristics narrow the differences between the two samples, this does not mitigate the fact that "a job with a secure future" was ranked most important by a significantly higher proportion of Detroit respondents than Yokohama respondents.

with increasing education in Detroit, going from 4.9 percent for the less than 12 years' education category to 14.8 percent for the more than 12 years' education group, suggesting both a more open opportunity structure and a more active search for job opportunities by the more educated. No such pattern is apparent in the Yokohama sample, where the proportion ranking promotion as important remains consistently insignificant. The importance attributed to working in a place where people are friendly and helpful declines sharply with increased education in Detroit, but shows only a slight decline in Yokohama. Overall, increasing education has some similar and some different impacts on the rankings of job characteristics in the two samples. One explanation for the observed differences is the more sharply differentiated reward structure in large and small firms in Japan, in combination with a heavier concentration of the more educated members of the labor force in larger firms which provide greater job security and benefits. However, a chi-square test on job preference by firm-size categories is not statistically significant, indicating that firm size alone does not have any uniform effect on the preferred job characteristics. This suggests that the relative lack of concern about job security in Yokohama is not a result of more highly educated respondents being in larger firms, but is a characteristic of those individuals with higher education and the occupations they occupy.

In summary, the lesser emphasis Yokohama respondents place on job security and the relative unimportance of promotion to them fits with the low volume of intra-firm job changing in Yokohama and suggests strong internal labor markets, but built on criteria other than a high level of job consciousness.

A third method to assess our interpretation is a good deal more tenuous but nevertheless an instructive exercise. If job consciousness is so much lower in Japan than in the United States, we might hypothesize that it takes a job change of some considerable magnitude to register as a job change in the minds of our Yokohama respondents, while in Detroit job changes of smaller magnitude would register. One way to examine this hypothesis is to see what proportion of those intra-firm job changes reported by respondents actually registered as occupational changes in the respective job classification schemes employed in the two countries.[12] We would predict that a higher proportion of those reporting intra-firm job changes in Yokohama would cross occupational categories in the job classification schemes as compared to Detroit. For the sake of completeness we may also include in our table a comparison of the proportion of respondents changing firms who also change occupations as measured in the job classification scheme. Table 24 reports the results for both samples.

It may be seen that the distributions are remarkably similar for both samples. Most notable in terms of our hypothesis are the last two categories, which

12. It may be argued that such a comparison is meaningless since we are using different coding schemes, which have different organizing principles. Although it is true that the organizing principles are different (e.g., the Japanese scheme gives more weight to industry), the two schemes do represent the best guesses of experts in both countries as to what the relevant occupational categories are. There are 393 three-digit codes in the Japan occupational classification, of which 226 actually occur in the dataset, and 296 in the U.S. counterpart, of which 204 actually occur in the dataset.

TABLE 24
Occupational Change[a] as a Proportion of All Reported Job Changes[b]
Classified by Intra- and Inter-firm Mobility

Firm Change	Occupational Change	Detroit	Yokohama
yes	yes	42	37
yes	no	16	18
no	yes	18	17
no	no	25	28
		100%	100%

[a] Occupational changes occur only if the three-digit occupational codes of successive jobs are not identical for the 1960 U.S. census code for the Detroit data and the 1970 Japanese standard classification of occupations for the Yokohama data.

[b] Job changes based on reports of respondents between the ages of sixteen and fifty-five. Table is constructed using a total of 1,732 job changes in Detroit and 548 in Yokohama. Jobs lasting less than six months are excluded.

refer to intra-firm job changes. Aggregating the two, we see that intra-firm job changes account for 43 percent of all reported job changes in Detroit and 45 percent in Yokohama. As noted in Chapter II, 25 percent of the intra-firm job changes reported by Detroit respondents did not involve a change in occupational code as measured by U.S. census categories; this compared to 28 percent for Yokohama. Conversely, 18 percent of the intra-firm job changes reported by respondents in Detroit did show a change in occupational code compared to 17 percent for Yokohama. The similarity in the two sample experiences is quite remarkable, though it is not clear that we ought to make too much of this, given that the key measurement instrument involves two different occupational classifications. In any case we find no evidence to support our initial hypothesis. Considering the precarious linkages postulated in the hypothesis as well as the problems of comparability in the measuring instruments, this is not a serious setback for the view that the diffuseness of the job concept in Japan is responsible for the low volume of intra-firm job changes reported.

In concluding this chapter a word is in order about the evaluation of Japanese practices. Western researchers have of late come to emphasize the great advantage of job diffuseness as a factor in Japan's remarkable rate of economic growth during the 1960s (Abegglen 1973). They point to the constraints that excessive concern with job jurisdictions poses for technological innovation, especially as exemplified in the obstructionist activities of U.S. unions. By contrast, the Japanese approach may be seen as a task-oriented, highly flexible and adaptive system that maximizes the interchangeability of job occupants in accordance with needs. Yet from the individual point of view the system reflects great dependency on the judgment of superiors and thereby strips individuals of initiative. This is a subject to which I will return in Chapter VIII.

Does Japan's reliance on internal labor markets contribute to rapid economic growth? One may argue that as an institutionalized practice its effectiveness is highly dependent on the rate of growth of the individual firm. In the sixties the rate of growth was sufficiently high in most industries for positions to be created fast enough to give employees the sense of upward movement in their work careers, as they moved from one job in the firm to another. But with the prospect now for a declining rate of economic growth and an aging labor force, the ability of firms to satisfy employees in this regard will be more limited.

Secondly, an evaluation of the efficiency of employer reliance on internal labor markets to adjust to changing technology must take into consideration the costs of recruitment and training from the external labor market. Western analysts have pointed to the covariation between rapid Japanese economic growth and reliance on internal labor markets and assumed causation. Yet there are alternative explanations that are quite compatible with the same set of observations. Specifically, we might suggest that it has been very expensive for employers to rely on internal labor markets in a period of rapid technological change. The education and training costs associated with having to upgrade established employees (who did not have the requisite skills) relative to recruitment on the external market may have been substantial (Inoue 1975). This would be especially the case of skills with a strong general training component. According to this interpretation, major Japanese firms have been able to bear the large costs of retraining because they enjoyed an oligopolistic position in the product market and because the Japanese economy was expanding. That is, selection of this option was based on having substantial slack in organizational resources. Perhaps the major benefits achieved by reliance on internal labor markets have been conformity to societal expectations and maintenance of worker morale. It is entirely possible that these do not translate into direct economic benefits for the firm. It may be that the major economic benefit from internal labor markets occurs in the context of *nenkō* and permanent employment, which enabled large firms to minimize their wage bill by paying large numbers of young workers below their marginal productivity.

A still different approach is to suggest that rapid economic growth contributed to the development of and reliance on internal labor markets. In high growth situations such as Japan has experienced, a firm which hires from within insures adequate firm-specific knowledge among those in new positions. This reduces problems associated with integrating the new position into the firm (Groves 1975, p. 281). We do not have evidence to substantiate these claims, but we ought not to prejudge the matter and simply assume that reliance on internal labor markets has made a major contribution to Japan's rapid economic growth.

Thirdly, reliance on the internal labor market mechanism in Japan means that the utilization of the full scope of individual talents tends to be limited by opportunities available in the firm one initially selects upon entering the labor market. This results not just in restrictions on the utilization of individual talents but implies costs to society of unused talent. It may be argued that under labor shortage situations the social costs of such misallocations are great.

*Karasu ga u no mane shite mizu
ni oboreru*
(The crow imitating the cormorant
drowns in the water)
Japanese proverb

CHAPTER V

BORROWING: THE CASE OF WORK REDESIGN IN JAPAN

The purposes of this chapter are twofold. First it will focus on the process of borrowing, with an examination of managerial decision making and subsequent adaptations of borrowed practices. The specific vehicle will be the movement for job redesign in the United States and its relation to similar developments in Japan. Secondly the chapter will serve as general background for the detailed examination of practices at Toyota Auto Body to follow in Chapter VI.

Simon Kuznets (1966, pp. 286–358), in his pathbreaking contribution to the study of industrialization, maintains that the increase in the stock of useful knowledge and the application of this knowledge are the essence of modern economic growth. This increase, in turn, rests on some combination of the growing application of science to problems of economic production and changes in individual attitudes and institutional arrangements which allow for the release of these technological innovations. As industrialization spread through the world, technological and social innovations cropped up in various centers of development. These innovations were the outcome of a cumulative testing process by

I am indebted to Professor Fujita Yoshitaka, my former classmate and dear friend, who helped me organize many of the ideas in this chapter and provided key background materials. His long experience as a researcher for the Japan Federation of Employers' Associations proved invaluable to my research. I am also indebted to Carol Yorkievitz, Leonard Lynn, and Terry Williams, who provided detailed critiques of an earlier draft of both this and the subsequent two chapters. William Whyte also made a number of critical suggestions. Finally Dr. D. Landen, Director of the Department of Organizational Research and Development at General Motors, was kind enough to read and comment on an earlier draft. None of the abovementioned individuals is responsible for the conclusions presented herein.

which some forms emerged superior to others; each historical period gave rise to new methods and solutions. The economic growth of a given nation came to depend upon adoption of these innovations. Kuznets (1966, p. 287) concludes by stressing the importance of the "worldwide validity and transmissibility of modern additions to knowledge, the transnational character of this stock of knowledge, and the dependence on it of any single nation in the course of its modern economic growth."

It is the accumulation of unutilized information and technique that lies at the heart of the late-developer hypothesis. The later a nation inaugurates the drive toward modern economic growth, the larger the unutilized store of transnational information available from which to choose, and the greater the opportunity for the nation to choose from among the most up-to-date techniques (see Veblen 1915). This means that the timing of the industrialization process may strongly influence the technological and organizational choices made. Yet, as we observed in Chapter I, even though there is growth in the transnational stock of knowledge, the choices made by any one nation depend not only on the timing of the process, but also on the historical experiences, relative power relationships, and resource base of that nation (see also Kuznets 1966, p. 293; Rosenberg 1976, pp. 184–85). In short there are a variety of constraints on the selection process beyond timing.

In this book we deal primarily with the borrowing and adaptation of social innovations. Although Kuznets speaks of both technological and social knowledge, his reasoning applies most forcefully to the realm of technological choice (physical hardware). It is here that the selection of the most progressive technique will be made most unambiguously in terms of cost-benefit analysis. For example, the blast furnace using a hot blast and a mineral fuel adopted in nineteenth-century America was clearly superior, in terms of reducing costs and increasing productivity, to its predecessor based on charcoal technology. These differences are easily measured and almost immediately obvious. With social knowledge and institutional arrangements the situation is more complex. To be sure certain institutional arrangements are fairly rapidly grasped, under the proper conditions, as essential to economic progress. Consider the spread of the joint-stock company, double-entry bookkeeping, and the diffusion of multidivisional decentralized management structure (see Chandler 1962; Murray 1930). Many other institutional innovations, however, are not easily compared and evaluated vis-à-vis existing arrangements. This is because social innovations often interact with a variety of other processes which obscure their respective contributions to economic growth. An additional consideration is that the output of social innovations is often not as easily quantified as is usually the case with physical hardware.

It is the lack of clarity in these relationships and the abundance of unwarranted inferences that lead to an element of fad in the adoption of social innovations and give free rein to arguments grounded more in ideology and power relationships than in tested generalizations. A rapid rate of diffusion of a particular social innovation may reflect these considerations more than the proven superiority of the innovation in question. Ironically, the claims to superiority of one social arrangement over another often are cloaked in the language of objective social science.

When the United States was unquestionably the most advanced industrial nation in the early postwar period, in addition to being the conqueror and occupying power of Japan, it was not surprising that the Japanese were willing and eager to learn from American management techniques. Generally the Japanese were willing to make the assumption that American management techniques must be the most advanced, independent of any objective confirmation. Now that Japan has emerged with a most remarkable and dynamic record of postwar economic growth and aggressive export development, it is not surprising that Westerners turn to the Japanese and ask what forms of social organization might be learned from them—a subject to be considered in the final chapter. Quite apart from policy considerations, there is an important scholarly issue that demands attention. One of the thrusts of recent Western scholarship emphasizes that the "social capability" to absorb technology makes the trend acceleration of the Japanese economy in the twentieth century particularly distinctive (Ohkawa and Rosovsky 1973). The description and analysis to be presented is intended as a contribution to our understanding of this social capability in the area of organizational technology.

Job Redesign

In the early 1970s there appeared in the United States extensive discussions of the need to humanize work and of the important role to be played by "job enrichment" and "job enlargement." The various programs and proposals designed to humanize work, whatever their labels, seem to have three bases. Job redesign, job enrichment and job rotation all involve an increase in employee participation in workplace decisions, an increase in job variety, and a more effective use of worker potential (HEW Special Task Force 1972, p. 105).[1] Advocates maintain that this approach enables employees to control those aspects of their work that directly affect their lives while allowing a worker "to achieve and maintain a sense of personal worth, to grow, to motivate himself, and to receive recognition and approval for what he does" (HEW Special Task Force 1972, p. 104). Sociologists stress that job redesign allows for the possibility of reducing worker alienation through providing meaning and purpose to individual functions, a sense of belonging and membership in society and specific work communities, a sense of control over one's work, and opportunities for self-actualization (see Blauner 1964, pp. 32–33).

The backdrop for the HEW proposals lay in the alleged growing alienation of American workers, which was purportedly manifested in such behavior as high absenteeism rates and lack of concern or even sabotage of the product they produced. All this was symbolized by the supposed disaffection of young auto workers at the new and highly automated General Motors plant in Lordstown, Ohio. The workers went out on strike and the event captured the imagina-

1. We have chosen to use the term job redesign, but it is not our intent to be limited by the narrow engineering connotations implied in the term.

tions of the journalists who wrote prolifically on the "blue-collar blues," though in fact the issue had caught their fancy well before Lordstown (e.g., Gooding 1970). The mass media were filled with reports of growing absenteeism and increased turnover rates. Government officials, concerned about adverse balance of payments and declining American competitive power in international markets, saw job redesign as one avenue to raising worker productivity. President Nixon gave impetus to the designation of job satisfaction as a matter of top policy interest when he stated in his 1971 Labor Day message:

> In our quest for a better environment, we must always remember that the most important part of the quality of life is the quality of work, and the new need for job satisfaction is the key to the quality of work.

It was in this context that the then secretary of health, education and welfare, Eliot Richardson, approved a broad study of the institution of work and its implications for health, education and welfare. This study culminated in the widely discussed report *Work in America*. The HEW report, like the flood of publications that have since appeared, draws heavily on the experiences of firms located in Western Europe. The Volvo and Saab experiments of assembling cars with small autonomous work groups who rotate job tasks sparked the interests of many. The HEW report lists thirty-four case studies upon which the authors build many of their observations; twenty-four are U.S. corporations, eight are from Western Europe, and two reflect the Yugoslav experience. In the growing American discussion of job redesign, almost no references to Japan exist.[2] Yet there is a literature in Japanese from which one might infer that the Japanese have come much further along this path of job redesign than the Americans, who are taking the first groping steps of the newborn.

Sources of Managerial Motivation

What is the nature of the motivation that propels Japanese companies to engage in job redesign? We can identify five possible explanations. The first would have it that we are dealing with a typical case of Japanese imitation of the West. The Japanese pay extraordinary attention to examining the latest developments in Western theory and practices. They have plucked up a variety of Western innovations, such as zero defect, quality control, the "human relations" approach, works councils, self-management, and management by objective. The source of interest in job redesign in the West lies in purported increases in worker dissatisfaction, alienation, and absenteeism. Yet these problems are hardly noticeable in Japan by Western standards. Consequently one might argue that there is no objective basis for undertaking job redesign practices; rather it must be a case of faddish borrowing. I would note parenthetically that many critics of job redesign in the United States also see the proposed reforms as the "fad of the 1970s."

2. It was not until 1975 that a brief account appeared in the *Monthly Labor Review*, one of the few periodicals that attempt to keep abreast of foreign labor developments (Mire 1975). Takezawa Shin'ichi (1972; 1976) is one of the few Japanese scholars whose work has reached an American public.

Since Japanese managers are already so sensitive to the needs and goals of workers, the argument goes, job-redesign practices are at best unnecessary. For example, American scholars and journalists often associate high voluntary turnover and absenteeism with high levels of worker alienation and dissatisfaction. Yet, as we reported in Chapter III, the rate of voluntary job changing in Japan is quite low by American standards. Absenteeism, generally speaking, is simply not a major problem for large-scale industry, nor does it appear likely to become one in the near future. This is true even in such mass production industries as the auto industry. A 1971 survey of 1,579 establishments in the machinery and metal manufacturing industry (response rate 52.6 percent) reports an average attendance rate of 94.9, with only minor variation by firm size. The method of calculation encompasses all absences, including paid leave days used for vacation, illness, or meeting family obligations. On this basis we may estimate an annual absenteeism rate of 5.1 percent (Ministry of Labor 1974, p. 77).[3]

The image suggested by the previous discussion is that of Japanese management simply responding to the fads of Western management. Yet this hardly does justice to the complexity and sophistication of Japanese management and government officials. Indeed, it is a conclusion based on the most superficial of analyses.

Hazama Hiroshi (1973, pp. 2–14) cites a second possible explanation of management interest in job redesign, one that is not incompatible, at least in part, with the imitation explanation. He likens the process of borrowing to the taking of a stimulant. Each technique has a temporary boosting effect. One after another, fads are enthusiastically adopted and then gradually dropped, having lost their ability to maintain a "high" in the subject. Without this succession of stimulants, Japanese employment practices, such as permanent employment, would lapse into mannerism and become lifeless and stagnant. As Albert Craig (1975, p. 23) notes, the potential for a drift toward formalism is strong as behavior becomes routinized. One way to interpret the various experiments in human relations, including the famous Hawthorne experiment at Western Electric, is that change in itself might stimulate increased productivity, regardless of its content. Consider the following exchange (Ushikubo et al. 1974a) during a public round-table discussion between Mr. Imazato, the personnel manager of Mitsubishi Electric, a firm known for its efforts in job redesign, and Mr. Kawamura, member of the Central Executive Committee of the All Telecommunications Workers Union:

> Imazato: Job enrichment and job enlargement may in theory be nothing more than a sleight of hand, but as long as there is a division of labor, there will be alienation and if this sleight of hand keeps alienation from progressing further, it is the responsibility of managers to try it.

3.
$$\text{Attendance Rate} = \frac{\text{Annual Workdays Actually Attended}}{\text{Total No. Employees} \times \text{No. Days Factory Opens in One Year}} \times 100$$

In the mid-1970s General Motors reported a roughly similar rate, but they exclude absences resulting from paid vacation time and illness lasting more than one full pay period (five days).

Kawamura: I think the opposite. Management has gone from one management or personnel technique to another. If management by results was so effective, why have job enlargement and job enrichment become fashionable? Isn't it because management by results did not solve the basic problems?

The difference in these positions is that Mr. Imazato is willing to concede that the basic problem may be insoluble; Mr. Kawamura is not. To suggest that change per se regardless of content is at the heart of management strategies, however, presents too simple a picture of Japanese management. To be sure the successive use of new techniques, particularly those borrowed from Western social science, conveys the image of progress, of moving forward to improve labor-management relations. The specific techniques are only vehicles in this sense. Yet at the heart of management strategy appears something more akin to a small-scale version of the Maoist permanent revolution, a subject to which we will return in subsequent chapters. It may be noted that some observers of job-redesign programs in the United States conclude that most enriched jobs will after a time become routinized and boring, as employees became accustomed to their new tasks. Consequently job-enrichment programs are "potentially limited and of short-lived effectiveness" (Van Maanen 1977, p. 142).

A third explanation for the motivation of Japanese managers lies in their attempts to be prepared for all contingencies. Throughout Japan there is an on-going evaluation of current and emergent problems and solutions relating to work relationships. This might well be called the age of employee attitude surveys. Newspapers, companies, unions, university scholars, and government agencies all conduct employee surveys. In 1972, 35% of all firms over 100 employees were conducting employee attitude surveys. The Japanese government conducted surveys of employee attitudes as early as 1890. The number of such studies and types of sponsors, however, increased dramatically in the late 1960s (see Take-zawa 1976, p. 32). Some of the results are proprietary in nature, such as the findings of many individual company surveys. However, a large body of public results are disseminated throughout the country by the various media and especially through the massive number of books and journals eagerly bought by the literate public. The results are further digested through the seemingly endless number of seminars, meetings, roundtable discussions, and speeches conducted by scholars, labor and management officials, and government bureaucrats. Some of the dominant themes in recent years include how to deal with growing worker alienation, job dissatisfaction, declining commitment to work, youth revolt, environmental disruption, and problems created by an increasingly leisure-oriented society. A major theme in these surveys is the changing attitudes of youth toward work and, more generally, changing worker consciousness.

This vast number of surveys and dissemination of results in the media hardly fits the image of a friction-free machine that some Westerners have of Japanese industrial relations, but it holds, in fact, one of the many important keys to the problem-solving success of the Japanese. There is no smugness or desire to dismiss incipient problems. Instead one finds intensive planning for all kinds of contingencies. It is not necessarily systematic planning; indeed it is often based on misconceptions of Western practices and ad hoc solutions to particular problems.

Westerners often assume that Japanese planning is the epitome of rationality, with decision makers carefully lining up all available options and carefully consulting all affected parties before making their final decisions. This hardly fits the pattern of borrowing and innovation under discussion. It is a considerably more chaotic process.

The signs of worker discontent and unrest that bubble to the surface remind Japanese managers all too much of the enormous problems to which they believe Western managers are increasingly subjected. In short they fear an increasingly recalcitrant labor force with growing political power. Japanese managers are determined to learn from Western experience and avoid it. For the Western observer this may appear to be a case of overkill. For Japanese managers and government officials it is part of a long historical tradition, in which Japanese elites have struggled to avoid Western labor problems through studying Western experiences and adopting solutions to these problems that fit the Japanese context. A generally accepted explanation of the diffusion of paternalistic practices in Japanese industry in the 1920s attributes this development to management efforts to avoid the rise of labor unions and the labor unrest that characterized Western economies.

Currently this is a period in which the inferiority of the immediate postwar period and consequent willingness to adopt Western and particularly American solutions to problems are long past. It is also a period in which the swing to the opposite side, of defending uniquely Japanese solutions, is on the decline. Instead it is a time of great eclecticism, with the Japanese eagerly studying problems and solutions in foreign countries and selectively applying and adapting these solutions to Japan. Japanese business and union leaders, for example, have flowed in a steady stream to examine job redesign and job-enlargement experiments at Volvo and Saab in Sweden. Ten key officials of Toyota Auto Body, the firm to be investigated in Chapter VI, have been to Sweden.

An examination of the report of a visiting Japanese team which surveyed the Swedish automobile industry in 1974 is quite revealing (Center for the Development of Human Abilities 1975, pp. 94–99). The team of ten was composed of management officials (especially auto industry-related), university professors and members of such organizations as the Japan Productivity Center. The report concluded that the incentives to innovate in job redesign were currently much higher in Scandinavia, in view of the severe recruitment and absenteeism problem. The affluence of Sweden (e.g., high levels of unemployment insurance) was stressed as increasing the alienation of those workers who engaged in repetitive tasks. Yet the team concluded that it was "just a matter of time before the solving of various social welfare and housing problems took place in Japan at which time the demands for humanization of the work environment would increase." The report also stressed the distinctive human relations practices in Japanese industry, and the unique values and societal organization which minimize worker alienation in Japan. For example, workers at the major Japanese firms, in which the threat of worker alienation is highest because of advanced technology, enjoy high prestige relative to workers in small firms, as a result of higher salaries and better working conditions. Nevertheless the team notes that differences by firm scale are diminishing and with them this protection against alienation. In point after point the report cites differences between Japan and Sweden, but then notes that things are changing in Japan and "we must give serious attention to job redesign." The team argues that job redesign may be easier to accomplish in Japan than in Sweden, because Japanese workers and unions do not emphasize job jurisdictions and a job-based wage system. The report concludes that the Japanese do not yet face problems of worker alienation on a scale of the West, but that these problems are coming and that counter-measures must be taken to deal with them. This kind of document is the type that Japanese missions to the West have been writing for one hundred years, though undoubtedly with increasing sophistication. In summary, Japanese managers acknowledge that they have relatively minor problems with worker motivation and commitment compared to many of the Western nations, but they state that they must work hard to maintain and, if possible, improve present levels of motivation.

The preceding discussion might lead one to believe that Japanese management and government officials are unusually prescient. From a decision-making perspective, however, we know that the stimulus for action can be and usually is quite slight compared with the response. This leads us to our fourth possible explanation. There were, in fact, a number of formidable developments in the 1960s and early 1970s that precipitated management action in the area of job redesign. These were sometimes different from the incentives for action in the West, but it would be extremely parochial to assume that an interest in job redesign could only arise from the same stimuli operative in the West.

What were these developments in Japan? First, Japanese employers found themselves faced with an increasingly tight labor market in the late 1960s and early 1970s (Minami 1973). This meant that it became more difficult to recruit those select employees they desired and, furthermore, management came to believe that it was increasingly difficult to retain such recruits. Although the evidence for the latter proposition (that rates of voluntary inter-firm mobility were increasing) is extremely hard to find, despite popular views, the recruitment problem, though selective, was real. Even though turnover is low by United States standards, it occurred in the context of severe labor shortage, especially of new male school graduates. This meant that replacement was both difficult and costly, because of the disappearance of a large pool of workers willing to take the most disagreeable jobs in the manufacturing sector. Such a pool exists in the United States, so that although turnover is high, replacements are also available (see Wool 1973, pp. 38–44).

Rising educational levels lead to an increasing proportion of workers who are reluctant to accept the least demanding jobs. Until roughly 1960 the small number of young people completing high school could be assured of white-collar jobs. With the rapid expansion in the numbers of those completing high school after 1960 a large minority of the annual output of these high school graduates increasingly had to face the choice between blue-collar jobs in manufacturing and jobs in the tertiary sector. As long as the tertiary sector was expanding at a high rate, many preferred jobs in this sector (though not necessarily the low-status jobs) to blue-collar jobs in manufacturing. Moreover the labor shortage was intensified for just those firms in the manufacturing sector that have the most standardized and routinized jobs. Highly automated industries with a preponderance of "gray-collar" technician jobs, such as in oil refineries, reported little difficulty in recruiting the desired personnel in the early 1970s. Industries still characterized by hard physical work under trying working conditions, and those requiring routinized job performance, had a good deal more difficulty. The problem is not simply one of recruitment but also one of retention. The previously mentioned survey of 1,579 establishments in the machinery and metal manufacturing industry reports that of the new employees recruited in spring 1969, 50 percent of both the middle and high school graduate recruits quit within the three-year period ending in spring 1972 (Ministry of Labor 1974, p. 72).

Mature industries, such as steel, reported severe recruiting problems in the early 1970s. A major steel firm set up a fifty-man department in 1973 devoted exclusively to recruiting 1,500 new employees annually, a ratio of one recruiter for every thirty new employees. A steel executive explained:

> High school graduates come in with strong views about what work they want to do —not like the old days when they were just happy to be part of the company and willing to do whatever job was assigned. After the war, employment in a big company meant security and that was what all strived for. But now with economic prosperity to be experienced everywhere, many young people prefer to work in smaller companies where they feel they can develop their individual talents. And those who do go to work for the major companies are much more demanding—and if they don't get what they want, they are more likely to quit than in the past.

That the economic slowdown of the mid-1970s will be of sufficient duration and intensity to put an end to such employee selectivity and return Japan once again to the scarcity mentality of the labor surplus economy is problematic. It will depend on the length and depth of the slowdown. For the period under discussion it is quite clear that labor shortage, affluence, and rising educational levels led employers to be extremely sensitive to the rising costs of recruitment and training. One strategy that emerged to increase company performance in these areas by increasing rates of retention was that of job redesign. Job redesign was perceived as an activity that would be useful in presenting a favorable image for recruiting purposes and, to the extent that it was successful, enable the company to reduce turnover and worker dissatisfaction (see Takezawa 1976, p. 36). A cursory examination of those companies noted for their innovative policies in the area of job redesign indicates that they are concentrated in just those industries suffering the most severe turnover and recruitment problems (e.g., steel, auto). This was also the case in Sweden.

A final factor in the long-range planning of Japanese employers in this regard concerns the rate of growth of the economy. As pointed out in the conclusion of Chapter IV, rapid economic growth and a favorable demographic structure have allowed for extremely rapid promotion in the past of large numbers of workers employed in expanding firms. This was a powerful factor that allowed the upward movement of employees to be viewed as a career and seemed to bear the stamp of progress. With lower rates of economic growth and an aging labor force already occurring for most major Japanese industries, employers will be more sorely put in the future to provide the annual increases in real wages and job upgrading that have prevailed in the past. For this reason employers are more kindly disposed to consider programs of job redesign as a means of replacing the functions of rapid economic growth in maintaining high levels of worker commitment. Whether in fact the investment in job redesign programs is compatible with the constraints imposed by lower economic growth rates is a moot point, one to which I shall return.

The last explanation for Japanese interest in job redesign lies in the seriousness with which Japanese managers take the potential contributions of the social sciences and American social science in particular. One is astonished by the attention the Japanese pay to Western developments. A significant component of the large literature on management and work in the Japanese language consists of translations of the work of Western scholars. One estimate puts it at 9% of some 1,000 books published a year. Peter Drucker's book, *The Age of Discontinuity*, was translated into Japanese and became a bestseller. The research and proposals of American organizational specialists such as Rensis Likert, Chris Argyris, and Douglas McGregor are widely diffused, and the use of their techniques is commonplace in large Japanese firms (see Takezawa 1976, p. 31). This may be seen as part of a larger "management boom," as it was called in Japan, during which American management formulas and techniques were introduced into all spheres of business administration from the late 1950s on; personnel administration was no exception (see Noda 1975, p. 128).

Perhaps the best publicized input into personnel relations, thought to be Western in origin, involved the introduction of a job-based wage system (*shokumukyū*) in the 1960s, as a replacement for the *nenkō* wage system. The job-based wage was actualized through the introduction of job-evaluation systems in most large Japanese firms, and was understood to be the basis for wage determination in the West. A sharp debate developed in Japan over the meaning of the job-based wage, with some seeing it as simply a modification of the *nenkō* wage while others saw it as having more fundamental consequences (Japan Federation of Employers' Associations 1960). Some scholars viewed *shokumukyū* as the equivalent of occupational wage rates in Western countries; other scholars disputed this interpretation (Soeda 1965). In any case, management used the perceived Western origin of job-based wages to legitimate the view that the Japanese adoption and adaptation represented a more modern form of industrial relations. Militant unions resisted this interpretation, insisting that it was a device to enhance management control.

In the area of job redesign the writings of Abraham Maslow (1954) and Frederick Herzberg (1966) have been widely discussed in Japan. Maslow asserts that the needs of human beings are hierarchical and that as each level is fulfilled, the subsequent level demands attention, thereby shifting the motivational focus. The order of needs is: 1) physiological requirements, 2) safety and security, 3) companionship and affection, 4) self-esteem and the esteem of others, and 5) self-actualization. Frederick Herzberg, on the other hand, maintains that the factors that reduce job dissatisfaction are not the same as those that produce job satisfaction. In his "motivation-hygiene theory" extrinsic factors such as increased pay, better supervision, and improved working conditions will reduce job dissatisfaction. Job satisfaction, however, is dependent on the nature of the job task, insofar as it allows individual achievement, recognition, responsibility, and advancement. Takezawa Shin'ichi (1972; 1976), a prominent Japanese scholar working in the area of job redesign, builds on Maslow's model in developing his position. As the Japanese economy develops, he maintains, worker orientations shift from subsistence to material acquisition to social recognition of the individual and, finally, to self-realization. He even provides specific dates for the entrance to these higher level states. The central argument is that achievement of these higher level states of consciousness means that workers will no longer tolerate meaningless and monotonous work, jobs that their elders once eagerly undertook. The advancing level of education among the young, and the increasing expectations that derive therefrom, promote these changes. It should be noted that the evidence for all these assertions is as weak in Japan as it is in the United States.[4] Insofar as managers believe these trends to be operative, however, these beliefs are real in their consequences. One of the consequences is to provide a strong rationale for management to undertake job-redesign programs.

On a different level, most of those companies publically identified as engaging in job redesign, such as Sony's Atsugi plant, Kantō Seiki's Omiya plant, Mitsubishi Electric, Nihon Radiator's Sano plant, TEAC's Toyōka plant, and Toyota Auto Body, began their efforts prior to the highly publicized Western experiments.[5] Their practices do not even necessarily get labelled as job redesign (Nakayama 1972). The time sequence suggests independent or simultaneous discovery. In the case of the widely influential experiments at Sony's Atsugi plant, innovations to humanize work began in the early 1960s with efforts to increase employee responsibility at the level of the work group. During a 1965 trip to the United States, Kobayashi Shigeru, the general manager of the plant, reported his great surprise upon hearing a lecture on the successful application of Frederick Herzberg's ideas to Texas Instruments. He found the description almost directly parallel to his own experience at Sony (Kobayashi 1966, pp. 225–28). These developments also indicate that Japanese management followed through on some of the logical implications of Western theories of worker motivation even before Western companies. Takezawa (1976, p. 31) states in a similar vein:

> The behavioral science model of management, however, is not perceived as an antithesis of the organizational reality, as it might be in the United States. Instead, Japanese managers tend to accept the model as an idealized goal which essentially

4. For the American critique of the empirical basis for the Herzberg dual factor theory see Steers and Porter (1975), especially pp. 104–37.
5. For a description of some case studies of these companies' experiences see Ushikubo et al. (1974; 1974a). For an abbreviated English language account see Takezawa (1976).

lies in the same direction as their own behavioral orientation. Often, they are puzzled to find out that American management in practice fits the scientific management model far better than that of the behavioral sciences.

One way to understand this "puzzle" is that the American engineering and managerial professions became locked into the earlier "solution" for raising worker productivity associated with scientific management, while the Japanese version of scientific management always allowed for more behavioralistic approaches involving attempts to increase worker motivation; e.g., as we saw in Chapter IV, the Japanese reconciled scientific management with famialistic paternalism in the 1920s.

Before proceeding let us summarize the conclusions of this section. We have examined a set of explanations that might produce Japanese managerial interest in job redesign. Superficial examination might lead one to question the need of Japanese management for such innovations. The first explanation simply attributed Japanese managerial motivation to an imitation of Western patterns. This was found by far to be the weakest explanation. It interacts, however, with a second explanation, which emphasizes the need for continual new innovations to stimulate existing institutions. Insofar as content is relatively unimportant, adoption of the latest fads in personnel management is not inconsistent with the stimulation explanation. In a third explanation we pointed out that Japanese management has long prided itself on planning for contingencies and harnessing worker discontent to advance company interests. There is evidence to support the importance of this causal factor as well. A fourth tack was to note that Japanese management has been experiencing a set of problems to which job redesign has appeared to provide a possible solution. Finally it was suggested that Japanese management appears remarkably receptive to the output of Western social sciences, and some possible reasons for this were discussed. At a minimum these Western ideas serve the interests of Japanese management by providing a series of new innovations to continually put forward to workers, cast as they are in the form of Western modernity.

The Job-Redesign Movement in Japan

Japanese management has increasingly moved toward a focus on employee participation in decision making and small-groupism (shōshūdanshugi). These developments began in the early 1960s and accelerated from the mid-1960s (see Yasui 1975, pp. 14–15). The various elements composing these developments incorporated Western management techniques grounded in the social sciences, but also grew quite naturally out of many traditional Japanese social practices. For example, the practice of paying workers for jobs they can do (highly touted in the HEW report as a desired form of job redesign) as in the General Foods plant experiment, has been standard in many large Japanese companies for some time. The broad social movement toward "all-employee management participation" included labor-capital conferences, roundtable discussions with employee groups, individuals or groups independently setting goals and communicating them to superiors, zero-defect programs, quality-control circles, and a variety of other volunteer groups, project teams and task forces.

A particularly interesting characteristic of this development was the leadership provided by high-level management groups.[6] The activities of the Japan Federation of Employers' Associations (Nikkeiren) were especially important. In October 1966 an Abilities First Principles research group was established by Nikkeiren's Labor Management Committee. In the group's report, *Nōryoku Shugi: Sono Riron to Jissen* (*The Ability Principle: From Theory to Practice*), released in 1969, it was pointed out that the period 1960–65 had been a turning point in Japanese labor management, as firms shifted from the reward by age and length-of-service system (*nenkō*) to the ability-first system. The report was the first to give a complete description of the change. Many of the factors contributing to this transformation are those we have already discussed: growing labor shortage, rising educational levels, rising technological levels, shifting value system and so on.

The report defines ability-first management as a matter of discovering the abilities of employees, developing these to the fullest, providing an environment, place, and opportunity for them to be used, and then rewarding them. According to the report all employees should be under the ability-first system, but in fact special attention is paid to white-collar workers, who were viewed as having the greatest potential for introducing change. The ability-first system developed rapidly, in a climate of rapid economic growth, as Japanese firms entered a new stage of large-scale capital prosperity and internationalization after 1966. At that time no one foresaw the recession caused by the successive shocks to the dollar-based world economic system in 1971. As employers sought countermeasures to cope with the increasingly difficult situation caused by these successive shocks, they included in their efforts a reassessment of personnel practices. As a consequence they became increasingly aware of the difficulties encountered in institutionalizing the ability-first principle. Although it was supposed to represent a revolution in enterprise consciousness, in actuality it was no more than a transformation of personnel management. Moreover the system often aroused intense opposition on the part of employees. Older workers, in particular, saw it as a threat to their privileges.

At Nikkeiren's general meeting in 1968 the president of Hitachi Shipbuilding gave a description of his company's experience with all-employee management participation. In the February 1966 issue of *Recruit*, Kawakita Jiro, Kobayashi Shigeru, and Komatsu Sakyo advocated a shift from the administered society to the participation society. Believing he perceived a trend toward all-employee management, the chairman of Nikkeiren, Mr. Sakurada, advocated support for this trend at a top management seminar in August 1970. The theme was that all-employee management participation did not stop at transforming personnel management practices. The slogan "Make Every Man a Manager" (*zen'in keiei*) is attributed to Mr. Sakurada, though apparently it had its origin at Texas Instruments (Jenkins 1973, p. 195). Other slogans include "Make Every Plant Worker an Engineer." Since this period Nikkeiren has engaged in a

6. This section, detailing the role of Nikkeiren, draws heavily on the contribution of Nakayama Saburo (1972). Since the book is published by the Japan Federation of Employers' Associations, it may overstate its role.

wide range of publicizing activities designed to explain and spread this participatory system.

What conclusions may we draw from this description? Notable is the high-level direction given to the spread of these new personnel developments. The mode of diffusion of this software organizational technology parallels the pattern that has been attributed to the Japanese style of industrialization. In the case of physical technology analysts have been impressed by the rapid diffusion of best practice in Japan. This has been facilitated by various industrial cartel arrangements in the past and by the key role of the Ministry of International Trade and Industry in the postwar period.[7] In the kind of organizational software we are discussing, it is clear that the identification of best practice is more difficult and subject to differing interpretations. Yet whether the selection of a given practice, such as all-employee participation, is in fact "best practice" is less important than the evolution of a consensus that identifies it as such. Nikkeiren, along with other management associations, plays a central role in determining "best practice" at any given time and rapidly diffusing this information to the most important of the potential users.[8]

A variety of surveys of managerial personnel practices confirms that these small group participatory practices are widespread. A major survey of 850 manufacturing firms by the Japan Federation of Employers' Associations in 1968 found that 72.5 percent of the firms were practicing some form of personnel policy emphasizing small groupism. This broke down to 26.1 percent for quality-control circles, 23.2 percent for zero defect, 23.2 percent for improvement groups, and 36.8 percent for management by objective.[9] Since some companies

7. For the prewar period, see Saxonhouse's (1974) discussion of the cotton-spinning industry.

8. Nikkeiren, while analogous in function to the National Association of Manufacturers in the United States, is a good deal more specialized in labor and personnel matters, and more prestigious and powerful in this area.

9. The case of the zero-defect movement (ZD) runs parallel to the evolution of the QC-circle movement to be discussed in the following section. The ZD movement had its origins in the Martin Marietta Company at their Orlando, Florida plant in 1961, based on their experience in the aerospace industry. The program focused on adopting practices that would reduce accidents, absences, and wasted time. It may be seen as a specialized type of performance-standards program, designed to set quantitative and qualitative performance levels for employees. General Electric adopted the ZD program in 1963, and the Defense Department advised all contractors to introduce ZD. As of 1965 an estimated 2,500 plants in the United States had ZD programs. The movement does not appear to have experienced notable expansion since that time. It has been criticized in the United States for the implicit coercion involved in "encouraging" workers to sign pledge cards and for leading to resentment among employees who interpreted the program as a criticism of their efforts (French 1974, p. 223).

In 1966 the Japanese Management Association dispatched a team to study ZD in the United States. Nippon Electric became the first to introduce these practices in 1965, but unlike firms in the United States, in which participation was for the most part voluntary, in Japanese firms all employees joined. ZD programs in Japan experienced immediate popularity and have grown rapidly. They have come to operate increasingly like quality-control circles.

register in more than one category, the total of 72.5 percent is probably more conservatively estimated at about 30 percent, though higher if only large companies were included (Japan Federation of Employers' Associations 1971). Since 1968 these activities continue to be diffused, so that experts estimate a figure closer to 50 percent today. The Fourth Personnel Management Census of the Japan Federation of Employers' Associations repeated the 1968 survey in 1974. They report a sharp increase in the proportion of firms practicing quality-control circles to 39.3 percent, and in those firms having improvement groups to 41.3 percent (extensive discussions of both types appear below). Slight increases were recorded for zero-defect groups to 25.8 percent and management by objective to 40.1 percent, with another 12.9 percent of the responses reporting different types of small group activity (Japan Federation of Employers' Associations 1975, p. 4). These various small group practices contain many of the elements of job redesign as American experts have come to define it.

The Development of Quality-Control Circles

We get a sense of the Japanese capacity to borrow and adapt Western organizational technology to their own needs through a brief tracing of the introduction of quality-control (QC) circles.[10] QC circles may represent the most innovative process of borrowing and adaptation in the personnel policies of large Japanese companies in the postwar period. A QC circle is a relatively autonomous unit composed of a small group of workers, usually led by a foreman or senior worker, and organized in each work unit. It is in principle a "spontaneously" formed study group, which concentrates on solving job-related quality problems, broadly conceived as improving methods of production as part of company-wide efforts. At the same time it focuses on the self-development of workers. This includes: development of leadership abilities of foremen and workers, skill development among workers, identification of natural leaders with supervisory potential, improvement of worker morale and motivation, and the stimulation of teamwork within work groups.

Before 1945 Japan had only moderate experience with modern methods of statistical quality control. William Deming (1970), a recognized expert on the subject, follows the classic definition of W. Shewhart (1931). He defines statistical quality control as "the control of quality through the application of statistical principles and techniques in all stages of production directed toward the economic manufacture of a product that is maximally useful and has a market." Dr. Deming was personally a major influence in the diffusion of

Management-by-objective is an American personnel approach which involves the establishment of goals for individual jobs and the periodic evaluation of performance relative to these goals. In some companies this is a highly autocratic program, while in others employees participate in the setting of goals (French 1974, pp. 384–88). Management-by-objective belongs to that class of performance-standards systems developed in particular for managerial and white-collar positions in the mid-1960s. It became quite popular among many large firms. The approach has been widely discussed and applied in Japan, with a strong emphasis on the participative components.

10. The historical treatment of QC circles in Japan and their functions draws heavily on Ishikawa (1968) and the Union of Japanese Scientists and Engineers (1975).

statistical quality-control practices in Japan on the occasion of his immediate postwar lectures there. Indeed the Deming Prize was established in 1950 to commemorate Dr. Deming's contribution to the diffusion of quality-control ideas in Japan; the annual competition by major firms for the award serves further to promote the spread of these ideas. Dr. Deming's visit to Japan was part of an early postwar effort by the American occupation to have American statisticians come to Japan and teach American wartime industrial standards to Japanese engineers and statisticians. These efforts were a major factor contributing to the formal adoption of Japanese Engineering Standards (JES) provided for by legislation in 1949 (see Tsuda 1977). The Korean War had a further impact on the acceptance of these standards. In order to win military procurement orders from the American military between 1954 and 1961, the quality standards defined by the Defense Department had to be met.

In 1954 Dr. J. Juran, a quality control expert, arrived in Japan for a series of lectures. He emphasized a newer orientation to quality control, stating that it must be an integral part of the management function and practiced throughout the firm. In practice, this meant teaching quality control to middle management. From 1955 through 1960 these ideas spread rapidly in major firms, but with an important innovation on the part of the Japanese. In the Japanese reinterpretation each and every person in the organizational hierarchy, from top management to rank-and-file employees, received exposure to statistical quality-control knowledge and techniques, and they jointly participated in study groups, upgrading quality-control practices. This is at the same time both a simple and a most profound twist to the original ideas propagated by the Western experts. Quality control shifted from being the prerogative of the minority of engineers with limited shop experience ("outsiders") to being the responsibility of each employee. Instead of adding additional layers of inspectors and reliability assurance personnel when quality problems arise, as is customary in many U.S. firms, each worker, in concert with his or her workmates, is expected to take responsibility for solving quality problems. This is in contrast to many American firms, where the general rule of thumb is that you do not have workers inspect their own work; implicit here is a basic lack of confidence and trust. It is just one more facet of an extreme division of labor. The implications of the different approaches may be seen in the ratio of inspectors to production workers. For example, at General Motors manufacturing plants we may estimate a ratio of about one inspector for every ten production workers, and in GM assembly plants one for every seven; by contrast Toyota Auto Company estimates the ratio to be one inspector for every twenty-five production workers in manufacturing plants, and one for every thirty in their assembly plants. This is a striking difference with significant cost implications, and both sets of ratios appear to be fairly typical of the industry.

Finally, the large number of inspectors in U.S. firms suggests that there are a large number of rejected items that need to be repaired before they can be further processed. Such is the case. At Ford Motor Company, the rule of thumb has been a 10 percent repair average. That is, 10 percent of their labor is engaged in repairing items that do not meet specifications. This percentage does not appear out of line with the industry average. The Japanese automobile companies, however, are able to rely more on "first time capability" of their employees. Again this cannot help but have significant cost implications.

The major organizational instrument for diffusing quality-control practices in the postwar period was the QC research group, organized in 1948 within the framework of the Union of Japanese Scientists and Engineers (JUSE). JUSE is composed of university professors in engineering and science as well as engineers from leading industrial firms. It is a national non-profit association dedicated to providing services to participating Japanese companies in the area of quality and reliability. This includes a large number of training programs. JUSE also serves as a major liaison between the private sector and the educational world.

In the early 1960s it was the QC research group within JUSE that took the lead in involving foremen directly in solving quality-control problems and in taking foremen outside their own companies to discuss problems with other foremen (Sugimoto 1972, p. 6). The low-priced magazine *Genba to QC (Quality Control for Foremen)*, published by JUSE beginning in 1962, was a major factor in stimulating the growth of QC circles. It puts particular emphasis on introducing case-study experiences of given companies to a broader audience of foremen. The magazine, which changed its name to *FQC* in 1973, increased its subscriptions from 6,000 in 1962 to some 70,000 by the mid-1970s. Training programs were begun using not only conventional textbooks but also radio and even television series.

The number of QC circles has grown explosively, from a total of 1,000 registered with JUSE in 1964 to 87,540 by February 1978. With an average of almost ten members a circle, the membership totalled 840,000. Unregistered QC circles are estimated conservatively to total an additional five times the number of registered circles, with a membership of some four million. With the total number of employees in the Japanese labor force standing at thirty-seven million in 1978, this means that approximately one out of every eight Japanese employees was involved in QC-circle activity. These summary figures are undoubtedly inflated because the data do not strictly discriminate between QC circles and some other forms of small group activity such as zero-defect programs, industrial engineering teams, improvement groups, and so on. Nonetheless we are dealing with a movement that has had a significant impact on managerial practices, especially among blue-collar employees in the larger manufacturing firms.

Characteristics of Quality-Control Circles

We may now turn to the details of quality-control practices in Japanese firms. Quality-control methodology is taught to managers in all functions—sales, accounting, purchasing, research, etc. This diminishes the need for specialist quality-control engineers. A key link in introducing quality control to the rank and file has been the intensive training programs given to foremen (commonly thirty to forty hours); the Japanese foreman has traditionally been less of an agent of management than a representative of the workers, so that the upgrading of the status of the foremen and enhanced training were vital for success. The content of QC training programs for foremen, as summarized by Ishikawa Kaoru, a recognized leader in the movement, includes:

1. Administering training as an integral part of the in-company training program which is given to all employees.
2. Teaching simple statistical methods for analysis and how to go about carrying out shop improvements.
3. Teaching in a way that is tied in closely with a given firm's own technology.
4. Emphasizing practical as opposed to academic training, building in the study of real cases.
5. Teaching participative management techniques.

The QC circle, designed, in turn, to link the training of the foreman with the rank and file, turned out to be the most innovative characteristic of the Japanese approaches to quality control.

QC-circle membership usually ranges from three to twenty people with circles of from five to ten members predominating. Ideally formation and activity of the QC circle are spontaneous, not forced on the employees by management. However, management often plays a behind-the-scenes role (critics would say manipulates), laying the groundwork through educational activities. The central idea is that participants engage in a study process designed to uncover and solve workshop problems. Members get together on a regular basis, learning statistical methods of problem solving and later discussing the selection and solution of actual problems, and setting timetables for completion of each phase of activity. They draw heavily on knowledge and techniques presented in QC textbooks, the examples presented in *FQC*, and their own skill and experience. Meetings are conducted both during regular working hours, with the approval of superiors, and outside regular working hours. Major tools of analysis studied by QC-circle members are the following seven: (1) Pareto diagram (a vertical bar graph ordered according to importance of measurement value), (2) Cause-and-effect diagram (defining effect and reducing it to contributing causes), (3) Histogram, (4) Check sheet, (5) Graph, (6) Scatter diagram, and (7) Control chart. Pareto diagrams, cause-and-effect diagrams, and graphs are the three most commonly used techniques. The appendix to this chapter presents two cases demonstrating the use of the various methods, taken from the journal *FQC* (Masutsugu 1975, pp. 41–45). A further understanding of QC-circle processes may be had from the account of a Toyota Auto Body foreman:

> We think that the first step of analysis is to see whether or not the work is being implemented in accordance with the job standard. Usually, we grasp this phenomenon by plotting the cause-and-effect diagram with the relevant factors contributing to production being reviewed one by one. This is a time-consuming but effective method which involves extensive data gathering by each member of the circle. If the job standard is not strictly followed, it will be fairly easy to discover the cause of defective units. They will arise either from worker error or from inadequate facilities. If worker error is not a problem, tools and materials are checked carefully. If defects still persist in the absence of worker error or material defects, the cause is considered attributable to an inadequate job standard. The task of the QC circle then becomes the development of a new job standard.

The remarkably high level of mathematical training in Japanese public education has been documented through large-scale systematic international comparisons. It means that all Japanese high school graduates have been exposed to a large extent either to the specific statistical techniques taught in the QC circles or to general modes of thinking that parallel them (Husén 1967).[11] In high school, mathematics is a compulsory subject until students graduate, with the standard being more than four hours a week. For non-college bound students math generally accounts for 10.5 percent of the eighty-five credits needed to graduate. Keeping in mind that over 92 percent of the relevant age cohorts now graduate from high school, this prior exposure undoubtedly facilitates the effectiveness of the training workers receive for QC circle participation once they enter the company.

A study of actual types of improvement activities carried on by QC circles reported by Ishikawa indicates that 50 percent of the activities are concerned with quality control narrowly defined, 40 percent with problems relating to productivity increase and cost reduction, and the remaining 10 percent with safety and other matters. Innovations relate primarily to production technique; there appears to be very little input on product innovation. Some additional characteristics of ongoing QC circles should be mentioned. The QC circle is not a response to specific problems. Rather it is a continuous study process operative in the workshop. Thus the QC circle performs "opportunistic surveillance" for the organization. Thompson (1967, p. 151) describes this as monitoring behavior which scans the environment for opportunities, does not wait to be activated by a problem, and does not stop its activities when a problem has been found and solved. He suggests that this is a rare quality in organizations, which when present greatly facilitates organizational self-control and increases adaptive capacity.

A survey of QC-circle meeting times found that 40 percent meet once a

11. An examination of the guidelines for teaching required mathematical courses in high school shows that among the subjects expected to be covered are:
(1) Change and its recognition.
   The teacher should enable the pupils, through concrete examples in real phenomena to express the change in a function's value on a graph and to approach it through the idea of changing ratios. With reference to the above, instruction should be given in the following:
   a) Change in a function's value and differential coefficients. Instruction in functions should be limited to the level of $y = ax^2 + bx + c$, $y = ax^3$
   b) Terms and symbols: Differential coefficients
(2) Recognition of uncertain phenomena.
   The teacher should have the pupils develop a statistical way of observation and thinking through the processing of data by means of surveys, observations, etc., and through probability tests. With reference to the above, instruction should be given in the following:
   a) Probability of simple events
   b) Simple sampling surveys
   c) Terms and symbols: Trials and event
In addition teachers are expected to cover one of the following three subjects: vectors and matrices, concepts of linear programming, and electronic computers and flow charts (Ministry of Education 1976).

month, 40 percent twice a month, and 20 percent three or more times a month. The average meeting time is between sixty and ninety minutes. At each circle meeting all members are given assignments which they are expected to complete by the next meeting, using both company and non-company time. These assignments commonly involve firsthand observation of specific phenomena in the workshop, and collection and analysis of data. At the QC-circle meeting itself, the brainstorming approach operates; each member is encouraged to participate and put forward his ideas. No idea is criticized and members are encouraged to voice all their ideas no matter how trivial or outlandish they might appear. Selection of study themes or improvement goals and the timetable for achieving the goals is generally done through the initiative of members utilizing Pareto analysis of problems. In some companies, however, management clearly "encourages" the selection of certain themes in as subtle a fashion as possible. One survey reports that 50 percent of projects are selected by workers and 50 percent by management.

Similarly procedures for overcoming the problems encountered are decided by the QC-circle membership as a whole, with management providing technical assistance as needed and available. All members are expected to acquire new knowledge, techniques, and practices that will help the achievement of the group goals. This is expected to lead to self-development and realization of worker potential. Each circle is formally independent of other circles but may meet with other circles in the company to jointly work on a common problem. Circles in one company are often encouraged to meet with circles in another company to exchange experiences and develop both incentive and new ideas for application (though not necessarily with competitors in the same industry). These visits are often arranged through the QC Headquarters at JUSE. Public demonstrations and awards serve as major devices for popularizing QC circles within the company. Commonly some provision is made for involvement of top management in these activities. Similar efforts are made outside the company through the numerous QC-circle conventions organized by the QC Headquarters at JUSE. Here companies present their most impressive successes. The number of companies participating in such conventions has expanded rapidly, as has the size of the audience representing still other companies. Again we may say that diffusion of best practice is rapid with respect to the diffusion of the software technology of the QC circle. Furthermore, companies report that a significant incentive for worker participation in QC-circle activity itself lies in their having the opportunity to travel to QC conventions to present the results of particularly successful cases. These conventions and company visits are intended to revitalize existing circles and prevent ritualism (*manerika*).

With respect to incentives, it is important to note that the financial rewards given to workers who make possible significant savings are quite small. Generally speaking symbolic payments under $10 are common, with rewards for even the best suggestions, leading say to a patent, seldom exceeding $600. A 1976 JUSE survey of 360 companies reports 52 percent of QC-circle meetings are held outside working hours (commonly after work), or both within and outside, depending on circumstances. Yet a 1971 survey reports that when they are held outside working hours, 24 percent of the circles are not paid any allowance, and in only 60 percent are workers paid their normal overtime rate.

This kind of behavior, in which immediate financial rewards are downplayed, becomes understandable in the context of the lifetime employment system in large firms, where workers closely identify the achievement of their own goals with the achievement of company goals. For a worker to refuse to have anything to do with the QC circles would be seen as a selfish act. That is, an employee is under strong pressure to "voluntarily" participate in QC circles, lest his or her career in the company be jeopardized. Successful participation in QC-circle activities affects management evaluation of employees for salary increases and promotion. This injects a potentially coercive note, but also allows workers an opportunity to demonstrate their talents. On the negative side even officials of large unions in the private sector, which adopt quite cooperative attitudes toward management's attempts to raise productivity, report that they must keep an eye on management to see that it does not abuse the QC circle by coercing workers to participate. Undoubtedly there is a significant minority of workers who do see the QC circles as coercive and still many more are apathetic. As the practice becomes institutionalized, it is seen more as a policy imposed by management than as spontaneous worker-initiated behavior. "Permanent revolution" is by no means easy to sustain. Perhaps some new form of personnel policy will arise to breathe new life into participatory management, as suggested by Professor Hazama. Toyota Auto found that initial enthusiasm for QC circles waned a few years after their introduction. They were able to reinvigorate them through the channeling of customer complaints through the QC circles. Revitalization is a continual concern.

The major characteristics of the QC circle may be summarized as follows:
1. Foremen training in participative techniques and statistical methods as applied to practical shop problems.
2. Foreman instruction of small groups of workers in their workshop.
3. Emphasis on spontaneous participation of workers and their participation in self-improvement activities.
4. QC circle as autonomous study group operating on a continuous basis.
5. QC circle as a group effort with all members of the circle participating.
6. Extensive staff and managerial assistance to QC circles provided by company.
7. Recognition of circle members through public demonstrations, company awards, and national and regional QC-circle conventions; financial incentives downplayed.

A Comparison of Motivational Strategies

Dr. Juran has carefully studied the QC-circle approach in Japan.[12] In 1967, he argued that it was a management tour de force which prepared the way for the Japanese to assume world leadership in quality control, and thus a much improved competitive position in world markets. Indeed, after the economic reces-

12. The following section draws heavily upon Dr. Juran's treatment of the subject (Juran 1967, pp. 329–36).

sion of the mid-1970s, one began to hear more often in Japan the assertion, "now that our prices are no longer cheaper than those for Western products, the major thing maintaining our competitive position in world markets is our reputation for quality and the world's most reliable delivery schedules." Dr. Juran sees the most remarkable feature of the development of QC circles to be the degree to which the Japanese have succeeded in harnessing the energy, ingenuity, and enthusiasm of employees to solve company problems. He is particularly struck that in the United States the Taylor influence has led to a strong separation of manufacturing planning from execution. The engineers perform the major planning activities and leave the execution of their plans to the production supervisors. In Japan, however, less formal planning is done by the engineers and the top managers. Rather, a good deal of the planning is left to the production supervisors. Production supervisors therefore develop much broader responsibilities than in the United States.

Dr. Juran compares the QC-circle concept to other motivational forms common in advanced industrial societies: the practice of piecework, the suggestion systems common in many American companies, the system of Stakhanovism and its derivatives as applied in the Soviet Union and Eastern Europe, the Scanlon plan of joint committees for improving productivity,[13] and the zero-defect movement. He finds the QC circle to be extremely innovative, in that it breaks with the traditional practices and assumptions implicit in most other motivational schemes. The QC circle has in common with most of the motivational schemes mentioned the principle of voluntary participation (with the exception of piecework systems). But the QC-circle practice of often conducting operations outside of regular working hours, frequently at reduced or nominal payment, has no counterpart among the other practices. It is simply not generally assumed that workers will voluntarily work on company projects after working hours in most industrial nations. Most significant is the fact that the QC circle starts with the assumption that the causes of poor quality performance are not known by either management or workers and that analysis is needed to discover and remedy these causes. Unlike standard motivational schemes, such as suggestions systems, the QC circle involves workers in a genuine study process, in which workers go well beyond simply telling management what they have known all the time. With the exception of the Scanlon plan the basic assumption of the other motivational schemes is that the workers know how to raise productivity and improve quality, but are holding back for no justifiable reason. Operator

13. The Scanlon plan is a combined group incentive, suggestion system and employee-participation program adopted by some small and medium-sized manufacturing firms. Each department in the adopting firm has a production committee composed of the foreman and employee representatives elected by departmental members or appointed by the union. This committee screens improvement proposals suggested by employees and management. If accepted the cost savings are paid to the work group rather than the person suggesting the proposal. Gains from increased productivity are paid as bonuses to all employees in proportional shares. Management receives its share of productivity gains in increased profits. Although advocates of the Scanlon plan argue strongly for its benefits, it has not been widely adopted (see Glueck 1974, pp. 427–28).

indifference or even sabotage are assumed to be the normal problems that management must combat. A corollary of the QC-circle assumption that the causes of poor quality performance are not known is to provide participants with the tools and the training necessary to discover causes and remedy them. Conventional motivational schemes assume that the employee himself will take the initiative in solving problems; or, in the case of formal suggestions systems, that the problems will be analyzed by management personnel. Furthermore the QC-circle approach involves group analysis rather than individual analysis, as is standard for the other motivational programs with the exception of the Scanlon plan. The QC circle emphasizes nonfinancial rewards such as contribution to the company and self-development. It shares this feature with Stakhanovism, though with the latter the emphasis is on building the socialist state rather than the company per se. The zero-defect schemes emphasize pride in workmanship, while piecework and suggestion systems provide money incentives, with the amount being determined by the value of the suggestion. Finally, the QC circle allows for employees to follow up on their proposals by instituting new procedures and insuring their effectiveness. With the exception of zero defect the other schemes make no formal provision for this.

In our subsequent examination of the operation of QC circles at Toyota Auto Body we shall have the opportunity to examine some of these claims. We will consider the QC circles' imperfections as well as the applicability of such programs to other nations. To the extent that the claims for QC circles' operations are validated, it seems clear that they represent a form of job redesign quite in line with the definition we offered at the beginning of this chapter. That is, they involve a fundamental increase in employee participation in workplace decisions, increase job variety, and make more effective use of worker potential. They offer workers the opportunity to achieve, grow, and relate to their job while receiving recognition and approval. In this sense quality control in Japan goes far beyond being a technical procedure. Japanese managers like to emphasize that it is a people-building not people-using strategy. Yet it must be seen also as part of the overall strategy of management getting workers to participate in decision making in ways which contribute to the achievement of company goals as management defines them.

With this introduction complete, we turn our attention to a description, analysis, and evaluation of job-redesign practices at Toyota Auto Body. We will examine these practices in the broad context of the company's employment policies and with special attention to comparisons with job-redesign efforts in the United States and Western Europe.

APPENDIX TO CHAPTER V

Experience I

Measures to Prevent Variance in Splicing Cement Viscosity
Learning the essence of quality-control methods through management and improvement activities.

by Eto Masutsugu
Press Team, Production Section
Tosu Works
Bridgestone Tire

Composition of the Quality-Control Circle: 9 males
Age of Members: Average age 28 years
Formation: September 1970
Theme History: Three cases
Meetings per Month: 1
Length of Meetings: 60 minutes (outside working hours)

This is an example that shows the rich results of using quality-control techniques in the form of control graphs and process ability indices in day-to-day management and in solving problems. There is a brilliant use of quality-control techniques at every stage. Moreover, when large differences between operatives became apparent, instead of jumping to the conclusion that each operative should show more responsibility, the team took the view that human nature is basically good, and looked for the causes of the differences.

1. Introduction
   Our plant specializes in the manufacture of radial tires. Since radial tires are used in high-speed driving, we make special efforts to improve quality at every stage of the production process. As an example of this, I would like to report on how our quality-control circle was able to reduce the variance in splicing cement viscosity as a result of various studies.

2. Outline of the Process (see Figure 1)
   At our workplace we blend rubber, rubber gasoline, and other chemicals to make rubber cement, the binding agent used in tires. Each shift includes four two-member teams in three cycles.

3. Reasons for Selecting the Theme
   1) At present there is considerable variance in splicing cement viscosity. In the future, with the automation of the coating process, it will be necessary to reduce this viscosity variance.
   2) In July, material shortages occurred as a result of inspection rejections due to substandard viscosity; this caused considerable trouble in the subsequent processes.
   The theme was adopted to solve the above problem.

4. Present Situation
   As of May-July 1972, in the transition of viscosity process abilities, the C_p (process ability index) was in the range of 0.67–1.00 with a C-class rating.

5. The Setting of Goals
   1) Raising the viscosity process ability C_p from Class C to Class A.
   2) Reducing variance and eliminating the occurrence of rejects due to variance.
   3) Based on the schedule for the automation of the coating process, the deadline was set at December 1972.

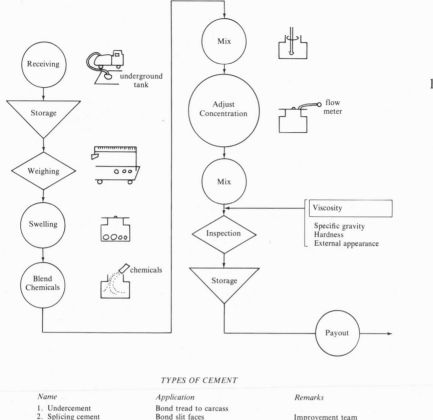

TYPES OF CEMENT

Name	Application	Remarks
1. Undercement	Bond tread to carcass	
2. Splicing cement	Bond slit faces	Improvement team
3. "Burekyua" cement	Exterior coating of raw tire	
4. Inner paint	Interior coating of raw tire	
5. Marking cement	Indicate type of tire	

Composition of the Circle
Number of personnel: 9
Average age: 29
Two individuals apiece from four work teams plus one leader

Figure 1: Outline of the Process (Flow Sheet)

These goals were drawn up into an operating plan by the entire team, and studies were begun based on this plan.

6. A Second Look at the Specific Factors Chart

We decided that the chart of specific factors drawn at a January 1972 brainstorming session should be re-examined first by all the members of the team; then those factors considered having strong effects on the inconsistency of viscosity should be confirmed. Those factors were: concentration adjustment, cutting method, swelling method and sampling method in the *operating method*; differences in performance and work experience in the individual performer; and rubber viscosity in *raw material* (see Figure 2).

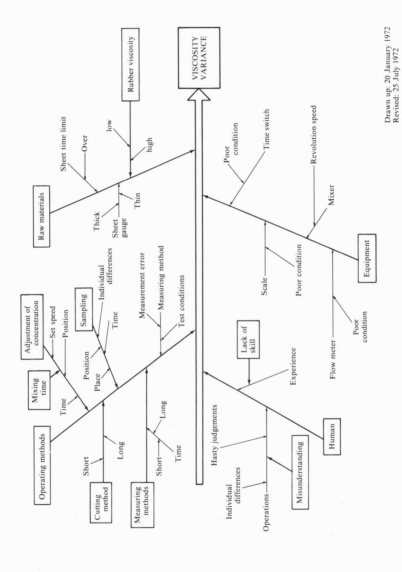

Figure 2: Specific Factors (Cause-and-Effect Diagram)

Drawn up: 20 January 1972
Revised: 25 July 1972

7. Analysis of Factors

   Human Factors

   First of all, as we are all subject to human variation, each operator was checked for the distribution of viscosity. The data showed that the standard deviation (σ) and the average viscosity ($\bar{x}$) both differed considerably in each operator. The problem might be in the method of operation.

   Operating Methods

   As a result of our analysis of operation methods, we found that the σ value (the standard deviation) was large for those with few years of experience and who relied on the operation standards. Conversely, we found that the σ value was small for skilled workers who did not follow the standards particularly faithfully. Consequently, we wondered if the problem lay in the standards themselves (see Figure 3).

8. Countermeasure

   Based on procedures using PDCA, a study of what type of operation method was most rational was made, taking Mr. Nonaka as an example of the small σ value and A-class C_p, and Mr. Tanaka as an example of comparatively good σ value and C_p. Their σ and C_p values were evaluated by factor analysis. (See Figure 3-2). After countermeasures were operationalized, the variance of the viscosity was successfully reduced as shown in Figure 5.

   The other factor was raw materials. In a study of the viscosity of rubber it became clear that the viscosity of the rubber and that of the cement are intercorrelated. Since the viscosity of the rubber was beyond our control, we requested that the viscosity of the rubber be set at 81 (the most reasonable value based on the regression line, see Figure 4), and that the variance of the viscosity be reduced to as small as possible.

9. Results

   Tangible:

   1) Improvement in C_p and G values with an A-class rating was attained in October.
   2) From the time the new measures were adopted in March 1973 until the present, there have been no defects.
   3) Before the measures there were considerable differences between operatives as to distribution and average values.

   After the measures were taken, individual differences can be judged to have disappeared.

   Intangible:

   We remembered the essence of quality control—if the problems are understood, it is easy to take measures to overcome them.

   There was an improvement in terms of quality in the morale of all members of the circle. Also with the advice of our superiors, we came to understand how to examine a control graph, and how to use statistical techniques in inspection. We want to carry out many activities from now on.

1) Distribution of Viscosities by Operative

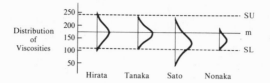

x̄ (mean)	170	178	130	150
σ (standard deviation)	26.6	18.4	31.0	13.2
η	16	16	12	18
C_P (process ability index)	C	B	C	A above
Operative	Hirata	Tanaka	Sato	Nonaka

2) Analysis of Operating Methods

Operative / Item	Standard	Hirata	Tanaka	Sato	Nonaka	Problem
Measuring distribution	Make sure set to 0; check with flow meter; verify with composition card	0	0	0 2 measuring mistakes	0	2 mistakes resulting from misjudgment
Rubber sheet cutting	3 bends of 10 cm	0	X 3 bends of 20 cm	Δ hardening	X judged to be 10 cm	Differing cutting methods
Swelling time	24 hours	X 18-24 hrs.	0	0	0	
Mixing time	3 hours	0	0	0	0	
Adjustment of concentration	15.3 l-g rubber; mix 30 m	0 0	0 X 20 m	0 0	Δ divided into 2; Δ 30m+40m	Those violating standard have lowest σ
Sampling	Collect from surface of liquid right after the adjustment of concentration	X Sampling after further mixing	X Sampling from bottom of vat because worried about tendency of viscosity to fall	0	0	Sampling method
Skill level		1 year	2 years	1 year	2.6 years	Large σ for inexperienced people

Figure 3: Analysis of Factors (Process Ability Index Calculated from a Distribution Curve)

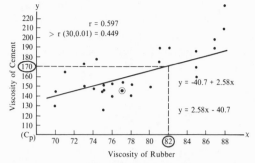

Figure 4: Relationship Between Viscosities of Rubber and Cement (Utilizing same principles as Pareto curve, but plotting best fitting line based on regression analysis.)

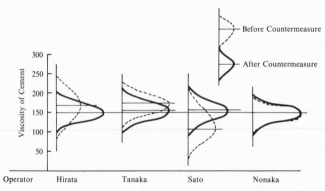

Figure 5: Comparison of Distribution of Viscosity of Cement Before and After Countermeasure for Individual Operative (Distribution Curve)

Experience 2

Rationalization of Inspection Process During Mass Production of New Products
Quality-control activities to develop human abilities.

by Hisahi Takahama
    Team 1, Inspection Section
    Shintoyo Work
    Aishin Seiki

Composition of the Quality-Control Circles: 7 males and 1 female
Age of Members: Average age 24 years
Formation: February 1973
Theme History: 6 cases
Meetings for This Theme: 18
Length of Meeting: 30 minutes (in and out of working time)

This report is a good example of the increasing capability of QC circles. The members studied and applied a technique which is usually employed by staff members for designing parts for production (possibly the first in the world). Application of a relatively simple technique of QC method was not fully successful. An FTA technique (see note) was therefore employed. This is a very good example of "development of infinite human capability," which is the basic concept of QC circle.

1. Introduction

Our plant manufactures several automobile parts. Our department is responsible for receiving, mid-line, and final inspections of bumper shock absorbers (described hereafter as B.S.A.).

This work started recently, and we have not yet had enough experience to discuss the efficiency of the day-by-day operation. We have reexamined our inspection practice while maintaining the quality of the products and have obtained good results.

2. Reasons for Selecting the Theme

To cover increasing production of B.S.A. for Toyota, our superior asked us to transfer one operator from our team to the night shift. However, we expected it would be difficult to maintain the whole operation with fewer operators.

We examined the problem by using the Industrial Engineering method but could not find a satisfactory resolution. So we decided to rationalize the inspection operation.

3. Situation at Beginning

1) Inspection time

After checking the time spent for each inspection, we found that the longest hours were spent on mid-line inspection (see Figure 6). Figure 6 shows the mid-line inspection in detail.

2) Rejection by mid-line inspection

Results of the mid-line inspection showed that 80% of the total rejection in the inspection was due to the lack of parts and improper assembling of parts (see Pareto Diagram, Figure 7).

Investigation of the lack of parts and improper assembling found during the inspection showed that only six kinds of defects can occur. This was proved by an inspection carried out by dismantling defective products.

3) Conclusion

Lack of parts and improper assembling can occur in the five operational steps shown in Figure 6. These defects are not easily found in the final inspection. However, if these can be found in the final inspection, the time needed for the mid-line inspection can be reduced.

4. Description of the Product

The B.S.A. is placed between the bumper and the body of the automobile. Four B.S.A.'s are used for each car, on both the right and the left sides of the front and the rear bumpers.

In collision, or when a shock is given to the bumper, the B.S.A.'s absorb

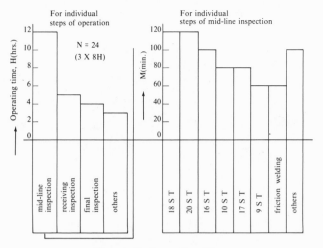

Figure 6: Operating Time

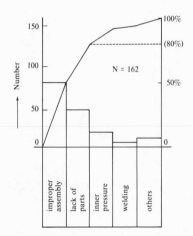

Figure 7: Pareto Figure of Defects in Mid-line Inspection

Improper Assembly
    (1) Improper assembly of parts—C, D
    (2) Two ring stoppers attached—E
    (3) Lower position of bearing—F
Lack of Parts
    (1) Lack of dust seal—A
    (2) Lack of ring stopper—B

the shock and protect the passengers. The B.S.A.'s also support the bumpers (see Figure 8).

5. Analysis of Factors (Part 1)

Investigation was made as to whether or not the six possible defects can be detected in the final inspection. The results are summarized in Table 25. Defects D and F are difficult to detect during the final inspection with the conventional method.

(1) Construction

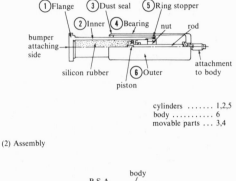

cylinders 1,2,5
body 6
movable parts ... 3,4

152

(2) Assembly

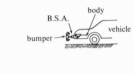

(3)

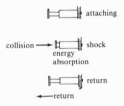

Figure 8: Explanation of Product

When the production of the B.S.A. was planned, staff engineers introduced a new method called FMEA* for inspection. We started studying FMEA in our circle, borrowing reference books from the staff. During this study, we found a method called FTA, and felt that it could be a possible way to solve the problem. We had six meetings on FMEA and FTA, including lectures by staff members. After the second meeting, leadmen and foremen also participated in the meetings.

The methods were new to all of us. All members studied hard.

6. Analysis of Factors (Part 2)
   1) Analysis by FTA
      From the diagram of "failure tree," it was found that the lack of parts and improper assembling can be detected by measuring the total length of the B.S.A. (see Figure 9).

      Example: If there is no ring stopper attached (B), the piston is slightly pushed out due to inner pressure, resulting in a longer length than the defect-free product.

*FMEA and FTA are methods of quality control. FMEA is analysis for minimizing failures and their effects. FTA is analysis by a "failure tree."

TABLE 25
Observation by Dismantling Inspection

Observation after Dismantling		Appearance of Product
Lack of parts	Lack of dust seal (A)	Paint comes out of folded joints
	Lack of ring stopper (B)	The body cylinder and the part connected to the bumper rotate
Improper Assembly	Improper combination of outer cylinder (C)	Larger size (136 → 141 mm)
	Improper combination of inner cylinder (D)	Undetectable by visual inspection in final stage
	Two ring stoppers attached (E)	Smaller effective stroke
	Lower position of the bearing (F)	Undetectable by visual inspection in final stage

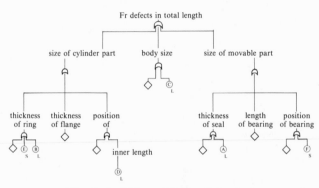

Figure 9: "Tree of Defect" Analysis
Note: L: Larger size
S: Smaller size
◇: Allowable deviation

2) Investigation of distribution of length

The results of investigation of the length of defective products are shown in Figure 10. The defective products in category E and F are shorter than the specified value, and those in category A, B, C, and D are longer.

7. Results of Analysis

The results obtained in the previous section are summarized in Table 26. We concluded that the measurement of the total length combined with other precautions can detect all possible defects in the production.

8. Action

The products which lack part(s) or are improperly assembled will be detected in the final inspection based on Table 26. The results of the inspection will be fed back to the production stages.

9. Confirmation of Effect of Revision

Time needed for inspection has been decreased by the revision as shown in

TABLE 26
Standard for Detecting Defects

Defect	Lack of Parts			Improper Assembly		
	A Dust seal	B Ring stopper	C Outer	D Inner	E Ring stopper	F Bearing
Parts with problems						
Total length	206 to 207	206 to 207	206 to 207	208 to 209	200 to 201	198 to 200
Appearance	Paint comes out of folded joints	The body cylinder and the part connected to the bumper rotate	Body size 141 to 141	Normal	Smaller effective stroke	Normal

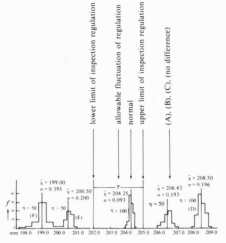

Figure 10: Comparison of Total Size

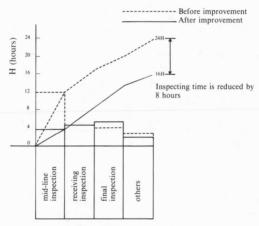

Figure 11: Inspecting Time
Note: After improvement has been done,
    mid-line inspection is:
    9 S T
    friction welding
    others

Figure 11. The release of one member from the inspection team has been accomplished. Detectability of defective products has also increased.

10. Closing Remarks

    Although we had solved several simple problems in the past, this project was our first major subject of QC involving cooperation with staff members. The accomplishment gave us much self-confidence. We believe that this experience was quite meaningful for the future of our QC circle activities.

*Two Chrysler assembly workers put a
13-hour stranglehold on the company's
huge Jefferson Avenue plant Tuesday
idling some 5,000 employees. The two
men scaled over a 10 foot high wire
crib and pushed the control button,
cutting off the electricity. . . . Workers
gave them a wire cable which they used
to secure the crib. More workers gave
them heavy chains and locks to further
secure their positions. When the men
finally came out at 7:11 p.m., they were
given a hero's ride out of the plant.*

Detroit Free Press
25–26 July 1973

CHAPTER VI

WORK REDESIGN IN JAPAN: THE CASE OF TOYOTA AUTO BODY

In this chapter we shall examine the personnel policies of a large Japanese auto assembly firm noted for its program of job humanization.[1] The selection of auto assembly production will permit us to examine the potential of job redesign as

1. In the fall of 1973, during a visit to Japan, I began to inquire about Japanese efforts in the area of job redesign. Through a newspaper article in *Mainichi Shimbun* (1973) I learned of the extensive activities being undertaken by Toyota Auto Body to enhance job humanization. The company even planned to build a new factory designed to reduce job monotony by shortening the assembly line, increasing the work span of employees, and introducing job rotation at fixed intervals. These plans have been held in abeyance as a result of the difficult economic situation facing Japan after 1974.

I visited the company headquarters and main facilities in Kariya and Fujimatsu, at which time Mr. Sato Ken'ichi, the then personnel department chief of Toyota Auto Body, strongly encouraged me to undertake a program of research. Since that time I have had extensive contacts with the company, including both site visits and the exchange of written communications. In addition the company kindly made available to me a variety of extremely useful company records.

I am very much in debt to officials of Toyota Auto Body who freely gave of their time and resources so as to enhance my capacity to understand the various policies and behavior described herein. In particular, Mr. Sato Ken'ichi proved an invaluable and

well as to "test" the validity of the propositions developed in Chapter IV. The choice of auto assembly operations is particularly apt. No other major industry better represents a highly structured and controlled work situation. The auto assembly line, in particular, symbolizes extreme division of labor, minimum spread of occupational requirements, machine pacing, short work cycles, routinization, and sharp delineation of job jurisdictions; it also promotes a high level of worker alienation (Blauner 1964; Chinoy 1955). We generally assume that the technological imperatives of the industry are immutable. An examination of the validity of these conclusions in the context of an analysis of job redesign in a Japanese automobile company will give us a better sense of just how far we might "bend" the technology variable. In particular I will show that it is possible to build career commitments in an industry generally characterized as having poor promotion prospects and low skill requirements, dictated by the technology of building automobiles (see Grinker et al. 1970; Chinoy 1955).

Toyota Auto Body: The Evolution of Job Redesign

Toyota Auto Body is part of the Toyota Motor Company Group. It is one of the 202 companies that belong to the Kyoho Association sponsored by Toyota Motors. The parent company needs little introduction.[2] It is the largest auto producer in Japan, the third largest in the world, and it is rapidly closing in on Ford Motor Company for number two ranking. It has experienced remarkable

---

frank informant. His willingness to discuss both the blemishes and the strengths of company personnel practices was most refreshing. Nevertheless, as a relatively disinterested student of the organization as well as someone with a different cultural perspective, I undoubtedly came to a number of conclusions that are not shared by company officials. Therefore my remarks cannot be interpreted as reflecting company opinion, and they are in no way responsible for the conclusions presented herein.

That company officials were willing to tolerate these differences, and indeed to allow me to name the company, is a reflection of the confidence with which they manage their industrial relations. I want also to thank Professor Koike Kazuo, who introduced me to officials at Toyota Auto Body and whose long experience as a student of internal labor markets greatly enriched my understanding. Leonard Lynn translated a large number of the critical company documents with great care. The chapter also benefitted from the critical comments of Gary Allinson. None of these individuals bears responsibility for the final product.

2. Toyota's public image in Japan does warrant some comment. One of the great men that every Japanese child used to learn about in elementary school in the pre-World War II period, when all textbooks were the same, was Toyota Sakiichi (1867–1930). Born of a poor family and with only four years of formal education, he went on to obtain almost eighty patents in his lifetime (see Taira 1970). He demonstrated successful entrepreneurial abilities as well, with his initiation of the Toyota Spinning and Weaving Company in 1918. His case served to stir a sense of pride among Japanese children in the ability and innovativeness of Japanese entrepreneurs, as well as in their capacity to hold their own in international competition. His was one of the early cases of reverse technological transfer, with the sale in 1929 of the technological know-how he had developed on the Toyota power loom to Platt Brothers of Ohlan, a British textile-machinery manufacturer. With funds acquired from these previous activities and under the technical leadership of his son Kiichiro (one of the first Japanese automobile engineers), automobile manufacturing was already an important part of Toyota Spinning and Weaving Company's activities by 1935. The Toyota Automobile Company was officially established

growth, with production more than quintupling in just the seven-year period from 1961 to 1968—from 200,000 units in 1961 to over one million in 1968. During this same period the number of employees tripled, rising from 12,000 to 35,200.

Toyota Auto Body separated from Toyota Motor Company in 1945 and became an independent company, although closely integrated into Toyota's production system. Of the eleven members of the board of directors, four are from Toyota Motor Company; 40 percent of the company stock is owned by Toyota Motor Company, and sales go almost exclusively to Toyota Motor Company. The company began as a truck body producer but has increasingly moved into passenger car and van production. It has its own production lines for pressing, sheet-metal working, painting, assembling and shipping. The major facilities are located in Kariya and Fujimatsu which are near Toyota City, the headquarters of Toyota Motor Company. Toyota Auto Body currently employs 5,500 people, of whom some 78 percent are blue-collar production workers. They are all male and this chapter thus deals primarily with male blue-collar workers. The proportion of employees who are blue-collar has shown only a slight tendency to decline over the last eight years. The average age of all employees is 30.9, with 7.1 years of service. Both figures have shown steady increases since the burst of company growth that took place in 1967–68 and temporarily depressed the average age and length of service. In 1967, for example, the average age was 26.5 and the average length of service 3.9 years. Employees are recruited from various geographical regions. Currently 25 percent are local recruits, 25 percent are from the island of Kyushu, and the remaining 50 percent are recruited from all over Japan.

The specific set of factors that led Toyota Auto Body's management to engage in widespread innovations in personnel policy arose with the completion of its new large-scale plant at Fujimatsu in 1967. As a consequence 1,200 new high school graduates were hired in 1967 and another 1,300 in 1968. These new employees accounted for almost half the total number of blue-collar workers in the company at that time. Although the company had assigned high school graduates to blue-collar jobs in the past, it had never before deployed to the

---

in 1937. With its major facilities located off the beaten path in Aichi Prefecture, some twenty kilometers east of Nagoya, the company retains a certain conservative image and sense of mission, together with its proven ability to innovate and compete in foreign and domestic markets. Even in the postwar period many older Japanese still take pride in the fact that Toyota alone of the major Japanese auto makers did not find it necessary to tie up with foreign auto makers in order to import technological know-how. Toyota's place in world auto sales is undoubtedly a continuing source of national pride among the older generation.

To keep matters in proper perspective, however, we should note that the major technological improvements in the Japanese automobile industry have been of foreign origin. As of 1967 Toyota and Nissan, the second largest Japanese automaker, together held only 400 patents. By comparison General Motors held 9,811, Ford 1,585, and Chrysler 861. The same disparity can be noted in the ratio of R & D expenditures to total sales. In the late 1960s the ratio stood at 1.94 for Toyota and Nissan, compared to 3.44 for General Motors, 3.0 for Ford and 2.5 for Chrysler. If we examine the ratio of research workers to all employees, the total stands at 5.9 for Toyota and Nissan compared to 6.0 for General Motors, 2.8 for Ford, and 3.8 for Chrysler (Uneo and Muto 1974, pp. 56–57).

workshop such a large number in one short period. The shortage of middle school graduates led them to rely on the high school graduates to meet their manpower needs. Company management feared that the new employees with a high school education would be dissatisfied with being assigned to the simple repetitive tasks associated with the typical mass-production system. In the past students could assume that going on to high school would assure them of a white-collar job. Furthermore, the high ratio of inexperienced workers to total workers sharply lowered the skill level in the entire company. Finally, the growing labor shortage made it difficult for the company to recruit the kinds of workers desired (middle school graduates). Consequently they were constrained to make work satisfying for those they did recruit, to reduce labor turnover. The labor shortage also resulted in a declining proportion of new employees coming directly to the company upon graduating from school. The distribution of employees stabilized in the mid-1970s, with the new school graduates accounting for 65 percent of all employees. The rest with prior work experience came mostly from smaller firms. The presence of large numbers of employees who had been socialized in other firms also concerned management.

For all these reasons, but most of all because of the enormous organizational strain associated with the doubling of the number of blue-collar workers, the company decided to design a new mode of personnel administration. The new system was designed to change working conditions and the reward structure in ways that would better meet worker needs as well as raise productivity. The form that this new personnel administration system would take was influenced by Western social science. In particular management carefully studied McGregor's "Y" theory (McGregor 1960) and Maslow's hierarchical-need theory. The head of the personnel department in the late 1960s, Mr. Nishiyama Daiso, together with Mr. Sabao Tsuyoshi, the general manager of the Fujimatsu Plant, found these ideas applicable to their own situation. Based on a set of inferences drawn from these theories, company officials formulated fundamental principles for human control to be used in the company. They are: (1) trust a man and entrust him with tasks, (2) present the targets so as to stimulate his creative power, (3) train for leadership to enhance the capacity for teamwork, (4) keep in close communication, (5) grasp the personal attitudes of workers, (6) reaffirm company commitment to education and training, and (7) positively perform technical skill training. The system to be described below suggests they have worked hard to operationalize these principles.

Mr. Nishiyama and Mr. Sabao found it necessary to legitimate their new program not only in terms of contemporary social science, but also in terms of the company founder, Toyota Sakiichi. They quote Mr. Toyota's admonition to engage in:

Exploitation:—Be ahead of the time and respect new ideas and times.[3]
Harmony:—Look for amity and cooperation by sincerity and trust.
Gratitude:—Cultivate an enterprising spirit through self-examination and learn the joy of life through labor. (Nishiyama and Sabao 1970)

3. Exploitation is used in the sense of exploiting opportunities.

Further attempts to legitimate the new approach appear in the repeated emphasis in company documents on the need to improve productivity, a need which arose in response to the threat of increased international competition following the opening up of the domestic market in the middle and late 1960s.

Building on the principles of control outlined above, as well as on existing practices and values in Japan, the company laid the fundamental blueprint for the current personnel administration in 1965 and 1966. The first direct steps, taken in 1967, involved increasing the job scope and responsibility of subleaders (assistant foremen) by delegating to the smallest unit (*kumi*), composed of an average of twenty members, the responsibility for plant safety. This function had been previously lodged in a separate group. The next move occurred in 1968 and involved shifting the responsibility for quality control on selected assembly lines down to the individual worker. This entailed giving each worker a button to stop the line when substandard quality products were produced. The new procedure provided for greater accountability by pinpointing the exact location where deficient products were being produced and thus minimizing the chance that they would influence subsequent stages of the assembly line. The company was sufficiently satisfied with the results in terms of contribution to productivity and quality control, as well as contribution to increasing workers' control over their work, to adopt this system for the whole company in 1972. One of the repeated findings of social scientists in the United States is that control over the pace of work is exceedingly important to workers (Blauner 1964, pp. 21, 98–100, 170–71). The button system was designed to encourage workers to believe they drove the conveyor belt, as opposed to being driven by it.

This innovation was not totally successful, however, because the company found that on long lines (of say 350 meters) workers tended to be reluctant to stop the line. The workers feared they would disrupt the system of production. As a result the company, where possible, has now designed the long lines in sections, with a "buffer" of three to five cars after every ten or so stations (one cycle). Thus when a worker presses his button he can stop only a short section of the line, thereby minimizing the disruption of production. We need only contrast this situation to the practices common in U.S. auto firms, in which the right to stop the line is limited to only a very select number of individuals (e.g., plant managers). Moreover, a line stoppage is of such major consequence in many American firms that it is undertaken with great reluctance and must later be justified to still higher-ranking officials.

QC Circles

The company became increasingly involved with quality control as part of the policy of the "Toyota family." The first QC circles in Toyota Auto Body were organized in 1964, at the same time as they were introduced into the parent company. With the rapid growth of the automobile industry at this time, and of Toyota Auto Body in particular, the introduction of QC circles may be seen as an attempt to minimize problems of maintaining quality standards, given the large number of new, untrained employees. Secondly, the QC circles may be seen as the organizational response to maximize control under conditions of explosive growth. The small group activities of QC circles are admirably suited for these purposes.

It became company policy to compete for the Deming Prize, and they achieved the distinction of winning the award in 1970. They were also awarded the gold medal from the QC Circle Headquarters in 1972. By 1976 the company had an impressive total of 763 QC circles operating, up from 285 in 1971. These circles include some 4,000 employees, with almost all blue-collar workers participating. Workers can be members of more than one circle. Circles tend to be organized around a particular job in the workshop, such as the "ceiling-glue group," or the "meter-fitting group." In principle there is voluntary participation. The QC circles are concerned not only with the reduction of goods deficient in quality, but also with almost every other kind of problem, including improvement of productivity, the speed and way of stopping the conveyor belt, job procedures, job training, and human relations problems. The company slogan is "Quality designed by the engineering personnel shall be realized by the production personnel."

When the QC circles first began in the company there were twenty members in each circle, with the foreman serving as leader. It was found that it was difficult to fully involve all workers with such large groups. Gradually the circles were made smaller and in 1968–69 the foremen were replaced by ordinary workers (who have achieved a specified job-grade ranking—see below). The company discovered that when the foremen were leaders the workers saw the QC circles as an extension of work relations and held back their spontaneous contribution. Since the shift to smaller circles with workers as leaders company officials believe the circles are making more substantial contributions to increased productivity. The shift toward having ordinary workers as leaders took place in many companies with developed QC-circle programs (in some companies leaders are elected). An attempt is made to rotate circle leadership to satisfy requests for the opportunity to lead a group. The emergence of leadership, however, is not entirely spontaneous. If a worker shows talent in participating and expressing himself, he is approached by a foreman and encouraged to assume the leadership of a QC circle. As the company sees it the number of groups depends on the combination of human needs and physical layout. Whether it be due to worker belief that this is a good outlet for their talents and a chance to demonstrate their worth, or pressure to fulfill company expectations, or some combination thereof, leadership of the circles has not proved a problem. Workers are paid about half the average hourly wage (were workers paid an hourly wage) for QC-circle activity after regular hours. The frequency of QC-circle meetings has increased from an average of one a month in 1968 to six a month in 1975.

The discussion thus far might suggest quite autonomous groups, each meeting and setting its own goals and then implementing them. In fact, however, the company carefully coordinates and regulates QC-circle activities. The general QC-circle reports directly to the factory manager and is responsible for companywide planning for all QC-circle activities. This includes arrangements for extracompany participation in QC-circle conventions to present successful cases. The number of these presentations is now running at some forty a year, up from twenty-two cases a year in the early 1970s. Secondly, at each departmental level office there is staffing for planning and promoting the QC-circle program in that department. This includes providing the training necessary for workers to partici- pate in the program. At the section level, staff are responsible for implementing the QC-circle training program and running intra-section meetings for QC-circle leaders. Monthly meetings are held for QC-circle leaders to exchange informa- tion, select performance themes and mutually assist in promoting each other's activities. This minimizes obstacles to solving problems when they involve other work stations and sections. A leader council has been established for every sec- tion; these councils consist of the workgroup leader, the foreman, and the leader of each QC circle. The council is designed to provide guidance for the activities of QC circles through identification of problems occurring in the implementation of QC-circle activities and for the coordination of QC-circle activities with com- pany policies. Leadership training includes how to conduct a meeting, get work- ers to express their opinions and induce participation among workers. Within each department there is a special QC reference room which employees are encouraged to use freely. In each section case competitions are held among QC circles and the best cases are selected for presentation in the monthly company- wide case competition. Unusually successful cases are then presented for the nationwide QC-circle competition. There is considerable competition among circles to participate in these events.

One of the problems that we might anticipate in the operation of QC circles is the absence of necessary technical expertise to solve workshop problems. In part this problem is met by the Industrial Engineering Project Team which is available to every workshop. It has some forty-five members, half of whom are engineers and half of whom are operatives from the shopfloor who have received more than sixty hours of company education. The combination of engineers and operatives in the same team is expected to produce different approaches to problem-solving than if the team were made up entirely of engineers. The project team works closely with QC circles, providing on-the-spot specialized analysis of problem areas. In this fashion technical expertise is made available to specific workshops when necessary.

Perhaps the point at which the QC circles depart most clearly from the voluntarist principle lies in the practice of prescribing a fixed number of sug- gestions to be allotted to each section, based roughly on the previous year's totals (with perhaps some increase over the prior year). A good many of these suggestions for improvements will arise from QC-circle activity. The personnel department officials estimate that group suggestions account for 75 percent of all suggestions (not all of which are from QC circles), with the remaining 25 percent being put forward by individuals. For the best suggestions the company pays a maximum of ¥50,000 ($227) to individuals and ¥60,000 ($272) to groups. The president of the company makes a public presentation annually to those individ- uals or groups who have been awarded the maximum award. Those receiving the maximum award also receive a two-days and one-night study-tour trip. The company even pays ¥500 ($2.27) for individual suggestions and ¥600 ($2.73) for group suggestions that are not accepted. The per capita number of suggestions has risen in the company from 0.29 in 1967 to 3.44 in 1973.[4] One might suspect that the allotment of a suggestion quota would be perceived to be coercive by workers and thus produce quantity rather than quality. Fortunately the company collects data which allow us to develop an indirect measure that sheds some light on this matter. The estimated yearly per capita cost of implementing employee suggestions has risen from $1,245 in 1967 to $3,382 in 1973.[5] If we deflate the 1973 value to allow for the moderate rise in input prices in the transport equipment industry (on an index of 100 for 1967, input prices rose to 120 in 1973), the revised per capita cost for 1973 is $2,817 (Nihon Ginkō 1974, p. 272). This is a 126 percent increase in the estimated yearly per capita cost of implementing employee suggestions over 1967. However, the number of suggestions per capita reported above rose 1,086 percent between 1967 and 1973. This discrepancy in increase rates suggests that although each individual may be making more valuable suggestions, there is a lot more "noise or static" in the system occasioned by a massive increase of relatively useless suggestions. This suggests that many are pro forma proposals which workers initiate to keep management "off their backs." On the other hand, since the per capita value of employee suggestions (as measured by the rough proxy of cost of implementing suggestions) has increased, the company still finds it to be a productive strategy to set suggestion quotas for each section.

Evaluation of the QC-Circle Program

This leads us to the need for systematic evaluation of company involvement with QC circles. There is no doubt that company officials regard the circles as a major success. They can point to an impressive number of new work arrangements and machinery that originated from QC circle suggestions. In addition there are the increasing number of successful cases presented in nationwide competition and the growing number of QC circles and increasing frequency of their meetings. The rising value of per capita suggestions does not fail to impress them. Company officials also cite the growth in productivity that has occurred in recent years despite a reduction of employees from 6,200 in 1969 to 5,500 in 1972. They point to the trend in the decline of defects per car completed, from 0.95 in 1968 to 0.60 in 1973, the reduction in the man-hours per car processed

4. For purposes of general comparison, we may report that GM runs a fairly vigorous suggestion program that in 1969 elicited 1,037,733 proposals, of which 279,230 were adopted. Seventeen million dollars, an average of sixty-two dollars a suggestion, was paid out to employees for their suggestions. Assuming that most suggestions derived from hourly employees, this works out to 2.4 suggestions proposed per employee. The comparable figures for 1976 show a considerable drop in suggestions proposed, those adopted, and suggestions proposed per employee. The totals are 345,059 suggestions proposed, 95,487 suggestions adopted, and approximately 0.80 suggestions proposed per employee. The average award increased to $133, but the total amount paid out dropped to $12.6 million. Needless to say, comparing General Motors with a company roughly 1 percent its size has but limited utility.

5. The cost of implementation is at best only a rough proxy for the value of the innovation.

from ten in 1968 to eight in 1973, and the decrease in the gross frequency of accidents per million work-hours from fifty-three in 1968 to almost zero in 1972. Employee turnover has also declined, with the rate of employee retention rising from 81.8 in 1968 to 91.5 in 1973. Finally they cite the company morale surveys investigating work satisfaction. These surveys show that the proportion of workers who believe their work is worth doing rose from 29 percent in 1967 (40 percent responded "don't know" and 31 percent reported they were dissatisfied) to 45 percent in 1973 (35 percent "don't know" and 19 percent dissatisfied).[6] Response to this same question on a national survey showed only 32 percent saying their work was worth doing, with 20 percent reporting "don't know" and 46 percent denying that the work was worth doing. The higher level of job satisfaction suggested by the Toyota Auto Body employee responses is particularly impressive, given the apparently alienating qualities of work in the auto industry even in Japan. In a replication of Blauner's (1964) study of alienation by industry, Fujita and Ishida (1970, p. 199) find the same tendency for workers in the Japanese automobile industry to score extremely high, relative to other industries, in the proportion of workers who feel their jobs make them work too fast, who regard their jobs as dull and tiresome, and who feel their jobs are too simple.

Particularly important for our interest in job redesign is the belief of company officials that through participation in QC circles workers have developed higher and broader skills in the context of improved teamwork.

In 1970, the year the company won the Deming Prize, they cited the following results of their QC-circle activity: better quality, assured delivery dates, and higher profits as the main tangible results; intangible results included enhanced quality consciousness, participation by everyone in quality control, realization of an improved management structure, and development of "thinking workers" (JUSE 1970, p. 53).

A final indirect measure of the success of management efforts relates to the strength of opposition to existing union leadership in the company. Since the union, as we shall see, has at least passively cooperated with the company efforts, opposition to the union leadership may be seen as one measure of worker acceptance of both the QC-circle concept and a variety of other innovations to be discussed below. The evidence here is clear-cut. The strength of opposition candidates vis-à-vis the incumbent union leadership is almost nil. This suggests the possibility that management policies have had considerable impact in mitigating worker opposition and committing workers to company policies.

At first glance one cannot help but be impressed by the various indicators of QC-circle effectiveness. The interpretation and attribution of causal links is, however, a good deal more complicated than may initially appear. In the first place QC-circle activity accounts for only a small proportion of any employee's working hours. Consequently it is difficult to separate out the impact of QC-circle activities from still other activities that might have influenced morale,

6. The Japanese question was: Anata no shigoto wa yarigai ga arimasu ka? (Would you say your work was worth doing?).

number of man-hours per car processed, turnover, union militancy and so on. It is possible that some significant proportion of the successes mentioned above derived not from QC circles per se but from the variety of innovations that we subsume under the rubric job redesign and which will be discussed in detail later in the chapter. It is also plausible that a good number of the recorded changes flowed directly from technological progress. The new Fujimatsu plant allowed for increased economies of scale and the new equipment permitted a more intensive operation of facilities.

Secondly, as noted earlier, a major influx of employees took place in 1967–68. It is only to be expected that initially work relations would be quite disorganized, leading to low morale, high turnover, high accident rates, lowered productivity and the like. As these employees acquired increased experience and skills (i.e., assuming normal learning curves) and the work force stabilized, we would expect that morale would improve, productivity rise, accidents fall and so on. Moreover, we are dealing here with the survivors of the major employee influx in the late 1960s; those most dissatisfied, and perhaps incompetent, quit or were forced to leave. These employees would tend to be the youngest and least skilled. We know from the company's morale survey that a higher proportion of the youngest employees tend to find their work not worth doing compared to older workers. Notwithstanding the permanent employment system, quit rates at auto firms are quite high by Japanese standards. Based on current experience, Toyota Auto Body anticipates that after one year of employment, 20 percent of new recruits have quit or proven unacceptable for some reason. After an additional year another 15 percent have quit, and after five years they have lost about 50 percent of the original cohort.[7] These figures are for new school graduates and those employees with prior employment. The point is that the large influx of new employees in the late 1960s was followed by a shedding of the more dissatisfied co-workers and the acquisition of more experience by those remaining. This was bound to lead to more satisfied and productive employees. To what extent the data cited above are explained by these phenomena is impossible to evaluate, though I would venture to suggest that these phenomena explain a significant proportion of the recorded changes.

Company officials themselves also recognize that the lack of strong support for opposition union candidates ought not to be overinterpreted. Although they would like to attribute it to the successes of their personnel policies, they recognize that, as a relatively small company, Toyota Auto Body can provide personalized management in a minimally bureaucratic environment. The rural location of Toyota Auto Body further helps it escape from many of the urban ills and frustrations that affect other factory employees. Worker opportunity to purchase their own relatively inexpensive housing near Toyota Auto Body facilities would be one important example.

The extent to which workers accept QC-circle activity is also problematic.

7. By comparison it is estimated that in the late 1960s American automakers with facilities in the major northern production centers were losing 60 percent of their entry-level unskilled employees within their first year of employment (Grinker et al. 1970, p. 53). General Motors loses about 50 percent in the first six months.

We have already seen that the number of suggestions grew much more rapidly than the value of these suggestions as measured in cost of implementation. In the company morale survey in 1975, 30 percent of the workers reported QC circles to be a burden (*omoni ni kanjiru*); the proportion registering dissatisfaction was up from 20 percent in 1972. Union surveys of employees find that quality-control circles increase the physical and mental burdens experienced by workers (Marsh and Mannari 1976, p. 302). At Toyota Auto Body, such feelings arise from competition between groups and pressure to submit suggestions. Moreover, circle leaders report member apathy to be a constant problem.

On the basis of these observations we might conclude that QC-circle activity has had negligible influence. Perhaps we are dealing here with a simple "halo effect," in which increased productivity and worker morale accidentally coincided with the introduction of QC-circle activity. This is quite consistent with Charles Perrow's (1972, p. 109) conclusion, after an exhaustive survey of organizational research findings, that the impact on productivity of moderately good or bad relations with subordinates appears to be small and difficult to separate from other considerations (though he does not specifically examine the worker-participation literature). The interpretation is also consistent with Hazama's "stimulant" hypothesis.

A further refinement of this view involves recognizing that Toyota Auto Body management is sophisticated enough to understand these relationships (i.e., the at best moderate contribution of QC activity to productivity), but for purposes of worker motivation, they prefer to emphasize the impact of QC-circle activity and other personnel policies. Company success and its attribution, in part, to QC-circle activity becomes part of management ideology designed to legitimate management power. Even if QC circles do not directly raise productivity or do only what industrial engineers can do at least as well, they may increase worker satisfaction and commitment to company goals by allowing for participation. In an indirect fashion this raises productivity by minimizing the likelihood of worker sabotage, worker turnover, and disruptive strikes. Furthermore, even if QC circles are not the cheapest way to solve problems, the workers tend to implement their own changes with enthusiasm. In contrast they will often resent those solutions arrived at and handed down to them by the engineers. This is particularly important in industries such as the auto industry, in which constant model changes and the like require new work layouts at regular intervals.

Let there be no doubt that company officials, based on their own first-hand observation, are sincerely convinced that QC-circle activity is a major factor in company success, and that the system will continue to generate output consistent with management goals. Certainly they have made a major investment of staff and worker time and other resources in QC-circle activity, and they are able to cite many concrete examples of its success. At the shop level QC circles are expected to present evaluations of their performance; for circles claiming to be successful, this typically includes trend charts detailing the decline in the number of defects (or accidents, etc.) observed. The number of reports claiming success rose from 1,222 in 1970 to 1,785 in 1976. Above all, QC circles mean education as it relates to work. The company, as we shall see, has invested heavily in this area. Management also recognizes the major contribution of technology and the new Fujimatsu plant to increased productivity. However, they argue that a momentum was built up as employees worked hard to win the Deming Prize in 1970. This momentum was maintained after 1970 and carefully guided by management (participation in QC circles was not voluntary at this time). QC-circle suggestions were actively solicited and implemented. Management attributes much of the sharp productivity increase in 1971–72 to these activities. They also report a ratio of inspectors to workers of less than 1:20; this is roughly comparable to the figures for the parent company reported in Chapter V. Moreover management reports that the ratio of inspectors to workers was considerably higher prior to the introduction of QC circles, though they do not have data to support this conclusion. It is impossible to judge whether comparable success would have occurred under some other system of personnel administration. Management at Toyota Auto Body does not believe this to be the case, but it may be that the variety of other small-group activities cultivated by Japanese management in this period would have yielded similar results (and did at other companies). According to this perspective QC circles provided a mechanism for the creation of a new mode of worker participation. It was a stimulant in Hazama's sense, but what was important was not the particular statistical techniques of problem solving (e.g., Pareto analysis) but that QC circles served as a vehicle for facilitating worker participation.

Finally, one additional tack to take in evaluating QC circles is to ask whether workers really learn to use the various statistical techniques associated with QC-circle activity. Management reports that all new employees learn the tools of QC as soon as they enter the company. They participate in a one-day course, and there is a more intensive six-day course for those employees who enter the company school. All employees learn the seven techniques reported in Chapter V. They learn by using them, so that QC-circle activity is not just a matter of the QC leader, who knows how to do it, getting employees to gather data. Yet management reports that although all employees learn to use these techniques there is variation in their ability to apply them. The best workers learn to classify variables to solve production problems. Others simply learn to classify variables. In short, while all learn how to identify problems, many don't learn to deal with the causes of the problem. Although the evidence here is mixed, it does appear that QC-circle activity has sufficiently penetrated the work force so that we cannot simply view it as a technique whereby qualified personnel use ordinary blue-collar workers to gather data for them in simple-minded fashion.

Personnel Administration Policy

The company's experience with QC circles led them to study very carefully the whole organizational system and the detailed characteristics of individual work. Through the QC circles they came to see the potential in small-group activity for involving workers in company goals. Many of the features of their current administrative policy grew out of the QC-circle experience, and the preceding evaluation applies to many of these activities as well.

We may now turn directly to the company's personnel administration policies.[8] For purposes of exposition we may divide these policies into eight categories: individual guidance, job-ranking system, wages, workshop administration, education for workers, education for leaders, life planning, and union relations.

Before proceeding it will be useful to describe the personnel department that operationalizes these policies. Of the 110 employees in the personnel department, 25 concentrate on recruitment, 20 on welfare facilities (13 of whom deal exclusively with housing, especially dormitories), 20 work on labor management matters, and the remaining 45 deal generally with personnel matters of a variety of types.[9] Given the size of the company the personnel department appears quite large from an American perspective. It constituted 2 percent of all company employees in 1974.[10] DeSpelder (1962) examines the ratio of personnel employees to the total number of production employees in a national sample of 561 American small-scale and medium-sized manufacturers of metallic automotive parts. He concludes that personnel needs as defined by these employers tend to assume a constant relationship to the size of the direct work force. On an overall basis, the typical company tends to employ 1 personnel employee for every 74 direct employees regardless of firm size; the ratio of personnel employees to total production employees stands at 0.014. In Toyota Body, however, the relationship works out to 1 personnel employee for every 39 direct employees, a ratio of 0.026. Even if we delete most of the recruitment section and assume a personnel section of 90 employees and a total of 4,290 direct production workers, there is 1 personnel employee for every 47 direct employees, a ratio of 0.021. This is still well above the figures reported by Despelder. The data suggest that Toyota Auto Body invests far more in the personnel department than we would expect among comparable American companies.[11]

8. I shall draw heavily upon Sato (1972, pp. 15–20) as well as on intensive interviews with company officials and examination of relevant company documents.

9. These totals include staff support as well as management. Arrangements relating to the maintenance of safety, a function commonly assumed by the personnel department in the United States, are handled by a separate safety department. The thirteen-person section devoted to housing is responsible for the 1,200 employees who live in bachelor dormitories and another 300 who live in married housing. Tenure in married housing is limited to seven years.

10. The proportion of personnel employees to the total number of production employees declined to about 1.6 by 1976, as members of the recruiting section were let go because of the company decision to discontinue large-scale recruitment of new employees. Members of this category were primarily retirees who had been rehired (*shokutaku*) to fulfill the recruiting function.

11. There are some limitations to this comparison, and it should only be regarded as suggestive. First, in DeSpelder's study the largest firms sampled were on the order of 2,000 employees, and it is possible that the relationship between personnel needs and total number of production workers might change at larger firm sizes. Secondly, it is also possible that the nature of the personnel function in the auto assembly operations charac-

The following sections, in delineating its functions, should make clear that this is indeed the case.

Generally it is preferred that managers in the Toyota Auto Body personnel department have experience in other departments rather than spending their entire careers in the personnel department. An examination of the 24 university graduates in the department who make up the managerial staff shows that they are all male; 5 majored in law in undergraduate school, 1 in education, and 18 in economics and administration. As is the case in most Japanese companies, the personnel department is not particularly powerful politically vis-à-vis other departments. Yet its members do not feel that they have any great difficulty convincing management to accept their views on matters relating to policy choice and implementation. Rohlen (1975, p. 186) claims that the status of personnel departments is higher in Japan than in the U.S., but he offers no evidence.

The central role played by the personnel department in instituting the innovations to be discussed below is of particular interest and a striking contrast to the position taken by personnel departments in the American automobile industry. In the American automobile firms personnel department members traditionally have had a strong "we versus they" orientation, based on years of labor-management conflict. As a consequence, they are often among the strongest opponents within management of worker participation in decision making. In the case of General Motors, for example, the firm that has shown the greatest interest in worker participation in shop floor decision making among the major U.S. automakers, it was necessary to separate the corporate personnel function into the Industrial Relations Staff and the Personnel Administration and Development Staff. This took place in 1971. The Department of Organizational Research and Development created in 1972 out of a broadened Employee Research Deparment was included under the Personnel Administration and Development Staff and had the major responsibility for company-wide efforts to foster worker participation in decision making. It would seem that the personnel development function does not conflict as much with existing labor relations practices at Toyota Auto Body as it did at GM. Consequently it was not necessary to separate the functions or create a new department in the case of Toyota Auto Body.

Individual Guidance

Management sees individual guidance as one of the central pillars in the company personnel policy. Through individual guidance the company seeks to develop individual work abilities. This development, in turn, is viewed as a

---

terizing Toyota Auto Body operations may be different than in the manufacture of metallic automotive parts. Furthermore employees concerned with safety are excluded from the Toyota Auto Body data, but included in the American data; the result is to make the reported differences all the more impressive. Although the relative size of the personnel function at Toyota Auto Body cannot be shown to be representative of Japanese firms through the data presented here, my intuitive experience is that the company is not particularly unique.

premise for better work performance and as indispensable for maintaining high work motivation. Individual guidance involves the construction of an "ability growth goal" for each employee and the development of training plans for the individual appropriate to that goal. This goal is subjected to periodic reexamination based on individual performance as evaluated through a variety of inputs, including the individual's own self-report. The goal is confirmed in interviews between each employee and his supervisor. The actual efforts to achieve the goal are carried out by differentiating those aspects that require on-the-job training (OJT) and those aspects that require off-the-job training (off-JT). In the case of OJT, one's superiors take responsibility for executing the training; in the case of off-JT, there is a formal program for which the personnel section assumes responsibility. Job rotation is carried out in cases where it is necessary to achieve the growth goal. OJT is practiced according to a standard OJT curriculum adapted to each constituent department and section. The OJT standard curriculum is prepared as a menu to provide possible choices for the individualized training plans. These training plans are formulated in an attempt to coordinate workshop personnel needs with individual requests.

In any investigation of this sort, it is always wise to keep clear the distinction between rhetoric and practice. This seems particularly the case in Japan because, as Ronald Dore has noted, the Japanese manager usually seems to need a good deal more hypocrisy to keep the wheels greased than is the case with his Western counterpart.

In the case of individual guidance, policy is operationalized in a very concrete fashion, through a set of individual employee records that are remarkably impressive in scope. This record-keeping and set of procedures existed in more simplified form prior to 1972; they assumed their present formality after 1973. At present a record of the ability-growth goal of each individual and his program of education is kept in a guidance note book. Included in the notebook is an evaluation of the education received and progress made toward the ability-growth goal. These records, compiled by the foreman in each section, in turn become the basis for further decisions on education, job transfers, and setting the classification grades for job assignments and ability. Of course other records, such as the individual's job duty record and a record of individual achievement evaluations, also form the basis for such decisions. The appendix to this chapter provides a translation of the guidance notebook.

It will be useful to review the guidance notebook briefly and outline its contents so as to grasp more fully its detailed and systematic character. Some of the key items included are: names of prior employers and work done; results of psychological tests (personality tests); company work history (division, department, and section); specification of jobs held; a record of job qualification certificates and licenses received; history of in-company and outside training received; record of conducting internal company seminars; accident record; individual characteristics favorable to pursuing company education, such as those dealing with the quality of home life and the progress made in developing proper work habits (e.g., "follows rules," "serious personality"); points individual needs to cultivate if he is to benefit more fully from company education and develop improved work habits (e.g., "lacks firmness as a leader," "needs to cultivate ability to harmonize with subordinates"); records of superior's interview with worker, including theme of conversation, content, results, and policy adopted (free-flowing discussion of work-related issues of concern to worker and superior, e.g., superior explains to worker basis for recent bonus decision); personnel evaluation of merit, including job and ability grades; wage changes; membership and use of company credit and insurance programs; evaluation of individual achievements (degree of inventiveness, creativity, and effectiveness of suggestions, e.g., "found a way to reduce amount of steel in building master model"); type of reward for recorded achievements (e.g., suggestion commendation); history of skill acquisition in company with name of each kind of work done and nature of requisite skills; guidance plan for year with month-by-month plans (e.g., June-July: "familiarize yourself with production process of master model"); records of education and activities actually undertaken during this period and results (evaluation); self-improvement record (this year's ambitions, goals to aim for, things accomplished, concrete steps taken to accomplish these goals, and individual's self-examination of this year's achievements).

It is apparent from this detailed apparatus of data-collection and record-keeping that a cornerstone of company personnel policy is a very individualized treatment of workers (*kobetsu rōmu kanri*), which involves the constant monitoring of individual plans and the actions designed to shape and produce the desired outcomes. In particular the focus on education is quite notable. Secondly, there is clearly an attempt to build into these plans individual hopes and aspirations. It should be noted that the only page the individual is allowed to see in this document is the fifth page (see appendix to this chapter) which lists the educational plans for the year and the records of education received, including an evaluation by one's superiors. Otherwise the document is open only to management; union officials have no significant input or right of access.

The individual guidance notebook and all the activities necessary to keep it up to date represent a concerted attempt by the company to facilitate career planning for blue-collar workers. From a company point of view career development is that part of personnel administration which is designed to develop paths by which employees progress in the organization over time. An expert on American personnel practices details the ingredients of career development as follows:

> Optimally developed with the encouragement of, and after consultation with, the employee involved, the career plan includes a program by which he can acquire information, attitudes, and skills. This is done in various ways: by training on and off the job, by counseling and coaching from superiors, and by planned rotation in positions of varying functions and in different locations. Fundamental to career development is the preparation of career paths and the counseling of employees about these paths. (Glueck 1974, p. 263)

Having said this Glueck also makes clear that career development is rarely practiced by business firms in the United States. Even for management it represents the exception and not the rule; for blue-collar employees it is simply not done! It is difficult even to imagine a major American company devoting the resources to compiling and utilizing the information necessary for blue-collar career guidance. The automobile industry in the United States would be one of the last places one would even think of looking for career development and guidance programs, given our image of the impact of technology on skill distribution and training requirements and the cyclical character of the industry. Glueck (1974, p. 276) predicts that formal career-development programs will become more common in the future in the United States. He notes that this area is already receiving more publicity and with accumulating case experiences, he believes, these programs will become more popular in large and medium-sized organizations with stable environments. There are already a number of indications that the auto companies are devoting more attention to career planning, especially for their managerial personnel. Whether this will "trickle down" to the bulk of salaried employees, much less blue-collar workers, is problematic at best.

If career development programs for blue-collar workers are notable for their absence in U.S. business firms, it needs to be emphasized that variations of these practices are quite common in large Japanese firms. The types run from highly formalized programs operated by top management, as in Toyota Auto Body and Honda Motor Company, to more informal practices based on custom and administered by foremen. The Fourth Personnel Management Census of the Japan Federation of Employers' Associations (a survey of 850 manufacturing firms) reports that 20 percent of all firms indicate they have some form of career development for regular employees, including blue-collar workers (Japan Federation of Employers' Associations 1975, p. 9). The number of companies actually practicing career development is probably underestimated, since many of those firms which informally practice career development do not report the practice. Annual self-assessment reports (*jiko shinkokusho*) were introduced in many large firms over a decade ago as a means of better coordinating individual aspirations with organizational needs. Fifty percent of all firms surveyed by the Japan Federation of Employers' Associations stated they practiced employee self-assessment (Japan Federation of Employers' Associations 1975, p. 21). The standard practice involves each employee stating in his report his own assessment of his present performance, suitability of job currently held, preferences regarding next assignment and willingness to participate in job rotation. In the past Japanese employers primarily relied on employees' receiving OJT by their superiors. Since the early 1960s, however, a major shift has occurred in the direction of planned educational development for all levels of employees. The development and systematization of educational investment at Toyota Auto Body as reported in this and other sections of this chapter must be understood in this broader context. In our discussion of the remaining seven categories of personnel policy we will have further opportunities to grasp how the career-development program is operationalized, particularly in the sphere of education.

Ironically it appears that innovative multinational corporations may play a key role in diffusing new personnel practices to Japan, practices which are not necessarily widely accepted in the country of origin. For example, the Mobil Oil affiliate in Japan is noted for its attempt to utilize "best practices" in both Japan and the United States. Its career-development program has been widely studied and emulated in Japan.[12] The program involves the solicitation of career preferences from non-represented employees. These preferences are reviewed both by the supervisors concerned and the career development committee, and are considered in planning career paths. Again the Japanese have gone beyond these original ideas in applying them to unionized blue-collar workers.

Job-Ranking System

The second element in the company personnel administration system is the job-ranking system. Figure 12 presents a distribution of production workers by their job-grade and ability-grade ratings for 1972. The higher the grade, the more skilled the employee in the sense of doing more difficult jobs and being able to do more jobs. The company began conducting job evaluations in 1964 and adopted them seriously in 1970. Each job is evaluated on the following criteria: knowledge, skill, mental pressure (tension—sense of being constrained), physical fatigue and work environment.

Job rating one is reserved for female employees, none of whom works on the production line. There are 324 women in clerical jobs (none in supervisory positions); the average age is twenty-two, and they have an average length of service of 3.2 years (compared to 10.4 years of service for males).[13] These female employees are generally expected to quit upon marrying or, in the case of a workshop marriage, to quit during pregnancy. There are no formal rules that require this, but it is informally understood. Company policy is not to hire any married woman, both because they believe married women do not have "any flexibility" in work hours and also because they can obtain sufficient numbers of unmarried women for their needs.

The immediate explanation for the absence of females among production workers lies in the protective legislation for females which makes their utilization in shift work difficult. There is a certain irony in this situation, since the labor shortage experienced by the Japanese auto companies has occurred in a context of the large availability of surplus female labor.[14]

Toyota Auto Body officials do state that they envision hiring women for blue-collar jobs in the future and think that their introduction will "make the

12. I am indebted to Mr. R. Pietsch, manager of personnel services and program development, Mobil Oil Corporation, for his observations on this matter. Personal communication, 8 July 1976.

13. Five percent of the female labor force have attained job grades two, three or four. They are not shown in Figure 12, which covers production workers alone. Females in job grades two, three or four are primarily clerical employees.

14. This is not to say that women don't get a chance to be exposed to assembly line work. There are a number of industries, such as electronics, with assembly line operations that rely heavily on female workers. On one of the same days I visited Toyota Auto Body, I spent the evening in a Nagoya cabaret and watched bar hostesses with transmitters tucked into their cleavage being directed by radio to proceed from one table of male customers to another at regular five-minute intervals. This guaranteed a most efficient utilization of resources and surely was just as thorough a rationalization of work as occurred in the factory.

Ability Grade   Number of Employees

Ability Grade	1	2	3	4	5
5				10	6
4			278	734	6
3		19	2167	30	
2		56	94		
1					

1   2   3   4   5

Job Grade

Figure 12: Distribution of Production Employees
by Job and Ability Grades (1972)

174

attitudes of male workers more peaceful, improve human relations in the work group and enhance teamwork." They say they are also prepared to recruit married females in the future, in response to social changes occurring in the country.

Job grade two is reserved for new employees. It is a probationary status that lasts for two years. When a new employee enters the company upon school graduation, he generally works for three months on the assembly line at half the span of the ordinary worker (e.g., attaching three parts instead of six). After six months the work load is increased to the span of an ordinary worker. After another three months the worker changes to a new job. In this whole first year the worker performs two full jobs. Once the first year is complete an attempt is made to expose the worker to one new job every three months, i.e., four jobs a year. The company policy is to train workers to do as many jobs as possible. The amount and speed of job rotation is left to the discretion of the foreman. The foreman is generally responsible for one section, which has on the average twenty workers. These job rotation practices are not uncommon in the Japanese auto industry; Honda Motor Company, for example, is also quite well known for similar practices.

Job grade three presumes that about half the work of a section can be done by the individual. This generally takes about three years of seniority. In Figure 12, we can see that 2,167 employees have achieved job grade three combined with ability grade three. Those with a higher ability grade than job grade are generally older employees who are not ready for job grade four (or perhaps there is no vacancy) but command higher abilities than reflected in their current jobs. However, this discrepancy between ability grade and job grade also reflects the continued strength of the age and length-of-service reward system. For older workers to have higher ability-grade ratings than job-grade ratings allows the company to pay the older workers more. The more infrequent situation in which a worker has a higher job grade than ability grade is generally reserved for younger workers (relative to a given job-grade cohort) who are making exceptionally rapid progress in mastering skills and displaying promise.

Job grade four is reserved for those employees who can do almost all the work in their section. This generally takes from five to six years of employment. As may be seen from Figure 12, 734 employees have achieved the number four job grade and a number four ability grade.

Ability Grade   Number of Employees

Ability Grade	Job Grade 1	2	3	4	5
5				137	9
4			546	692	
3		12	1848	11	
2		44	5		
1					

1   2   3   4   5

Job Grade

Figure 13: Distribution of Production Employees
by Job and Ability Grades (1974)

Job grade five is composed entirely of a small number of high-level craftsmen. Foremen, though not shown in Figure 12, also have a job grade of five assigned to them. Company records show that 4.7 percent of the 5,500 employees in the company are first-line foremen. Blue-collar workers in the fifth grade are eligible to climb up the management hierarchy from subsection foreman to section foreman to department head if they have the ability and quality necessary for each status. Clearly not many are able to make the ascent to department head, but the company does point to numerous section chiefs who have risen from the ranks.

The higher job grades entitle employees to become candidates for a variety of desired openings in the company, such as improvement group membership, QC-circle leadership, recreation group leadership, training instructorship, etc. Finally, there is extensive job rotation in and out of the maintenance and the high-status experimental section.

The job system described above is not without its problems. Figure 13 presents the distribution of job and ability grades for 1974 (Figure 12 reported the distributions for 1972). The most notable difference lies in the significant increases in those workers with higher ability grades than they have job grades (i.e., in job grades three and four). The company policy is to encourage all workers to strive to achieve number four job-grade status. There are those who have made insufficient efforts to master the necessary skills, however, and there is a shortage of grade four jobs, so that it is impossible to give all production workers grade four status. In a survey of worker satisfaction with that portion of their wages determined by job grade, dissatisfaction rose from 26 percent in 1969 to 58 percent in 1973. The company discovered that the majority of dissatisfied workers were the 546 workers in grade three jobs with ability-grade four rankings. These workers wanted the opportunity to qualify for job-grade four jobs or at least have more internal differentiation in the ability-grade four group. The company reports that it still is difficult to make the ability grade of workers correspond to their job grade; as a consequence, they were making efforts in the mid-1970s to supplement wages for those whose ability level is higher than their job grade. Officials recognize that they may have to consider a new job system if disproportionately large numbers of employees end up in job-grade four jobs.

Perhaps the major observation to be made here is that despite extensive job evaluation the meaningful job grades are few in number. Yet job analysis, as it developed in the United States, rests on the standardization and detailed classification of large numbers of occupations and pay rates.

To be sure the cross-referencing of the job grade and ability grade at Toyota Auto Body allows for somewhat more differentiation than is provided for in the simple job-grade system. This cross-referencing, however, also introduces a mechanism for maintaining the age and length-of-service reward system. Company officials have clearly recognized the need for internal differentiation of the job-grade system as reflected in worker sentiments. Yet the amount of job-grade differentiation still remains minimal compared to what one would anticipate in an American manufacturing firm (see Chapter IV; also Livernash 1957). Nor does this arrangement seem unique by Japanese standards.

Wage System

The third element in the company personnel administration is the wage system. Numerous treatments of the actual content of the Japanese wage system have appeared in English; consequently we will focus only on the broad content as it relates to the theme of job redesign (see Dore 1973; Funahashi 1973). Prior to 1966 the company had a rather standard wage system that gave primary weight to reward by age and length of service. In connection with various changes in the mid-1960s, the company officials noted that conveyor belt production methods were becoming increasingly dominant. Skilled production work was subjected to a differentiation of functions whereby it was being replaced by simple standardized jobs. As a consequence of these changes personnel officials believed the basis of the *nenkō* system was being undermined. They adopted three principles that were to become the basis of a new wage system:
1. Wages would be designed to reward the development of workers' ability to carry out their job duties at a high level.
2. Wages would reflect the content of work carried out by employees as well as their ability to execute this work.
3. Wages would be designed to promote the stability of worker livelihood.
Building on these principles they established a wage system based on a basic wage, a job wage, and an ability wage. These account respectively for 40, 54, and 6 percent of the total wage. The basic wage is designed to protect worker livelihoods through recognizing the increased financial responsibilities of workers as they move through the life cycle; it is premised on a marriage age of twenty-six. Payments are calculated on the basis of one-half of the standard cost of living, estimated by government statistics for each age group in the city of Nagoya. It is intended as a guide for life planning for young workers as well as being designed to guarantee the livelihood of the core workers in the enterprise.

The job wage is based on job analysis, so that the burden of a job and its necessary qualifications can be evaluated relative to other jobs. Time-and-motion studies are used indirectly to measure mental pressure and physical fatigue, two of the five components of job evaluation. These studies are used directly to determine the best kind of equipment to use, the appropriate amount of work for one person, the best job order, and the number of people needed to do a particular job. Job knowledge and job skill requirements, the two key additional components of job evaluation, are measured in three categories: ability to improve, ability to train others, and ability to perform usual duties. As management recognizes, this is in reality a measure of job performance rather than an objective measure of the skill or knowledge requirements of the job. The measures are also vague enough to lead one to believe that informally seniority may play a significant role. Management, however, emphasizes that it is truly a job rate because each job grade has a definite number of positions. They believe that the method of job analysis is essentially the same as that which exists in the United States. A change in job grade produces a change in the job wage.

Within each of the effective job grades (three, four, and five), there is a range which is determined primarily by length of service in grade. Job duty content is reexamined annually according to union agreement; the classification of job duties relative to other jobs is reexamined twice a year at fixed intervals. This continual monitoring is necessary because of the rapid technological changes that have engulfed the auto industry. In addition, because of extensive job rotation, there is some problem in keeping job rates current. Since workers may experience three or more jobs a year through job rotation, the agreement specifies that the worker shall be paid the job rate for that job which he had three or more months during the preceding six months.

The ability wage was established both to stimulate the growth of ability among employees and to plug the gap between the distribution of ability and the prescribed number of employees for each job. Through experience Toyota Auto Body management found that there are often insufficient jobs of higher quality relative to the number of employees with the skills to execute them. We have seen that the category of high ability grade cross-referenced with a lower job grade often contained older workers who were not promoted, some because of lack of ability but many because of insufficient vacancies. It should be noted that the ability portion of the wage bill is considerably higher in other large Japanese companies.

Finally mention should be made of the bonus system. Bonuses are paid semiannually, as is common to Japanese firms, and total some five months' salary annually. The amount available for the bonus is decided through negotiations between the company and the union, based on the company's business results and the general economic situation. The amount a given individual receives is based on his age, job, and skill, with adjustments upward or downward based on individual performance. The evaluation of the individual's performance is made by his superiors based on standards outlined in the guidance notebook (see appendix to this chapter). The assessment of individual performance is calculated so that it implicitly encourages competition among workers of a given section for a limited number of high ratings. This involves use of the forced distribution method of evaluation which is analogous to "grading on the curve" (Glueck 1974, pp. 295–96). The results of an individual's performance evaluation are announced to the individual, and there is a discussion with him of the reasons for the evaluation and of his progress toward his work objectives in the future. The results are recorded in the guidance notebook and in such a fashion there is a mutual reconfirmation of individual progress.

These practices are central to the company policy of associating specific rewards with the setting of explicit goals and clear criteria for evaluating individual success in achieving these goals. It is not clear how successful the company has been in the latter respect, but they report that the system has not produced major complaints by workers, though officials insist they must be on guard to insure that the system of evaluation remains open and fair.

The current wage system is not without its problems, but management believes the system has won increasing acceptance by workers, as judged by their responses to annual surveys. We noted earlier, however, that the job-wage portion has encountered some difficulties. Quite apart from the components of the wage system and their weights, workers continue to register strong dissatisfaction with the wage level as well as the amount of company expenditure for welfare facilities. The company consciously maintains its wages at a level comparable to the average auto industry wages and, of course, real wages in the auto industry have risen substantially over the last fifteen years. Critics, however, would point out that they did not rise as fast as productivity. The company position is that no matter what they do, workers are going to be dissatisfied with wage levels and the extent of welfare facilities.

Company officials would like to be able in the future to put still greater weight on the job and ability wage and move further away from the life-cycle and *nenkō* approaches. Their ability to do so is constrained by the extent to which the government will more fully develop the social security system and thereby relieve companies of this responsibility. Perhaps more problematic, however, is how far Japanese managers will go toward greater specificity of authority and responsibility in their industrial reward system. The movement away from age and length of service as explicit wage determinants is not limited to Toyota Auto Body. It has been a powerful force throughout Japanese industry. Some Japanese labor scholars see the basis for management success in the past in the diffuseness of responsibility and authority, which allowed for great flexibility in organizing work and introducing new procedures.

One of the key questions is whether the specification of authority and responsibility will be located at the individual level or at that of the small group. There is no clear trend yet as to which factor will be emphasized by Japanese industry, though I would guess that it is likely to be the latter. At Toyota Auto Body, although management speaks of enhancing the responsibility of individuals, much of the actual activity can be interpreted as the enhancement of responsibility for small groups. For example, the company calculates the proportion of inferior goods to total production for each three- to five-man crew (*gumi*). It also calculates the proportion of down time to total operating time for each three- to five-man crew. This suggests again the ability of the company to play on the competition between small work units. A number of the companies that went the furthest toward fixing wages according to individual job duties in the late 1960s have since modified their systems to allow greater weight for age and length of service and to obtain greater flexibility in the development of their labor force. Unions have also pressed management for going too far in this direction and forced many companies to build in greater rewards for middle-aged workers.

The fourth element in the company's personnel administration policy involves what they call workshop administration. This is essentially an attempt each year to relate individual goals to company goals. A yearly plan is announced each year with specific goals alloted to each management division. In turn each department sets specific management goals and activities for each administrative level down to the individual workshop. At each workshop the process unfolds in the activities centered on the quality-control circles, based on the leadership of supervisors, and various subcircles, which are led by subleaders. It is through the activities of such small groups as these that the company attempts to give substance to its goals in such a way that the evaluation of results can be directly observed by the employees themselves. The company consciously aims at keeping workers from alienation through attempting to strengthen the connection between organizational goals and individual goals. The policy of self-administration through individual guidance (*kobetsu shidō ni yoru jiko kanri*), the first element in company personnel policies, is similarly designed to achieve these same goals.

It is impossible to evaluate directly just how successful these activities are. Are we dealing here with a charade of paper goals and lip service or do managers indeed succeed in having workers internalize company goals? To pose the question in this fashion probably does not allow an answer. It is unlikely that these are just paper goals. The QC circles do seem to function in a way that management desires. Moreover it is hard to believe that they would devote the amount of resources necessary to implement this system were they not convinced that they were having some success. On the other hand, it is also hard to believe that workers fully internalize management goals. We have already seen that 30 percent of the workers reported that the quality-control circles were perceived as a burden. The truth then lies somewhere in between. We will have the opportunity in examining other facets of company personnel administration to more fully explore this theme, albeit in a more indirect fashion. In the final chapter the specific relation between individual and company goals will be confronted.

The practice of workshop administration, as described above, is common among large Japanese firms. In one variation, Hitachi Shipbuilding has its managers tour the plants at the beginning of each year, holding roundtable discussions with employees. This is an effort to have company strategy for the year permeate the company and have employees develop a sense of participation by making their opinions known. My personal evaluation of these procedures is that they are not very effective in inducing the convergence of individual and organizational goals. Rather they belong to that category of characteristically ritual occasions designed to reinforce the solidarity of the organization, a behavioral form at which the Japanese excel (see Rohlen 1975, pp. 185–209). They provide the ideological cement, but more directly important for building the convergence of individual and organizational goals are the institutionalized practices that reward employees for committing themselves to company goals. Chapter VIII deals explicitly with this matter.

The practice of workshop administration does represent an approach that we have had occasion to write about more than once in these chapters. It is one of the many procedures for mobilizing support for decisions made at higher levels. There are also some striking parallels to the Maoist organizational style. Whyte (1973, p. 152) describes the "mass line" approach as follows:

> A new policy is announced and explained, and then subordinates break into regular discussion groups to go over each point in detail. In these groups efforts are made to convince everyone of the need for a change in routine, to elicit suggestions and ideas, and to get "activists" to encourage their co-workers to support the change.

This comparison with Chinese practices will be dealt with in greater detail in the following chapter.

Education

The fifth element in company personnel administration is its educational program for workers. We have already explored in some detail this issue in the section dealing with how individual guidance policies are operationalized. Consequently the discussion here will focus on the practice of improvement groups, the "workshop university," and the automobile-repair classroom.

As the quality-control circles developed a variety of other questions had to be faced. Who was to follow up and evaluate the suggestions flowing from the QC circles? How could the company arrange for quick feedback for worker suggestions so that incentives to contribute would not be lost? The company made the basic decision not to leave the implementation of proposals to industrial engineers. Instead in 1968–69 they created improvement groups for each section in the operational lines. These improvement groups were created to insure quick action on QC-circle proposals. They build machines and jigs and generally implement proposals for improving equipment and production that emanate from the QC circles and individuals.

Members of improvement groups are selected from among production workers and appointed for a fixed term as part of the company's job-rotation system. These are full-time assignments. Generally membership is for six months to one year, although about 20 percent of the members stay longer. Those with longer tenure generally show special talents or get involved in long-term projects. Workers may be reassigned to the improvement groups as needs and interests coincide. Workers qualifying for the improvement groups have a grade four job classification, or are those who are able to perform any task in their work groups. Even without these qualifications a worker may be assigned to the improvement groups if he has made an interesting proposal, or if the team leader judges that an individual would benefit from such exposure. Success in improvement-group activities becomes an important arena for workers to demonstrate they are worthy of promotion. Perhaps the best evidence that we are dealing with a serious commitment on the part of management is that some 5 percent of all grade four job holders are assigned to the improvement groups at any one time. This is an impressive commitment of resources. Moreover, engineers are assigned to improvement groups as needed. If proposals cost less than $1,130, the improvement groups need no special approval to design and build new equipment and institute new procedures.

We have here a situation in which specific proposals for improvements in production processes are generated by workers themselves and put into practice through the activities of the improvement groups. The willingness and ability of the company to draw upon worker talents in this fashion is quite striking. The labor-saving equipment and jigs produced out of the activities of the improvement groups are designated as "improved machinery." There is a large amount of "improved machinery" operating in various sections of the company, as can be verified by a tour of the plants. In recent years the company has been awarded two patents on ideas suggested by production workers. One was for a design for improvements on automatic welding procedures. The other allowed two presses to be arranged in such a fashion that they could be manned by one person instead of the usual two. The workers in question will receive royalties if they are forthcoming.

Significant here is not simply the ability of the company to draw upon and utilize worker talents. Just as important are the opportunities opened up by improvement-group membership for job rotation and career development. This rotation prevents the stagnation of talent among those working on the simple standard production line. It serves the larger purpose of "broadening" the employee by enlarging the contents of the work of line operatives and, in effect, extending the progression of skill acquisition. Skill acquisition becomes not simply acquiring increasingly complex job skills (of which there is a relatively limited supply in auto assembly plants). Rather, a whole new dimension is added by the quality-control circles and improvement groups.

The importance that Toyota Auto Body managers attach to tapping the basic intimate information that all workers have about their work is characteristic of Japanese management. Success in tapping this reservoir of information is only possible if workers accept that it is in their own individual interests to share this knowledge with management. To a varying extent Japanese management attempts to provide workers with the tools to improve production methods and participate in improvement groups, and to provide the training that makes it possible for workers to follow up on their own suggestions. These activities give release to native talents, lengthen the job ladder and undoubtedly are a major element in the process of convincing workers that there is an identity of interests between themselves and their employers.

It is easy for many critics, including this one, to question whether workers really get their share of the reward for this impressive contribution. The answer is that financially they do not. There is clearly a strong element of co-optation and manipulation here. This is not to say that the rewards simply go to the managers. There is no evidence to suggest that Japanese managers are appreciably better paid than their American or Western European counterparts relative to blue-collar workers (e.g., Dore 1973, pp. 265–69).[15] A rough check of the most comparable statistics suggests that ordinary production workers earn on the order of slightly over one-third of what department chiefs do in both Japan and the United States. Moreover, the gap between workers and managers appears to have closed rapidly in Japan over the last fifteen years. The bonus of the average union member in manufacturing rose steadily from 19 percent of that of department chiefs in 1965 to 33 percent in 1974, while the average basic wage of male middle school graduates for all industries rose from 30 percent of the earnings of department chiefs in 1965 to 40 percent in 1974 (model wage data). This represents a remarkable closing of occupational and status differentials in a very short period (Ono 1975, pp. 32–33; *Chūō Rōdō Iinkai* 1966–75). These developments are part of the strong egalitarian thrust in both attitudes and behavior in the postwar Japanese business organization.

The evidence suggests that to a large extent profits have been reinvested in the company rather than simply being used to better the relative position of management. Ultimately, of course, this benefits the stockholders. The social democratic position—one to which I subscribe—is to reorganize the relationship so that workers share more fully and immediately in the monetary rewards generated by their labor and ingenuity. In addition as may be seen in the Western European experience, workers are capable of exercising more control over higher-level policy decisions that affect the organization of work. As it now stands in Japanese industry workers are left to exercise their participation in a narrow range of production-related areas circumscribed by management authority.

Be that as it may, the system does operate in a capitalistic framework and even one committed to a social democratic solution must entertain the possibility that this is a more humane way to organize work relationships than one is likely to experience in an American auto factory. Notwithstanding the elements of co-optation and manipulation referred to above, we must recognize that if these practices give meaning and direction to workers' lives in an otherwise rather alienating work environment, then workers do indeed draw important non-monetary rewards. The research of Melvin Kohn (1976, pp. 111–30) is relevant here. He examined those variables having the greatest effects on various measures of alienation in a national sample survey of 3,101 males, representative of all men employed in civilian occupations in the United States. The results indicate that the major factor in alleviating alienation is the ability to give the worker meaningful control over the conditions that impinge directly on his opportunities to exercise initiative, thought and independent judgment in his work. It is precisely here that the Japanese have put their emphasis.

One has only to compare the description of Toyota Auto Body practices

15. Ono (1975) argues that a particular characteristic of the Japanese compensation structure is its markedly continuous character. To preserve the appearance that anyone can rise in the ranks (even if everyone does not), the wage-compensation structure avoids any marked discontinuities between categories.

outlined above with the one offered by Ely Chinoy (1955) in his classic study of work in an American automobile factory to appreciate the differences. He found that after age thirty-five most workers who have not made foreman lose their aspirations to upward mobility, except in their fantasy world (e.g., want to buy a farm, open up a gas station, etc.) and in passing their aspirations on to their children. Moreover, the position of foreman is apparently not perceived as very rewarding, since many foreman jobs in the auto industry go begging for want of applicants. Chinoy attributes the extensive sense of alienation among auto workers to the limited structural opportunities for upward mobility and ambiguous criteria for promotion. The work cycle is a process of the worker adjusting his aspirations downward as he comes to grips with and accepts the realities of factory life. The problem of mental health associated with this process seems severe (HEW Special Task Force 1972, pp. 84–85). Lest these observations be considered dated, consider the conclusions arrived at in a recent study:

> The assembly line of the automobile plant, though one of the most economical production processes today, is nevertheless one of the most tedious types of work one can perform. It is repetitive, requires only minimum skill and judgment, and requires a constant pace. As a result of the boring work, absenteeism and turnover are relatively high and many intelligent workers are unwilling to work on assembly lines long enough to be selected for a supervisory position, or else they are absent too often to qualify for promotion.
>
> When employees do remain for extended periods of time, they often become fearful of trying something new. The hourly work is well paid and involves little responsibility. However, those that do accept positions as first line supervisors are under constant pressure. One line manager reported that at least five first line supervisors had heart attacks and indicated the heavy pressures as a contributing factor. Assembly line work, then, can affect both the turnover rate among present and potential supervisors, and actively discourage hourly employees from seeking supervisory positions. (Northrup et al. 1975, pp. 74–75)

This description is in sharp contrast to the situation described at Toyota Auto Body.

A second outgrowth of the QC circles has been the "workshop university." Although engineers are available to the improvement groups as consultants, the decision was made the the production workers should themselves develop their own skills in the course of carrying out improvement-group activities. This again was a conscious decision not to rely on an elite corps of engineers but rather to build on the natural talents of workers. The workshop university was created to enable ordinary workers to acquire the technical knowledge that they needed to carry out their projects. At first workers were simply enrolled in special training teams in designated locations to acquire these skills. Since the operatives were high school graduates and studied in a special location, the whole procedure became designated as the workshop university. The practice has evolved so that those completing the program of study receive a diploma awarded by the section chief. Company officials draw the analogy with regular school and after-hours homework and research. In this case regular work in the factory corresponds to the school and the workshop university is the outside research. Although the title and procedures as well as these analogies may strike one as pretentious at best, they appeal to strongly held prestige and status needs of workers. The program is especially popular among the middle school graduates and to a lesser extent among high school graduates who feel inferior for not having gone on to receive a college education. In a society in which close to 50 percent of the relevant male age cohort now goes on to college, this comparison takes on very real meaning.

Training in the workshop university takes the form of guidance from technical engineers, transfers to the improvement section, and transfers to those sections of the company enabling one to acquire particular expertise. The actual form is decided on a case-by-case basis according to the team's program. At present, they have developed three courses, for production equipment, administrative technology, and specific skills. Each section of the operation line has one university covering one or all of these three courses. In 1975 some 150 students were enrolled as workshop university students. Graduation is authorized by the operations section chief, who serves as the school president. It occurs in accordance with the following criteria: realization of an improvement proposal, submission of a treatise based on team training, and evaluation of individual skills. No special treatment is given to the graduates in terms of monetary rewards, although successful completion of the program enhances opportunities for promotion to foreman. A given individual's program takes from one to three years, with the average being two. Study time for the workshop university is entirely outside working hours with the form of study and type of training varying according to conditions. In some cases the major study requires the reading of textbooks at home so that guidance of reading will be limited to a few hours a month in class. In other cases the acquisition of skills on the job might require two hours a day. Again we have a rather impressive attempt to draw upon the natural talents of regular production workers and make opportunities for education available to them.

Before we embrace the Japanese practices too closely, let it be clear that they are not without their own problems. Management reports that some 50 percent of the projects undertaken by workshop university students are failures. There is clearly a lot of trial and error; workers will often underestimate the practical problems they face and overestimate their own abilities. Yet perhaps any loss deriving from trial-and-error procedures, which might be avoided by more experienced engineers, may be offset by the ability of workers with their on-the-spot experience to identify the sources of problems that need correcting. Secondly, there is the potentially enormous payoff in workshop morale with management enforcing policies which recognize publically that workers can make important contributions to solving workshop problems. Management has consciously eschewed the alternative policy of sending employees to technical schools to accomplish these same ends. They clearly believe that the benefit that accrues to the company through having workers select problems directly related to workshop problems, and the building of employee commitment to solving organizational problems, justifies their decision to provide this training within the company.

The company introduced a third mode of enlarging the scope of work in the late 1960s. This involved making available to workers an automobile repair classroom. Workers are taught to repair their own cars and do their own inspections. This allows them to go beyond the kinds of skills required in their own jobs to develop still broader skills. So, for example, an employee specializing in sheet metal might spend his time in the classroom specializing in engine work or paint retouching. The company provides the facilities; teachers are ordinary workers who are dispatched from the shop with teaching status to provide training. These trainers receive special compensation. The classes are conducted after regular working hours. There are two kinds of courses offered. The first is for those seeking a third-rank auto repair license (government approved); this can be used to qualify for certain jobs in the company, such as assembly inspection. Others use the license to return home to open their own repair shop and farm; commonly these are oldest sons who will inherit the family property. Still others have no specific purpose in mind. Some forty students are recruited twice a year for this course; the training takes place over a half-year period on Sundays for eight hours a meeting. The second type of course is for those who would like to learn how to repair their own car; it runs for one month and enrolls some 200 individuals per month. We have here a rather modest investment by the company which enables workers to go beyond the scope of their own work, become more familiar with car operations, and learn to repair their own automobiles. My prior research on the Japanese automobile industry indicates that a significant proportion of young workers choose to work in the industry because of their interest in cars. The automobile classroom clearly appeals to and capitalizes on these interests. Jenkins (1973, p. 57) notes that young men everywhere seem to have a remarkable interest in tinkering with automobiles. Yet most auto companies have managed the considerable feat of transforming this fascinating activity into the world's most hated workplace.

185

A final word on investment in education and training is in order. Estimates of company investment in training are notably unreliable for many purposes, excluding as they commonly do such costs as the loss of production by experienced workers who are helping trainees (see Mincer 1962, p. 52). Yet to the extent that they measure the same things across firms they can give one a picture of relative standing of a particular firm. Toyota Auto Body spends approximately 0.7 percent of its monthly wage bill for education. This amount includes payments for job training at 300 yen an hour, fees for lecturers, pay for workers who take courses outside the company, and costs of training materials, e.g. textbooks. This figure compares to an estimate of 0.3 for all of manufacturing and 0.5 in the transportation equipment and machine industry in 1974 for firms employing thirty or more workers. It should be noted that the transportation equipment and machine industry, along with the chemical industry, records the highest levels of investment in education of any industry subcategory within manufacturing (Ministry of Labor 1975, p. 112). In firms of over 5,000 employees expenditure for education in the transportation equipment and machine industry rises to 0.6. These rough estimates should be interpreted with great caution, but they do suggest that Toyota Auto Body makes investments in formal education that are comparable to those of other firms of a similar size in the transportation equipment and machine industry.

Training and Education of Supervisory Personnel

The sixth element in the company personnel policy focuses on the training and education of supervisory personnel. In 1967–68, when the company recruited some 2,400 new employees, the problem involved not only the quality of the workers recruited but the quality of the leadership that was to be given to these new employees. A series of several meetings, which included section and departmental heads as well as the whole personnel section, was held to try to develop effective programs. Out of these brainstorming sessions, the company developed a personnel study meeting for each department and section as well as monthly personnel administration meetings. A supervisory education manual involving 140 hours of training was also created. At present the company is using the General Electric Manual for all foremen and section chiefs. The 140-hour training course emphasizes the human relations approach and need for foreman sensitivity to worker needs. It was introduced to the company through the former education section chief of an electrical equipment manufacturer. Materials from American Telephone and Telegraph's human assessment and managerial grid programs were also used. The latter materials were diffused throughout Japan by the activities of the Industrial Efficiency Junior College (Sangyō Nōritsu Tanki Daigaku) and are based on the Blake-Mouton program. The managerial grid is an approach to managerial development that has been very fashionable in the United States in recent years. It is a team management approach designed to make supervisors aware of their own leadership styles and develop a concern with both production and people (Glueck 1974, pp. 378–79). It seems quite suited to Japanese conditions. At American Telephone and Telegraph the human assessment program is used to evaluate personnel. Toyota Auto Body managers, however, use it exclusively for leadership education.

A format specific to Toyota Auto Body involves having superiors take responsibility for training subordinates under their direct control at each management level. The supervisory training designated F.T.P. (foreman training program), in force for all supervisors, has the following contents: human relations, operations training, workshop administration, operations improvement, and safety administration. For department chiefs, section chiefs, supervisors, and foremen, monthly training meetings are held on a voluntary basis. These study groups continue to produce various innovations and refinements in personnel policy; the input of the study-group recommendations into company policy is insured through presentation of recommendations at personnel study meetings on section and departmental levels.

It is clear that the company has taken quite seriously the need to retrain its foremen and supervisors to insure that new policies will be successfully executed and institutionalized. Their training programs have been heavily influenced by comparable U.S. programs but, as we should expect, they have been adapted to meet the specific situation present at Toyota Auto Body. A central focus of company efforts has involved upgrading the foreman role and making foremen more responsible for worker evaluation functions previously lodged in the personnel department. This upgrading was central to development of QC-circle activity.

Guidance for Life Planning

An additional characteristic of company personnel policy lies in the emphasis placed on assistance and guidance for life planning. This includes various company activities designed to guarantee the future of employees in their activities as citizens and community members. Foremost among practices developed to insure this future is the provision of the basic wage. It constitutes, the reader will recall, 40 percent of the total wage and is geared to the life-cycle expenses of workers. Secondly, the company has a goal of enabling workers to own their own home by age twenty-six. Central to implementation of this goal is a saving system for home ownership, company loans for home ownership at low interest rates, personnel available to employees for consultation on home purchasing, and company involvement in selling real estate to employees and generally assisting them in real estate purchases. The land prices in the geographic areas near Toyota Auto Body plants have not risen to the astronomical heights which they have in large metropolitan areas, so these policies can be quite effective. These policies are typical of the Toyota companies and strongly encouraged by the various unions in the Toyota group. A 1977 Toyota Auto Union pamphlet entitled "Vision for Lifetime Livelihood" calls for employee home ownership at age thirty-one, at a cost of $55,000 with a floor space of eighty-six square meters.

The company makes available to employees a large range of recreational activities as is common in large Japanese companies, from flower-arranging classes for female employees to baseball diamonds and outings for male production workers. As the five-day week gradually becomes established (currently employees have two Saturdays off a month) and the number of work hours decreases, the company has become even more concerned about guidance of workers' free time activities. The issue is more pronounced for Toyota Auto Body than it is for many other companies because of the relative isolation of the area in which its plants are located; this means that some kinds of commercially available recreation are minimized. This should not be overdone. It is reported that in 1972 Kariya had more bowling alleys per capita than any other city in Japan. Nevertheless, both through formal and informal groups the company seeks to maximize its guidance in this area and assure that workers pursue "healthy" outlets. This would include insuring that they do not become involved in communist youth groups. Generally speaking the range and extent of company activities in these areas seems quite comparable to what one would expect of Japanese companies of this size.

In the context of life planning, it should be noted that the retirement age is set at sixty. Toyota Auto Body is among those firms that went the furthest in raising the retirement age from the traditional fifty-five during the labor shortage of the late 1960s and early 1970s. The trend in retirement age has gone in the opposite direction in the U.S. auto industry as a result of industry and union negotiated incentives. In 1954 the average General Motors hourly-rated worker retired at sixty-seven; in 1977, the average such worker retired between fifty-eight and fifty-nine.

Unions

The last feature of the company's personnel administration is its relationship with the union. The union at Toyota Auto Body was organized in 1946, just one year after the company was organized as a separate entity. In 1955 the company carried out large-scale discharges that led to a fifteen-day strike. This was a pattern that was common to many auto companies in the early 1950s, though union resistance to management actions was notably weaker at Toyota companies than at Nissan Auto and many other auto makers. Even at this time, management recalls, the union leaders were not very radical. One of the first union chairmen is now a department head. The Toyota Auto Body union is a member of the Tokai Shibu, an organization of affiliated Toyota unions that allows for cooperation in formulating policy among members.

Company officials summarize their current relation with the union as follows:

> In our company, the union's role is interpreted by the company in terms of it being an organization which absorbs the ideas (demands) of employees and represents them. Labor-management consultation is exchanged sincerely in all sorts of areas of management. Of course, we cannot avoid having different (conflicting) claims based on different viewpoints but, while respecting the viewpoints of both parties, various kinds of conferences, roundtable discussion and committees at each and every level are held in an atmosphere of clear fact-finding, and in this way problems of various kinds are solved.

Conversations with union leaders produce similar kinds of statements. These statements, however, do not capture the rather passive quality of union activity. The company was careful to consult with union representatives throughout initiation of the new personnel programs. The union policy was not to actively support these changes, but they did not actively oppose them either. According to union officials themselves, they played a rather passive role. There were no major points of dispute, though there were disagreements on specific aspects. For example, the union objected to including the criterion of responsibility in job analysis because they thought it overlapped with the assessment of knowledge, skill, and tension present in a given job. The company gave in on this point, believing that the overall cooperation of the union was more important than their victory on this particular matter. Generally union leaders (who are elected for a two-year term) say that they support the many changes associated with job enlargement because they reduce monotonous work by increasing job rotation and giving workers an opportunity to participate in interesting sections like improvement groups. However, the union itself is not strongly involved in the new arrangements. They have no input on the guidance notebook and do not monitor it; they are not involved in regulating job transfers and job rotation. These are the almost exclusive prerogatives of the foreman, supervisor, and section chief.

Union officers were questioned on their position toward speedups, a common problem in American industry and one to which U.S. unions pay a great deal of attention. The Toyota Auto Body union officials claim that they do not have any policy with regard to labor intensification, because it is hard for them to get information on how many people are actually needed for a given amount of work. There is an institutionalized grievance procedure to which the union is a party. It is designed to deal with individual grievances against an individual management decision such as the occupational ability rating given an individual. If the individual is not satisfied with the resolution of a complaint in his discussions with his superior and files a formal grievance, it becomes a matter of negotiation between union and management in a labor-management committee. It does not appear that this apparatus is often used. The company states that it gets information on worker views through annual surveys and various meetings at the workshop level which are held at regular intervals.

The union activities described above seem to fit the pattern of the Toyota group of companies. They suggest passive support of company policies. The roots of these policies lie in the history of Japanese trade unionism and the historic strength of Japanese management. They also lie, however, in the history of particular companies. For example, the unions in the Nissan companies, the second largest auto producers in Japan, more actively support company production goals; they are institutionally more enmeshed in the day-to-day operations of the company. By contrast the Toyota unions tend to focus their greatest activity on wage negotiations, with less institutional involvement in the day-to-day operations of the company.

Whether it be passive or active support of management production goals, it is clear that contention with management over working conditions and job assignments is not central to the activities of Japanese auto unions. This fact has been true at least since the late 1950s, when most of the militant early postwar unions were replaced by those of today. For purposes of comparison we may note that disputes over working conditions and local plant issues account for the greatest proportion of major work stoppages recorded in the American auto industry between 1950 and 1971.[16]

This completes our summary of the central element in the company's personnel administration. In the next chapter we turn to the question of how the various arrangements described fit with the ideas of participatory management as understood in the United States and other nations.

16. There were thirty-nine such stoppages, which accounted for 47 percent of all workers involved in strikes; more significantly almost 68 percent of the total man-hours of idleness during these twenty-two years were related to disputes over working conditions and local plant issues (U.S. Department of Labor 1973a). To qualify as a major stoppage 100,000 workers or more must have been idled.

190

FACTS TO SERVE AS POINTS OF REFERENCE IN GUIDING EMPLOYEE (Education, homelife, work habits)		CODE NAME	
YEAR/ MONTH	GOOD POINTS	YEAR/ MONTH	POINTS NEEDING CULTIVATION
	DATE	INTERVIEW TOPICS, CONTENTS, RESULTS, STRATEGIES	
RECORD OF INTERVIEWS			

	YEAR	JOB GRADE	NAME OF JOB	ABILITY RATING	SUMMER BONUS	WINTER BONUS	REMARKS
PERSONNEL EVALUATION OF MERIT; RANKING							

	YEAR OF REVISION	BASIC WAGE		ABILITY WAGE	OTHER	TOTAL WAGE
		Livelihood Wage	Job-related Wage			
WAGE CHANGES						

MEMBERSHIP AND USE OF (CREDIT UNION) PROGRAMS	EMPLOYEE SAVINGS PLAN HOUSING CREDIT PLAN TRAFFIC ACCIDENT INSURANCE	OPTIONAL LIABILITY INSURANCE OPTIONAL COMPREHENSIVE INSURANCE FUND FOR PURCHASE OF A CAR	HOUSING FUND EMERGENCY FUND

	DATE	CONTENT: Instances of innovations, ideas, etc. proposed by employee	REMARKS
ACHIEVEMENTS DEVELOPED			(type of reward etc.)

	TYPE OF WORK	ESSENTIAL SKILL ELEMENTS	(Name of production process)	PERIOD IN CHARGE	DATE APPROVED
ACQUIRED SKILLS					

GUIDANCE NOTEBOOK

NAME	DATE OF ENTRY TO FIRM

BIRTHDATE	BLOOD TYPE	DATE PROMOTED TO STATUS OF REGULAR WORKER

PRESENT (As of) ADDRESS	TELEPHONE

CONTACT IN CASE OF EMERGENCY	NAME	RELATIONSHIP	TEL:

SCHOOLING:

GRADUATED FROM THE _____ DEPT. OF _____ SCHOOL, _____ PREFECTURE, IN 19 ___

WORK[1] HISTORY	PERIOD	PLACE OF EMPLOYMENT	TYPE OF JOB

FAMILY COMPOSITION

ADDRESS				
RELATIONSHIP	NAME	DATE OF BIRTH	OCCUPATION	PLACE OF EMPLOYMENT OR NAME OF SCHOOL

NOTEWORTHY ITEMS	(Facets of Medical History, Character, etc. Deserving of Mention)

KRAEPELIN TEST[2]	CLASSI-FICATION	STAGE	YG TEST[3]	CLASSI-FICATION	STAGE	WORK INTEREST	DIVISION

LOCKER NUMBER	AUTO OWNERSHIP	
	MAKE:	LICENSE NUMBER

1. Prior to entry into Toyota Body.

2. A personality test named after the German psychologist Kraepelin, used as a basis for job assignment.

3. A Japanese version of the Guilford-Martin personnel inventory test, a personnel test also used by the company as a basis for job assignments. The test is known as the Yatabe-Guilford Personality test, so named after Prof. Yatabe of the Psychology Department of Kyoto University who developed refinements that made the test even more accurate than the Guilford-Martin.

WORK HISTORY WITHIN FIRM	DATE OF TRANSFER	PLACEMENT (AFFILIATION)		REMARKS
		DIVISION DEPARTMENT SECTION		

JOB SPECIFICATION	DATE OF ACCESSION	TYPE OF WORK	DATE OF ACCESSION	TYPE OF WORK

RECORD OF LICENSES AND QUALIFICATIONS	DATE OBTAINED	TYPE	DATE	TYPE

TRAINING COURSES ATTENDED WITHIN OR OUTSIDE FIRM	DATE	COURSE TYPE	NUMBER OF HOURS	INSIDE FIRM?/ OUTSIDE?

HISTORY OF CONDUCTING SEMINARS AT FIRM	DATE	CONTENT		

ACCIDENTS ILLNESSES AND INJURIES	DATES OF ONSET/RECOVERY	TYPE OF INJURY/ ILLNESS	COMMENTS (Causes, Counter-measures)

194

| RECORD OF "GUIDANCE" (19 ___) | GRADE | ABILITY RATING | NAME CODE | NAME |

YEARLY GUIDANCE PLAN (DEVELOPMENT)	GOALS	
		FOREMAN[1]
		SUPERVISOR
		SECTION CHIEF

FIRST HALF OF FISCAL YEAR RECORD OF GUIDANCE	(CONCRETE MEASURES TAKEN— THINGS TAUGHT, TESTS GIVEN— SPECIFICALLY CONCERNED WITH ACTUAL JOB PROCESS)	
		FOREMAN
		SUPERVISOR

1. Entries in these right hand columns call for the seals of the individual worker's superiors.

LATTER HALF OF FISCAL YEAR RECORD OF GUIDANCE				

EVAULATION	GOOD POINTS	APRIL THROUGH SEPTEMBER		OCTOBER THROUGH MARCH
	NEED DEVELOPMENT			

SELF IMPROVEMENT RECORD	THIS YEAR'S AMBITIONS	AREA	GOALS TO SHOOT FOR	THINGS ACCOMPLISHED TOWARD GOALS
		WORK		
	REFLECTIONS ON THE CURRENT YEAR	HOBBIES LEISURE SPORTS LIFE PLANS OTHER		

*It is not so difficult to present a
brief account, for example, of the
bureaucracy, of the financial houses,
of the armed forces, or of the political
parties, but to ascribe to each group its
own proper position, its relation to
other parties of societies, to judge
between any of these groups and say
this one is master and that one servant,
this would be something of a Sisyphean
task, but one which none the less ought
to be shouldered.*
E. H. Norman, 1940

CHAPTER VII

WORK REDESIGN IN JAPAN:
AN EVALUATION

The purposes of this chapter are twofold. The first is an overall evaluation of work-redesign efforts in Japan seen in comparative perspective. The second, concluding the chapter, involves consideration of our findings for the earlier inferences drawn from our interpretation of the Detroit-Yokohama comparison of job-mobility patterns.

In summarizing characteristics of the rather minimal experience with participatory management in the United States, the HEW task force report *Work in America* (1972, pp. 103–10) delineated the range of decisions in which workers participate. They may determine:
1. Their own production methods.
2. The internal distribution of tasks.
3. Questions regarding internal leadership.
4. What additional tasks to take on.
5. When they will work.
With regard to job content the emphasis in the American literature on job redesign and job enlargement has been on expanding the scope of individual jobs and job rotation in particular. The HEW report also places strong emphasis on the need for profit sharing to be associated with these innovations.

At first glance these foci seem not inconsistent with the descriptions presented in the preceding chapter. To leave the matter here, however, ignores some subtle though, in the last analysis, fundamental differences in the style, content and direction of participatory management in the two nations.

The Basic Differences

The reorganization of work at Toyota Auto Body is more radical than most U.S. activities in this area. The head of the personnel section summarizes their approach as follows:

> We believe that an individual job and the way it is performed must be activities into which are woven the original ideas of workers, not to be thought of as simply a fixed job which superiors order one to perform. The individual jobs must be carefully thought out with this aim in mind.

We may ask ourselves what obstacles would have to be removed in the United States before we could imagine successful institutionalization of these seemingly utopian assumptions. First, it may be noted, machine design is by and large not a function of each specific company. Rather, it is a highly centralized operation that came into being in the middle of the nineteenth century in the United States. The machine-tool industry developed as a response to the common processes and problems in the production of a wide range of disparate products in a variety of different industries. This technology involved the spread of specialized machines, each designed to insure speedy performance of limited tasks. This presumed a sequential productive process involving large numbers of special-purpose machines, with each one advancing the product one small step further toward its completed form. It was the growing nineteenth-century success in development of machine technology which culminated in the assembly-line system in the early twentieth century. The tendency towards "pre-set tools" which culminated in the revolutionary numerical-control machine technology of the post-World War II period reduced the skills required by the machine operator (Rosenberg 1972, pp. 98–110).

Yet this perspective is based on a conceptualization of technological change exclusively in terms of large-scale innovations. Nathan Rosenberg (1972, p. 164) notes that much less attention is paid to small-scale, often anonymous, improvements in design and minor adjustments and modifications of practices. Stinchcombe (1974, pp. 8, 17–18, 30) makes the same point in resisting "the easy theoretical distinction between innovation and routine administration." Only by innovation can the routine problems of production be solved. The cumulative impact of frequent small-scale changes can be enormous, and without their consideration approaches to technological change are incomplete. These small-scale changes, often introduced by workers and foremen, are far more critical to raising industrial efficiency than is commonly realized. It is here at the "margins," in short, that workers may have their most significant opportunity of determining production methods. The extent to which the opportunity is exploited may be treated as variable. In this connection, American organizational sociologists generally assume that because a task is routinized, job occupants do not have the potential for non-routinized decision making. They interpret this situation as one in which job designers are simply responding to a universal organizational logic in situations of high clarity of task objectives, high predictability of expected problems and high capability in developing regular procedures for handling these problems (e.g., Dornbusch and Scott 1975, pp. 82–83). Our analysis suggests to the contrary that the potential organizational benefits of greater employee discretion may be higher in routinized tasks than is commonly recognized. In this sense American organizational sociologists confuse organizational logic with the political power of engineers to make a particular set of decisions.

Historically in Japan and the United States, as with all successful industrializers, industrialization has been associated with the breaking down of traditional skills. Concomitant with this development has been the separation of work associated with conception (intellectual work) from that associated with execution (manual work). As Frederick Taylor himself wrote:

> Establishing a planning department merely concentrates the planning and much other brainwork in a few men especially fitted for their task and trained in their especial lines, instead of having it done, as heretofore in most cases, by high priced mechanics, well fitted to work at their trades, but poorly trained for work more or less clerical in nature. (Taylor 1947, pp. 65–66, cited in Braverman 1974)

Historically this involved a process of management systematically gathering up knowledge of the work process and then distributing it to individual workers in the form of detailed instructions. Such arrangements do not begin to tap the potential for training and knowledge that workers have. Indeed it is a strategy systematically to denude workers of this potential (Braverman 1974, p. 84).

Within the Japanese automobile industry the process of breaking down traditional craft skills and substituting semiskilled jobs and assembly-line operations took place in the 1950s and 1960s. Toyota Auto Body did not establish its first fully mass production operation until 1957; at the time the No. 1 Kariya assembly plant was the industry's most modern facility. Now Toyota Auto Body managers are seeking to reverse these historical processes.

In the United States, as a "natural" corollary of having engineers design the basic machinery, the engineers, along with line managers, have assumed responsibility for job design as well (Glueck 1974, p. 111). Industrial engineers generally adopt the norm that a machine design which breaks the operation down to (cheaper) less skilled operations is a superior one. These are the labor "requirements" which shape their design (Braverman 1974, pp. 199–200). In the American auto industry it is not uncommon to hear industrial engineers talk about the need to design equipment that is "idiot proof." They mean, of course, that it must be designed to minimize any possible interference by those blue-collar workers who must operate it on a daily basis. Toyota Auto Body managers are increasingly questioning these assumptions, and they are doing so in two ways. First they are bringing the industrial engineers into working relationships with the workers and line managers through such activities as QC circles and improvement groups, and secondly they are trying to upgrade the level of worker competence through education; this permits workers to participate more fully in the design of the production process.

The following discussion should give us further insight into the implications of these different strategies. When a persistent quality problem develops the tendency of American auto companies is to turn not only to the inspectors, as noted earlier, but to the engineers, to see if the problem can be designed away. Thus, for example, the American auto producers are increasingly moving away from nut-and-bolt assemblies to rivets. The reason is that nuts must be tightened with just the right torque to insure that they will not loosen when subject to vibration. This has been a significant problem for U.S. auto companies, as reflected in consumer complaints. Unwilling to wrestle with the task of upgrading worker quality, they are turning to rivets, which require considerably less worker skill and discretion. As an alternate solution an auto parts firm began in 1977 to market a newly developed "microencapsulated epoxy" that automatically creates a permanent seal when nuts are fastened to bolts. In both developments we see the tendency of the U.S. auto industry to look for technological solutions to their quality problem. A similar response may be seen in the change of types of welding operations for putting panels together. The U.S. auto industry joins exterior body panels by flanging the panels and welding the flanges. The Japanese carmakers often use lap joints with exposed welds where the panels overlap. The flanged joint offers two "advantages":

1. Dimensional control does not require dependence on worker care and skill.
2. Appearance does not require as precise positioning of the weld gun.

The contrast with the Japanese auto industry in these respects is instructive. In terms of design one might call Toyota "backward," since they still rely heavily on nut-and-bolt assemblies and lap joint welding operations. Yet they have consistently produced a superior product as measured by independent quality ratings; it is a more labor intensive operation relying on higher quality labor. They have been able to do so by working to upgrade labor quality rather than seeking to simplify skill requirements whenever quality problems arise. But to present the matter in this fashion conceals the nature of the ongoing process. Because labor quality is high they have fewer incentives to seek out technological solutions which lower skill requirements. This particular example should not be overdone. There has been an enormous amount of technological innovation in the Japanese auto industry over the last decade, often involving the simplification of tasks and including, for example, welding operations. But the primary incentives for these innovations have been the labor shortage, and a desire to reduce physically exhausting and tedious tasks and increase international competitive ability (see Koshiro 1977).

Our discussion thus far suggests that a major obstacle to institutionalizing the participation of workers in job design is the conflict with the jurisdiction of industrial engineers. Our conclusion, however, is that the jurisdictional boundaries are not as fixed as at first appears. A second obstacle to increasing worker involvement in job design lies in the attitudes and vested interests of workers, managers and unions in existing job structures. Grinker and associates (1970, p. 9) summarize the American situation as follows:

> Even if an industry wanted to alter significantly certain job structures quickly, these patterns have been enforced by unionism and entrenchment of existing workers to

the extent that they are almost immutable without cataclysmic consequences, or so most employers and union leaders believe.

Although U.S. manufacturers have a relatively free hand to reorganize jobs below the level of skilled worker, there can hardly be meaningful job enrichment if semiskilled workers are systematically excluded from the job tasks requiring the greatest discretion and responsibility. Monopolization of these tasks by skilled workers is a serious barrier to job redesign. The contrast with the approach adopted by Toyota Auto Body managers is stark. In the context of diffuse job definitions the Japanese manager seeks to organize job duties around qualified individuals. From an employer point of view the costs resulting from ambiguity in job definitions are compensated for by great flexibility in adaptive capacity. The union adopts a hands-off policy. From an employee point of view there is the benefit of having a higher probability of being assigned to jobs that suit one's interest and/or serve company goals. On the cost side there is less protection for the worker in terms of insuring that individual interests will not be sacrificed to company interests. In America, the employer benefits from having clearly defined jobs so that job occupants can be more easily treated as replaceable parts. This provides an important kind of flexibility for employers, though it is, so to speak, a flexibility "between" occupants, while the Japanese emphasize a flexibility in using the occupant himself. These differences may reflect the different supply-and-demand functions for labor in the respective nations. Historically labor surplus and weak unions in Japan have allowed employers to take the initiative in constructing job structures. These different strategies may also rest on different conceptions of human nature. In assessing the distinctive job-related worker evaluation strategies practiced by India, Malaysia, Singapore, Pakistan, Canada, and the U.S.A., as compared to ability-based evaluations in Japan and Thailand, Shiba (1973, p. 65) concludes:

> Those countries relying on job-related evaluation presuppose inequality of human ability and believe that these differences must be recognized and assessed and jobs allocated accordingly. The basic assumption in countries like Japan and Thailand, however, seems to be that human ability is basically constant; that any employee satisfying minimum requirements will, given experience, be able to do any job.

He attributes these differences in perception to the degree of cultural homogeneity in a given society, with the belief in equality of human ability stemming from a more homogeneous cultural base.

It is interesting that the American and Japanese educational systems have been contrasted in exactly the same terms. Cummings (1976) notes the strong egalitarian character of Japanese elementary schools relative to U.S. schools. In contrast to the American schools, which assume that individuals have different abilities, Japanese teachers are less ready to concede the point and act accordingly. Instead they assume that differences in performance result from lack of effort and other factors that can be overcome.

In summary, the HEW report's list of decisions in which workers participate gives us a sense of tinkering, while managers at Toyota Auto Body are acting to enable workers to control the content of the job itself. In the analysis of most Western scholars and engineers, technology is usually designated as the critical causal agent. In line with the heritage of scientific management, work is assigned and jobs designed on the basis of the perceived imperatives flowing from the mechanical processes to be carried out by relating the machine and the man, in a way which maximizes efficiency. This conception limits our capacity to examine all available options, though its dominance, no doubt, reflects the 201 social, political, economic, and cultural conditions prevailing in America. This is not to say conditions are so different in Japan that managers at Toyota Auto Body have entirely succeeded in their efforts to weave worker ideas into the very concept of the job itself. They themselves see this as a policy to be seriously pursued, though hardly at all costs.

The Japanese efforts do have many parallels to the new approaches being explored in Western Europe. In particular, the methods developed at the Tavistock Institute in London and applied in Norway and Sweden through the work of Einar Thorsrud appear quite similar (Emery and Trist 1969; Thorsrud 1969). The emphasis in their approaches is on the development of the organization as an "open socio-technical system" which focuses on the interaction of social and technical factors. The aim is to develop small work groups which maintain a high level of independence and autonomy. As a consequence it is expected that jobs will be enriched, individual responsibility increased, and learning possibilities enhanced. These same statements could be applied to the Japanese efforts.

Controlled Participation

A second characteristic of job redesign at Toyota Auto Body is that the emphasis is not on participation per se, but rather on achieving the consent of workers for policies which management wants to pursue, as well as on guiding workers in the direction in which management would like to see them move. This is apparent in the rhetoric the company uses; the term *sanka* (participation) is not used, rather the focus is on *nattokusei* (consent) and *kobetsu shidō* (individual guidance). Quite apart from rhetoric, the variety of documents and practices discussed in the previous chapter should amply demonstrate this characteristic. We have here a carefully controlled participation in which management often takes the lead informally or formally in initiating policies that workers are then guided to accept and pursue. The operation of the QC circles clearly corresponds to this description, as do the programs for career guidance and life planning. In a similar vein, when asked if the job redesign program at the company was aimed more at the increase of responsibility of each individual employee rather than at employee participation in management, a company official stated:

> Yes, this is correct. We believe that the heavier duties (more important jobs) will enhance employees' motivation to see their jobs as a challenge. We believe that taking jobs with heavier duties is related to employees' participation. . . . The QC circles in our company necessarily result in participatory management because they heighten job quality.

Job redesign occurs in a context of unquestioned management authority at Toyota Auto Body, though the maintenance of this authority is something that the managers self-consciously work very hard to uphold. The belief that they can build increasing responsibility into employees' jobs suggests the considerable trust and confidence that Japanese managers have in their employees. Above all, they do not appear to be concerned that given worker groups will acquire the power to keep their area of work under their own control free from outside interference. Crozier (1964, pp. 153–59) describes such an outcome in a French firm; it is a situation where the power of (maintenance) workers is insured by their exclusive knowledge and the resultant unpredictability of their behavior. There are a number of possible explanations for Japanese management's self-confidence in this regard. The increased responsibility given to workers occurs in a context in which management controls the training, the amount of job rotation, and the content of career patterns. This gives management enormous leverage in preventing the hardening of worker privilege. Furthermore, foremen maintain responsibility for QC circles in their workshop; thus the existing structure of line authority is not threatened. Moreover management cultivates the ideology of shared organizational goals to legitimize still further its attempt to limit "selfish" efforts devoted to the exclusive enhancement of worker rights and privileges. It is, of course, possible that management may be misreading the situation. There is a line of reasoning about organizational change and worker participation, in particular, which emphasizes its incremental character (Jenkins 1973, pp. 291–93). Small changes work their way through the system gradually modifying structural arrangements, so that in the long run profound changes, often unnoticed in the beginning, end up transforming organizational practices and power relationships. Whether this will be the case with job redesign in Japan is not something we can predict with confidence. As yet management maintains firm control of the innovative process.

Another approach to examining the degree of control management retains over the work process is to directly examine decision making concerning the determination of the speed of production, number of items to be produced, and the size of the workgroup. These are crucial decisions for both the firm and employees. We would expect that if job redesign were being implemented in the fashion envisioned by the report *Work in America*, workers would have significant inputs into the decision-making process. Instead we find that at Toyota Auto Body the speed of production, number of units to be produced, and size of the workgroup are decided through consultation at three levels, by the department chief, the section chief, and the supervisor and foreman. These production decisions are made for the section level, not for individual jobs. It is the responsibility of the section chief and lower-level supervisors to set the workpace for the workgroup or individuals where appropriate. Workers and unions have no direct input into the determination of workpace, amount of production, and size of workgroup. To be sure they can make their views known indirectly through complaints to the foreman if they feel that staffing is inadequate or the workpace too rapid. What about QC-circle activity? Is this not a realm in which they have a direct impact? Apparently this is not the case. Company representatives set the production goals for each workgroup; QC circles act to implement these goals whenever there is a gap between the goal and actual performance. In short, QC circles act in the framework of decisions determined by management.

This leads many Japanese scholars to see QC circles as a device to break worker collective resistance and rebuild group solidarity on the basis of management goals. Our understanding of decision making in organizations must rely heavily on a grasp of the distribution of power in the organization and how power is used. This ought to be a commonplace observation. Yet, while social scientists have treated the subject of power in organizations (e.g., Thompson 1967; Zald 1970), the subject has only recently been receiving more systematic attention (Salancik and Pfeffer 1974, pp. 135–51). The failure to recognize the role of power in organizational decision making is even more apparent in the work of American social scientists studying Japan, many of whom still treat Japan as a consensual society with "bottom-up" participation (Vogel 1975). What our analysis reveals is that the heavy expressive and instrumental reliance on consensus in a Japanese organization is in no way incompatible with the strong exercise of management power and authority.

It is here that Japanese efforts may be clearly distinguished from Scandinavian ones. In the Swedish and Norwegian developments, the aim is to achieve a fundamental change in the basic structure of the organization, with rather open-ended possibilities for worker influence. There is a high level of public discussion, with the dialogue punctuated by concern for democracy and social justice. This has heightened worker expectations. The forward movement has been sustained by labor governments and strong union support. These conditions are not present in Japan and consequently management has been able to proceed without making radical commitments, conceding only those areas in which it is convinced its interests are being fully served. The Japanese effort focused on blue-collar employees in the private sector while as noted the Scandinavian efforts developed more as a national social and political movement. Consequently, the Scandinavian approach included public sector as well as white-collar employees. In the case of the Japanese public sector, strong conflict between the government and public sector unions discouraged any such effort. On the other hand, there is a strong class consciousness and a certain mistrust which interacts with a pragmatic cooperation between management and labor in the Scandinavian private sector that has no counterpart in Japan. This class consciousness focuses attention on relative and absolute wage levels. No discussion of new forms of work organization takes place in Scandinavia without raising important issues of wage equity and giving rise to union and worker suspicion of management motives. These are not significant issues in Japan.

One should not exaggerate these differences. Although the Swedish and Norwegian unions and the social democratic politicians have strongly shaped the public debate and thereby constrained management behavior, they have not been so active at the individual firm level. The central labor union federations fear (especially in Norway) that the existing centralized decision-making process of wage determination would be threatened by the new increase in shopfloor decision-making. Consequently, although the unions support the movement in principle, they have adopted a much more passive and defensive role at the firm level than is commonly recognized. This has allowed management to play the dominant role in the articulation of shopfloor participation. Still, there is no doubt that Scandinavian management has been constrained by anticipated reactions from the unions, the social democratic parties and the workers to an extent that has no counterpart in Japan.[1]

It was not until the late 1970s that some Japanese Socialist party and union theoreticians began seriously to consider *jishu kanri* (workers' self-management) as a new route to increased democratization and socialism (see Hori 1977, pp. 10–15). They see this decentralized approach as an alternative to the centralized Soviet model, advocated by many extreme leftist members of the Socialist party, and as a means to rejuvenate a shattered Socialist party. The popular socialist leader Asukata Ichio, chairman of the Socialist Party, is particularly attracted to the Yugoslav model.

The Chinese and Yugoslav Cases: Some Comparisons

In fact, the nature of Japanese controlled participation has a number of similarities with the socialist model. The most widely studied socialist case is that of Yugoslavia, with the practice of "self-managing socialism" (e.g., Hunnius 1973). This system calls for the gradual introduction of direct management of both politics and the economy by the workers, a radical solution which, of course, has little in common with what Japanese managers have in mind. But the central building blocks thus far set in place in Yugoslavia are the "basic organizations of associated labor," which contain from six to several hundred workers each. Within a carefully defined framework of rules each unit is supposed to hold its own meetings, decide what work is to be carried out and how, as well as decide the distribution of rewards. Members of the League of Communists carefully guide the proceedings at all levels to insure the achievement of designated goals. As in Japan, despite the controls from above, workers do participate in decisions affecting their workshop, and control by peers is more likely in Yugoslavia than in Western nations such as Italy and the United States (Tannenbaum et al. 1974, p. 210). The range of decisions made by workers, however, is much wider in Yugoslavia than in Japan. Yet although the range of decisions is wider, the results achieved are not necessarily superior. Notwithstanding the extensive controls built into the Yugoslav innovation, enormous losses of productivity are said to occur just as a result of endless meetings. Poorly motivated workers continue to plague the operation of the economy (Browne 1975). To be sure a labor force characterized by low levels of education and limited industrial experience further limits the effectiveness of workers' self-management. Whatever the reason, the structure of control exercised by Japanese management appears far more effective than the controls built into the Yugoslav experiment. The

1. I am indebted to Professor Sigvard Rubenowitz for the opportunity to meet with his research staff at the Department of Applied Psychology of the University of Göteborg. We had numerous discussions in the summer of 1978 concerning similarities and differences between Swedish and Japanese modes of worker participation.

ability to reconcile the power and control of superiors with voluntaristic participation by subordinates is, after all, at best a most delicate matter—and Japanese managers seem very good at it. Perhaps a cultural inheritance of collective organization explains Japanese success here.

There is another difference between the Japanese system and the socialist model as represented by Yugoslavia, which may explain the seemingly different results. The Japanese manager, despite some occasional claims to the contrary, is constitutionally unable to take the broader interests of consumers and society at large into consideration unless pressured by the government. Such pressure has occurred quite rarely in postwar Japan, where until recently it seemed to many that the interests of the society were enhanced by letting management pursue its corporate goals. Practically speaking, it is difficult to take into account the interests of society at large and consumers because the participants in the whole range of worker-participation and labor-management consultation activities are company employees (Shirai 1975, pp. 70–77). In contrast, Yugoslav enterprises are public institutions. The League of Communists, the trade unions, the local commune, the banks and the territorially-based industrial associations all operate to exercise powerful social controls on the enterprise. These social controls, though somewhat curbed in recent years, insure that society's interests—as perceived and interpreted by the party—are taken into consideration (Hunnius 1973, pp. 286–91; Jenkins 1973, p. 98). This system of social control means that workers see less direct payoff for advancing their own short-run interests through positive cooperation with self-managing socialism. There is indeed evidence that persistent attitudes of "excessive self-interest" at the expense of wider community interests are quite prevalent (Hunnius 1973, p. 309). This being so it would in all likelihood be reflected in lesser rates of productivity increases than would otherwise be the case where worker motivation is a factor.

We might also note that it is in this area of taking the wider interests of society into consideration that the Japanese model diverges most sharply from the Maoist organizational model. The highly publicized charter of the Anshan Iron and Steel Company, promulgated in the early 1960s, lays down the fundamental principles for running Chinese socialist enterprises as follows:

> keep politics firmly in command; strengthen Party leadership, launch vigorous mass movements; institute the system of cadre participation in productive labour and worker participation in management, reform irrational and outdated rules and regulations, and close cooperation among workers, cadres and technicians; and go full steam ahead with technical innovations and the technical revolution. (Peking Review 1976, p. 9)

Yet, apart from keeping politics in command, it is also clear from this statement that there are a number of interesting similarities between the Maoist organizational style and the Japanese approaches outlined above. For more explicit comparisons, we reproduce Whyte's (1973, p. 157) comparison of Western and Maoist ideal organizational types (see Table 27). Our previous discussions suggest that the Japanese score closer to the Maoists than to the Western type on

TABLE 27
Contrasting Organizational Styles in China and the West[a]

Western Conceptions	Maoist Conceptions
	Contrasts	

Western Conceptions	Maoist Conceptions
1. Use criteria of technical competence in personnel allocation	1. Use both political purity and technical competence
2. Promote organizational autonomy	2. Politics takes command, and openness to outside political demands
3. Legal-rational authority	3. Mass line participative-charismatic authority
4. Informal social groups unavoidably occur	4. Informal groups can and should be fully co-opted
5. Differentiated reward to office and performance encouraged	5. Differentiated reward to office and performance deemphasized
6. Varied compliance strategies needed, depending on the organization	6. Normative and social compliance should play the main role everywhere
7. Formalistic impersonality	7. Comradeship
8. Unemotionality	8. Political zeal encouraged
9. Partial inclusion and limited contractual obligations of office-holders	9. Near total inclusion and theoretically unlimited obligations
10. Job security encouraged	10. Job security not valued, and career orientations not encouraged
11. Calculability through rules and established procedures	11. Flexibility and rapid change valued, rules and procedures looked on with suspicion
12. Unity of command and strict hierarchy of communications	12. Collective leadership and flexible consultation

Similarities	
1. Organizations have specific goals	1. Same
2. Organizations utilize a hierarchy of specialized offices	2. Same
3. Authority and rewards greater at the top of an organization	3. Same, although efforts to deemphasize
4. Universalistic hiring and promotion criteria	4. Same, although criteria differ
5. Files, rules, and written communications regulate organizational life	5. Same, although not always viewed positively
6. Offices separated from office-holders	6. Same

[a] Reproduced from Martin Whyte, "Bureaucracy and modernization in China: The Maoist critique," *American Sociological Review* 38: 149–63.

many of these conceptions. The major discrepancies appear in the emphasis on organizational autonomy (number 2) promoted by the Japanese in contrast to the Chinese, and the Japanese firm's emphasis on job security and career orientations (number 10), which the Chinese disdain (at least in theory).

What explains the surprising similarities in organizational style between Japan, a highly industrialized nation, and China, still in the early stages of industrialization? Several possible explanations come to mind. The first is that one of the two nations is studying the other's experiences and learning from them. An examination of the Japanese managerial literature suggests that it is not the Japanese who are studying the Chinese, nor does it appear that the Chinese have been paying particular attention to Japanese personnel methods. One possible variant of this diffusion thesis is that during World War II the Chinese were exposed to Japanese managerial methods in China and absorbed them. It is suggestive that many of the key management models spread from the Northeast (Manchuria) to other parts of China in the 1950s. It is in Manchuria, especially in large firms, that most plants were exposed to Japanese influence (e.g., Anshan Iron and Steel Company). Most large plants there were controlled and run by Japanese managers and engineers. Moreover the Japanese stayed on in key roles until as late as 1953 in some cases (Office of the Prime Minister 1956, pp. 245, 262, 298–99). Yet whatever the impact of the Japanese it should be kept in mind that they would have been inculcating prewar Japanese patterns; such patterns were a good deal more authoritarian and less oriented towards participation than the postwar patterns. The possibility that this channel of influence was important represents a provocative hypothesis, but unfortunately no current research results are available which allow for a disposition of the thesis.[2]

A second explanation is that the two nations, as late developers, share the common need of late developers to mobilize their population on behalf of political goals. This explanation does seem to have some potential in explaining twentieth-century revolutionary movements, such as that of China, which base their legitimacy on mass support. The explanation, however, hardly fits the pre-World War II Japanese experience. The late-developer hypothesis cannot be stretched to cover two such diverse historical experiences as those of Japan and China, in this regard at least.

A third explanation sees common organizational outcomes as a result of common cultural heritages (see Brugger 1976). The rapid spread of QC circles to South Korea and Taiwan is suggestive in this regard. Ronald Dore (1973, pp. 401–2) makes the following rather pertinent observation:

> The modified Confucian world-view which prevailed in late nineteenth-century Japan assumed original virtue rather than original sin. Confucianists in positions of authority—whether in Tokugawa samurai bureaucracies, in Japanese nineteenth-century railway workshops, or in modern Peking party offices—have been rather less predisposed than their Western counterparts to see their subordinates as donkeys responsive to sticks and carrots, and more disposed to see them as human beings responsive to moral agents.

Perhaps the clearest indication of this disposition in Japanese firms is the reliance on a succession of publicly announced goals, policies, annual objectives, programs, and slogans designed to mobilize worker activity on behalf of the company. For example, in the evolution of personnel management at Toyota Auto Body each new program (e.g., workshop university, QC circles) is inaugurated with great fanfare and a series of slogans. In the case of QC-circle activities, each of the four periods into which the company divides QC-circle development had its own slogan: "Please everybody gather," "Let's try to-

2. This analysis draws heavily on the observations of Thomas Rawski.

gether," "Let's study harder," and "To be a powerful QC circle." In every new activity undertaken by the company the slogan writers are busy at work. The president of the company commonly plays the key ritual role of announcing goals, slogans, and policies. The successive attempts to revitalize worker participation are also characteristic of the Chinese efforts. As Whyte (1974, p. 213) notes, campaigns recur "precisely because their efforts tend to wear off in time" (see also Andors 1971 and Skinner and Winckler 1969).

Finally, we ought not to overdo the extent of these similarities. In this post-Mao era the new Chinese leaders are charging that in preceding years production goals were continually sacrificed to political ends. This simply has not been the case in Japan. Moreover, although many Western observers see a renewed Chinese interest in raising production in the future, all signs now point to a downplaying of the participatory approach under the new leadership.

Organizational Control and Coordination

A third feature of the job-redesign policies present at Toyota Auto Body involves the extensive emphasis on the responsibility of small work units. This theme appears in the Western job-redesign literature as well, though it does not appear to be as central to U.S. efforts as in the case of Japan and Scandinavia. The emphasis on responsibility of small work units is hardly novel to Japanese job-redesign efforts but is rather a continuing feature of Japanese work organization. It includes a strong implicit, if not explicit, focus on the stimulation of competition among small-group units. The operation of the QC circles discussed previously amply demonstrates the existence of these practices. Historically the stimulation of small-group competition in order to coerce workers to perform according to management desires has had an important place in the arsenal of management techniques. Tekiji Kobayashi's classic proletarian novelette *Kani Kosen* (The Cannery Boat), written in 1927, is one of the most graphic literary descriptions of exploitative aspects of this technique (Motofuji 1973, p. 34). Present-day practices are a far cry from the openly coercive prodding of competition that was all too common in the pre-World War II period. Since the current management ideology and practice calls for obtaining worker consent for management policies, the emphasis is on a voluntaristic competition. No doubt this is more effective than the coercive methods of the past, at least when a high level of worker skill is required. Yet it is clear that a coercive element remains even in the contemporary approach, as seen in the fact that QC circles are often established on orders from top management and with the requirement that all employees participate. Moreover, socialist and labor union militants emphasize that Japanese management uses worker self-management primarily to rationalize the firm and raise production (Hori 1977, p. 14).

Whatever success the Japanese have had with QC circles, zero defect and the like is not explained simply by their ability to apply statistical methods to production. These various practices are built on the submerged portion of the iceberg reflecting traditional Japanese human relations. The ability to integrate hierarchy with the traditional small-group collective organization separates the

Japanese experience with job redesign from the more technological character of the movement in the United States. Emphasizing small-groupism, to the extent that it is accepted by workers, brings the weight of informal ties to the commitment-building process, thereby adding affective and normative pressures to the instrumental company ties (see Rohlen 1975, p. 188).

This leads us to a consideration of hierarchy. Job redesign and participatory management require decentralization; this is true by definition and certainly characterizes the Japanese experience. Yet decentralization at Toyota Auto Body has been accompanied, if anything, by an increase in the authority and role of the foreman. There certainly has been no diminution of foreman authority.

Yet the Western literature on the subject is full of suggestions of the "withering away of the role of the foreman" as workers come to take up the full range of decision making affecting their work lives. This must be understood in the broader context of the attack on bureaucracy and the particular evil identified as hierarchy in the United States. Indeed the very same people who believe that job mobility must increase in the modern organization of the future are also those who would maintain that hierarchy in organizations is doomed (e.g., Bennis and Slater 1968). They reason that hierarchy in bureaucracy is inconsistent with the "turbulent environment" that characterizes advanced societies and the increased importance attached to democratic principles. The decline of hierarchy is also a major theme of those who see the Chinese model as the wave of the future—even as the Chinese leaders now move to modify their approach. Students of Japan also argue that as Japanese organizations move toward a more participatory mode of decision making, hierarchy will decline and worker morale will improve (Azumi and McMillan 1976, pp. 225–26).

It is one thing to argue that there is variation in the power and privilege associated with hierarchy across organizations and societies, but it is quite another to demonstrate that hierarchy is doomed or rapidly declining (Tannenbaum et al. 1974). The prophets of industrial democratization are on extremely shaky empirical and theoretical grounds, as Charles Perrow (1972) among others has demonstrated. An examination of the literature on complex organizations suggests in fact that hierarchy and decentralization may be joined together to meet certain organizational contingencies. One organizational response to increased internal and external complexity is to choose "tall hierarchies" and decentralized decision making (see Chandler 1962; Blau 1968; Blau and Schoenherr 1971; Child 1972). The need to reduce operating overhead by eliminating supervisory levels provides one such incentive. This is the response of some U.S. auto companies to having to scale down their cars and accept the lowered profit margins associated with the downsizing. Job redesign constitutes a mode of decentralization whereby workers assume greater responsibility for their work behavior, thereby reducing some supervisory overhead costs. This does not mean that hierarchy or the supervisory authority that persists will be diminished; indeed it may be strengthened. Hierarchical control implies a source of authority located at the top of the organization, but is not inconsistent with decentralization (Child 1972, p. 174). In short there is no strong basis for predicting that were job-redesign efforts successful in the United States, they would involve substantial reduction of foreman authority. Of course, we can build such a reduction of foreman authority into our definition of job redesign, but then we are dealing with tautology.

Japan's experience here is enlightening, and Toyota Auto Body's practices are not particularly unique in this respect. If it can be demonstrated that foreman authority is not diminished as job-redesign efforts are institutionalized in an advanced industrial society such as Japan, it becomes difficult to take seriously the argument that hierarchy is inevitably slated to disappear.

Japanese managers see nothing inconsistent in the continuation of hierarchical principles of organization as they develop participation. The situation at Toyota Auto Body is rather clear-cut in this regard. Hierarchy is not diminished by the various developments we have described. It has been shown how the QC-circle activity is very carefully orchestrated, and operates within the boundaries designated by management; it fits into the existing structure of line authority. The chief of the personnel section makes it clear that he is in charge of the job-redesign plan, though it is done in consultation with the heads of other departments. The role and authority of the foreman in this area involve:

1. The enforcement of job rotation within teams.
2. The operationalization of job-redesign plans received from his superiors into workable plans at the respective workshop levels.
3. The fair evaluation of worker performance under these plans in terms of what the workers can do and what they have actually done.
4. The provision of education and training for subordinates.

Workers do not select their foremen in any formal sense. Moreover the foreman role has probably been strengthened, as discussed in the previous chapter. Management has sought to upgrade foreman leadership abilities; this was central to its whole reorganization plan. Management's idea was that by strengthening the role of the foreman through shifting many functions previously carried out in the personnel department to the shop level, they would be able to increase worker participation. This is because the foreman can more effectively absorb the ideas of subordinates than can distant functionaries. In short, there appears to be no conflict between increasing worker participation and the strengthening of the foreman role. The Japanese brand of worker participation clearly relies on principles of hierarchical control.

Interestingly, when the Toyota Auto Body managers were asked what work-related and personnel policy-related problems are caused by decentralization, they did not mention either growing worker power or threats to hierarchical control through a diminution of foreman authority. Their concern was with hierarchical control, but at the level of departments—exactly what we might expect, based on the classic studies of business organizations (see Chandler 1962). The head of the management planning office explained:

> If the chief of each department had complete freedom to make policy then management of the whole organization would collapse. If, for example, as sometimes happens, department heads emphasize a different aspect of individual guidance, it

creates a big problem for the organization as a whole. To combat this we have adopted several measures:

1. The personnel department collects data by department and feeds the information back to each department so that each knows what the others are doing.
2. Every month meetings are held between the personnel department and department heads and section heads. In these meetings the personnel section representatives raise issues and try to smooth out differences.
3. Four times a year campaigns are initiated company-wide to deal with issues of concern to all. Thus in one recent campaign the goal was to have a company-wide assessment of educational training. The results of these campaigns are then fed back to each department so that they can work to bring themselves into line if necessary.

In summary, the company tries to deal with the classic problems of organizational control and coordination stemming from ongoing decentralization. These problems are sources of continued difficulty, but they are problems with at least partial solutions—solutions which involve development of new modes for coordination and hierarchical control. This is not to say that decentralization cannot lead to a reduction of hierarchy. In Sweden and especially Norway, the early movement for job redesign stressed the absorption of the foreman role by autonomous groups. More recently, the trend is to recognize the necessity of the foreman and emphasize the transformation of the foreman role to that of long-range planner and coordinator. Similar developments seem to be taking place in Japan.

The "Profit Motive"

The fourth characteristic of participatory management at Toyota Auto Body is its disdain for engaging in direct worker participation in profits. Central to the ideology of the job-enlargement movement in the U.S. is the view that direct worker participation in profits is necessary if workers are going to avoid believing that "participatory management is merely a refined Tayloristic technique for improving productivity at their expense" (HEW Task Force 1972, p. 105). Profit sharing is the solution proposed by the HEW report in order to avoid having workers believe they have been manipulated into raising productivity for the employer's benefit. Moreover it is emphasized that profit sharing must be tied to the productivity of the individual worker or to that of his or her small group as opposed to the profitability of the entire firm. The rationale here is that workers must be able to relate their efforts to raise productivity to specific rewards. The HEW report also urges that the return on increased worker productivity must be immediate. Annual profit-sharing plans are inadequate, because the reward may be too far in the future to affect worker or group performance. Finally, the profit-sharing arrangements must be contractual to avoid workers seeing them as paternalistic or capable of being arbitrarily rescinded by management.

Although Toyota Auto Body officials pay great attention to measuring productivity increases at the individual and small-group levels, we have seen from our examination of the wage system that it is only loosely tied to productivity increases (the semiannual bonuses constitute a partial exception).[3] Nor is this approach unusual for large Japanese firms. If we accept that Japanese managers have had as much or more success in motivating the work force as their American counterparts, how are we to explain this discrepancy? Workers believe that their activities in raising productivity through participation in QC circles and the like do lead to company growth, and that this should be reflected in increased wages. There is no attempt, however, to measure these relationships. This relaxed approach makes sense in the context of the delayed-reward system built into arrangements for career advancement. Where probability of job changing is low; delayed gratification becomes much more acceptable policy from the viewpoint of both employers and employees.

The HEW recommendation on profit sharing reads like a stereotyped Skinnerian model of resurrected economic man. Inherent in the presentation is the view that instant reward is necessary to reinforce desirable behavior, lest it be extinguished. Perhaps in the context of a higher rate of job changing and little management commitment to career planning for blue-collar workers, this model does make sense. Yet it seems to be based on a perception of workers as narrowly self-interested automatons to be used by management as it sees fit. The Japanese approach highlights an alternative which permits the elaboration of some very different kinds of behavioral models. The alternative model assumes a conception of the worker as having socio-psychological needs which, if nurtured, will yield economic returns to the firm.

Career Enlargement

The most distinguishing feature of the Toyota Auto Body approach to job redesign lies in the company's emphasis on career enlargement rather than job enlargement. Their achievements are particularly impressive in that they occur in an industry notorious for its early occupational ceiling and preponderance of routine semiskilled work. Would not the potential to pursue such policies be much higher in industries that already have a good deal of variety built into the technological constraints?

The American approach, as summarized in documents such as the HEW report, is focused on the narrow concept of job enlargement and job enrichment. Toyota Auto Body, however, operates from the assumption of long-term employee commitment (even if not in fact always true). They seek to operationalize policies based on career enlargement. This involves attention to individual blue-collar aspirations, job progressions carefully coordinated with heavy investment in educational and training inputs, and policies designed to maximize the utilization of worker knowledge and talents in designing jobs and raising productivity.

3. Sixty-five percent of all Japanese companies listed on the national stock exchanges report some sort of employee stock-ownership program in 1974. However this accounted for only 0.59 to the total volume of stock issued by the listed companies, and only 1.8 percent of the total amount of stock held by Japanese private investors. In short, employee stock-ownership programs do not constitute a significant portion of private investors, nor does employee stock-ownership appear to be a major employer strategy for mobilizing worker identification with the goals of the firm (Zenkoku Shōken Torihikijo 1975, p. 17).

The company has increasingly drawn back from the policy of relying on university-trained technical engineers to implement proposals for changes in work and production organization. Again Toyota Auto Body practices appear not as unique innovations of recent vintage but rather as characteristic Japanese practices. Rohlen (1975, p. 207) observes, for example, that Japanese work groups tend to be granted a great deal of autonomy within the company and that experts are not expected to solve ongoing operational problems. This would be viewed as outside interference, leading to an undermining of group morale and leadership.

The reliance on segregated units to initiate and execute innovations is the commonplace American organizational solution, and it fails to efficiently utilize the talents and training of ordinary workers. Victor Thompson (1965, pp. 1–20) refers to this situation as the "overspecification of resources whereby jobs end up requiring only a small part of the worker's training and knowledge."

Toyota Auto Body managers have instituted practices designed to maximize the blue-collar workers' opportunities for skill development and for contribution to productivity increase. One is reminded of the oft-mentioned observation of Japanese managers: "American managers are much better at performing managerial functions than the Japanese but Japanese production workers perform much better than U.S. workers." Generally speaking it may be said that fairly extensive educational opportunities are open to the roughly 16 percent of the U.S. blue-collar autoworkers who may be characterized as skilled tradesmen. The remaining 84 percent of blue-collar autoworkers who are overwhelmingly operatives benefit, however, from only the most rudimentary on-the-job training (Grinker et al. 1970). They are expected to look out for their own interests or trust in union regulations, especially seniority, which guarantee job rights and insure some degree of wage progression with increased length of service (see Northrup et al. 1975, p. 23).

A different way to examine these arrangements is to describe the forms and scope of training programs for acquiring higher-level skills open to American blue-collar workers. In the case of General Motors two forms of training are open for hourly-rated production employees to acquire skills. They are the formal apprenticeship program and the employee-in-training (EIT) program. EIT primarily involves on-the-job training and the taking of specified courses outside the company, which the company pays for at the straight hourly rate the employee is currently receiving. This program is particularly suitable for older married employees. In addition the company runs a formal apprenticeship program (in conjunction with the UAW) which involves considerably more schooling and is particularly suited for younger workers. Of the 400,000 hourly-rated employees there are roughly 12,000 enrolled in EIT and 5,500 in the apprenticeship program, a total of 4.4 percent of all hourly-rated employees. Moreover General Motors undoubtedly invests more in this training function than do its American competitors. It is to the bulk of unskilled operatives, left for the most part untouched by the formal training efforts of U.S. auto employers, that Toyota Auto Body managers have sought to expand educational opportunities. We have shown in the preceding chapter that Toyota Auto Body policies on career enlargement represent fairly standard policies in large Japanese firms.

The impact of the rapid economic growth of the automobile industry on the development of career enlargement policies deserves some elaboration. It is quite clear that in Japan the automobile industry has been a growth industry for the past twenty years. The producers exploited an almost virgin domestic market and rapidly expanded exports. This provided ample organizational opportunities and resources for worker upgrading; talented workers knew that they would be required to spend only a few years on the assembly lines. The normal blue-collar worker could expect promotion to subforeman before the age of thirty, and even promotion to foreman was a realistic expectation for normally qualified workers (see Osako 1973, pp. 150–51, 154). Heavy educational investment by the company could be recaptured because the vacancies being created required increased skills. In the United States, however, the automobile industry has been a cyclical industry over the last twenty years. Employment in the industry has risen and fallen with fluctuations in consumer demand. If we examine the postwar period, employment in the U.S. auto industry (motor vehicles and equipment) in 1971 stood at 842,100, just slightly above the total of 833,300 in 1951 (with about 80 percent classified as blue-collar workers). In the twenty years from 1951 to 1971, total annual employment in the industry increased twelve times over the previous year and declined eight times (U.S. Department of Labor 1973, p. 268). By contrast, employment in the Japanese automobile and parts-manufacturing industry rose almost steadily from 101,000 in 1951 to 617,062 in 1972 (Ueno and Muto 1974; Office of the Prime Minister 1973a, pp. 8–9). The aggregate data, of course, do not necessarily mean that all firms are growing; indeed many firms either merged or went out of business. Yet for the many Japanese firms in which the aggregate data do reflect the company experience it is clear that planning for manpower development must have been greatly facilitated by these growth rates. In contrast, the U.S. situation has been one in which the opportunities for worker upgrading and career planning have been sharply constrained by the lack of growth in organizational employment. Employers have not been able to anticipate vacancies to insure that educational investment will be recaptured.

This analysis has important implications for industrial sociology and, more generally, for the sociology of complex organizations. In recent years Western sociologists have devoted an enormous amount of scholarly attention to the character of technology in their interpretation of work behavior (e.g., Blauner 1964; Woodward 1970; Perrow 1970). In some versions the degree of uncertainty in an organizational task imposed by technology is viewed as critical (Crozier 1964; Thompson 1967). Rates of growth of an industry or firm have not been given their due consideration. A major reason for this bias is that analysis of work organizations, like most sociological research, relies primarily on cross-sectional data. Institutional variables, such as technology and the organization's relation to the environment (e.g., location, public policy, and product market), can easily be measured at one point in time (see Northrup et al. 1974). The research of William Form (1976) demonstrates some of the problems with this approach; using just four national cases surveyed at one point in time to construct a measure of the technological complexity of automobile production, he proceeds to make broad generalizations concerning the impact of the industrialization process on work and non-work behavior. By contrast, inclusion of rates of growth as an independent variable requires more dynamic models of work behavior than have heretofore been developed.[4]

In this light it would be interesting to compare rapidly growing industries in Japan and the United States, such as the basic computer industry, to see whether the options for career development are exercised equally by managements in both industries. A cursory examination of IBM personnel policies indicates that great importance is attached to avoiding layoffs whenever possible, high investment in employee education, early exploration and development of job-enrichment programs, emphasis on respecting individual dignity, and utilization of behavioral science approaches (Foy 1975). Although it remains to be seen just how similar these programs are to Japanese arrangements, the initial similarities are striking. One logical implication of the above line of reasoning is that the slowdown in the rate of growth of Japanese industry may make it exceedingly difficult for Japanese industry to maintain career-development policies. The constraints imposed by a slowdown were discussed at the conclusion of Chapter IV. Most importantly, the reduction in the rate of creation of new vacancies and an aging labor force will put severe pressures on existing management policies. With respect to the Japanese automobile industry, a government advisory organ to the Ministry of International Trade and Industry estimated in 1976 that the average annual production increase will be only 2.8 percent in the period 1974–85. This compares to the spectacular average annual growth rate of 17.4 percent recorded in the period 1965–73. The upshot of these projections is that the European and American pattern of sales rising when the economy is strong and falling when it fares poorly is expected to take root in Japan within the next ten years. The implications of this shift for employment and personnel administration policies should be profound.

Additional Participatory Practices

The aforementioned arrangements do not exhaust the forms of participatory management currently operative at Toyota Auto Body. There is also a production conference, held once a month, at which management and union officials discuss in advance how to achieve the company's monthly production plans. Workshop consultation meetings (*shokuba kondankai*) are then held at which management and union representatives in each workshop discuss how to achieve those parts of the goals agreed on in the production conference that apply to them.

These arrangements are part of the broad labor-management consultation systems (*rōshi kyōgisei*) that have evolved in postwar Japan. They derived orig-

4. To be sure those who have emphasized the impact of different kinds of technologies have often pointed out the incompleteness of their analysis. Blauner (1964, p. 9) writes, for example, "Whereas technology sets limits on the organization of work, it does not fully determine it, since a number of different organizations of the work process may be possible in the same technological system." Yet these caveats came to be ignored in subsequent scholarship. One scholar who has explicitly focused on the causal implications of rate of organizational growth is Arthur Stinchcombe (1974, pp. 123–50).

inally from an amalgam of practices including the prewar factory committees, the Whitley Committee in Great Britain, and the *Betriebsrat* in Germany. They also drew strength from post-World War II conditions in which management took the initiative in responding to the aggressive character of the labor movement by seeking to prevent stress and increase productivity. A third phase developed between 1955 and 1965, in which management began to make extensive use of human relations techniques stressing the importance of communication. This was an attempt to harmonize workers' desires with the goals of the firm. From 1965 to the present there has been an intensification of use of more sophisticated types of management techniques grounded in the social sciences; these provide a basis for further elaborating the joint consultation systems (see Keiya 1972, pp. 247–48; Yasui 1975, pp. 2–16).[5] Unions also took the initiative in many cases in establishing joint councils. A 1972 Ministry of Labor "Survey on Labor-Management Communications" found that over 60 percent of all firms surveyed had some system of joint consultation in which employers and employees discussed management policies and plans—the larger the firm, the greater the likelihood of its having such a system. Some 90 percent of those firms employing 1,000 or more employees have joint consultation systems. In these firms the consultation generally takes place at the plant level, though both firm- and plant-level consultation may exist in the same firm. Industry-level consultation exists in such industries as shipbuilding and textiles, but generally it remains weakly developed. The subjects of joint consultation meetings, as reported in the 1972 survey, included "dealing with the running of the workshop" (92 percent of the establishments), "dealing with the workshop environment" (85 percent), and "involving management policy, programs and workshop organizations" (58 percent).

The distinction between collective bargaining and joint consultation is not sharply drawn. It is not unusual for issues that cannot be resolved through joint consultation to be taken up in the collective bargaining process (Shirai 1975, p. 275). Joint consultation does, however, provide a framework for negotiations on working conditions to be conducted on a continuous basis. The system is not seen by participants as providing the primary basis for increased worker participation in management. In the aforementioned 1972 survey only 6 percent of the unions involved reported that the objective was increased participation in running the operation (see Okamoto 1974, p. 7). Rather the focus was on improvement of communications between management and labor (29 percent), improvement of working conditions (28 percent) and stabilizing labor relations (18 percent). Subsequent surveys by the Japan Productivity Center come to the same conclusion.

Interestingly enough when Japanese managers and, to a lesser extent, unionists are pressed as to why the joint-consultation system is being advanced in Japan instead of formal labor participation in management, the answer is com-

5. In addition to these named sources the following section draws upon Okamoto (1974) and the Japan Institute of Labour (1973).

monly that the joint-consultation system already in operation is quite sufficient.[6] Yet in many of the Western European nations the major emphasis is not on job enlargement as described earlier nor on the kinds of labor-management consultation just mentioned. Rather it is on having worker or union representatives sit directly on corporate boards of directors. Labor participation in management is already legally required in some form in such countries as West Germany, Sweden, Norway and the Netherlands (Levinson 1974, p. 95). In these countries it is required by law that every corporation above a minimum size have its workers represented on its board of executives, or auditors, or equivalent machinery. Although some Japanese unionists and academics have proposed having a union representative participate as an auditor, these suggestions have not had much currency in Japan. Unions in the Domei Federation, representing the majority of workers in the private sector, until recently were interested in having representatives on boards of directors; the Textile Workers Union (Zensen Domei) has pursued this goal. However, none of these unions have strongly advocated legislative enactment, a common pattern in Western Europe. Unions in the more militant Sohyo Federation, which dominates the public sector, have tended to be opposed to worker participation on boards of directors. The Chemical Workers Union (Gōkarōren) maintains that such proposals would lead to a co-optation of labor and a sapping of union vitality. There are indications, however, that the grass roots support among Sōhyō union leaders for worker representation on boards of directors is quite strong, notwithstanding the official Sōhyō position (Hanami, Koshiro and Inagami 1977).

217

Japanese management is strongly opposed to legislating worker representation on boards of directors, with the Federation of Employers' Associations urging members to do everything possible to forestall such moves. In 1976 the Japan Committee for Economic Development (Keizai Doyukai) also announced its opposition to worker participation in management. These organizations agree only to the need for expanding the "quite effective" labor-management consultation system currently in operation. They also cite the success of small-group participatory activities such as QC-circle activities at the workshop level. With respect to the former, management concedes labor only the commitment to consult. It still retains the initiative in introducing subjects, so that questions of company productivity plans and equipment investment policies dominate much of the discussions. Yasui (1975, p. 16) notes that matters relating to the operation of the firm, production, and personnel are most often settled by company notification or explanation. It is generally only matters relating to health, safety and working conditions that are settled by binding consultation (*kyōgi kettei*).

In short, management retains its prerogative to act unilaterally but, where possible, uses the joint consultation system to elicit worker and union opinion. With regard to small-group participatory activities, we have seen that management carefully controls and guides the activities into channels which flow toward

6. For a sample of union comment see the remarks of Mr. Asano representing the Japan Automobile Workers Union (International Metalworkers Federation—Japan Council 1974, p. 23).

the achievement of basic management goals. No surprise then that management would seek to forestall more direct threats to its prerogatives through legislation.

The United States and Japan have almost entirely avoided the form of representative participation on boards of directors.[7] This reflects the absence of the powerful political role of labor as manifest in the labor parties of Western Europe. Instead management is much more firmly in control of labor-management practices, though this is modified in the case of the United States by the powerful influence of collective bargaining on workshop operations. In the case of the United States the movement for increased worker participation takes the form of calls for job redesign and job enlargement. This has the characteristics of the typical American search for solutions when confronted with social problems —that is, to look for the solution in technical virtuosity, whether it be physical hardware or organizational software. This contrasts with an approach that recognizes differing interests and makes adjustments in power relations. At the same time there is an almost utopian quality to the proposals for job redesign in the United States. The call for worker control of all shopfloor decisions relating to them has relatively little backing from organized labor. Government interest, as shown in the now defunct National Center for Productivity and the Quality of Working Life, reflected a primary concern with creating an environment for improved productivity, rather than participation per se. The major advocates of worker participation appear to be a small but vocal minority among intellectuals, selected union leaders, and occasional foundation officials. Although not to be dismissed, they hardly provide the organizational force to bring about the innovation in question. The enormous academic literature on organizations is seldom applied to worker participation and job design. In those few firms and industries in the United States in which labor has cooperated with management in trying to institute new approaches to job redesign, the efforts have been voluntary. They are designed to solve specific productivity problems rather than being programmatic responses to well-articulated demands for worker participation (Weinberg 1976, pp. 13–22). They arise from the traditional concerns with job security and company or industry survival.

In the case of Japan, despite enhanced participation at the lower levels, it may well be that management has not given up any of its prerogatives; the net result, in fact, may be a strengthening of management and the bureaucratic structures of the firm (see Yasui 1975). This is potentially the greatest paradox of worker participation in Japan. In the mid-1970s the tone of Japanese labor's pronouncements on participation in management began to shift from a concentration on democratization of the workshop to joint determination of economic policies on a national level by management and labor (Inagami 1975). The Federation of Iron and Steel Workers (Tekkorōren) has taken the lead in this area. At their 1977 convention, they called for the establishment of a "social contract" involving the creation of a consultative organ among government, labor and management to discuss economic management and wage determination. The

7. In 1975 Hitachi Shipbuilding and Engineering became the first major Japanese firm to conclude a union contract providing for union participation in management.

slowdown in economic growth, the gradual weakening of the Liberal Democratic party and the likelihood that they would be forced into a coalition government with at least one of the opposition parties no doubt served as background for these developments.

Conclusions

We may conclude by considering the implications of our findings on job redesign for the inferences developed in Chapter IV. The research at Toyota Auto Body provides a unique opportunity to "test" some of the conclusions drawn from analysis of the Detroit-Yokohama comparative study.

One observation on the analytical strategy adopted here is in order. The conventional practice is to state that case-study research is designed to develop hypotheses that can later be tested systematically through careful sampling methods, commonly in a survey research format. Those who collect case study data are usually quite defensive on this matter, rushing to point out the limitations of their research as if to defuse their critics in this age of quantification in the social sciences. The strategy adopted here is quite contrary to this convention. We are saying instead that the use of systematic sampling and survey techniques has permitted us to generate a set of propositions and their corollaries. We would like to examine the validity of these propositions and corollaries in a specific case. If our propositions fit the empirical realities of this case we will claim support for them (though of course we cannot empirically demonstrate the correctness of these propositions through the use of only one case). Similarly, if the propositions do not hold, we may conclude either that they are wrong or that the case selected is somehow unique.

The specific task is to ask what we would expect the job system of a specific company to look like if the analysis presented in Chapters III and IV were correct. We can summarize the conclusions of Chapter IV as they apply to a typical Japanese factory job system with the following two propositions and their corollaries.

I. The social organization of a Japanese firm is characterized by a lack of sharp jurisdictional definition of job duties.
   a. Low concern with promotion to particular jobs but existence of rough categorizations designed to locate employee progress in company.
   b. Job performance not a major determinant of wages.
   c. Extensive job rotation.
   d. Task performance perceived as a goal of work group (group production norms) rather than individual—strong work-group ties.
   e. Low commitment of employees to particular jobs.
II. The social organization of a Japanese firm is characterized by a strong internal labor market (relative to the importance of the external labor market) with employees manifesting a career commitment to the company.
   a. Low quit rate.
   b. Strong company training programs designed to sustain and adapt worker skills throughout employment with company.

c. Minimal concern of employees with job security.

d. Selective recruitment of new employees.

e. Job assignments primarily a management prerogative with low union involvement.

Parenthetically, these propositions and their corollaries represent ideal conditions for the introduction of extensive job-redesign programs. Indeed, were such characteristics as extensive job rotation already present, we would be right to conclude that many of the goals of the job-redesign movement as articulated in the United States have already been achieved in Japanese firms.

We turn now to our first proposition, that the social organization of the Japanese firm is characterized by a lack of sharp jurisdictional definition of job duties. It is apparent that over the last ten years Toyota Auto Body has moved strongly into the area of job-evaluation systems and shifted the wage system to give greater weight to job rankings. This transition became quite common in major Japanese firms as the slogan "ability first" took hold. Clearly this sharpened the jurisdictional boundaries between jobs. Yet on balance one cannot help but be impressed that, by American standards, job boundaries are grouped in extremely broad categories for purposes of wage remuneration. Although the job wage accounts for 40 percent of the total wage (excluding bonuses), we have seen that the bulk of production employees are grouped in only two job grades. Although we report no data on the degree of employee concern for promotion, we can document the existence of an extremely rough categorization of employees by job and ability grades. These grades are designed to locate employee progress in the company (corollary a). In short, the payoffs are not for the detailed job classifications but for extremely broad categories. Job performance is a significant determinant of wages, contrary to corollary b, but not in the sense of providing detailed internal differentiation of jobs and job holders. We do find associated with this outcome the existence of extensive job rotation, as predicted in corollary c. Task performance does appear to be perceived as a goal of the work group rather than the individual (corollary d); the most clear-cut manifestation of this lies in QC-circle activity and the overall ability of the company to foster small-group activity and establish the small group as the locus of responsibility. We do not have direct evidence concerning the degree of employee commitment to particular jobs and therefore cannot arrive at a definitive judgment on the applicability of corollary d. Overall, Proposition I and the associated corollaries find substantial support in our examination of Toyota Auto Body. They do, however, underestimate the role of job performance as a determinant of wages.

Proposition II predicts that the social organization of the factory will be characterized by a strong internal labor market with career commitment by employees to the company. Our evidence supports this proposition with the important exception that turnover is relatively high; the company reports a loss of 50 percent of the annual cohort of new recruits after five years. This requires modification of corollary a. Turnover is generally high in the Japanese automobile industry relative to other manufacturing industries, but it is still remarkably low by American automobile industry standards. On the other hand, high turnover of new recruits may be seen as a continuation of the selection process. Since the selection process for initial entry to the labor market is never perfect, a further sorting out before the internal labor market takes over seems like a rational qualification of the dominance of internal labor markets in Japan. Viewed from a comparative perspective, this initial sorting-out process appears quite similar to Western market economies. The Japanese Ministry of Labor (1973, p. 69) reports that in France 50 percent of non-university school graduates change jobs within three years of entering the labor force, while in the United States 30 percent of high school graduates change jobs within two years. The ministry estimates that in Japan some 30 to 40 percent of high school and middle school graduates change jobs within two years and 50 percent within three years. In short, the volume of turnover seems roughly equivalent. If the internal labor market does operate differently in Japan, and we think it does, it is only after this initial period.

In the case of Toyota Auto Body, as reported above, the annual retention rate has been high and has been rising in recent years. The company has systematically pursued a policy of career enlargement. Although we are unable to report any subjective measure of career commitment by employees, the objective structure of career enlargement does appear to have been institutionalized to an unusually high degree. Closely associated with the structure of career enlargement is an intensive development and systemization of educational opportunities within the firm, reaching down to blue-collar workers. This training is not reserved for an elaborately screened elite who qualify for skilled tradesman jobs; rather it is available to all regular blue-collar workers. The amount of company investment in employee training is impressive, though it comes primarily in the form of on-the-job training and is not directly obvious (corollary b). We can report no direct subjective data on the concern workers express for job security (corollary c). However, the strong worker involvement in individual and group suggestion systems, as institutionalized through QC-circle activity, suggests that for many employees working themselves out of a job is not a major preoccupation. The rapid growth of the auto industry over the last ten years has meant that workers who demonstrated their ability did so in a relatively open opportunity structure, which allowed them to be rewarded in the firm through upgrading. The persistence of the selective recruitment which we would expect to be associated with strong internal labor markets is a bit more difficult to evaluate (corollary d). It would seem that selective recruitment has on balance been weakened. The higher proportion of new recruits with prior work experience suggests that the company, under pressure from the labor shortage, has had to lower its standards considerably. These new recruits enter the firm with work habits not necessarily suited to the personnel policies enforced by management. By contrast, new school graduates, being without work experience, are more amenable to shaping by the company. The second element in an evaluation of selective recruitment involves the shift from recruiting primarily middle school to high school graduates. This shift has been enforced by the rapid increase in the proportion of middle school graduates going on to complete high school. The companies have not eagerly sought to recruit high school graduates. They were increasingly forced to do so as a consequence of the disappearance of middle school graduates who were prepared to enter the labor force.[8] For routine blue-collar jobs one might argue that the shift to high school-educated recruits reflects on balance a lowering of recruitment standards from the perspective of existing organizational practices in large Japanese firms. This is because large Japanese firms have been accustomed to recruiting young middle school graduates whom they could train and mold to the form desired by the company.

Finally, it is clear that management determines job assignments and unions do not (corollary e). The unions do exercise some indirect influence over job assignments through their participation in the monthly production conference and the workshop consultation meetings, but this is a secondary rather than primary function of these meetings. Moreover the union has no established power base for gaining acceptance of its view in this area.

In summary, there is considerable evidence in our study for support of Proposition II and its corollaries, although again with some qualifications. The notable exception is the high rate of turnover for each annual cohort of new recruits.

In conclusion, we find substantial support for both propositions and their corollaries, although with some qualifications. Since we did not collect data on workers' subjective perceptions, we can only address some of the corollaries indirectly. As noted earlier the prediction of one case cannot confirm the inferences developed in Chapter IV, particularly when the one case was selected for its atypicality in the area of job redesign. Nevertheless, as repeatedly demonstrated throughout these last two chapters, Toyota Auto Body may be atypical in its systematic approach to job redesign, but many of the characteristics we have discussed are demonstrably present in a majority of large-scale Japanese firms. Thus we may conclude that the data presented in this chapter do provide substantial support for the inferences developed in Chapter IV.

To further summarize our discussion in this chapter it is appropriate to suggest a third proposition and associated corollaries that seem to underlie many of our findings concerning management strategies and policies.

III. Management operates with a model of human nature which stresses the perfectibility of human nature.
   a. Development of QC circles.
   b. Provision of extensive training and encourage skill acquisition.
   c. Career development programs evolve.
   d. Research findings of the social sciences acted on.

8. General Motors executives claim that the situation has been quite similar for them. The proportion of those General Motors employees in assembly plants classified as modal production workers with a high school education or more rose from 30 percent in 1950 to 67 percent in 1972. Moreover of that 67 percent 7 percent were college graduates, 10 percent had more than a high school education, and 50 percent were high school graduates. General Motors executives assert that this was not part of a general strategy, but that they simply drew from the existing labor force. The federal affirmative action guidelines have, if anything, forced the company to reconsider its selection procedures and encouraged more aggressive recruitment of non-high school graduates.

Whether it be based on Confucianist values, cultural homogeneity, rapid economic growth, or some combination thereof, the Japanese manager views his employees as having socio-psychological needs, which, if nurtured, will yield economic returns to the firm. Japanese management sees all regular male employees as resources with substantial potentialities for human growth. Because they apply these views to all regular male workers they are prepared to accept a quite egalitarian distribution of rewards and status. As a consequence, moreover, they are prepared to invest in the various strategies listed above as corollaries of the initial proposition.

It must be noted that these benevolent views of human nature were hardly characteristic of much of pre-World War II industry; nor are they necessarily dominant in small-scale industry today. A set of facilitating conditions has, however, come into being since World War II, which has allowed these evolving managerial attitudes to become dominant in large-scale firms. The most notable enabling conditions have undoubtedly been the growth of an educated managerial class, the spread of democratic ideology, the rapid growth of the economy and associated development of strong internal labor markets, and the crushing of the militant left-wing unions of the early postwar period, though not until they had brought about the diffusion of many white-collar privileges to blue-collar workers. To be sure, enlightened views on the perfectibility of man do not necessarily spring from the noblest of antecedents. Nor do they necessarily apply to female employees.

There is one analytical concept which links our study of mobility in Chapters II–IV and our study of participation and job redesign in Chapters V–VII. We have throughout been concerned with the analysis of boundaries: boundaries between organizations and job boundaries within organizations. It is the strength and permeability of these boundaries that constitute the major variables of our study. Moreover, the permeability of one boundary is inextricably linked with the permeability of the other. Our major finding is that the restricted job movement between organizations in Japan is closely associated with a strong internal labor market characterized by relaxed jurisdictional boundaries for jobs within the organization. Indeed, these boundaries are so permeable that the very concept "job" takes on a different meaning in Japan than in the United States. This permeability lends itself, in particular, to the institutionalization of many social arrangements we characterize in America as job redesign. We will have the opportunity to pursue this theme further in the next chapter, in which we consider the historical basis of employee attachment to the firm.

Our company, beloved company,
With its bright future rising.
Closing lines from the Suntory Ltd.
company song

CHAPTER VIII

THE JAPANESE WORK ETHIC

Not long ago an American journalist looking for that magic key to explain rapid economic growth in Japan was reduced, seemingly in desperation, to conclude that "the Japanese have achieved their unparalleled economic success in the postwar period by 'plain hard work.'" In the American popular media this has already replaced low wages as the purported secret behind Japanese economic success in the postwar period, though it has to share the limelight with such factors as the close cooperation between Japanese management and government. Similarly the Japanese increasingly respond to criticism of their export drives with claims that Westerners will just have to learn to work as hard as the Japanese. To claim that Japanese economic success lies in "plain hard work," however, is more a confession of ignorance than an explanation. Rather than contributing to our understanding, it systematically distorts our perception of the meaning of work, the importance of work for productivity, and the nature of labor problems in Japan. We are left with the simplistic image of regimented workers subordinating themselves to group interests for the greater glory of Mitsubishi, Mitsui, etc. Moreover the fashionable practice of using the strong Japanese work ethic as a weapon to berate American workers for their seeming loss of will to work and shoddy workmanship contributes little to our understanding. This is not to say that there is no such thing as a Japanese work ethic. It is simply a far more complicated phenomenon than commonly realized, with its roots in a set of relationships not usually recognized in the West. This has significant implications for those who would learn from the Japanese. Our task in this chapter is to explain what the Japanese work ethic means sociologically,

Arthur Stinchcombe was kind enough to read and comment on this as well as on the subsequent chapter. The citations in this chapter should make clear that my debt to him goes well beyond his comments. The author alone, however, is responsible for all conclusions presented herein.

to present with analytic clarity its various components, and to detail its socio-structural basis in Japanese organizations.

If we are to understand the potential impact of a strong work ethic, we must first accept that in a complex industrial society like Japan productivity is not determined by any single factor such as how hard workers work. Rather, productivity increases are generated by the interaction of technology and labor, guided by management, and influenced by the social structure and work organization prevailing in the given country. It is this complex interaction pattern that makes it so difficult to disentangle the contribution of the Japanese work ethic. Our discussion of the QC circles should have demonstrated this.

On the other hand we see in the United States a strong tendency among industrial engineers, economists and management to underestimate the potential of harnessing worker cooperation to raise productivity. The industrial engineers focus their attention primarily on the introduction of new technology in producing productivity gains (HEW Task Force 1972, p. 19). That they minimize the role of work commitment may reflect their vested interest in the technology explanation; it is the way they justify the existence of their own jobs. The economists' analysis of productivity increase stresses such factors as the growth of capital, technological change and innovation, and the related impact of advances in scientific and engineering knowledge. Concentrating on large-scale scientific and engineering advances, their approach is subject to many of the limitations discussed in the previous chapter. The impact of variables such as effort and motivation on output has been almost totally ignored in microeconomic theory (see Leibenstein 1976).

Many economists fall back on Japan's high rate of investment as an explanation for its high rate of economic growth. In the twenty year period 1950–70, fixed capital formation averaged well over 30 percent of the GNP, most of it being private productivity investment; for the U.S.A. the comparable investment shares stood at 17 percent. Initially this may appear to be a quite convincing explanation of Japan's rapid economic growth. We may ask, however, what lay behind this high rate of investment. First we find that personal savings constituted an especially significant source of finance for domestic investment. In the 1960s personal savings were about 20 percent of disposable income, as compared to 7 percent in the United States, 5 percent in the United Kingdom, and 10 percent in France. The explanation for this high ratio will be treated below, but certainly it constitutes one of the possible meanings of the strong Japanese work ethic, in the sense of employees displaying a marked frugality which involves working hard and maintaining conservative consumption patterns. A second factor in the high rate of investment is the high expected rate of return on capital, especially notable in the postwar period. Although a number of factors are responsible for this situation, especially the high rate of productivity increase engendered by the absorption of foreign technology, we may identify as significant the historic lag in wage increases relative to productivity increases (Ohkawa and Rosovsky 1972). There are a number of levels of explanation for this phenomenon, but we can interpret the wage lag as prima facie evidence for a work ethic that emphasized diligence and commitment to employer goals while demanding only moderate compensation in return. To be sure this wage lag also coincided historically with a labor-surplus economy and a powerful alliance of management and government. Finally, a major aspect of Japan's allegedly unusual social capability to absorb technology presumably has involved the willingness of employees to innovate, accept management's direction, and demand relatively little monetary compensation in return.

American management has also been inclined to write off worker cooperation and motivation in raising productivity. Basic to such thinking is the view that increased efficiency comes not from worker initiatives or commitment but from management guidance based on superior education and training, and from developing better technology.[1] At the root of these operating assumptions is the perceived inevitability of adversary relationships between workers and management. Workers and management are seen to have diametrically opposed interests. It is the classic low trust situation which is institutionalized in work rules, job descriptions, supervisory styles and general control systems, and informal work practices (Fox 1974). Under these circumstances management writes off worker cooperation because it is seen as either irrelevant or impossible to achieve. These are, of course, gross generalizations made in the context of broad national comparisons. If we were comparing, say, the United States and Great Britain, we might be struck by the relative flexibility of American management in these matters. Be that as it may, the HEW Task Force (1972, p. 37) reports that perhaps the most consistent complaint reported to it by U.S. workers was the failure of superiors to listen to workers who wish to propose better ways of doing their jobs. "Workers feel that their bosses demonstrate little respect for their intelligence; superiors are said to feel that the workers are incapable of thinking creatively about their jobs." This conclusion, however, exaggerates actual survey findings. Thus, in the 1972–73 Quality of Employment Survey, Quinn and Shepard (1974, p. 200) interviewed 1,496 members of the labor force using a national probability sample of dwellings. One set of questions dealt specifically with worker evaluation of supervisors. Asked whether supervisors encouraged innovative behavior on the job, 41.8 percent reported that it was very true that their supervisor encouraged those he/she supervised to develop new ways of doing things, 31.1 percent reported this was somewhat true, 16.6 percent reported that it was not too true, and 10.5 responded that it was not at all true. Yet it may also be that these survey findings simply reflect the low levels of expectation that employees have come to accept as normal (Shelly and Company 1971, p. 4).

Even when management recognizes that workers have a contribution to make to raising productivity, it regards the workers, not its own policies, as the greatest obstacle. A *Business Week* survey of conditions in some major U.S. industries in the early 1970s reported that employers overwhelmingly cited union rules and worker attitudes as a major drag on productivity. They tend to accept

1. Witness this statement by Alfred Sloan Jr., former chairman of the board of General Motors. "In the end, increased efficiency flows not so much from the increased effectiveness of workers, but primarily from more efficient management and from the investment of additional capital in labor saving devices" (Sloan 1964).

these as given constraints within the parameters of which they must operate. Consequently employers tend to dismiss worker cooperation as a strategy to raise productivity.

Worker commitment and cooperation do appear to have significant potential for raising productivity. Unlike American management, Japanese managers strongly emphasize the important contribution that hard work, worker cooperation, and commitment to the company make to increasing productivity, and specifically to achieving technological innovation. Moreover they do so not only in their public pronouncements but, as we have seen in earlier chapters, in their employment policies as well.[2] This is not to deny that Japanese managers have an ideology which may well overestimate the importance of worker motivation. Our evaluation of the contributions of the QC circles suggests that this may indeed be the case. Japanese management also clearly recognizes that management decision making and technological innovation take precedence over worker motivation as factors in raising productivity (see Marsh and Mannari 1976, p. 282). Yet the priority accorded to raising worker motivation is demonstrably high.

The Ideology of the American Work Ethic

Ironically American management's belief that the potential for worker motivation to influence productivity is small coexists with the commonplace view that Americans have traditionally had an unusually strong work ethic. Only in recent years, it is argued, has the American work ethic been weakened as a result of rising levels of affluence and union control. This is a widely shared perspective. In a national cross-sectional Harris Poll of 1,519 adults, hard-working people were seen by 87 percent of those polled as a major cause of American greatness in the past, ranking third on a list of twenty-three important contributions to American greatness. Only 78 percent, however, saw hard-working people as a key to the future greatness of America. Hard work dropped from third to sixth in the ranking (*Detroit Free Press* 1975).

Yet these views of the hard-working Americans of yesteryear rest on a romanticized image of an idealized past. It draws more upon the alleged characteristics of Yankee ingenuity and the inventive activity of a small minority of the labor force than it does upon the industrial experience of millions of new industrial workers. One major reason for the perpetuation of the view that American workers are characterized by an unusual commitment to work lies in the failure of labor historians to integrate immigrant experience with work experience in America (Gutman 1976). The American working class was continually changed as a result of the successive waves of immigrants that came to dominate much of America's industrial experience. These new workers, from both the farm and outside the national borders, hardly brought to work the commitment

---

2. Some interesting evidence for this view comes from a recent survey of the practices of foreign-owned subsidiaries in the United States. Jedel and Kujawa (1976, p. 34) conclude that Japanese-owned subsidiaries in the United States tend to place more strategic importance on employee motivation and behavior than do American firms, and are concerned with adapting traditionally successful Japanese employment practices to their U.S. operations.

and disciplined work habits so integral to the imagined American work ethic. Instead they had to learn to adapt to the new demands of the emergent industrial society. Their responses covered the full range of possibilities, including withdrawal (prior to World War I out of every 100 immigrants who entered the United States 44 went back to their country of origin), production restriction, continual job changing, self-employment, adaptation of older patterns of work and life to their new country, investment of minimal psychic energies in the work situation, and challenge through collective action. In the first quarter of the twentieth century employers became increasingly aware of enormous employee turnover and the costs associated with it. Indeed this was a major incentive for the initiation of personnel departments in American industrial firms. At Ford Motor Company's Highland Park plant, the model of progressive factory design at the time of its construction in 1910, it was discovered that 52,000 men were hired to fill 13,000 jobs in 1913. Foremen were responsible for discharging some 8,000 (Nelson 1975, pp. 149–50).

Often the new industrial workers brought behavior patterns to the factory totally at variance with management expectations. In major American cities, where much of the new industry came to be concentrated, foreign-born workers quickly became a major force. For example in 1873 four-fifths of the children in Detroit schools were of foreign parentage (Conot 1974, p. 103). The foreign-born and native-born children of foreign-born parents constituted 71 percent of male employees in the car building and repairing industry in 1907–8. These percentages were quite typical of other industries as well. An examination of the national data shows that the male foreign-born population constituted 24 percent of all males over twenty-one years old at the turn of the century, and as late as 1920 they still constituted 22 percent of the total male population over twenty-one years old (U.S. Bureau of the Census 1961, p. 65). Moreover with low levels of skill and education the bulk of the immigrants tended to be concentrated in industrial jobs.[3] Gutman (1976, p. 18) observes that the changing composition of the American labor force caused by continued infusion of new immigrant groups led to a continual recurrence of "premodern" forms of collective behavior usually associated in other nations with the early stages of industrialization. The subsequent migration of rural blacks to northern urban centers to fill the bottom-rung jobs in industry repeated the process once again. The crude methods of worker recruitment operative well into the second decade of the 1900s were hardly conducive to establishing a good match between workers and jobs (Nelson 1975, pp. 79–85).

If to this interweaving of labor, immigration and migration history we add the characteristic boom-and-bust economic cycles that marked much of Ameri-

3. For the prior occupations of immigrants by year of entry see the U.S. Bureau of the Census (1961, p. 60). In every decade from 1841 to 1930 laborers constituted the largest category among those immigrants reporting an occupation (Eckler and Zlotnick 1949, p. 96). Moreover, the proportion of skilled workers is probably overstated. To increase the probability of being accepted, immigrants often inflated their skills. To paraphrase Irving Howe about one stream of immigration, how many Jewish tailors could there have been?

can industrialization, it is indeed difficult to see the basis on which workers could consistently develop a strong commitment to their work. One can only conclude that the existence of an ingrained work ethic among American workers is at best problematic, and in all probability could not have existed under the kinds of conditions described above.

One reason we have so much difficulty accepting this conclusion is that we confuse the concept of a commitment to work with a commitment to economic betterment. It seems reasonable to conclude that the Europeans who migrated to the United States did not constitute a random sample of the European labor force, but were a self-selected population. The basis for this selection may indeed have been a high responsiveness to economic incentives and a willingness to experience deprivation in search of a better life (see Rosenberg 1972, p. 33). Yet a consequence of this sensitivity may well have been a very rapid recognition that factory employment constituted a dead end. High rates of labor turnover are not at all inconsistent with a desire for economic betterment, but they are inconsistent with commitment to work in a particular setting. It was not until the 1920s that employers came to recognize that ethnic succession in the factories was only one aspect of the more general problem of high rates of turnover (Nelson 1975, pp. 85–86).

It has always been difficult to persuade white native males to take those jobs they believe suitable only for immigrants, blacks, women, and children. One way to think about the work ethic in historical perspective is that the range of unacceptable jobs has steadily grown as labor force participants have raised their expectations about what constitutes a respectable job. Instead of thinking of this as a decline in the work ethic, however, we might think of it as a democratization of expectations.

The Ideology of the Japanese Work Ethic

Although a large influx of immigrants was not characteristic of the formation of the Japanese labor force, it is undoubtedly true that the image of the dedicated, hard-working Japanese employee also does a grave injustice to the historical experience of Japanese labor. Because of the relatively homogenous background of Japanese workers, the rulers of Japan have been able systematically to cultivate the image of the hard-working Japanese employee, from well before industrialization began and throughout the industrialization process itself. In preindustrial agrarian Japan the official ideology stressed that the welfare of the family depended on the diligent efforts of the family head, and a decline in family fortunes was viewed as resulting from abandonment of these efforts. In the industrial period the position taken by the Kyōchōkai (Labor Management Cooperative Society) in the interwar period was not atypical. The government-funded society, in addition to preaching familistic paternalism by industry and containing a special section on scientific management (see Chapter IV), also advocated a particular view of work. These views were often utilized by Japanese business spokesmen in the 1920s and 1930s. The society downplayed the material rewards associated with work as an incentive to individual effort, and instead stressed an ethic of work performance in which work was an end in itself. Work made possible human progress and was consequently an important social virtue (Marshall 1967, p. 97). To this day the at least partial success that Japanese management and the state have had in instilling this ideology into the population may be seen in the responses individuals give in describing traits most characteristic of the Japanese. In the national character surveys conducted at five-year intervals, respondents have consistently selected "diligent" as the trait that most describes the Japanese people. Indeed, perhaps as a response to postwar economic success, the proportion choosing "diligent" has risen in each survey from 55 percent in 1953 to 66 percent in 1973. Generally the higher the age, educational and occupational status, the higher the proportion choosing "diligent" (Institute for Statistical Mathematics 1975, pp. 162–64).

The cultivation of an image of diligent workers and its partial acceptance, however, does not begin to capture the full historical experience. The treatment of the evolution of the permanent employment practice in Chapter I should point up the incompleteness of such understanding. In particular the element of sheer coercion involved in early Japanese industrialization has hardly been accorded proper recognition. It has also been proposed that the formation of a permanently employed industrial labor force was far slower than commonly thought. Throughout industry high rates of turnover in the labor force are reported well into the 1920s and early 1930s (Taira 1962). This does not fit our image of the diligent Japanese worker.

Work and Leisure

We turn now to an examination of the experience of contemporary Japanese employees. Even for today's worker firm evidence is at best elusive, but we will try to piece together the relevant information. One way to proceed is to examine the relation between work and leisure. Although actual working hours are declining in Japan, the average Japanese employee continues to work more hours than his American counterpart. Those who are critical of the international and domestic consequences of Japan's high rate of economic growth are apt to interpret the high average number of hours or days worked in terms of a compulsive need to work—a nation of "workaholics" some would say. Those inclined to view the same data more favorably refer to a powerful work ethic. In 1973 the number of hours worked per week in manufacturing, including holidays, was 42 in Japan and 38.3 in both the United States and West Germany (Japan Productivity Center 1975, p. 170).[4] Of the three countries, however, Japan showed the steepest decline in hours worked over the last decade in both absolute and percentage terms.[5] The five-day week, though slowly spreading in Japan, is still not experienced by most employees on a regular basis. Okamoto (1971, p. 6) estimated that in 1970 there were about seventy days off annually in Japan compared with more than 130 in the United States and 120 in West Germany. To be sure the number of hours or days worked does partially reflect worker preference and attitudes.

4. The method of calculation is not exactly comparable.
5. After falling to 40.2 in 1976, the number of hours worked began to increase again. Many large firms sought to cope with the prolonged economic slowdown by increasing overtime and reducing the number of employees.

Worker attitude surveys during the late 1960s and early 1970s reveal that many employees believed their working hours were too long (Bennett and Levine 1976, p. 480). In a 1974 survey 40 percent of those surveyed preferred more leisure to more income, while only 30 percent gave the opposite response (Economic Planning Agency 1975, p. 140). Yet the number of working hours also reflects the impact of government action, managerial needs, the level of economic activity, union bargaining strategies, and international demonstration effects. The Japanese government, for example, has encouraged the spread of the five-day week. To a great extent this is a response to international pressures, showing sensitivity to the charge that the Japanese is an "economic animal." In summary, the number of hours or days worked is the outcome of a complex interaction, of which worker preferences are only one component. Number of hours worked must not be equated with amount of effort expended.

A more promising line of analysis is to examine some aspects of leisure-time consumption. A national survey of individuals' perceptions of their need for lifetime education conducted by the Ministry of Education found that among those interviewed who were already in the labor force some 74.2 percent selected subjects related to work as those they wished to study (Economic Planning Agency 1972, p. 47). For those under thirty-nine years of age the percentage rises to 85 percent. Studies of the actual consumption of leisure time show that Japanese employees are not well accustomed to utilizing their discretionary time on an individual basis. Much leisure time is consumed with fellow workmates, often in activities organized under the auspices of one's employer (Vogel 1963). In other words the work relationship tends to carry over into the utilization of leisure time. A still different approach is to examine the consumption of annual paid leave received by employees. A 1970 national survey reports that only one-fifth of the people surveyed took all of the paid leave available to them and 40 percent of them utilized only a half or less (Economic Planning Agency 1972, pp. 86–88). The underutilization of paid leave is particularly notable among older age groups, who have fewer alternatives to their current employment and stronger commitments to work by virtue of higher wages and benefits. Some 70 percent of male workers from age forty to forty-nine took less than half of the paid leave to which they were entitled. The purpose given by people for taking their paid leave is also revealing. Over 50 percent of both males and females gave "unavoidable" reasons such as illness, fatigue, and social and familial obligations such as marriages and funerals. Only 23 percent of the males and 20 percent of the females indicated that the paid leave was spent in activities of their own choice. In short the whole notion of a fixed vacation time taken for personal enjoyment free from the work situation is relatively unestablished in Japan. These attitudes exist despite the Japanese labor standards law which specifies the amount of annual vacation with pay accorded to employees by their length of service and type of enterprise. It is even specified that employees may take those holidays when they wish, either consecutively or separately. Not only are these provisions underutilized in Japan, but the amount of paid leave available to employees lags far behind that of most advanced industrial nations. It is only a fifth that of Sweden and about half that of the United States (Economic

Planning Agency 1972, p. 107). The situation in Japan is all the more remarkable since there are, by and large, no financial incentives for not taking paid vacations. Employees do not generally receive additional compensation for not taking the vacation time to which they are entitled. They choose to work when they could receive compensation simply by staying home.[6]

For comparative data on attitudes toward work we may turn to a recently conducted attitude survey of youth between the ages of eighteen to twenty-four in eleven countries (Office of the Prime Minister 1973). The advanced industrial nations of England, West Germany, France, Switzerland, Sweden, and the United States were included in addition to Yugoslavia, India, the Philippines, and Brazil. Representative samples of 2,000 respondents were drawn in each nation. In one question respondents were asked, "Why do you think man works?" and were offered the choices: to earn money, to do his duty as a member of society, or to find self-fulfillment. Japanese youth scored the highest percentage among the advanced industrial nations of those seeking self-fulfillment in their work, with 34.5 percent of the sample making this choice. This stood well above the 13.8 percent making the same choice in England, 15.3 in West Germany, 14.2 in France, 23.5 in Switzerland and 14.9 in Sweden. Interestingly enough the U.S. sample scored 30.3 on this same question. Only the Brazilians scored higher than the Japanese in choosing this answer, with some 42.4 percent doing so. Only 54.5 percent of the Japanese sample chose the response "to earn money," which was well below the proportion selecting this response in most of the other industrialized nations. About 11 percent chose "to do his duty as a member of society," a proportion quite similar to that in the United States, West Germany, Switzerland and Sweden but well above that of England and France.

Both males and females were interviewed and there were no significant differences by sex in the proportion choosing "to find self-fulfillment" in work in the Japanese sample. Among the industrial nations, only in France and Sweden were there significant differences by sex in the proportion choosing this response, with females in each of the two cases showing the higher proportion selecting "to find self-fulfillment." The percentage choosing self-fulfillment increases in the Japanese sample with a rise in the educational qualifications of respondents, as well as with rising occupational status. This pattern holds for most other industrial nations as well, although the positive relationship with education does not hold for France and the relationship with occupation is not as clear in many of the other countries, including the U.S.

Before concluding this discussion it must be emphasized that commitment to work should not be equated with work satisfaction or work morale. In the

6. There are some companies which "buy" vacation time from individual employees. Usually employees can keep their right to paid vacations for two years, after which unused vacation days are lost. Some companies compensate this lost right to paid vacations by paying the sum equal to the number of unused vacation days multiplied by the worker's straight time wage rate. In such cases, employees can convert their paid vacation into money, and to this extent the practice works as an incentive not to take vacation time. This practice of purchasing vacations is interpreted as illegal under the Labor Standards Law, however, and it is primarily in small firms that it exists.

just-mentioned survey, Japanese youth also showed the lowest proportion of those satisfied with their jobs—59.5 percent compared to 82.4 percent in the U.S. sample and 85.6 percent in the English sample. The Detroit-Yokohama Comparative Work History Project also permitted us to compare job satisfaction in the two samples. Using the kinds of indirect measures of work and job satisfaction that have been found to be the most revealing, we asked respondents (the self-employed were excluded) if they would advise a friend who was properly qualified to take a job at their current employer (HEW Task Force 1972, pp. 13–17; Kahn 1972, pp. 159–203; Robinson et al. 1969, pp. 25–69). We also asked respondents whether or not they would go into the same kind of work they were doing now, if they could do it all over again. In both cases the Detroit respondents recorded higher satisfaction with their current work. Seventy-one percent of the Detroit respondents would have advised their friend to take a job with their current employer, compared to only 44 percent among Yokohama respondents. Similarly 54 percent of the Detroit respondents would choose the same work if they had it to do over again, compared to 33 percent of the Yokohama employees. To further untangle the nature of work commitment manifested by Japanese workers we need to pursue additional comparative data on the subject.

Diligence: Some Comparative Data

Whitehill and Takezawa (1968) conducted a worker-attitude survey in large unionized firms in several industries, interviewing some 1,000 American and Japanese rank-and-file production workers each. One measure, in particular, was designed to tap the nature of worker diligence as measured by attitudes. The findings are reproduced in Table 28. If we take choices one and two as constituting the core "diligence worker attitude," we see relatively little difference in attitudes between the two samples of production workers. Although there are some significant differences in the distribution of choices by the respondents in the two societies (chi square = 135.48, significant at 5.01 level), the overall distribution between the diligent and non-diligent appears quite similar. The relatively higher proportion of workers selecting item one in Japanese firms than in American firms is explained by Whitehill and Takezawa (1968, p. 119) in a fashion quite consistent with the conclusions we drew in Chapter IV. Specifically jobs tend to be organized in U.S. business firms with a standard performance level established for each job. There tends to be a one-to-one relationship between the individual and the job, with the goal being to ensure accountability. Under these circumstances it is not surprising that "diligent" American workers tend to choose item two rather than item one. Indeed to help co-workers complete their task may often involve a violation of company rules. In Japanese firms, however, the ideology and cultural values stress cooperative group activity. Therefore item one constitutes a quite proper response though, as we may see from Table 28, hardly the dominant one.[7]

7. By age and sex subgroups the data reveal no significant differences among the U.S. respondents choosing item one. Among Japanese respondents choosing item one, however, older male workers show the highest support. For those respondents choosing

TABLE 28
I Think It Is Desirable for My Co-Workers To:

	Unit: Percent U.S.	Japan
1. Work at maximum capacity, without endangering their health, helping others when their own tasks are completed	9	24
2. Work at whatever level is necessary to perform their own jobs well	84	73
3. Work at whatever level is set by older members of their work group as being a normal day's output	1	3
4. Work at the minimum level necessary to keep their jobs, since this will spread the work among more employees	6	0

SOURCE: Adapted from Whitehill and Takezawa (1968, p. 118).

In the Detroit-Yokohama project we also included measures designed to tap worker diligence. We therefore have the opportunity to compare these findings with those of Takezawa and Whitehill. We constructed a scale based on three items from our questionnaire. These are:

1. How often do you work harder than your employer or supervisor requires?
2. How often do you get so wrapped up in your work that you lose track of time?
3. How often do you spend some time thinking of ways you can do your job better?

Each item allowed the following possible responses: very often, fairly often, once in a while, and never. A work-commitment scale was created by the simple addition of the values of the responses for the three items (very often = 3; fairly often = 2; once in a while = 1; never = 0). The maximum possible work-commitment score of an individual on the three items was 9, and the minimum score was 0.[8]

Table 29 reports the mean work-commitment scores for 459 Yokohama respondents and 567 Detroit respondents by educational level. The sample mean for Detroit is 5.64 (standard deviation 2.23) and 5.23 for Yokohama (standard deviation = 2.19), an inter-city difference of 0.41. This difference yields a t-score of 3.0131 which is significant at 0.00013. Although the difference is

---

item two older females show the highest support in the U.S. sample and younger females in the Japanese sample.

8. Several steps were taken to assess the reliability of work commitment scores for each of the two samples. The results suggest moderate reliability. Treating the work commitment score as an interval scale, intercorrelations between the items making up the scale were calculated. The correlations did not vary too widely, with the Detroit correlation matrix ranging from 0.2616 to 0.3198, and the Yokohama correlation matrix ranging from 0.2569 to 0.3235. Item analysis (the correlation of each item with the scale excluding the item) also showed minimal variance, ranging from 0.3253 to 0.3673 for Detroit and 0.3198 to 0.3706 for Yokohama. Finally, a standard measure of reliability, Cronbach's coefficient of alpha, was calculated. The values (0.5415 for the Detroit sample and 0.5401 for the Yokohama sample) suggest a moderate degree of internal consistency. Goodman-Kruskal's Gamma and Kendall's Tau-B, two measures which do not require the assumption that the items making up the scale are interval scales, were also calculated. The values suggest again that our scaling is reasonably reliable.

TABLE 29
**Distribution of Scores on Work Commitment Scale
by Education and City**[a]

City		Under 12 Years	12 Years	12 Years or More	Total
		Educational Achievement			
Yokohama					
	Mean	4.87	5.45	5.57	5.23
	(N)	(203)	(129)	(127)	(459)
Detroit					
	Mean	5.36	5.63	5.96	5.64
	(N)	(199)	(188)	(180)	(567)

[a] Only respondents employed by others and answering all three questions were included.

statistically significant it would not appear to be substantively significant. We also used the work-commitment scale to examine the impact of education on work commitment. In Table 29 we see that in both cities increased education produces higher work-commitment scores. Assuming that education is a reasonable proxy for occupation, it stands to reason that the increased education associated with more rewarding higher-status jobs induces greater work commitment on the part of their occupants. It is also apparent that overall differences between the two cities are preserved in each of the educational categories. Detroit respondents consistently score higher on the work-commitment scale than do Yokohama respondents.

What conclusions may be drawn from this discussion? There is not much evidence to suggest a markedly different commitment to work being manifested by respondents in the two cities. Certainly there is no evidence to suggest that Yokohama respondents score higher even when we control for education. Whatever differences do exist suggest stronger work commitment on the part of Detroit respondents. However, taking measurement error into consideration and the possibility that the boundaries of response categories may differ between the two cities (behavior that Detroit respondents categorize as very often might be categorized as often by Yokohama respondents), we are not inclined to argue that a substantive difference exists. There is in fact some basis for believing that Japanese respondents are less willing to select extreme choices in survey interviews. We must also be cautious in relying on measures involving subjective assessments of worker involvement in their jobs. We cannot assume that subjective assessments reflect behavior—in particular, that workers are willing to share their thoughts with management. Indeed Marsh and Mannari (1976, p. 262), in their examination of worker attitudes and behavior at two Japanese firms, found that there was only a modest association between their subjective measure of thinking about making suggestions and their behavioral measure reporting how many times suggestions were actually made (0.30 in one factory and 0.50 in the other). In short we have no basis for knowing what proportion of thoughts about improving the job translate into action. We might think of this in terms of a "conversion rate." That is, what is the rate at which thoughts about improving the job convert into action? If this concept is valid then we must allow for the possibility that the conversion rate is different in the two societies. There may, for example, be stronger institutional arrangements designed to produce a higher conversion rate in one society relative to the other (e.g., such as QC circles). Finally it should be noted that our measure focused specifically on the job held by the respondent and did not ask more generally how often workers were active in seeking to improve the productivity of their workshop. It is quite possible, for example, that workers might be reluctant to think about ways to improve their own jobs for fear that it might affect their income and job security (especially in Detroit), but be more willing to think about ways to improve the productivity of their workshop in general. In summary, our findings of the relatively small differences between Detroit and Yokohama respondents on our work-commitment scale parallel Whitehill's findings.

There is one additional set of data that we ought to examine in evaluating the view that Japanese employees are more highly motivated to work than are American employees. Marsh and Mannari (1976, pp. 99–118) conclude that the image of the fanatically work-oriented Japanese requires some modification on the basis of their findings. They base their conclusion on such data as the fact that "only" 51.2 percent of rank-and-file workers aged thirty-three and older, in the electric factory they surveyed, selected the response "work is my whole life, more important than anything else." (The other two choices measure pleasure and family value preferences.) Marsh and Mannari imply that this response constitutes low support, but low relative to what? If one has an image of robot-like workers at the disposal of omnipotent management, the fact that only 51.2 percent of rank-and-file workers over age thirty-three took this position may indeed be low. If one has a less stereotypic image, however, and thinks about how Western workers might respond to the choice "work is my whole life, more important than anything else," then 51.2 percent may be a remarkably high percentage (Dubin 1956, pp. 131–42; Goldthorpe et al. 1968). Without comparative data, Marsh and Mannari have little basis for arriving at their conclusion.

Takezawa and Whitehill (1968, p. 111) do report comparative data using a somewhat similar measure.[9] The results appear in Table 30. The data (chi square = 377.43, significant at <0.01 level with three degrees of freedom) reveal a markedly greater willingness on the part of Japanese production workers to identify with their company.[10]

A final set of comparative data allows us to examine worker attitudes over time in Japan. To what extent do we find a weakening of the commitment to work in Japan as a consequence of advanced levels of industrialization, citizen affluence, increased leisure, and rising educational achievement? Do the gener-

9. The question has some problems since it taps not just the one dimension of company versus non-company commitments, but also the dimension of whether workers prefer to think of these dimensions as separate or non-separate.

10. Older males are the subcategory which shows the strongest support for item one in both samples. Younger workers in the United States show the strongest support for item two, as do younger females in Japan. Relatively minor differences in the frequency distributions by age and sex subgroups appear in the responses to items three and four in both samples.

TABLE 30
I Think of My Company As:

	Unit: Percent	
	U.S.	Japan
1. The central concern in my life and of greater importance than my personal life	1	9
2. A part of my life at least equal in importance to my personal life	22	57
3. A place for me to work with management, during work hours, to accomplish mutual goals	54	26
4. Strictly a place to work and entirely separate from my personal life	23	8

SOURCE: Adapted from Whitehill and Takezawa.

ally less work-oriented attitudes recorded by younger workers in most surveys reflect life-cycle changes whereby the work orientation grows progressively stronger as workers age? Or do these youthful attitudes indicate long-term historical change? An examination of four nationwide surveys at five-year intervals by the Research Committee on the Study of Japanese National Character permits us to answer these questions.[11] The specific question used in successive surveys asks respondents to give their attitudes toward life in terms of six precoded responses. It was found that traditional attitudes stressing sacrifice, service, and living a pure life gave way over successive surveys to more easygoing responses (e.g., don't think about money or fame, just live a life that suits your own tastes). Examining the data by birth cohort, a strong age effect was found in each of the four surveys. Younger members of the population consistently showed higher support for the easygoing responses. Further analysis of the birth-cohort data over time revealed that the age effect derived not from individual life-cycle experiences, but rather from the different historical experiences of the more recent birth cohorts. As a consequence the data indicate a secular trend, beginning in the prewar period, toward moderation of a strong work ethic. We must, of course, be careful once again not to confuse attitudinal change with behavioral change.

A Reconceptualization of the Findings

We have now completed a presentation of the data available to us which bear on the proposition that Japanese workers display an unusually strong work ethic. If the reader is somewhat confused as to what conclusion to draw, there are good reasons for this ambivalence. How are we to make sense of these often disparate findings? The discerning reader will be aware of a number of seeming contradictions in the data reported above:

1. The Japanese record a high need to find fulfillment in work relative to employees in other nations, but they also record lower levels of work satisfaction.
2. The data indicate few differences in the frequency distributions of American and Japanese employees on measures designed to tap worker diligence.

11. For a more elaborate analysis of the data see Cole 1976, pp. 200–207.

3. Higher levels of identification with the company are recorded for Japanese than for American employees.
4. Many Japanese workers do not take all the vacation time available to them, but they report on surveys that they would like more free time.
5. Time series data from Japan suggest a secular trend toward moderation of a strong work ethic. Yet young Japanese workers record a higher need to find self-fulfillment at work than do young workers in Western nations.

We need to find ways of reconceptualizing the data to allow for the possibility that these findings are more logically related than they might otherwise appear. At the same time we cannot dismiss the possibility that the world is more disorderly than we would otherwise like to admit.

One last caveat is in order. The datasets reported in the previous pages come from very diverse sources and the samples are often of relatively homogenous populations of workers (e.g., young workers). Consequently one must be careful in generalizing to larger populations. The reconceptualizations proposed below should be treated, therefore, as suggestive ones that require further testing, with controls for industry, technology and type of work.

The Japanese display a high need to find fulfillment at work and at the same time register low levels of job satisfaction relative to employees in Western nations. This fact deserves our attention first because some scholars who have "discovered" the lower work satisfaction of the Japanese employee, as it manifests itself in survey data, have concentrated on this facet alone. They have thereupon proceeded to the unsubstantiated inference that Japanese workers are neither so highly motivated nor have notable organizational attachments (Azumi and McMillan 1976, pp. 215–29). Odaka (1975, pp. 134–35) also notes the higher job satisfaction registered in Western nations in comparing his Japan findings with those reported by Inkeles. Odaka speculates that these differences stem from more skillful personnel management in the West and the greater freedom Western workers have in their workshop activities. Yet a simpler explanation is at hand, which is no less plausible than either of those proposed above. Because Japanese workers are so highly committed to finding fulfillment in their work, they expect a good deal more from work and are therefore likely to display greater dissatisfaction when their expectations are not met. In short, high expectations vis-à-vis work may coexist with low job satisfaction. Indeed this may be the most likely outcome. This perspective is quite consistent with the current social psychological literature. Steers and Porter (1973, p. 287) see job satisfaction as the sum total of an individual's expectations which are met on the job. The more an individual's expectations on the job are met, the greater his job satisfaction. An alternative route to the same conclusion involves questioning the relation between job satisfaction and work motivation. Stinchcombe (1974, pp. 133–34) speculates that workers are motivated by a set of rewards (monetary, rank, authority, etc.), not by job satisfaction. If they receive these rewards they will be highly motivated regardless of other factors that might depress their job satisfaction. For example in a rapidly growing economy with many rapidly growing firms, as has been the case in Japan especially in the postwar period, organizational members will confront a relatively open opportunity structure (i.e., high availability of rewards) and be highly motivated to perform. Yet they may also register high levels of job dissatisfaction, because they see many around them being promoted to supervisory positions and believe their own progress is not proceeding at a pace consistent with their abilities. Samuel Stouffer, in his well-known study of the psychological effects of different promotion rates in the various branches of the armed forces, arrived at a rather similar observation (Stouffer et al. 1949, cited in Stinchcombe 1974, p. 133). Stouffer and his associates developed the concept of relative deprivation to account for feelings of dissatisfaction, particularly in those cases where the objective situation would seem unlikely to provoke such feelings (Merton 1957, p. 235).

Western social scientists have gradually come to the realization that high worker morale or job satisfaction do not necessarily correlate with high worker productivity, despite some simplistic theorizing to the contrary by early human relations scholars (Perrow 1972, pp. 106–8). In an analogous fashion a high commitment to finding fulfillment at work does not necessarily translate into more diligent workers. This would be consistent with our failure to find any significant differences between Japanese and American workers on our measures of worker diligence. We also pointed out, however, that Japanese workers record unusually high levels of identification with the company in which they are employed. This is consistent with the findings of a number of other scholars as well (e.g., Marsh and Mannari 1976; Dore 1973; Osako 1973). How is this possible? The core of the proposed reconceptualization involves making two distinctions. The first, referred to above, involves recognizing that a strong need to find fulfillment at work does not guarantee high levels of job satisfaction. The second involves recognizing that the need to find fulfillment at work must be further broken down so that we distinguish three levels of employee identification and commitment: commitment to larger organizational goals, to subgroup goals (e.g., those of the informal work group), and to specific job tasks. Many analysts have a tendency to talk indiscriminately about commitment to the job, the work group, and the firm, without ever making clear the referent of the discussion. It makes a great deal of difference whether you ask a worker if he is committed to his job, his work group, or his company. By fusing these different levels of analysis we end up with contradictory results. There is no reason to assume that commitment at all three levels ought to be consistently in the same direction.

One of the repeated findings of industrial sociologists in America is that informal subgroup goals are often at variance with formal organizational goals. We have not provided much evidence bearing on the nature and extent of Japanese workers' commitment to subgroup goals relative to their Western counterparts. It may be that Japanese workers do not have a greater commitment to these subgroups than Western workers (Western views notwithstanding). The difference between Japanese and Western workers may rather be that the goals of the informal work groups for Japanese workers are not as often at variance with formal organizational goals. The reasons for this hypothesized reduced variance will be outlined in the following section.

We do conclude, based on the evidence presented in the preceding pages, that Japanese workers' commitment to or identification with the work task itself is no stronger than among their Western counterparts. Moreover it is our thesis that commitment to and identification with the company or work group is quite compatible with strong dissatisfaction with one's job task and working conditions. Osako (1973) arrives at a parallel observation in her study of a major Japanese automobile manufacturer. She notes that the company personnel policies constrained workers to differentiate between their status as employees who were members of the company community (e.g., club member, dormitory resident) and their status as assembly-line workers. It is the strong identification with the company that partially explains the high expectations employees have toward work as well as the ability of the company to mobilize subgroups on behalf of larger organizational goals. Yet it is not surprising that Japanese workers would be quite dissatisfied with their specific job tasks. Satisfaction with specific job tasks is likely to be based primarily on the nature and extent of intrinsic job rewards. Such intrinsic rewards are difficult to influence by standard company policies.

One way to summarize the relationship of Japanese employees to the Japanese company is to stress that the former share with management a strong sense of participation in the company as a "community of fate." That is to say, failure to achieve organizational goals is seen as damaging to the individual employee. Conversely organizational success is thought to enhance individual interests. Consider the previous example of the failure of Japanese employees to take their paid vacations, despite survey evidence that many wanted more leisure time. Initially we might attribute this outcome to an unvarying internalized work ethic that did not allow workers to take their vacations despite a conscious desire to do so. If we examine the matter a little more closely we learn that the provision of the Labor Standards Law referring to paid vacations specifies that they must be taken so as not to disrupt the normal operation of the business. This is a critical clause, for it allows the company to mobilize enormous formal and informal pressures to discourage workers from taking their full vacations. For large numbers of employees to take their full vacations would conflict with the company goal of raising productivity. If we assume high identification of individual employees with organizational goals, this would be unwise. It would conflict with individual self-interest in improving one's own situation, in particular promotion, since maximizing organizational interests tends to maximize individual interests.[12] Evidence for this interpretation comes from a 1971 Ministry of Labor survey in which employees who used less than half of their allotted vacation time were asked to give the reason (Ministry of Labor 1972). Only 4.4 percent chose to respond "because I am happy when I am working." Rather,

12. An aggressive forty-year-old steel executive with major responsibilities remarked to me in 1974 that he was taking his first two-week vacation in his fourteen years of employment at the company. In an embarrassed fashion he explained to me that he was sensitive to the criticism of "economic animal" leveled by Westerners against the Japanese. The fact of the matter, though, was that there was some slack in the work of his department and his superiors had encouraged him to take the time off. It would not have occurred to him to insist on this time off as a matter of right.

the majority stressed the "pressure of work" (38 percent), "the atmosphere of work is such that it is hard to take off" (23 percent), and "intend to add them up and use them later" (11 percent).

We asserted in this section that Japanese employees have unusually strong identification with the company, but not necessarily high job satisfaction or strong commitment to the performance of specific job tasks. The evidence in support of these propositions has been of a nature that provides an unusually good understanding of the fit among work ethic indicators. Instead of simply relying on logic, however, we can also detail the specific institutional arrangements and historical configuration of events that have led to the strong need to find fulfillment at work and the high level of identification with company goals.

Anatomy of the Japanese Work Ethic

We have found that when talking about a strong Japanese work ethic we are in fact talking about two very specific dimensions: the need to find fulfillment in work, and the identification of individual interests with organizational interests. One may reasonably attribute the strength of these two factors to existing institutional arrangements. We may point to the permanent employment system, heavy emphasis on in-company training, career orientation of workers, payment by age and length of service, and enterprise-based unions. Certainly many of these arrangements seem directly associated with the two dimensions of the work ethic that we have isolated. Indeed they are so closely tied that we are easily led to tautologies. We can, however, push the explanation back one step and ask what is responsible for the institutional arrangements that have developed in postwar Japan. We may proceed by examining the nature of organizational imperatives and motivating factors available to managers at given points in time.

Daniel Katz (1975, p. 259) cites three basic behavioral requirements for an effective ongoing organization. People must be recruited to the organization and induced to remain in the organization. Secondly, they must perform their role assignments in predictable fashion. Thirdly, they must be willing to innovate in achieving organizational goals when role specifications are inadequate. He further suggests that there are six major motivational patterns for securing these desired performances. Some motivational patterns may be more effective in achieving one particular behavioral requirement than another. The six motivational patterns are: (1) conformity to rule compliance, (2) instrumental system rewards (e.g., resulting from the perquisites of seniority), (3) instrumental individual rewards (e.g., resulting from piecework pay system), (4) intrinsic satisfaction from role performance, (5) internalization of organizational goals and values, and (6) involvement in primary group relationships.

An examination of the literature on Japanese organizations as well as of the data presented in our previous discussion suggests that the distinguishing characteristic of Japanese organizations is their attempt, with some measure of success, to rely heavily on (5) internalization of organizational goals and values and (6) involvement in primary group relationships. As a seventh motivational pattern I add the need to find fulfillment at work. Japanese employers have been able to capitalize on this factor as well. The singling out of these three motivational patterns does not mean that the others are not utilized by Japanese organizations. In particular the rapid increase in real and nominal wages of Japanese workers (2) must have been a major asset to management. Similarly the other motivational strategies are also heavily relied upon, but Japanese business organizations do appear distinctive for their reliance on motivational patterns five, six and seven.

When individuals accept the achievement of organizational goals as consistent with the achievement of their personal goals, the organization is in a particularly strong position to draw upon the spontaneous innovative potential of its members. Our interpretation is consonant with the report of a 1974 Japan Productivity Center mission to the United States. They concluded that although both American and Japanese employers try to reconcile individual and organizational goals, the Japanese tend to focus on adapting organizational practices to employee needs. The American managers, however, tend to be more oriented toward bringing about employee adaptation to the organization. In the context of our evaluation of Toyota Auto Body policies we saw that the Americans emphasize changing the organization of work to fit with formal organizational goals and the perceived imperatives of technology. In Japan the emphasis, where possible, is on changing the organization of work to meet employee needs as long as it does not endanger high level management goals.

To say that Japanese business organizations have been relatively successful in this area does not mean that they have been completely successful (see Chapter V). Complete internalization of organizational goals tends to be very rare, especially in business organizations, and Japanese firms are no exceptions. Alienation from work as measured in a sense of powerlessness, self-estrangement, meaninglessness, and isolation is hardly absent from Japanese organizations. Meaninglessness, in particular, is relevant to our discussion; the individual experiences meaninglessness when his or her individual roles are not seen as fitting into the total system of organizational goals (Blauner 1964, p. 32). Japanese firms have not been left unscarred in this respect, as a consequence of rapid technological change, rationalization of the firm, and growing impersonality. It is because the process of internalization is incomplete in Japan as well that we see high levels of job dissatisfaction, and that a comparative analysis of worker diligence does not show Japanese workers to be unusually committed to their specific work tasks. There is every reason to believe that there persists a fundamental conflict in Japan between workers who seek higher wages to guarantee their livelihood and employers who seek to cut the costs involved in producing a product or service.

Dependency

This discussion suggests the utility of conceptualizing the individual's relation to organizational goals in terms of the degree of unity between organizational and personal goals. High levels of internalization involve a willingness of organizational members to see themselves as participating in a community of fate. Loyalty and commitment to the organization stem from the organization being the focus of normative solutions to central life problems faced by individual members. When this occurs the organization provides the framework through which individuals crystallize their personal identities (Stinchcombe 1975). We are more inclined to think of medieval guilds and slavery as communities of fate than we are business organizations. Although the elites of business organizations are rather closely tied to the fate of their organizations (think of stock options and bonuses), subordinates tend to be less so.[13] McGregor (1960, p. 26) argues that in contemporary American industry employees are in a state of partial dependence. In large Japanese organizations, however, we have a situation where those lower down in the organizational structure have been more closely tied to the achievement of organizational goals. Employees tend to see the company not simply as a safe haven, a place to secure income, or a place to work, but as a community to which they can devote their entire lives. In contrast to the findings of Robert Dubin (1959, pp. 125–32), who reported that for most American industrial workers, work and the workplace do not constitute central life interests, we believe the data indicate that work in large-scale Japanese firms does provide this focus for regular male employees.

It is not accidental that the Japanese have a phrase which captures the essence of this discussion. The term is *kigyō wa unmei kyōdōtai de aru*, which might be translated as "the enterprise and its employees share a common destiny." In complementary fashion the Japanese organization also appears quite effective in motivating employees through the mobilization of primary-group relationships (see Rohlen 1974). Western scholarship indicates that identification with one's work group does not always contribute to increasing productivity, but can detract from it. Highly cohesive work groups may not be task-oriented. However, together with high penetration of informal work groups by the company, primary-group relationships can be a powerful force contributing to the achievement of organizational goals. It is exactly this combination of motivational sources that Japanese managers have been most effective at mobilizing, again without excluding reliance on the other standard motivators outlined by Katz.

If we accept these observations on the distinctive motivational bases of the Japanese work ethic—need to find fulfillment at work, company identification, and primary-group penetration and mobilization—we still need to inquire into the process by which these social outcomes are produced. Arthur Stinchcombe

13. However much they might otherwise want it to be, most American management officials would probably agree with the following description by Levitan and Johnston (1973, p. 37):

> The ideal of communal effort in which a group of individuals are united by common beliefs to achieve a common aim is foreign to large corporate enterprises. The firm is interested in profits, with most other goals being measured by how they affect this single variable. The firm's employees, especially the production workers, are concerned with improving their lives, a goal only incidentally connected with the corporation's success and in part opposed to it because there is only one corporate revenue pie to be divided. By its nature, the corporation is not primarily concerned with workers' lives. Unless corporate enterprise were to radically alter its functions to make the welfare of its employees its first reason for being, it is hypothetical to talk of internalizing the firm's goals.

(1970) provides a strategy for analysis in his discussion of the degree of dependency members have on the organization. When we say the organizational commitment of Japanese employees is high we are saying, in effect, that they are unusually dependent on their organizations relative to their Western counterparts. Why should this be so?

　First, as Stinchcombe notes, the degree of dependence of subordinates upon superiors is a function of the existence and availability of alternative sources for the satisfaction of needs. For our purposes the issue is whether comparable terms of employment are available elsewhere. To the extent that they are, "exit" from the organization is encouraged instead of "voice" as a course of action to improve one's condition. The terms are those of the economist Albert Hirschman (1970); "voice" refers to the ability to protect and improve one's condition from within the organization. With the exception of certain high-skill categories, Japan has, however, until recently been a labor-surplus economy. Throughout much of her industrial history, especially in the less skilled categories, there has been an industrial reserve army of unemployed and underemployed ready to take over potentially vacant positions. As a consequence, voluntary "exit" and to some extent "voice" have been limited. This has been a major factor operating to produce loyalty to the firm and contributing to the identification of workers with organizational goals. The crystallization of the permanent employment practice in the postwar period amply demonstrates the lack of alternative options. It meant that to leave a large firm generally resulted in getting pushed down to the bottom of the dual economic structure, a bottom made up of small firms which paid lower wages, had poorer working conditions and were unable to guarantee employment security. The best evidence for the pressure exercised by this reserve army of underemployed is that historically wage income has lagged behind increases in labor productivity.

Moreover when alternative opportunities for comparable benefits are not perceived as available employees tend to evaluate their existing employment more highly, even if their objective working conditions and rewards are low when compared to those of other industries and workers (or other nations for that matter). Robert Blauner (1964), in his comparative study of American industries, reached the same conclusion when trying to explain the relatively high work satisfaction manifested by Southern textile workers located in small company towns. Without recourse to alternative sources of employment in their isolated geographical setting, they displayed high work satisfaction compared to other industries, even though their objective working conditions were poorer.

On the micro-level of work groups the literature on Japanese industrial organizations emphasizes the dependency of the individual on the work group (Rohlen 1975). As noted in earlier chapters, work relations are structured so that the focus is not on individual responsibilities and tasks but rather on integrating the individual into the group to accomplish tasks assigned to the group. Ideally individuals are not coerced to sacrifice their interests to those of the group, but are able to advance their personal goals as they advance the interests of the group. Only in this fashion does the individual achieve esteem, social status and emotional security (see Yoshino 1968; Nakane 1970; Rohlen 1975). Moreover it is understood that the group will retain sufficient autonomy to allow these relationships to take on significant meaning for participants (Rohlen 1975, p. 193).

On another level there is the dependence of the work group on their supervisor. Historically this is expressed in the patron-client relationship (*oyabun-kobun*), one of the fictive kinship patterns established between group leaders and their followers. It was particularly notable in the early stages of Japanese industrialization and survives today in a variety of attenuated forms, such as the senior-junior relationship (*senpai-kohai*) (Cole 1971; Rohlen 1974, pp. 121–34). The foreman is seen as part of the work group, sharing with it a common destiny. Hazama (1973) maintains, on the basis of his comparison with English workers, that the Japanese supervisor is expected routinely to check a subordinate's work during the course of the work. If he doesn't the subordinate will feel that the supervisor is not concerned about him. There is the need to constantly depend upon superiors. By contrast Hazama suggests that British workers are content to have their work evaluated after it is done. To be constantly checked while doing the work would be interpreted by subordinates as negative behavior. Ideally in Japan there is a reciprocal relationship; the superior is expected to look after the interests of those who work under him. In short, he is expected to be dependable. Conversely workers are expected to respond with behavior reflecting loyalty and commitment to group goals as defined by the superior.

These interpersonal dependencies are said to be deeply rooted in basic patterns of family socialization. Takeo Doi (1973, pp. 28, 86) sees the desire to be dependent (*amae*) as the basis of Japanese social structure. He believes the psychological prototype of *amae* lies in the infant's desire to be close to its mother (Doi 1973, p. 75). Somehow this unwillingness to face "objective reality" is prolonged in Japan, so that it plays a major role in adult life. Similarly George De Vos (1974) tries to explain the achievement orientation of the Japanese by focusing on familial obligations, writing that "rather than fear of punishment, there is more often a fear of rejection and abandonment on the part of those on whom the person places his ultimate dependence." Glazer (1976, pp. 852–53), drawing upon the work of De Vos and Doi, sees dependency (or interdependency), along with the yearning for nurturance and security, as providing the basis of the Japanese achievement ethic. These factors are said to correspond in function to the role played by personal autonomy and early independence in the formation of the Western achievement ethic.

In addition to dependence as a structural characteristic of Japanese interpersonal relationships we can pursue the matter of dependence on a macroinstitutional level. Japanese employees in large firms are dependent on their employers not only for good wages and working conditions but, as we have seen, for a variety of other benefits, including housing, the use of their leisure time, and so on. It is estimated that company housing alone accounts for some 6.9 percent of all household dwellings in Japan. This is even more than publicly run rental housing, which accounts for 5.8 percent. The lack of public housing, the high costs of land and private housing, the high cost of education, the high cost of private leisure activities, and the relative absence of public facilities all strongly reinforce this dependence. The dependence is indexed on such measures as housing space, diffusion of water supply and sewerage, and area in city parks; Japan lags notably behind other industrial nations in these categories (see Bennett and Levine 1976). The ratio of social capital stock to national income dropped sharply during the 1950s and has not increased appreciably since then. If we calculate just the living-related social capital stock—housing, living environments, health and sanitation, security and education and culture—as a percentage of the gross national product, the total stands at 7.4; the comparable estimates are 8.3 for the United States and 14.6 for the United Kingdom. The figures for the United Kingdom are fairly representative of Western Europe. The greater seriousness of the environmental pollution issue in Japan further reflects this neglect. In summary, the relative absence of public investment in social capital stock means that employees have been unable to rely on the government to solve some of their major life problems and thus lack alternatives to reliance on the corporations for the satisfaction of many basic needs. The corporations have been only too willing to fill this void. These structured dependency relationships are a primary factor in the Japanese employee's high level of commitment to organizational goals and need to find fulfillment in work.

A second source of dependency suggested by Stinchcombe lies in the capacity of inferiors to organize in opposition to superiors. This raises the question of management's power to enforce its views at a societal level. Here the extent to which management can count on the cooperation of the state is paramount. Historically the power of Japanese management, buttressed by the state, continually struck down worker efforts to collectively organize in defense of their interests. It has been a powerful factor inducing workers to conform to company discipline. Combined with paternalism and the mobilization of traditional social relationships, the management-government alliance operated to secure high employee commitment to organizational goals. If paternalism represents the carrot, the stick was never far from sight.

The crushing defeat suffered in World War II, the occupation reforms, and the organization of unions administered a severe shock to the prewar structure of management power and authority. With the recovery of management confidence and with the strong support of the Japanese conservative government, however, this dominant position was, to some extent, restored in the postwar period. To be sure workers were extended civil and political rights (e.g., freedom of speech, right of association and combination, right to vote and have access to public office), but they have been unable to reap the social and economic benefits. Indeed the failure of workers to achieve political power, or to have direct influence on its exercise, in both the prewar and postwar periods, meant that they were denied full civic incorporation into the state. That is, they were denied citizenship in the sense of full participation in the political and economic community and all that this entails (see Bendix 1964, pp. 74–104). Certainly the rise of nationalism in the prewar period gave many Japanese a sense of participating in a national mission for a brief period of time. The "income doubling" slogans of the postwar period were also designed to give workers a sense of sharing in a national effort. It was, however, an effort whose locus was the business enterprise. Each new success of Japanese management in raising the lowered standard of living in the immediate postwar period redounded to the benefit of the organization and a restoration of management's authority. With a discrediting of other values, especially national greatness, the success of Japanese corporations became a measure of Japan's very success as a nation. The government supported this resurgence indirectly through the allocation of resources in a way that met the major needs of the industrial corporations. Throughout the 1960s the low rate of both individual and corporate taxation in Japan—a political decision—guaranteed an increasing gap between the resources available for expansion of production in the private sector and the resources available to the public sector for public welfare. Plainly put, the leaders of private corporations had enough political clout with the ruling Liberal Democratic party, which they financed, to see to it that private corporate investment received first priority. The failure to allocate sufficient resources to provide for housing, education and public facilities was matched by the failure to build a strong social security system. Old-age pensions still are particularly inadequate. Social insurance payments as a percentage of national income were 6.7 in 1973, an increase of only 0.6 over 1966. By comparison, the figure stood at 8.1 for the United States (1966), 21.8 for West Germany, 19.7 for France, 17.3 for Sweden (1966), and 15.0 for the United Kingdom (Economic Planning Agency 1975, p. 113). The inadequacy of social insurance arrangements in Japan is part of the explanation for the high rate of personal savings in Japan, much of which becomes available as investment capital for business. Another factor is the lack of an installment consumer credit system. The four primary reasons for savings given in recent surveys rank as follows: saving for illness, child's education, retirement, and land or house purchase (and house repairs). In other words, we are not dealing with a simple matter of the intrinsic frugality of the Japanese. Some might argue that the Japanese solution of letting individuals save for themselves is more "rational" from the point of view of investment decisions. The point is, however, that the majority of the labor force who are employed in small and medium-sized firms have little or no economic security guaranteed to them in their old age. Secondly, for those in large firms reliance on the firm to provide retirement pensions heightens employee dependence on the firm.[14] Moreover employees continue to depend on business firms to provide cash income even after the official retirement age. Families supported by those aged sixty-five or older depend on wage income for an overwhelming portion of their cost of living in Japan. In comparison social security benefits and pensions cover nearly 80 percent of living expenses in West Germany and 65 percent in Britain (Economic Planning Agency 1975, p. 110).

14. One might ask why there is so much greater dependence in Japan compared to the United States when the U.S. also has relatively little investment in social capital stock and social insurance. As a consequence of the lower per capita income in Japan—approximately two-thirds that of the United States—individuals have fewer personal financial resources, and consequently are more dependent on their firms for satisfying basic needs (assuming the same low level of social capital investment in both societies).

A third factor influencing the degree of dependence of subordinates on superiors consists of the heritage of values, ideology, and past practices which are brought to bear as constraints on current choices. This heritage both reflects past distributions of power in society and has an independent life of its own, influencing the kinds of options perceived and choices made. By any criteria Japanese management has had an enormous advantage in imposing the arrangements described in the preceding pages. They have had available a coherent set of preindustrial values and practices that could be mobilized to provide the ideological justifications for the dependency relationships which emerged. The mobilization of these values and practices around the permanent employment practice has been detailed in Chapter I.

Ironically it is in the postwar period, when many of the values of dependency were, at least on the surface, being rejected, that we see a greater acceptance by employees of dependency relationships. To be specific, structurally based dependency grew at the expense of personally based dependency relationships. The postwar dependency was based on the rapidly increasing material rewards offered to employees in the major corporations. The growing scale of rewards made available to employees in the postwar period may have been enjoyed at a substantial cost to individual freedom, with resultant conformity and subordination of individual to organizational interests. It is, after all, not always possible to dovetail personal goals with organizational goals.

One may ask how it is that the Japanese would come to accept these costs of dependency. A simple answer, of course, is that the rewards have outweighed the costs. To take this position, however, we need to know something about the values of a society, values in the fundamental sense of the preference ordering assigned to various cultural standards. Dependency as a social value has extraordinarily pejorative connotations in the context of American values (see McGregor 1960, pp. 26–27). That is to say, it ranks quite low as a desired value and is an emotional matter of great sensitivity.[15] Nor is this simply a matter of American uniqueness. Crozier (1964, p. 222) observes that face-to-face dependency relationships are perceived as most difficult to bear in the French cultural setting. The emphasis is on the elimination of direct dependency relationships through reliance on impersonal rules. This is not the case for the Japanese, where the value of dependency has ranked fairly high on the scale of ideal behavior. Dependency—within limits—is perceived as a necessary part of successful work relationships in Japan and, more generally, is often regarded as a positive aspect of social relations (Rohlen 1975, p. 205; Lebra 1976, pp. 50–66). Crozier (1964, p. 233) observes that this is also the case with British organizations, which still place great reliance on old patterns of deference that bind inferiors and superiors within necessary limits.

The Japanese solution to the potential problem is, however, only partially that of defining the dependency relationship positively. In the postwar period many dependency relationships came to be labelled as feudal, and developed

15. In fact Americans tend to be quite ambivalent about dependency. To be taken care of is both satisfying and frustrating. Similarly independence is satisfying, but can be threatening if the risks are too great.

pejorative connotations. Such was the case with *oyabun-kobun* relations, which became associated in the public mind with the bonds that hold gangster groups together. Furthermore the continuing, if not strengthened, appeal among many Japanese of setting up one's own business testifies to the desire for independence as opposed to dependence. The solution to the problem of dependence, and the Japanese citizen's increasingly ambivalent attitude toward it, has been to define the problem away and thereby deny its existence.

The postwar rhetoric of the Japanese manager and supervisor focuses less on the positive aspects of dependency than it does on the value of interdependency. Societal values emphasize interdependency as ideal practice. Thus the focus is shifted away from possible discussion of the costs of dependency to the exercise of cooperation, teamwork, and mutual support to achieve mutual goals. Conversely the exercise of individual freedom is seen as selfish and has pejorative connotations. At least this is the position taken by management. We see here the strength of social values and traditions which allow for the possibility of redefining the social situation from bad to good, from dependency to interdependency. The converse is often the case in social movements which challenge established power. Witness, for example, the rhetoric of much of the American women's liberation movement, which redefines the heretofore dominant value of interdependency in marriage relationships as the negative value of dependency. This is consistent with the sociological maxim that social behavior has little intrinsic meaning, but derives its meanings from the interpretation actors, imbued with values, give it. Western scholars have often uncritically accepted Japanese rhetoric without distinguishing between interdependency and dependency (e.g., Glazer 1976). The "real" issue is one of reciprocity. If there is symmetrical reciprocity the relationship is one of interdependency. If the relationship is asymmetrical in the distribution of rights and obligations, then one party is more dependent on the other.

In summary, we can identify the historical sources of worker dependency in Japan that led to strong employee identification with company interests and a high need to find fulfillment at work. We have also examined the bases for the persistence of those phenomena in the postwar period. There are some grounds for thinking that the level of employee dependency on the organization is declining and will continue to decline in the future. Moreover, conversations with Japanese corporate officials in the mid-1970s suggest a growing uncertainty about organizational goals. In the past it was sufficient to hold up company growth as the corporate goal that all employees could share and benefit from. With the prospects for economic growth now sharply curtailed, especially in the manufacturing sector, this is no longer possible. Management fears a sharp diminution of employee commitment to company goals. Under these circumstances employees are much more likely to define dependency negatively.

We can say that throughout much of the post-World War II period the large-scale Japanese business organization appears to have been remarkably dominant in solving the central life problems of its regular employees relative to their expectations. The range of services provided by these large-scale organizations, at a macro and micro level, has significantly amplified the areas of worker dependency. The territorial segregation indexed by limited inter-firm mobility, long working hours, and extensive company housing similarly amplifies dependency and the potential for building worker commitment to organizational goals. Yet for an internalization of organizational goals to take place, so that the individual identifies his personal success with organizational success, dependency per se is not adequate. Indeed dependency alone may well lead to employee resentment and a sense of coercion. We faced this same issue in our treatment of permanent employment in Chapter I. Business firms had to establish a set of positive rewards to serve as incentives. They had to become dependable in the eyes of the employees by contributing to the solution of the central life problems of employees. The extent to which this was done for more than a small minority of the labor force in the prewar period is difficult to gauge. Certainly the element of coercion was not absent in many work situations. Although large-scale firms achieved a more dominant place in the economy during the postwar period, and undoubtedly became more "dependable" for larger numbers of employees in the sense described above, the process is far from complete. Indeed we have argued that it may be more problematic in the future.

Employer dependability is not simply a matter of paying higher wages and improving working conditions. Stinchcombe (1975) suggests that it is dependency, plus worker participation in and influence upon the organization, that leads individuals to willingly identify with the goals of the organization—to see themselves as full-fledged members. In this regard Japanese employer mobilization and penetration of primary-group relationships among workers, while allowing these groups sufficient autonomy to assume meaningful roles, is critical to understanding the willingness of employees to identify with organizational goals. It is in these primary-group relationships that workers can develop a sense of participation in the organization. The ideology of participation and its policy implementation is primarily—though not exclusively—a postwar phenomenon, and we can be assured that the process of worker participation is far from satisfactory from the viewpoint of many employees. Yet, as should be apparent from the descriptions and analyses of preceding chapters, Japanese managers are moving rapidly to expand the scope of worker participation in the narrow range of production-related decisions. It is carefully controlled participation, and it remains to be seen whether management can contain it in a way that does not threaten their prerogatives.

"When in doubt, throw 'em out."
Management saying at a U.S. auto plant

CHAPTER IX

CAN WE LEARN
FROM THE JAPANESE?

This final chapter concerns the potential for borrowing from the Japanese in the area of work practices. Here we depart from our scholarly efforts to advocate particular values and policy positions.

We may begin our discussion of the potential for learning from the Japanese with an evaluation of our analysis of the Japanese work ethic. If the Japanese work ethic is seen as a unitary phenomenon there is no reason to believe we can or would want to learn from the Japanese. In the context of the complex interaction of variables that underlie the Japanese employee's relation to the organization it is difficult to believe we could apply Japanese practices in toto. Yet our discussion should make it clear that it is not particularly fruitful to see the Japanese work ethic as a unitary concept. It is a multidimensional phenomenon and the potential for borrowing must be examined with respect to specific dimensions.

We found no evidence to show that the Japanese are more committed to work, as defined in its narrow sense of task performance and job satisfaction as reported by workers. This hardly, therefore, seems a desirable avenue for transfer of organizational know-how. Japanese employers do appear quite effective in the area of penetration and mobilization of primary work groups on behalf of organizational goals. This is an area, however, in which success rests most heavily on culturally unique patterns of behavior that cannot easily be absorbed by other nations. Japanese leadership patterns and the individual's relation to the group in Japan are approaches that could not easily be replicated in the United States. Workers and unions would not likely be receptive to the attempts by companies to penetrate and mobilize informal work groups on behalf of organizational goals. Indeed they have a history of resisting such efforts.

In the more general sense of the need to find fulfillment at work, we did find that the Japanese recorded unusually high levels relative to Western European nations. Americans also recorded a strong need to find fulfillment at work, though not quite as high as the Japanese. The differences were not so great, however, as to make this a likely area for borrowing, assuming that it was a need we valued highly in the first place. This leaves the matter of the strong identification with and commitment to the company. We have explained this relatively strong organizational attachment in terms of the historical dependency of workers upon employers in providing normative solutions to central life problems faced by individual members.

What then can we learn from the Japanese? On the one hand there is a fundamental humaneness about the mode of organizing people. Individuals belong and they have goals that give clear-cut direction to their lives. This by no means applies to all members of the labor force, but for those privileged males in large firms (and this does include blue-collar workers) the results appear impressive. Worker alienation, although hardly absent in Japan, seems to be minimal relative to that experienced by Western workers. This is no small achievement, as is only too apparent when we look at the indirect indicators of alienation in the United States as measured in high unemployment, turnover, and absenteeism rates, and the suburban fragmentation and urban cancer that strike at the heart of the American body politic.

At the same time the various dimensions of the Japanese work ethic rest ultimately on a fundamental power relationship that brooks no misunderstanding. Among corporate management in the industrialized market economies, there is no doubt that it is the Japanese managers, above all, who maintain most of their traditional managerial prerogatives and hold firm to the reins of power. Worker participation, worker commitment, company training, and so on, must all be understood in this context. For those committed to democratizing the firm this hardly represents an ideal to be emulated.

In view of the different trajectory taken by Western industrialized nations it is difficult to conceive of the Japanese employee's organizational attachment, based as it is on worker dependency, serving as a feasible model for Western organizations. Indeed the industrial-paternalism model was a solution that Americans explored in the first quarter of the twentieth century, and dropped as unsatisfactory in the face of the great depression and worker militancy. Certainly the idea of individual dependency on corporate paternalism is currently an unacceptable solution. Apparently the idea of the welfare state sits more easily with citizens of contemporary Western nations. Except for those who are ideologically opposed to the welfare state, and those who are "dropouts" for one reason or another, the relationship between citizen and state is perceived not as dependency but as one of reciprocal exchange of rights and obligations. In this context Ronald Dore's assertion (1973) that Japan, by a peculiar set of historical circumstances, is riding the high tide of evolutionary development in its acceptance of welfare corporatism, seems strangely archaic.

Yet to leave the matter here, while perhaps satisfying in a scholarly or ideological sense, leaves much to be desired from a practical point of view. We have seen in the case of quality-control circles and other personnel management strategies that the Japanese have been willing and able to select out particular practices, literally ripping them from their causally ordered network of relationships, and adapting them to Japanese needs and circumstances. This does violence to the social scientist's neatly ordered world of cause-and-effect relationships. One might argue that the Japanese, through historical experience, have developed a remarkable facility for borrowing and adapting that makes them unusually adept in this area, but it hardly seems a skill that Americans could not choose to cultivate more fully. It is true that in the area of worker-manager relationships Americans have historically kept themselves unusually insulated from the experiences of other industrial nations—notwithstanding the ideas brought to our shores by successive waves of immigrants. No doubt this is a function of the unique relationship worked out in the course of our history between human and natural resources in a relatively isolated geographical setting.

In the light of the preceding discussion we may rephrase the question of what we can learn from the Japanese mode of organizing work relationships. At the heart of the distinctiveness of the Japanese approach is the attempt to maximize the harmonization of individual and organizational goals. Most of the key postwar personnel innovations can be understood in this light. Moreover this attempt is made not only by providing incentives for workers to adopt management-defined organizational goals, but also by attempting to maximize the achievement of worker-defined goals so long as they do not conflict with high-priority management goals.

That American organizations might benefit from an attempt to increase the harmonization between personal and organizational goals is hardly a novel idea. Indeed the subject is one which is much discussed in the scholarly literature and among practitioners (e.g., March and Simon 1958; McGregor 1960; Steers and Porter 1975). The potential to learn from the Japanese lies in the borrowing of selected practices that might increase this harmonization while respecting worker goals. To be sure one might argue that we ought not to be limited to innovations that do not conflict with high-priority management goals, but Japan has little to offer in this regard. What we can learn from Japan is limited by its own historical experience, which grew out of management's superior power. An attempt to increase the integration between personal and organizational goals need not, however, be characterized by the thoroughgoing dependency of the individual upon the organization which has been the case in Japan. Just as the Japanese have selectively borrowed and adapted practices to fit their own organizational and societal needs, so may Americans.

QC circles provide an interesting case in point. They promote worker self-development, including skill acquisition and leadership training, as well as shop-floor participation in decision making on production-related matters. At the same time, however, they contribute to high-priority management goals, such as improving product quality and the more efficient organization of work methods. American management and quality-assurance experts have, in fact, shown increasing interest in QC circles and the possibility of adapting them to U.S.

industry. The professional journal of the American Society for Quality Control, *Quality Progress*, has carried a number of articles on Japanese quality-control practices.

The Missiles Systems Division of Lockheed Missiles and Space Company adopted QC circles in 1974 and claims considerable success with their operation (Schleicher 1977, pp. 14–17). Other companies, such as General Motors, are experimenting with similar programs. The General Motors Assembly Division plant at Tarrytown, New York, adopted a problem-solving group for blue-collar workers in the glass installation area in 1973–74. This area had been a major trouble point for the company and union alike. Within just six months the volunteer circle of some thirty workers (out of sixty workers on two shifts) produced a remarkable turnaround in workshop attitudes and a sharp decline in glass breakage and leakage. A United Auto Workers official cites the following results of instituting the problem-solving group: discipline stopped being a problem, worker morale rose sharply, absenteeism dropped from 12 to less than 3 percent, and attitudes toward management personnel, union officials, and co-workers were much improved. More generally, workers now felt that they were being treated like human beings, and that someone was listening to them; there was a new-found dignity.

The company responded to the 1974 recession, however, as they often do in the case of innovative organizational programs; they wiped out the model circle as a shift was lost due to layoffs. One of the striking characteristics of the Tarrytown plant management's presentation on the subject is their emphasis on the long evolutionary process involved in getting them to the point where they were willing to actively consider involving workers on a regular basis in participative decision making. Yet it would appear that they have not reached the point at which institutionalization of job redesign can take place. There seems to be little planning for contingencies which may threaten the program. This observation is consistent with the findings of Tichy (1976, pp. 63–80) in his comparison of the approach of Volvo and General Motors to job redesign. He found a primarily pragmatic, let's-do-it orientation at General Motors. One half-worked-out program succeeds another at relatively short intervals. At Volvo Tichy found a more comprehensive model of social and technological determinants of production, with more forethought to the monitoring and correction of emergent problems. One footnote to this discussion is in order. In somewhat uncharacteristic fashion the Tarrytown experiment was not lost to the organization. The experience was sufficiently positive so that with the upsurge in the auto industry in 1976–77, plans were made at the Tarrytown plant to renew the program on a large scale. All hourly-rated employees are to be trained in problem-solving and small group participative techniques under the joint sponsorship of management and the local union. Furthermore, the initial experience is being held up to other General Motors divisions as a potential model for involving workers in decision making.

It remains to be seen whether the QC circle can be successfully applied to the United States. There are those who would argue that they have their basis in Japanese cultural and institutional conditions, with their unique group orientation, practice of permanent employment, and strong employee commitment to organizational goals. Consequently they are held not to be applicable to the United States. My own judgment is that they may well be applicable if appropriate adaptations are made to accommodate the circles to U.S. conditions. One would think, for example, that in the absence of permanent employment, worker rewards and recognition ought to be more immediate and oriented to financial benefits, so that workers could share resultant productivity gains. Yet it should not be assumed that non-material incentives, such as allowing workers to make contributions to organizational goals and symbolic recognition of these contributions, would not appeal to American workers. It is the intellectual snobbishness of the left that assumes such rewards are meaningless to workers under capitalism (though not under socialism), because the financial rewards go to the firm and not the state. In addition the unions should be more heavily involved in the operation of QC circles than they are in Japan. This would especially be the case in the planning and supervision of their operation to insure that worker interests are respected, and that workers identify QC circles with the union as well. Finally we would expect that any meetings held after regular working hours would be compensated at the normal overtime rate.

Career Enlargement and Job Security

Perhaps the area in which the Americans have the most to learn from the Japanese is that of career enlargement, as elaborated in Chapter V. Career enlargement involves the preparation of career paths and the availability and application of company resources, especially training, to individual employees, so that it is profitable for both company and employee to actualize these career paths. It involves a recognition that all employees, with proper training, have the potential to make significant contributions to organizational goals. This is a far more ambitious program than job enlargement as currently advocated in the United States (see Chapters V and VI). The recent emphasis on "upgrading" and "new careers" in the United States does, however, point in some of the same directions, though as yet these new orientations have had limited impact (National Manpower Policy Task Force 1970).

The practice of career enlargement, not just for white-collar employees but for blue-collar workers as well, is most feasible in the context of lifetime employment, or at least striving toward this ideal.[1] Consequently for career enlargement to make sense to American managers on a large scale they would have to learn to accept the idea that you do not adjust your labor force up and down with the vagaries of the business cycle. Instead you operate with the assumption that an attempt will be made with every employee hired to train, educate, and expand his or her job horizons, and above all to keep employees until retirement age. This would involve designing jobs and job structures so that learning and the acquisition of new skills are part of the ongoing job experience. The institution of these policies would reduce employee incentive to change jobs. This would reduce the heavy costs to management associated with voluntary turnover, e.g.,

1. I refer hereafter to the permanent employment practice as lifetime employment.

recruitment and training costs, and unemployment compensation contributions. Only on the assumption that they will keep an employee until retirement age can the firm operate to capture sufficient returns against the costs of investment in education, training and personalized attention that are involved in the practice of career employment. A partial exception occurs when the employee is willing to finance his or her own educational investment through lowered wage increases.

Certainly were the decision made to pursue these policies it would go a long way toward meeting a major American worker need, as identified in numerous surveys (see Table 21, Chapter IV). Job security is commonly rated among the most important job characteristics by American employees; generally, the lower the occupational status, the greater the dissatisfaction with the current job in this respect (Robinson et al. 1969, pp. 25–75, especially p. 50). Although laissez faire ideology would have it that job insecurity is the most effective prod to keep workers in line and insure proper performance, this canard goes against the basic findings of modern psychology. It is positive not negative sanctions that are capable of eliciting high levels of motivation to perform role assignments in predictable fashion and, especially, to produce innovative behavior on behalf of organizational goals when role specifications are inadequate.

Is such a proposal as we have outlined feasible? Do career enlargement and guaranteed job security meet high-priority management goals as well as worker needs? In rapidly growing firms there seems to be no problem. Declining industries, small firms, and those industries peculiarly subject to sharp fluctuations in product demand would, however, be hard put to maintain such policies. In addition really sharp fluctuations in the national economy, such as occurred in 1974, put severe pressure on the ability to maintain such policies. Yet perhaps we can learn from the Japanese here as well.

The mid-1970s recession also had a great impact in Japan. Yet the lifetime employment practice did not disappear. Apart from company attempts to limit the impact of the recession on employment by resorting to shorter working hours and the like, the government made a policy decision that lifetime employment was too valuable a practice to let simply die. New legislation was drawn up in the shape of the 1974 Employment Insurance Act, providing for government subsidies to designated firms which carry employees on their rolls until the economic situation improves. The subsidies are drawn from the unemployment insurance reserves. The new law enables employers to avoid dismissals by receiving grants to cover partial wage payments to workers put on work furloughs extending for one-third or longer of the month (one-fourth or longer for small and medium-sized firms). Those firms qualifying can receive grants for six months. Extensions for as long as nine months have been granted, but generally only three-month extensions are anticipated. The important thing is that large Japanese enterprises, by resorting to these Japanese-style layoffs rather than "temporary discharges," hold their surplus regular workers within their own organizations rather than throwing them out into the street. Between January and August of 1975 some two million workers benefited from the program, with the Ministry of Labor estimating that the grants saved 150,000 to 200,000 workers from possible discharge.

One might argue that the same function could have been achieved by paying out unemployment benefits, but this position entails an exceedingly narrow view of the costs of unemployment. We argued in Chapter IV that the social and psychological costs of severing the employment relationship are profound; nor should this be surprising, since it is through work that employed men and women come to define their own social and personal worth. Moreover the economic costs should not be underestimated. The potential loss of productivity, through the disruption and later renewal of the employment relationship with a new or even the same employer under altered circumstances, is often substantial.

A reorientation of American management and government toward acceptance of the ideal of lifetime employment may initially strike one as unrealistic. Yet we should keep in mind, as one unhappy American businessman who operates factories in a number of nations told me, that America is really odd man out on this matter. In most of the other nations a variety of restrictions make it difficult for employers to simply dismiss employees without "just cause." They also find it difficult to dismiss workers when minor weaknesses in the economy develop. These restrictions on management prerogatives take many forms; they are based on statutory law, labor agreement, and social customs. In Japan, as we saw in Chapter III, worker protection is based largely on custom. In the United States we have no general unjust dismissal statutes, nor do we provide much protection through custom. We have the odd situation where only unionized employees have access to the developed body of arbitration law which recognizes that employees have property rights in their jobs and effectively protects them against unjust dismissal. Yet even unionized employees have little protection in the face of economically-based dismissals, although arbitration law does insure that unionized employers must use some objectively measurable standard for layoffs and dismissals rather than relying on their subjective evaluation of individual employees. In addition to seniority, American unions have relied on work sharing (in some industries) to distribute the incidence of layoffs, and in certain industries supplementary unemployment insurance and/or severance pay have cushioned the impact of unemployment. Unlike workers in a number of Western European countries, American workers (and Japanese workers for that matter) do not have the legal right to be consulted well in advance of layoffs, and the ability to delay and sometimes to prevent them (Weinberg 1974, p. 3). For the almost two-thirds of the American labor force that is unorganized, there is practically no protection. They have recourse only to the common law rules which deny the existence of any job rights and deny employees any protection from even the most arbitrary dismissals. The major exceptions, where employees have been given statutory protection, are in the statutes of the National Labor Relations Act of 1935, prohibiting an employer from discriminating in employment to encourage or discourage union membership, and the Civil Rights Act of 1964, which prohibits discrimination on the basis of race, creed, nationality, and sex. In short, the United States is one of the few industrial nations that does not provide general legal protection against unjust dismissals (Summers 1976). It is one of the minor ironies of our times that foreign firms increasingly treat us as an underdeveloped nation. They see the absence of statutory protection against unjust dismissal and other restrictions on their rights to discharge as a significant incentive for locating their plants in the United States. They have greater flexibility than in their native countries to adapt output and employment to changing demand conditions. This compensates, in part, for the higher labor costs they must bear in the United States.

258   Apart from statutory regulation, in a number of nations such as Sweden and, as we have seen, Japan, employees are subsidized by the government through a variety of devices during economic downturns, so that they can maintain employees on the payroll. Indeed many prominent Japanese are coming to recognize that if permanent employment is to be maintained in a period of low economic growth rates, it will require significant increases in government investment to "stabilize employment." Fujita Yoshitaka (1976) argues that permanent employment has survived as a custom in Japan in a period of rapid economic growth. If it is to survive in periods of economic downturn, however, he believes that they must institutionalize long-term and large-scale government subsidies as in Sweden. Koike Kazuo argues that there must be statutory protection, particularly to protect older workers.

In a similar fashion, Americans have hardly exhausted the potential of public policy for smoothing out the business cycle. One might argue that we have barely begun. With respect to unemployment it is clear that many existing programs are of dubious value. After all the billions of dollars spent on manpower training programs for unemployed workers, the consensus seems to be that these programs have for the most part failed (see HEW Task Force 1972, pp. 167–71). Is it not possible that we could elaborate policies which contain incentives for employers to retain and train their employees? There is reason to believe that such programs would be more effective than those designed to train the unemployed. Evidence for this proposition may be derived from the observation that on-the-job training appears to be more successful in placing enrollees of manpower training programs in permanent jobs than is the practice of training the unemployed (HEW Task Force 1972, p. 170). Encouraging employers to retain and retrain their employees would thus diminish the inflationary impact of job creation relative to the standard approaches.

To subsidize firms would involve shifting the payment of unemployment insurance to the firm of worker origin, rather than directly to the worker. Since this goes against the principle of vesting, it might well be met with political opposition in the United States (i.e., would this make the worker too dependent on the firm?). Moreover the administrative problem of insuring that firms do not arbitrarily inflate their financial problems to qualify for the subsidy must be handled carefully. There was some speculation, for example, that the new Japanese law was being used by some firms to lay off their workers rather than helping them to deal with layoffs when they were really needed.

Yet these are not insurmountable problems. In the case of Japanese firms, in order to qualify for government subsidies the firm must produce documents which satisfactorily demonstrate to the Ministry of Labor that production has decreased more than 20 percent over the previous year. Even then the subsidy is only one-half of the basic wage payment in large firms and two-thirds for small and medium-sized firms. In short, the government subsidy is limited to industries hard-hit by economic downturns, and the employer must still bear a significant portion of the wage payment. The basic approach is to treat government subsidies as counter-cyclical grants rather than permanent subsidies.

Although it is hardly inevitable that such arrangements will come to pass in the United States, the ideas are perhaps not as farfetched as might initially seem the case. In the legislative arena, job tax credits have been proposed as payments to business firms for employing new workers; these wage subsidies are intended as incentives for hiring new employees.[2] Nor must the initiative always come from the state. In 1955 the United Automobile Workers and the Ford Motor Company agreed on a contract providing "supplemental employment benefits." Under this contract a percentage, now 95 percent, of a worker's pay continues even if he or she is laid off. This was a major step forward to stabilizing the work force. Yet job security has continued to be a dominant issue in company-union relationships. It was the dominant issue at the 1976 United Auto Workers bargaining convention as the union readied for contract negotiations with employers in a year of tentative economic recovery. The demands adopted at the convention were the characteristic ones associated with spreading the work as a response to shrinking job opportunities and cyclical declines in the demand for labor. The proposed solutions involved shorter working hours, reduced subcontracting, improved pension plans to encourage early retirement, controls over subcontracting, and an end to the practice of supervisors—who are former UAW members—"bumping back" to hourly-rated jobs during layoffs. Although the institution of all these proposals would certainly create more jobs and although the union, in fact, won some of these demands, they hardly attack the core of the problem. This core involves the strong incentive that employers have to lay off workers with even the slightest dip in the economy. Similarly the practice of encouraging extensive overtime rather than bearing the costs associated with new hiring testifies to the disincentives toward stabilizing the labor force at high levels.

For a while it looked as though the next breakthrough in this area would come from the steel industry. The United Steelworkers of America selected a lifetime job guarantee as one of their bargaining goals at their 1976 union convention for the 1977 contract negotiations. The union seeks "a lifetime security program, guaranteeing that a steelworker will have a job and will receive full pay irrespective of circumstances outside his or her control." The union proposal involves a combination of a reduction in working days per year and various jobs and income guarantees, such that the steel companies would move toward providing employees with lifetime job security. Nor is the boom-and-bust quality of steel industry production seen as an insurmountable obstacle. The union argued that the prior historic agreement to send unresolved issues to arbitration, and

2. These proposals are, of course, still quite different from policies that would encourage upgrading and long-term investment in existing employees. Moreover tax-credit legislation is not necessarily the most efficient policy option for job creation. There is the danger that it would be giving firms tax incentives to do what they would have done anyway.

thereby do away with strikes and stockpiling, also did away with the major causes of the roller-coaster character of production in the industry. They reasoned that this created the basis for successful implementation of the new union proposals. The union further argued that lifetime job security would relieve employers of all unemployment insurance payments and further stabilize the job force. The 1977 contract did achieve a new security package for those with twenty or more years of seniority on the job. It provides layoff pay for up to two years and a three-hundred-dollar-a-month supplement for those who take their pension upon layoff prior to age sixty-two. The contract also creates a task force to decide what further steps should be taken to achieve lifetime job and income security. This still falls short of the goal, as was made painfully evident by large-scale steelworker layoffs late in 1977.

The longshoremen's contract for workers at the ports of New York and New Jersey provides a model whereby workers are guaranteed compensation for 2,080 hours of work a year until retirement age. In the New York port, of the 12,000 longshoremen on the active working rolls in 1977, some 3,000 collect the guaranteed annual income. The quid pro quo for job security here is the granting to management a freer hand in the internal deployment of the labor force and in the introduction of new technology (i.e., containerization).

It may be time for Americans to reflect more on whether the welfare society can have any real meaning if we persist with the anachronistic practice of making selected workers arbitrarily vulnerable to protracted periods of unemployment. Equity requires that we either share the burden more widely or provide jobs for all those who want to work full time. Japanese practices highlight the benefits to be obtained from maximizing policy outputs that reinforce the lifetime employment principle. The advantages of adopting policies such as counter-cyclical subsidies to companies in order to avoid dismissals are threefold. It would contribute to removing a major fear and insecurity among workers stemming from the absence of job security, lay the groundwork for career enlargement, and contribute toward a greater harmonization of personal and organizational goals.

The kind of cyclical unemployment for which we have proposed solutions should not be confused with that unemployment arising from structural weaknesses of the economy. The fundamental problem is that our economy, as currently structured, does not create enough jobs for everyone who wants to work. To deal with structural unemployment involves some combination of monetary and tax policy, educational policy, public works projects, and specific programs tailored to the needs of the most disadvantaged, the young, and the minorities.

The Japanese have been able to maintain a low level of structural unemployment, not because they have figured out a better mix of these various alternative policies, but because their economy has grown at such a rapid rate. This growth, simply put, has created a sufficient number of jobs. Throughout the mid-1960s and early 1970s, the unemployment rate stood at about 1.3 percent: it rose to 1.9 percent in 1975.[3] With lowered economic growth rates, we begin to see

3. The official unemployment figures are based on labor force surveys rather than the number of registered insured workers. They tend slightly to underestimate the inci-

some problems developing. The full unemployment effects of the long-term decline in Japanese economic growth rates have yet to be experienced. Although firms have been able to hold redundant employees within their fold as they tided over the immediate effects of the recession, the financial reserves of such structurally depressed industries as steel and shipbuilding are being rapidly depleted. Large-scale dismissals may yet have to take place as makeshift solutions such as employee transfers to affiliated companies and government measures prove inadequate. It has become increasingly difficult for small affiliated firms to absorb the excess labor of the major enterprises as they have done in the past. One possibility is for a contraction of lifetime employment to take place, limiting it to a more select core of employees with greater restrictions on the benefits associated with this guarantee. In practice, this might not be so different from what exists in many Western economies.

Yet Japanese government officials in the Ministry of Labor and Ministry of Trade and Industry seem determined to preserve the permanent employment practice since they and many businessmen see it as the key to industrial harmony and indeed societal harmony. To this end, significant new legislation has been enacted and more is proposed to deal with structural unemployment. Notable is the Employment Stabilization Project (1977) designed to stabilize employment through facilitating job transfers from depressed or declining industries. Under this program, an employer who has "temporarily laid-off" employees due to business fluctuations or the need to make changes in business activities is entitled to rebates from the Employment Stabilization Fund (two-thirds of wages in smaller enterprises and one-half in larger enterprises). Similarly, these provisions also apply to employers who respond to the same problems by providing training to employees while paying them their normal wages. Still another notable feature is rebates to employers who shift their employees to affiliated firms while bearing the costs. The Ministry of Labor is responsible for designating industries that require a shift to new business activities (i.e., structurally depressed industries). For the time being, employers bear the major costs of funding the new programs through increases in the employers' insurance premium rate.

The strategy involves designing incentives for firms in structurally depressed industries to shift to new more profitable lines of business. This is consistent with long-term government policy which steers and sometimes coerces Japanese firms in directions that the government believes will enhance their competitive power. The Ministry of Trade and Industry, in particular, is assigned the task of developing the fiscal and tax incentives to encourage firms to move toward new lines of business. It is not an unfamiliar task for the Ministry. Recently, this has involved encouraging major firms to establish new affiliated firms to which employees are transferred. To take one example, Ishikawajima Harima

---

dence of unemployment relative to other nations because of the relatively loose definition of being employed and the rather strict definition of unemployment. In addition there is a strong discouraged-worker effect, in which individuals withdraw from the labor market when employment prospects appear poor (Shimada 1972, p. 21).

Heavy Industries, a major shipbuilding firm, recently established the Ishikawa-jima Harima Sound Reduction Company which specializes in designing sound reduction construction machinery to facilitate nighttime construction and reduce occupational sound hazards. Other manufacturing firms are venturing into real estate and a variety of other service sector industries.

At the same time, the Ministry of Labor assumes responsibility for developing programs that provide incentives for employers to retrain their own employees in the skills necessary for new lines of business. For example, shipbuilding employees are to be taught skills in land construction projects such as bridge building. It is too early to assess the impact of the new legislation; much will depend on the rate of economic growth Japan is able to sustain. There are also a variety of more traditional policies that are being advocated within the Ministry of Labor including the encouragement of labor mobility between firms and industries and increased job training for the unemployed. Yet, from an American perspective, the legislation suggests a boldness absent from the discussions of American policy makers. Who in America is talking publicly about the need to shift firms in declining industries like textiles, where we are no longer internationally competitive, into new lines of business and to provide the financial incentives to employers to do this as they retrain their existing labor force? Who in America has the political courage to advocate such policies? Certainly not Richard Nixon at the time of the textile crisis several years ago. Certainly not Jimmy Carter as he seeks to pacify rising protectionist sentiment. Yet, if these shifts are not made, how are we to accommodate the rising clamor from third-world nations for an increasing share of the economic pie?

Before we grasp so eagerly at Japanese solutions we need to further clarify some similarities and differences in Japanese and American economic structure and public policy as it impinges on employment policy. American government policies are hardly laissez-faire as regards the stimulation of new industries. The U.S. government engages in a variety of individual programs through its tax policies (e.g., rules for depreciation) and public expenditures (e.g., defense budget) that promote new industries. Often, however, these are uncoordinated programs with the results deriving as second-order consequences from pursuing other primary goals; cost-benefit ratios are high as a consequence. The spinoff industries generated by the defense industry are a case in point. There is, moreover, no systematic policy to encourage firms and workers in structurally depressed industries to shift into new more promising growth industries.

Ultimately, any attempt to learn from the Japanese must take into consideration some fundamental differences in economic structure and the nature of the unemployment problem in the two economies. In the U.S., the public sector is an important component of total employment and we rely heavily on expansion of the public sector in stimulating employment; in Japan, the public sector plays a relatively minor role, though public works programs are large. Solution of the U.S. unemployment problem involves learning how to improve the employability of unskilled and uneducated labor, workers who often have never experienced a regular job. This, in turn, is entwined with youth and minority unemployment. These have not been major problems for the Japanese and consequently, it is reasonable to think that solutions to the respective employment problems would be quite different.

Finally, for all the recent scholarly emphasis on the fundamentally egalitarian quality of Japanese firms (Dore 1973; Glazer 1976), the economic slowdown calls attention to certain fundamentally unegalitarian qualities in Japanese social and economic institutions.

A detailed analysis of the effects of the 1974–1975 recession reveals that, although the core workers in large firms were fairly well protected from its effects, substantial employment adjustments in the system came through discrimination against the non-elites (Shimada, 1977). In particular, large firms resorted to dismissing temporary workers while small firms more often resorted to selective dismissals, the solicitation of early retirements, and the dismissal of temporary workers. Substantial numbers of secondary workers, in particular, housewives, left the labor force. As many as 600,000 women left the labor force in 1974–1975, despite an overall growth in the number of women in the productive age category. In short, employment security is much better for white-collar workers than blue-collar workers, for young workers than older workers (over fifty), for employees in large firms than small firms, and those with regular employee status than those without it (including family workers, casual workers, and temporary and part-time workers).[4] Last but perhaps most important, employment security is much better for male workers than female workers. Thus the egalitarian quality of certain organizational practices in large firms, such as lifetime employment, must be weighed against the shape of the total stratification system. This overall system, with its ascriptive age and sex discrimination and dualistic labor market practices, hardly represents a model for the solution of the problems facing the United States. We have all too much of our own inequality. If the job security benefits achieved by the American auto workers and steelworkers come at the expense of others less powerful in the economy, then overall societal justice can hardly be said to have been enhanced. The issue becomes how to spread these benefits more widely among the population. Rapid economic growth has not required the Japanese to face up to these inherent inequalities in the past. The future offers no such luxuries in either Japan or the United States.

---

4. With respect to age, 75 percent of those large firms with a fixed age retirement system have the retirement age set between fifty-five and fifty-seven.

BIBLIOGRAPHY

Abegglen, James.
   1958. *The Japanese factory*. Glencoe, Ill.: Free Press.
   1973. *Management and worker: The Japanese solution*. Tokyo: Sophia University
      Press.
Andors, Stephen.
   1971. Revolution and modernization: Man and machine in industrializing society,
      the Chinese case. In *America's Asia: Dissenting essays on Asian-American
      relations*, ed. Edward Friedman and Mark Selden. New York: Vintage
      Books.
Armer, Michael, and Schnaiberg, Allan.
   1972. Measuring individual modernity: A near myth. *American Sociological Re-
      view* 37:301–16.
Asahi Publishing Company.
   1930. *Nihon keizai tōkei sōkan (Special edition on Japanese economic statistics)*.
      Tokyo: Asahi Shinbunsha.
Augustine, Joseph.
   1972. Personnel turnover. In *Handbook of modern personnel administration*, ed.
      Joseph Famulero. New York: McGraw-Hill.
Azumi, Koya, and McMillan, Charles. ͂
   1976. Worker sentiment in the Japanese factory: Its organizational determinants. In
      Japan: The paradox of progress, ed. Lewis Austin. New Haven: Yale Uni-
      versity Press.
Bank of Japan.
   1974. *Keizai tōkei nenpō (Economic statistics annual)*. Tokyo: Bank of Japan Sta-
      tistics Department.
Barby, Steven.
   1969. Economic backwardness and the characteristics of development. *Journal of
      Economic History* 29:449–73.
Becker, Gary.
   1964. *Human Capital*. New York: National Bureau of Economic Research.
Bendix, Reinhard.
   1964. *Nation-building and citizenship*. New York: John Wiley and Sons.

1967. Preconditions of development: A comparison of Japan and Germany. In *Aspects of social change in modern Japan*, ed. Ronald Dore. Princeton, N.J.: Princeton University Press.

Bennett, John.

1967. Japanese economic growth: Background for social change. In *Aspects of social change in modern Japan*, ed. Ronald Dore. Princeton, N.J.: Princeton University Press.

————, and Levine, Solomon.

1976. Environment and the postindustrial society in Japan. In *Japanese industrialization and its social consequences*, ed. Hugh Patrick. Berkeley and Los Angeles: University of California Press.

Bennis, Warren, and Slater, Philip.

1968. *The temporary society*. New York: Harper and Row.

Benson, J.

1977. Organizations: A dialectial view. *Administrative Science Quarterly* 22:1–21.

Berger, Suzanne, et al.

1975. New perspectives for the study of Western Europe. *Items* 29:34–37.

Bishop, Yvonne; Feinberg, Stephen; and Holland, Paul.

1975. *Discrete multivariate analysis*. Cambridge, Mass.: MIT Press.

Blau, Peter.

1964. *Exchange and power in social life*. New York: John Wiley and Sons.

1968. The hierarchy of authority in organizations. *American Journal of Sociology* 73:453–67.

1974. Parameters of social structure. *American Sociological Review* 39:615–35.

————, and Dudley Duncan.

1967. *The American occupational structure*. New York: John Wiley and Sons.

————, and Schoenherr, Richard.

1971. *The structure of organizations*. New York: Basic Books.

Blauner, Robert.

1964. *Alienation and freedom*. Chicago: University of Chicago Press.

Braverman, Harry.

1974. *Labor and monopoly capital*. New York: Monthly Review Press.

Brenner, Harvey.

1973. *Mental illness and the economy*. Cambridge, Mass.: Harvard University Press.

1975. Social stress and the national economy: Recent findings on mental disorder, aggression, and psychosomatic illness. Testimony to the Joint Economic Committee of the Congress of the United States. Washington, D.C., December 8.

Bright, James.

1958. *Automation and management*. Boston: Harvard University, Graduate School of Business Administration, Division of Research.

Browne, Malcolm.

1975. Yugoslav output off, cracking down on loafers. *New York Times*, 11 September, p. 10.

Brugger, William.

1976. *Democracy and organization in the Chinese industrial enterprise, 1948–1953*. London: Cambridge University Press.

Business Week.

1972. Japan paces the world. September 9. P. 118.

Byrne, J. J.
    1975. Occupational mobility of workers. *Monthly Labor Review* 98, no. 2, pp. 53–59.
Cain, Glen.
    1976. The challenge of segmented labor market theories to orthodox theory: A survey. *Journal of Economic Literature* 12:1215–57.
Caplan, Robert.
    1971. Organizational stress and individual strain: A sociopsychological study of risk factors in coronary heart disease among administrators, engineers, and scientists. Ph.D. dissertation, University of Michigan.
Center for the Development of Human Abilities.
    1975. *Ningensei kakuho no tame no man-mashin shisutemu no kaihatsu ni kansuru chōsa kenkyū* (*Studies on the development of man-machine systems to reaffirm humanity*). Tokyo: Ningen Nōryoku Kaihatsu Sentā.
Chandler, Alfred, Jr.
    1962. *Strategy and structure: Chapters in the history of the American industrial enterprise*. Cambridge, Mass.: MIT Press.
Child, John.
    1972. Organization structure and strategies of control: A replication of the Aston study. *Administrative Science Quarterly* 17:163–77.
Chinoy, Ely.
    1955. *Automobile workers and the American dream*. Garden City, N.Y.: Doubleday.
Chūō Rōdō Iinkai.
    1966–75. *Chūō Rōdō Jihō* (*Central Labor Review*), Wage Conditions Survey.
Cole, Robert E.
    1971. *Japanese blue-collar*. Berkeley and Los Angeles: University of California Press.
    1972. Permanent employment in Japan: Facts and fantasies. *Industrial and Labor Relations Review* 26:615–30.
    1973. Functional alternatives and economic development: An empirical example of permanent employment in Japan. *American Sociological Review* 38: 424–38.
    1974. British factory–Japanese factory. *Contemporary Sociology* 3:389–92.
    1976. Changing labor force characteristics and their impact on Japanese industrial relations. In *Japan: The paradox of progress*, ed. Lewis Austin. New Haven: Yale University Press.
————, and Tominaga, Ken'ichi.
    1976a. Japan's changing occupational structure and its significance. In *Japanese industrialization and its social consequences*, ed. Hugh Patrick. Berkeley and Los Angeles: University of California Press.
Conot, Robert.
    1974. *American odyssey*. New York: William Morrow.
Craig, Albert.
    1975. Functional and dysfunctional aspects of government bureaucracy. In *Modern Japanese organization and decision-making*, ed. Ezra Vogel. Berkeley and Los Angeles: University of California Press.
Crawcour, Sidney.
    1965. The Tokugawa heritage. In *The state and economic enterprise in modern Japan*, ed. W. W. Lockwood. Princeton, N.J.: Princeton University Press.

Crozier, Michel.
:   1964. *The bureaucratic phenomenon*. Chicago: University of Chicago Press.
Cummings, William.
:   1976. Egalitarian education. Unpublished paper, University of Chicago.
Dahrendorf, Ralf.
:   1967. *Society and democracy in Germany*. New York: Doubleday.
:   1970. On the origin of inequality among men. In *The logic of social hierarchies*, ed. Edward O. Laumann et al. Chicago: Markham.
Deming, William.
:   1970. *Statistical control of quality in Japan*. Proceedings of the International Conference on Quality Control, 1969. Tokyo: Union of Japanese Scientists and Engineers.
DeSpelder, Bruce.
:   1962. *Ratios of staff to line personnel*. Bureau of Business Research, Research Monograph No. 106. Columbus: Ohio State University.
Detroit Free Press.
:   1975. U.S. losing faith in military might. November 27.
De Vos, George.
:   1974. Achievement orientation, social self-identity, and Japanese economic growth. In *Modern Japan*, ed. Irwin Scheiner. New York: Macmillan.
————, and Wagatsuma, Hiroshi.
:   1973. The entrepreneurial market of lower class urban Japanese in manufacturing. In *Socialization for achievement: Essays in the cultural psychology of the Japanese*, ed. George De Vos. Berkeley and Los Angeles: University of California Press.
Doeringer, Peter, and Piore, Michael.
:   1971. *Internal labor markets and manpower analysis*. Lexington, Mass.: Heath.
Doi, Takeo.
:   1973. *The anatomy of dependence*. Tokyo: Kodansha International.
Dore, Ronald.
:   1973. *British factory–Japanese factory*. Berkeley and Los Angeles: University of California Press.
:   1974. *Late development—or something else? Industrial relations in Britain, Japan, Mexico, Sri Lanka, Senegal*. Institute of Development Studies Discussion Paper No. 61. Brighton, England: University of Sussex.
Dornbusch, Sanford, and Scott, W. Richard.
:   1975. *Evaluation and the exercise of authority*. San Francisco: Jossey-Bass.
Dower, John, ed.
:   1975. *Origins of the modern Japanese state*. New York: Random House.
Drucker, Peter.
:   1954. *The practice of management*. New York: Harper.
:   1971. What we can learn from Japanese management. *Harvard Business Review* 49, no. 2, pp. 100–22.
Dubin, Robert.
:   1956. Industrial workers' worlds: A study of the "central life interests" of industrial workers. *Social Problems* 3:131–42.
:   1958. *The world of work*. Englewood Cliffs, N.J.: Prentice-Hall.
Duncan, Otis, ed.
:   1964. *On culture and social change*. Chicago: University of Chicago Press.

Durkheim, Emile.
   1947. *The division of labor in society.* Glencoe, Ill.: Free Press.
Duus, Peter.
   1976. *The rise of modern Japan.* Boston: Houghton Mifflin.
Dyck, Richard.
   1975. A sociological analysis of Japan's research and development system. Ph.D. dissertation, Harvard University.
Eckler, A., and Zlotnick, Jack.
   1949. Immigration and the labor force. *Annals of the American Academy of Political and Social Science* 262:92–101.
Eckstein, Alexander.
   1966. Individualism and the role of the state in economic growth. In *Political development and social change*, ed. Jason Finkle and Richard Gable. New York: John Wiley and Sons.
Economic Planning Agency, Japan.
   1972. *The Japanese and their society.* Part II of the Report on National Life. Tokyo: Economic Planning Agency.
   1975. *Economic survey of Japan, 1974–75.* Tokyo: Japan Times.
Eisenstadt, S. N.
   1956. *From generation to generation.* Glencoe, Ill.: Free Press.
   1965. *Essays in comparative institutions.* New York: John Wiley and Sons.
   1973. *Tradition, change, and modernity.* New York: John Wiley and Sons.
Emery, F. E., and Trist, E. L.
   1969. Socio-technical systems. In *Systems thinking*, ed. F. E. Emery. London: Penguin Books.
Featherman, David.
   1971. A research note: A social structural model for the socioeconomic career. *American Journal of Sociology* 77:293–304.
Feldman, Gerald.
   1966. *Army, industry and labor in Germany: 1914–1918.* Princeton, N.J.: Princeton University Press.
Forbes, A. F.
   1971. Markov chains for manpower systems. In *Manpower and management science*, ed. D. J. Bartholomew and A. R. Smith. London: English Universities Press.
Form, William.
   1968. Occupations and careers. In *The international encyclopedia of the social sciences.* Vol. 11. New York: Macmillan and Free Press.
   1976. *Blue-collar stratification.* Princeton, N.J.: Princeton University Press.
Fox, Alan.
   1974. *Beyond contract: Work, power, and trust relations.* London: Faber and Faber.
Foy, Nancy.
   1975. *The sun never sets on IBM.* New York: William Morrow.
Frank, Andre G.
   1967. Sociology of development and underdevelopment of sociology. *Catalyst* 5:20–73.
French, Wendell.
   1974. *The personnel management process.* Boston: Houghton Mifflin.

Friedson, Eliot.

    1977. The division of labor as social interaction. In *Work and technology*, ed. Marie Haug and Jacques Dofny. Beverly Hills, Ca.: Sage Publications.

Fuchs, Victor.

    1967. *Differentials in hourly earnings by region and city size 1959.* Occasional Paper 101. New York: National Bureau of Economic Research.

Fujita, Wakao.

    1961. *Nihon rōdōkyōyakuron (An analysis of collective agreements in Japan).* Tokyo: Tokyo University Press.

Fujita, Yoshitaka.

    1976. Omoni ni natta shūshin koyō (The heavy burden of permanent employment). *Gekkan Ekonomisuto* 7 (March): 28-35.

————, and Ishida, Hideo.

    1970. *Kigyō to rōshi kankei (The enterprise and labor management relations).* Tokyo: Chikuma Shobō.

Funahashi, Naomichi.

    1973. The industrial reward system: Wages and benefits. In *Workers and employers in Japan*, ed. Kazuo Okochi, Bernard Karsh, and Solomon Levine. Tokyo: University of Tokyo Press.

    1975. Naibu rōdō shijō to nenkō seido (The internal labor market and the *nenkō* system). *Nihon Rōdō Kyōkai Zasshi* 17 (March):2–12.

Geertz, Clifford.

    1964. Ideology as a cultural system. In *Ideology and discontent*, ed. David Apter. New York: Free Press.

Gerschenkron, Alexander.

    1962. *Economic backwardness in historical perspective.* New York: Praeger.

Gibbs, J., and Martin, W.

    1962. Urbanization, technology and the division of labor: International patterns. *American Sociological Review* 27:667–77.

Gilbreth, Frank.

    1911. *Motion study.* New York: D. Van Nostrand.

Glaser, Barney, ed.

    1968. *Organizational careers.* Chicago: Aldine.

Glazer, Nathan.

    1976. Social and cultural factors in Japanese economic growth. In *Asia's new giant*, ed. Hugh Patrick and Henry Rosovsky. Washington, D.C.: Brookings Institution.

Glueck, William.

    1974. *Personnel: A diagnostic approach.* Dallas: Business Publications.

Goldthorpe, John, et al.

    1968. *The affluent worker: Industrial attitudes and behavior.* Cambridge: Cambridge University Press.

Gomberg, William.

    1955. *A trade union analysis of time study.* 2nd ed. New York: Prentice-Hall.

Gooding, Justin.

    1970. Blue-collar blues on the assembly line. *Fortune* 82, no. 1, pp. 69 ff.

Goodman, Leo.

    1971. The analysis of multidimensional contingency tables: Stepwise procedures and direct estimation methods for building models of multiple classifications. *Technometrics* 13:33–61.

Grinker, William; Cooke, Donald; and Kirsch, Arthur.

    1970. *Climbing the job ladder*. New York: E. F. Shelley and Co. Reprinted ERIC Reports, National Institute of Education, U.S. Department of Health, Education and Welfare.

Groves, Robert.

    1975. Intra-employer status mobility: The role of the firm in wage and occupational achievement. Ph.D. dissertation, University of Michigan.

Gusfield, Joseph.

    1967. Tradition and modernity: Misplaced polarities in the study of social change. *American Journal of Sociology* 72:351–362.

Gutman, Herbert.

    1976. *Work, culture, and society in industrializing America*. New York: Alfred A. Knopf.

Hage, Jerry, and Aiken, Michael.

    1967. Relationship of centralization to other structural properties. *Administrative Science Quarterly* 12:72–92.

Hall, John.

    1962. Feudalism in Japan: A reassessment. *Comparative Studies in Society and History* 5:15–51.

Hamel, H. R.

    1967. *Job tenure of workers, January 1966*. Special Labor Force Report No. 77. Washington, D.C.: Bureau of Labor Statistics.

Hanami, Tadashi; Koshiro, Kazutoshi; and Inagami, Takeshi.

    1977. Worker participation in management today. *Japan Labor Bulletin* 16, no. 8, pp. 5–8.

Hannan, Michael, and Freeman, John.

    1977. The population ecology of organizations. *American Journal of Sociology* 82:929–64.

Hartmann, Heinz.

    1959. *Authority and organization in German management*. Princeton, N.J.: Princeton University Press.

Hauser, William.

    1974. *Economic institutional change in Tokugawa Japan*. Cambridge: Cambridge University Press.

    1974a. The diffusion of cotton processing and trade in the Kinai region in Tokugawa Japan. *Journal of Asian Studies* 33:633–49.

Hazama, Hiroshi.

    1964. *Nihon rōmu kanrishi kenkyū* (*A study of the history of personnel management*). Tokyo: Daiamondosha.

    1973. Nihon teki keiei no tokushitsu (Characteristics of Japanese-style management). *ZD Kenkyū Repōto* (*Zero Defects Program Research Report*), pp. 1–14. Published by Nihon Nōritsu Kyōkai (Japan Management Association), May 1973.

Herzberg, Frederick.

    1966. *Work and the nature of man*. Cleveland: World Publishing Co.

Hirschman, Albert.

    1970. *Exit, voice, and loyalty*. Cambridge, Mass.: Harvard University Press.

Hirschmeier, Johannes, and Yui, Tsunehiko.

    1975. *The development of Japanese business, 1600–1973*. Cambridge, Mass.: Harvard University Press.

Hodge, Robert, and Siegel, Paul.
    1966. The classification of occupations: Some problems of sociological inter-
        pretation. *Proceedings*, American Statistical Association, Social Statistics
        Section.
Holli, Melvin, ed.
    1976. *Detroit*. New York: New Viewpoints.
Hori, Masao.
    1977. Atarashii shakaishugi e no michi (Road to a new socialism). *Ekonomisuto* 55
        (No. 36, August 30): 10–15.
Horie, Yasuzo.
    1966. The transformation of the national economy. In *The modernization of Japan*,
        ed. Seiichi Tobata. Tokyo: Institute of Asian Economic Affairs.
Hoselitz, Bert.
    1966. Main concepts in the analysis of the social implications of technical change.
        In *Industrialization and society*, ed. Bert Hoselitz and Wilbert Moore. The
        Hague: UNESCO Mouton.
House, James.
    1974. The effects of occupational stress on physical health. In *Work and the quality
        of life*, ed. James O'Toole. Cambridge, Mass.: MIT Press.
Hunnius, Gerry; Garson, G.; and Case, John, eds.
    1973. *Workers' control*. New York: Random House.
Hunter, Lawrence, and Reid, Graham.
    1968. *Urban worker mobility*. Paris: Organization for Economic Cooperation and
        Development.
Husen, Torsten, ed.
    1967. *International study of achievement in mathematics: A comparison of twelve
        countries*. New York: John Wiley and Sons.
Hyodo, Tsutomu.
    1971. *Nihon ni okeru rōshi kankei no tenkai* (The development of industrial rela-
        tions in Japan). Tokyo: Tokyo University Press.
Inagami, Takeshi.
    1975. Keiei sanka to rōdō ishiki (Worker participation and worker consciousness).
        Nihon Rōdō Kyōkai Zasshi 17 (September):2–14.
Inoue, Shozo.
    1975. Aspects of international labor markets: The Japanese case. Unpublished
        manuscript.
Institute of Statistical Mathematics, Japan.
    1975. *Dai 3 Nihonjin no kokuminsei (The national character of the Japanese peo-
        ple: Volume 3)*. Tokyo: Shiseido.
International Labour Office.
    1975. *Yearbook of labour statistics*. Geneva: International Labour Office.
International Metalworkers Federation—Japan Council.
    1974. *Sabu, Borubo, sagyō saisoshiki seminā: Sanka hōkoku (Saab and Volvo—
        work reorganization seminar: Joint report)*. Tokyo: International Metal-
        workers Federation.
Ishida, Takeshi.
    1971. *Japanese society*. New York: Random House.
Ishikawa, Kaoru.
    1968. *QC circles activities*. Tokyo: Union of Japanese Scientists and Engineers.
Jagdeo, Tirbani.

1975. Guyana and Trinidad: Comparative analysis of social conflict. Ph.D. dissertation, University of Michigan.

Japan Federation of Employers' Associations.
1960. *Chingin taikei no kindaika to shokumu bunseki (Modernization of the wage structure and job analysis).* Tokyo: Japan Federation of Employers' Associations.

1971. *Waga kuni rōmu kanri no genkyō (The present situation of personnel management in our country).* Third Personnel Management Census. Tokyo: Japan Federation of Employers' Associations.

1975. *Waga kuni rōmu kanri no genkyō (The present situation of personnel management in our country).* Fourth Personnel Management Census. Tokyo: Japan Federation of Employers' Associations.

Japan Institute of Labour.
1973. Labor management communications and worker participation. *Japan Labor Bulletin* 12 (October): 6–8.

1974. *Japan labour statistics.* Tokyo: Japan Institute of Labour.

1975. *Haichi tenkan o meguru rōshi kankei (Industrial relations centering on job transfers: Survey results).* Tokyo: Japan Institute of Labour.

Japan Productivity Center.
1975. *Katsuyō rōdō tōkei (Practical labor statistics).* Tokyo: Japan Productivity Center.

1976. *Katsuyō rōdō tōkei (Practical labor statistics).* Tokyo: Japan Productivity Center.

Japanese National Commission for UNESCO.
1972. *Technical and technological education in Japan.* Tokyo: Japanese Commission for UNESCO.

Jedel, Michael, and Kujawa, Duane.
1976. *Management and employment practices of foreign direct investors in the United States.* Atlanta: Georgia State University.

Jenkins, David.
1973. *Job power.* New York: Doubleday.

Johnson, Richard, and Ouchi, William.
1974. Made in America (under Japanese management). *Harvard Business Review* 52, no. 5, pp. 61–69.

Johnson, Terrence.
1972. *Professions and power.* London: Macmillan.

Juran, J. N.
1967. The QC circle phenomenon. *Industrial Quality Control* 23:329–36.

JUSE (Union of Japanese Scientists and Engineers).
1970. *1970 nendo Demingushō jushōsha narabi ni Demingushō jisshishō jushōsha hōkoku kōen yōshi (Announcement of the essential lectures for the 1970 Deming Prize winners as well as the Deming Prize winners for best execution).* Tokyo: JUSE.

Kahn, Robert.
1972. The meaning of work: Interpretations and proposals for measurement. In *The human meaning of social change*, ed. Angus Campbell and Philip Converse. New York: Russell Sage Foundation.

Kasl, Stanislav.
1974. Work and mental health. In *Work and the quality of life*, ed. James O'Toole. Cambridge, Mass.: MIT Press.

————; Gore, S.; and Cobb, Sidney.
　1975. The experience of losing a job: Reported changes in health, symptoms and illness behavior. *Psychosomatic Medicine* 37:106–22.
Katz, Daniel.
　1975. The motivational basis of organizational behavior. In *Motivation and work behavior*, ed. Richard Steers and Lyman Porter. New York: McGraw-Hill.
Kawashima, Takeyoshi.
　1964. *Ideorogī toshite no kazokuseido* (*The family system as ideology*). Tokyo: Iwanami Shoten.
Keiya, Yoshio.
　1972. Some aspects of workers' participation in industry in Japan. In *Proceedings of the 1971 Asian Regional Conference on Industrial Relations*. Tokyo: Japan Institute of Labour.
Kelly, Jonathan.
　1973. Causal chain models for the socioeconomic career. *American Sociological Review* 38:481–93.
Kerr, Clark.
　1964. The Balkanization of labor markets. In *Labor mobility and economic opportunity*, ed. E. W. Bakke et al. Cambridge, Mass.: MIT Press.
————, and Siegel, Al.
　1969. Inter-industry propensity to strike. In *Collective bargaining: Selected readings*, ed. Allan Flanders. Harmondsworth, England: Penguin Books.
————, et al.
　1960. *Industrialism and industrial man*. Cambridge, Mass.: Harvard University Press.
Kindleberger, Charles.
　1967. *Europe's postwar growth: The role of labor supply*. Cambridge, Mass.: Harvard University Press.
Kirchheimer, Otto.
　1965. Confining conditions and revolutionary breakthroughs. *American Political Science Review* 59:964–74.
Kishimoto, Eitaro.
　1962. *Nihon chinginron-shi* (*History of wage problems in Japan*). Kyoto: Mineruva Shobō.
Kobayashi, Ken'ichi.
　1974. Kigyōnai rōdō shijō to rōdōsha ishiki no henka (Internal labor market and the changing attitude among workers). *Nihon Rōdō Kyōkai Zasshi* 16 (March): 13–28.
Kobayashi, Shigeru.
　1966. *Sony wa hito o ikasu* (*Sony revitalizes its employees*). Tokyo: Nippon Keiei Shuppan Kai.
Kohn, Melvin.
　1976. Occupational structure and alienation. *American Journal of Sociology* 82:111–30.
Koike, Kazuo.
　1962. *Nihon no chingin kōshō* (*Wage bargaining in Japan*). Tokyo: Tokyo University Press.
　1975. Internal labor markets and industrial relations systems on the floor in Japan. Unpublished manuscript.
Koshiro, Kazutoshi.

274

1975. Bijon no iki o dekinai Nihonteki keiei sanka ron (Theory of Japanese-style management participation is no better than an ideal vision). *Gekkan Ekonomisuto* 18 (August):80–86.

1977. Humane organization of work in the plants: Production techniques and the organization of work in Japanese factories. Paper presented at the Sixth Japanese-German Economic and Social Conference, Düsseldorf, October 3–9.

Kraar, Louis.

1975. The Japanese are coming—with their own style of management. *Fortune* 91, no. 3, pp. 116–21, 160–64.

Kuznets, Simon.

1966. *Modern economic growth*. New Haven: Yale University Press.

Landes, David.

1965. Japan and Europe: Contrasts in industrialization. In *The state and economic enterprise in Japan*, ed. William Lockwood. Princeton, N.J.: Princeton University Press.

Large, Stephen.

1976. Nishio Suehiro and the Japanese social democratic movement, 1920–1940. *Journal of Asian Studies* 36:37–56.

Lebergott, Stanley.

1968. Labor force and employment trends. In *Indicators of social change*, ed. Eleanor Sheldon and Wilber Moore. New York: Russell Sage Foundation.

Lebra, Takie.

1976. *Japanese patterns of behavior*. Honolulu: University Press of Hawaii.

Leghorn, Rex.

1976. Inter-firm mobility as a stochastic process: Organizational attachment in work careers of men in Detroit and Yokohama. Ph.D. dissertation, University of Michigan.

Leibenstein, Harvey.

1976. *Beyond economic man*. Cambridge, Mass.: Harvard University Press.

Lester, Richard.

1967. Pay differentials by size of establishment. *Industrial Relations* 7, no. 1, pp. 57–67.

Levine, Solomon.

1965. Labor markets and collective bargaining in Japan. In *The state and economic enterprise in Japan*, ed. William Lockwood. Princeton, N.J.: Princeton University Press.

Levinson, Charles.

1974. *Industry's democratic revolution*. London: George Allen and Unwin Ltd.

Levitan, Sar, and Johnston, William.

1973. Job redesign, reform, enrichment—exploring the limitations. *Monthly Labor Review* 96, no. 7, pp. 35–41.

Levy, Marion.

1966. *Modernization and the structure of societies*. Princeton, N.J.: Princeton University Press.

Livernash, Robert.

1957. The internal wage structure. In *New concepts in wage determination*, ed. George Taylor and Frank Pierson. New York: McGraw-Hill.

McGregor, Douglas.

1960. *The human side of enterprise*. New York: McGraw-Hill.

Magota, Ryohei.

1965. Senji rōdōron no gimon (Some questions on wartime labor). *Nihon Rōdō Kyōkai Zasshi* 7 (July):11–23.

Mainichi (newspaper).

1973. Sagyō ni "ningenmi" o konbeyā hoshiki e kaizen (Improving conveyor belt methods to bring about humanity on the production line). 21 September.

Mannheim, Karl.

1940. *Man and society in an age of reconstruction*. New York: Harcourt.

March, James, and Simon, Herbert.

1958. *Organizations*. New York: John Wiley and Sons.

Marsh, Robert, and Mannari, Hiroshi.

1971. Lifetime employment in Japan: Roles, norms and values. *American Journal of Sociology* 76:795–812.

1976. *Modernization and the Japanese factory*. Princeton, N.J.: Princeton University Press.

Marshall, Byron.

1967. *Capitalism and nationalism in prewar Japan*. Stanford: Stanford University Press.

Maslow, Abraham.

1954. Motivation and personality. New York: Harper and Row.

Masutsugu, Eto.

1975. Supuraisusemento nendo no baratsuki taisaku (Measure to reduce variance in splicing cement viscosity). *FQC* 2:41–45.

Matossian, Mary.

1966. Ideologies of delayed industrialization. In *Political development and social change*, ed. Jason Finkle and Richard Gable. New York: John Wiley and Sons.

Matsumoto, Y. Scott.

1970. Social stress and coronary heart disease in Japan: A hypothesis. *Milbank Memorial Fund Quarterly* 48:9–36.

Matsushima, Shizuo.

1962. *Rōmu kanri no Nihonteki tokushitsu no hensen (Characteristics and changes in Japanese personnel management)*. Tokyo: Daiamondosha.

Men-Koy Wong, Lawrence.

1973. Managerial ideologies in industrial society: The construction of the corporate world-view. Ph.D. dissertation, University of Michigan.

Merton, Robert.

1957. *Social theory and social structure*. Revised ed. Glencoe, Ill.: Free Press.

Minami, Ryoshin.

1973. *The turning point in economic development: Japan's experience*. Tokyo: Kinokuniya Shoten.

Mincer, Jacob.

1962. On-the-job training: Costs, returns, and some implications. *Journal of Political Economy* 70 (Supplement):50–79.

1970. The distribution of labor incomes: A survey with special reference to the human capital approach. *Journal of Economic Literature* 8:1–26.

Ministry of Education, Science and Culture, Japan.

1976. *Course of study for upper secondary schools in Japan*. Tokyo: Ministry of Education, Science and Culture.

276

Ministry of Labor, Japan.

1972. *Kinrōsha seikatsu ishiki chōsa hōkoku: showa 46 (Report on the attitude survey of wage earners' livelihood: 1971)*. Tokyo: Ministry of Labor.

1972a. *Koyō dōkō chosa hōkoku: 46 (Survey of employment trends: 1971)*. Tokyo: Ministry of Labor.

1973. *Rōdō keiei no bunseki: Showa 47 (Analysis of the labor economy: 1972)*. Tokyo: Ministry of Labor.

1974. *Koyō kanri shindan shihyō (Indicators of the conditions of employment administration)*. Tokyo: Employment Security Office.

1975. *Rōdō hakusho: Showa 49 (Labor white paper: 1974)*. Tokyo: Ministry of Labor.

1975a. *Rōdōsha fukushi shisetu seido to chōsa hōkoku (Research results of worker welfare benefits systems)*. Tokyo: Statistical Information Bureau.

1976. *Rōdō hakusho 50 (Labor white paper: 1975)*. Tokyo: Ministry of Labor.

Mire, Joseph.

1975. Worker's morale in Japan. *Monthly Labor Review* 98, no. 6, pp. 49–53.

Montagna, Paul.

1977. *Occupations and society*. New York: John Wiley and Sons.

Moore, Wilbert.

1962. The attributes of an industrial order. In *Man, work and society*, ed. Sigmund Nosow and William Form. New York: Basic Books.

Morrisset, I.

1958. The economic structure of American cities. *Regional Science Association, Papers and Proceedings* 4:239–56. Washington, D.C.: U.S. Government Printing Office.

Motofuji, Frank.

1973. *"The factory ship" and "the absentee landlord."* Tokyo: University of Tokyo Press.

Murray, David.

1930. *Chapters in the history of bookkeeping accountancy and commercial arithmetic*. Glasgow: Jackson, Wylie and Co.

Muto, Sanji.

1963. *Mutō Sanji zenshū (Collected works of Mutō Sanji)*. Tokyo: Shunjūsha.

Nagai, Michio.

1971. *Higher education in Japan*. Tokyo: University of Tokyo Press.

Naikaku Tōkei Kyoku.

1935. *Rōdō tōkei yōran (Handbook of labor statistics)*. Tokyo: Government Bureau of Statistics.

Nakane, Chie.

1970. *Japanese society*. Berkeley and Los Angeles: University of California Press.

Nakayama, Ichiro.

1974. *Rōshi kankei no keizai shakai gaku (The economic sociology of labour-management relations)*. Tokyo: Japan Institute of Labour.

1975. *Industrialization and labour-management relations in Japan*. Tokyo: Japan Institute of Labour.

Nakayama, Saburo, ed.

1972. *Zen'in sanka keiei no kangaekata to jissai (All-employee management participation: Viewpoints and practices)*. Tokyo: Japan Federation of Employers' Associations.

National Manpower Policy Task Force.
>   1970. *Conference on upgrading and new careers*. Washington, D.C.: National
>   Manpower Policy Task Force.

Nelson, Daniel.
>   1975. *Managers and workers*. Madison, Wis.: University of Wisconsin Press.

New York Times.
>   1977. Management: In-house education by companies. June 11.

Nishiyama, Daiso, and Sabao, Tsuyoshi.
>   1970. Technical skill evaluation system. *Proceedings*, International Conference on
>   Quality Control, 1969. Tokyo: Union of Japanese Scientists and Engineers.

Noda, Kazuo.
>   1975. Big business organization. In *Modern Japanese organization and decision-
>   making*, ed. Ezra Vogel. Berkeley and Los Angeles: University of California
>   Press.

Northrup, Herbert, et al.
>   1975. *In-plant upgrading and mobility patterns*. Final Report: Office of Research
>   and Development Manpower Administration, U.S. Department of Labor.
>   Miscellaneous Series No. 21. Philadelphia. Industrial Relations Unit,
>   Wharton School, University of Pennsylvania.

Odaka, Konosuke.
>   1967. The structure of Japanese labor markets. *Kikan Riron Keizaigaku (Economic
>   Studies Quarterly)* 18 (June):25–42.

Odaka, Kunio.
>   1961. Sangyō no kindaika to keiei no minshuka (Modernization of industry and
>   democratization of management). *Chūō Kōron* 26 (July):25–44.
>   1975. *Toward industrial democracy*. Cambridge, Mass.: Harvard University Press.

Office of the Prime Minister, Japan.
>   1956. *Chūkyō tekkōgyō chōsa hōkokusho (Survey report on the steel industry of
>   Communist China)*. Vol. 1. Tokyo: Office of the Prime Minister.
>   1967. *Nihon no shūgyō kōzō (Employment structure of Japan: Summary of the
>   results of 1968 employment-status survey)*. Tokyo: Bureau of Statistics.
>   1970. *Nihon hyōjun shokugyō bunrui (Japan standard classification of occupa-
>   tions)*. Tokyo: Administrative Management Agency.
>   1972. *Kokusei chōsa hōkoku, Showa 45 (1970 population census of Japan)*. Vol.
>   3, part 14, Kanagawa ken. Tokyo: Bureau of Statistics.
>   1973. *Sekai seinen ishiki chōsa hōkokusho (Report on the world youth attitude
>   survey)*. Tokyo: Youth Policy Office.
>   1973a. *Jigyōsho tōkei chōsa hōkoku (1972 establishment census of Japan)*. Vol. 1.
>   Tokyo: Bureau of Statistics.
>   1974. *White paper on schoolchildren and youth*. Tokyo: Bureau of Statistics.
>   1975. *Shūgyō kōzō kihon chōsa hōkoku, Showa 49 (1974 employment status
>   survey)*. Tokyo: Bureau of Statistics.
>   1976. *Nihon no jūtaku (House of Japan: Summary of the results of the 1973
>   housing survey of Japan)*. Tokyo: Bureau of Statistics.

Ohkawa, Kazushi.
>   1962. *Nihon keizai bunseki (Analysis of the Japanese economy)*. Tokyo:
>   Shunjūsha.
>   ———, and Rosovsky, Henry.
>   1973. *Japanese economic growth*. Stanford: Stanford University Press.

Oi, Walter.
    1962. Labor as a quasi-fixed factor. *Journal of Political Economy* 70:538–55.
Okamoto, Hideaki.
    1971. Work and leisure in Japan. *Japan Labor Bulletin* 10, no. 10, pp. 1–8.
    1974. The union management relationship at the enterprise level. *Japan Labor Bulletin* 13, no. 7, pp. 5–8.
    1975. Jizen kyōgisei no ronri (The logic of the prior consultation system). In *Haichi tenkan o meguru rōshi kankei*, ed. Nihon Rōdō Kyōkai. Tokyo: Japan Institute of Labour.
Okochi, Kazuo.
    1965. The characteristics of labor-management relations in Japan. *Journal of Social and Political Ideas in Japan* 3 (December):44–49.
Okuda, Kenji.
    1968–71. Nihon no nōritsu undōshi (History of the Japanese movement). *IE Review*, nos. 9–12.
Ono, Tsuneo.
    1973. Intra-firm labor markets: Personnel practices and mechanisms for adjustment. *Japan Labor Bulletin* 12, no. 4, pp. 13–16.
    1975. Kanri shoku no chingin kettei (Salary determination for managerial personnel). *Nihon Rōdō Kyōkai Zasshi* 17 (May):28–38.
Organization for Economic Cooperation and Development (OECD).
    1965. *Wages and labour mobility*. Paris: Organization for Economic Cooperation and Development.
    1973. *Manpower policy in Japan*. Paris: Organization for Economic Cooperation and Development.
Ornstein, Michael.
    1976. *Entry into the American labor force*. New York: Academic Press.
Osako, Masako.
    1973. Auto assembly technology and social integration in a Japanese factory: A case study. Ph.D. dissertation, Northwestern University.
Palmer, Gladys.
    1963. *The reluctant job changer*. Philadelphia: University of Pennsylvania Press.
Parsons, Carole, ed.
    1972. *America's uncounted people*. Washington, D.C.: National Academy of Sciences.
Peck, Merton, and Tamura, Shuji.
    1976. Technology. In *Asia's new giant*, ed. Hugh Patrick and Henry Rosovsky. Washington, D.C.: Brookings Institution.
Peking Review.
    1976. Always act as a locomotive in grasping revolution, promoting production. November 12. Pp. 9–10.
Perlman, Selig.
    1928. *A theory of the labor movement*. New York: Augustus Kelley. Reprint 1968.
Perrow, Charles.
    1972. *Complex organizations: A critical essay*. Glenview, Ill.: Scott, Foresman and Co.
Piore, Michael.
    1974. Upward mobility, job monotony and labor market structure. In *Work and the quality of life*, ed. James O'Toole. Cambridge, Mass.: MIT Press.

1975. Notes for a theory of labor market stratification. In *Labor market segmentation*, ed. R. Edwards et al. Lexington, Mass.: Heath.

Portes, Alejandro.

1973. Modernity and development. A critique. *Studies in Comparative International Development* 8:247–49.

1976. On the sociology of national development: Theories and issues. *American Journal of Sociology* 82:55–85.

Pugh, D. S., et al.

1969. Dimensions of organizational structure. *Administrative Science Quarterly* 14:211–28.

Quinn, Robert, and Shepard, Linda.

1974. *The 1972–73 quality of employment survey*. Ann Arbor, Mich.: Institute of Social Research.

Ranis, Gustav.

1957. Factor proportions in Japanese economic development. *American Economic Review* 47:594–607.

Rees, Albert, and Schultz, George.

1970. *Workers and wages in an urban labor market*. Chicago: University of Chicago Press.

Reubens, Beatrice.

1973. Manpower training in Japan. *Monthly Labor Review* 96, no. 9, pp. 16–24.

Reynolds, Lloyd.

1951. *The structure of labor markets: Wages and labor mobility in theory and practice*. New York: Harper and Row.

1974. *Labor economics and labor relations*. 6th ed. Englewood Cliffs, N.J.: Prentice-Hall.

Robinson, John; Athanasious, Robert; and Head, Kendra.

1969. *Measures of occupational attitudes and occupational characteristics*. Ann Arbor, Mich.: Institute for Social Research.

Rohlen, Thomas.

1974. *For harmony and strength*. Berkeley and Los Angeles: University of California Press.

1975. The company work group. In *Modern Japanese organization and decision-making*, ed. Ezra Vogel. Berkeley and Los Angeles: University of California Press.

Rosenberg, Nathan.

1972. *Technology and American economic growth*. New York: Harper and Row.

1976. *Perspectives on technology*. Cambridge: Cambridge University Press.

Rosovsky, Henry.

1966. *Industrialization in two systems*. New York: John Wiley and Sons.

Roth, Guenther.

1963. *The social democrats in imperial Germany*. Totowa, N.J.: Bedminister Press.

Rueschemeyer, Dietrich.

1977. Structural differentiation, efficiency, and power. *American Journal of Sociology* 83:1–25.

Ryder, Norman.

1965. The cohort as a concept in the study of social change. *American Sociological Review* 30:843–61.

Sahlins, Marshall, and Service, Elman.

1960. *Evolution and culture*. Ann Arbor, Mich.: University of Michigan Press.

Salancik, Gerald, and Pfeffer, Jeffrey.

1974. The bases and use of power in organizational decision making: The case of a university. *Administrative Science Quarterly* 19:135–51.

Sato, Ken'ichi.

1972. Toyota Shatai ni okeru rain no jinji kanri (Personnel administration on the line at Toyota Auto Body). *Hyōjunka to Hinshitsu Kanri* 25 (September): 15–20.

Saxonhouse, Gary.

1974. A tale of technological diffusion in the Meiji period. *Journal of Economic History* 36:149–65.

In press. Productivity change and labor absorption in cotton spinning: 1891–1935. *Quarterly Journal of Economics*.

Schleicher, William.

1977. Quality control circles save Lockheed nearly $3 million in two years. *Quality* (May):14–17.

Scott, Richard.

1975. Organizational structure. *Annual Review of Sociology* 1:1–20.

Shelly and Company.

1971. *Upgrading the workforce: Problems and possibilities*. Washington, D.C.: U.S. Department of Health, Education and Welfare, Office of Education.

Shewhart, W. A.

1931. *The economic control of quality of manufactured products*. New York: Van Nostrand.

Shiba, Shoji.

1973. *A cross-national comparison of labor management with reference to technology transfer*. Institute of Developing Economies Occasional Papers Series No. 11. Tokyo: Institute of Developing Economies.

1973a. *Rōdō no kokusai hikaku (An international comparison of labor)*. Tokyo: Tōyō Keizai Shinpōsha.

Shimada, Haruo.

1968–69. *Nenkōsei no shiteki keisei ni tsuite-senzen Yahata Seitetsujo no jirei kenkyū (Historical formation of the lifetime-employment system: A case study of the Yahata Steel Corporation)*. Management and labor Studies Series No. 227. Tokyo: Institute of Management and Labor Studies, Keio University.

1974. The structure of earnings and investments in human resources: A comparison between the United States and Japan. Ph.D. dissertation, University of Wisconsin.

1975. Nenkōseiron to kokusai hikaku no hōhō (The concept of the *nenkō* system and the methodology of international comparison). *Nihon Rōdō Kyōkai Zasshi* 17 (May):17–27.

1976. Kajō koyōron o kangaeru (Thoughts on an analysis of surplus employment). *Nihon Keizai Shinbun*, April 11–12.

1977. The Japanese labor market after the oil crisis: A factual report. Supplementary paper presented at the 423rd Experts' Meeting of OECD (March): 1–42.

Shirai, Taishiro.

1975. Nihon teki keiei sanka no mondaiten (Key questions concerning Japanese-style management participation). *Tōyō Keizai*, special issue, no. 31 (January), pp. 70–77.

Siegel, Paul, and Cole, Robert E.

1976. Inter-firm mobility in comparative perspective. Working paper, Center for Social Organization, University of Michigan.

Simon, Herbert.

1965. *Administrative behavior*. 2nd ed. New York: Free Press.

Skinner, William, and Winckler, Edwin.

1969. Compliance succession in rural Communist China: A cyclical theory. In *A sociological reader on complex organizations*, ed. Amitai Etzioni. 2nd ed. New York: Holt, Rinehart and Winston.

Sloan, Alfred.

1964. *My years with General Motors*. Ed. John McDonald with Catherine Stevens. New York: Doubleday.

Smith, Thomas.

1955. *Political change and industrial development in Japan: Government enterprise, 1868–1880*. Stanford: Stanford University Press.

1959. *The agrarian origins of modern Japan*. Stanford: Stanford University Press.

1963. Pre-modern economic growth: Japan and the west. *Past and Present* 60: 127–60.

1969. Farm family by-employments in preindustrial Japan. *Journal of Economic History* 29:687–715.

Soeda, Mitsuteru.

1965. *Nihon no shokumukyū (Job-based wages in Japan)*. Fukuoka: Kyūdai Keizaigaku Kenkyū.

Somers, Gerald, and Tsuda, Masumi.

1966. Job vacancies and structural change in Japanese labor markets. In *The measurement and interpretation of job vacancies: A conference report*, ed. National Bureau of Economic Research. New York: Columbia University Press.

Sørenson, Aage.

1974. A model for occupational careers. *American Journal of Sociology* 80:44–57.

1975. The structure of intra-generational mobility. *American Sociological Review* 40:456–71.

1975a. Growth in occupational achievement: Social mobility or investments in human capital. In *Social indicator models*, ed. Kenneth Land and Seymour Spilerman. New York: Russell Sage Foundation.

Steers, Richard, and Porter, Lyman.

1975. *Motivation and work behavior*. New York: McGraw-Hill.

Stewman, Shelby.

1975. Two Markov models of open system occupational mobility: Underlying conceptualizations and empirical tests. *American Sociological Review* 40: 298–321.

Stinchcombe, Arthur.

1959. Bureaucratic and craft administration of production: A comparative study. *Administrative Science Quarterly* 4:168–87.

1970. Organized dependency relations and social stratification. In *The logic of social hierarchies*, ed. Edward Laumann et al. Chicago: Markham.

1974. *Creating efficient industrial administrations*. New York: Academic Press.

282

1975. Social structure and politics. In *Handbook of political science* ed. Fred Greenstein and Nelson Polsby. Vol. 3. Reading, Mass.: Addison-Wesley.

Stone, Katherine.

1974. The origins of job structures in the steel industry. *Review of Radical Politi cal Economies* 6 (Summer):113–73. Reprinted in a slightly briefer versira in *Root and branch*. Greenwich, Conn.: Fawcett Crest.

Stouffer, Samuel, et al.

1949. *The American soldier*. Vol. 1. Princeton, N.J.: Princeton University Press.

Sugimoto, Yasuo.

1972. The advancing QC circle movement. In *Japan quality control circles*, ed. Asian Productivity Organization. Tokyo: Asian Productivity Organization.

Sumiya, Mikio.

1958. *Nihon chinrōdōshiron (An analysis of wage labor in Japan)*. Revised ed. Tokyo: Tokyo University Press.

1966. The development of Japanese labor-relations. *Developing Economies* 4: 449–518.

1974. Nihon teki rōshi kankeiron no saikentō (Japanese labor-management relations revisited). Part I. *Nihon Rōdō Kyōkai Zasshi* 16 (August):2–10.

1974a. Nihon teki rōshi kankeiron no saikentō (Japanese labor-management relations revisited). Part II. *Nihon Rōdō Kyōkai Zasshi* 16 (October):2–11.

Summers, Clyde.

1976. Arbitration of unjust dismissal: A preliminary proposal. Unpublished manuscript, University of Pennsylvania.

Suttles, Gerald.

1973. *The social construction of communities*. Chicago: University of Chicago Press.

Taira, Koji.

1962. Characteristics of Japanese labor markets. *Economic Development and Cultural Change* 10:150–68.

1970. Entrepreneurship, management, and growth of firms: Cases from Japanese business history. Paper delivered at the Conference on Micro Aspects of Development, Chicago.

Takahashi, Ko.

1965. *Nihon rōshi kankei kenkyū (Research on Japanese type labor-management relations)*. Tokyo: Miraisha.

Takezawa, Shin'ichi.

1972. *Changing worker values and their policy implications in Japan*. International Conference on the Quality of Working Life. Harriman, N.Y.: Arden House.

1976. The quality of working life: Trends in Japan. *Labour and Society* 1:29–48.

Tanaka, Hirohide.

1977. Koyō kankō no Nichibei hikaku to kigyō taishitsu mondai (Questions concerning the character of the enterprise and U.S.-Japan employment practices). *Economy Society Policy* 10:36–41.

Tannenbaum, Arnold, et al.

1974. *Hierarchy in organizations*. San Francisco: Jossey-Bass.

Taylor, Frederick.

1911. *Shop management*. New York: Harper and Brothers.

1947. *Scientific management*. In *Compiled writings*. New York: Harper.

Thompson, E. P.

1963. *The making of the English working class*. New York: Random House.

Thompson, James.
   1967. *Organization in action*. New York: McGraw-Hill.
Thompson, Victor.
   1965. Bureaucracy and innovation. *Administrative Science Quarterly* 10:1–20.
Thorsrud, Einar.
   1969. *Mot en ny bedriftsorganisasjon* (*Toward a new performance organization*). Oslo: Tanum.
Thurow, Lester.
   1975. *Generating inequality*. New York: Basic Books.
Tichy, Noel.
   1976. When does work restructuring work? Organizational innovations at Volvo and GM. *Organizational Dynamics* 5, no. 1, pp. 63–80.
Tipps, Dean.
   1973. Modernization theory and the comparative study of societies: A critical perspective. *Comparative Studies in Society and History* 15:200–26.
Toffler, Alvin.
   1970. *Future shock*. New York: Random House.
Totten, George.
   1966. *The social democratic movement in prewar Japan*. New Haven: Yale University Press.
Treiman, Donald.
   1970. Industrialization and social stratification. In *Social stratification: Research and theory for the 1970s*, ed. Edward Laumann. New York: Bobbs-Merrill.
Tsuda, Masumi.
   1959. *Rōdō mondai to rōmu kanri* (*Labor problems and personnel management*). Kyoto: Mineruba Shobo.
   1968. *Nenkōteki rōshi kankei ron* (*Discussion of Nenkō-style industrial relations*). Kyoto: Mineruba.
   1975. Rōdōsha Jūyakusei no hatten to Nihon e no teigen (Development of worker-directorship in Europe: A proposal for Japanese industrial relations). *Nihon Rōdō Kyōkai Zasshi* 17 (January):4–17.
   1976. *Nihonteki keiei no yōgo* (*Protecting Japanese-style management*). Tokyo: Tōyō Keizai Shinposha.
   1977. Study of Japanese management development practices. *Hitotsubashi Journal of Social Studies* 9 (May):1–12.
Ueno, Hiroya, and Muto, Hiromichi.
   1974. The automobile industry of Japan. *Japanese Economic Studies* 3 (Fall): 3–90.
Umetani, Shun'ichiro.
   1968. Selected case studies of vocational training in Japanese manufacturing firms. M.S. dissertation, University of Wisconsin.
Union of Japanese Scientists and Engineers.
   1975. *QC sākuru kōryō* (*Main points of QC circles*). 9th printing. Tokyo: Union of Japanese Scientists and Engineers.
U.S. Bureau of the Census.
   1952. *Census of population, 1950*. Vol. 2. Characteristics of the population, Part 22, Michigan. Washington, D.C.: U.S. Government Printing Office.
   1961. *Historical statistics of the United States: Colonial times to 1957*. Washington, D.C.: U.S. Department of Commerce.

1971. *Alphabetical index of industries and occupations.* Washington, D.C.: U.S. Government Printing Office.

1972. *1970 census of population, Michigan, general social and economic characteristics, PC(1)–C24.* Washington, D.C.: U.S. Government Printing Office.

1972a. *Census of the population: 1970 detailed characteristics. Final report PC(1)* D24 Michigan.* Washington, D.C.: U.S. Government Printing Office.

1973. *Census of population, 1970.* Vol. 1. Characteristics of the population, Part 24, Michigan. Washington, D.C.: U.S. Government Printing Office.

U.S. Department of Health, Education and Welfare Special Task Force.

1973. *Work in America.* Cambridge, Mass.: MIT Press.

U.S. Department of Labor.

1964. *Formal occupational training of adult workers.* Manpower Automation Research Monograph No. 2. Washington, D.C.: Office of Manpower, Automation and Training.

1973. *Employment and earnings: United States, 1909–1972.* Bulletin 1312.9. Washington, D.C.: Bureau of Labor Statistics.

1973a. *Collective bargaining in the motor vehicle and motor vehicle equipment industry.* Washington, D.C.: Bureau of Labor Statistics.

Ushikubo, Hiroshi, et al.

1974. Foramu: "shokumu jūjitsuka" no Nihon teiki tenkai, II (Forum: Development of job enrichment in Japan, II). *Nihon Rōdō Kyōkai Zasshi* 16 (February):44–56.

1974a. Foramu: "shokumu jūjitsuka" no Nihon teki tenkai, III (Forum: Development of job enrichment in Japan, III). *Nihon Rōdō Kyōkai Zasshi* 16 (March):42–55.

Van Maanen, John.

1977. *Organizational careers: Some new perspectives.* New York: John Wiley and Sons.

Veblen, Thorsten.

1915. *Imperial Germany and the industrial revolution.* Ann Arbor, Mich.: University of Michigan Press. Reprint 1966.

1934. The opportunity of Japan. In *Essays in our changing order*, ed. Leon Ardzrooni. New York: Viking.

Verba, Sidney, et al.

1970. Sequences and development. In *Crises and sequences in political development.* ed. Leonard Binder et al. Princeton, N.J.: Princeton University Press.

Vogel, Ezra.

1963. *Japan's new middle class.* Berkeley and Los Angeles: University of California Press.

1967. Kinship structure, migration to the city, and modernization. In *Aspects of social change in modern Japan*, ed. Ronald Dore. Princeton, N.J.: Princeton University Press.

———, ed.

1975. *Modern Japanese organization and decision-making.* Berkeley and Los Angeles: University of California Press.

Wallerstein, Immanuel.

1974. *The modern world-system.* New York: Academic Press.

Weber, Max.

1947. *The theory of social and economic organization.* Glencoe, Ill.: Free Press.

Weinberg, Edgar.

1976. Labor-management cooperation: A report on recent initiatives. *Monthly Labor Review* 99, no. 4, pp. 13–22.

Weinberg, Nat.

1974. Multinationals and unions as innovators and change agents. Paper delivered at the Conference on Industrial Relations Problems Raised by Multinationals in Advanced Industrial Societies, Michigan State University, November 10–13.

White, Harrison.

1970. *Chains of opportunity: Systems models of mobility in organizations.* Cambridge, Mass.: Harvard University Press.

White, James.

1974. Tradition and politics in studies of contemporary Japan. *World Politics* 26:400–27.

Whitehill, Arthur, and Takezawa, Shin'ichi.

1968. *The other worker.* Honolulu: East-West Center Press.

Whyte, Martin.

1973. Bureaucracy and modernization in China: The Maoist critique. *American Sociological Review* 38:149–63.

1974. *Small groups and political rituals in China.* Berkeley and Los Angeles: University of California Press.

Wilensky, Harold.

1961. Orderly careers and social participation: The impact of work history on social integration in the middle class. *American Sociological Review* 26:521–39.

1964. Work careers and social integration. In *Comparative social problems*, ed. S. N. Eisenstadt. New York: Free Press.

Wilkinson, Thomas.

1965. *The urbanization of Japanese labor, 1868–1955.* Amherst, Mass.: University of Massachusetts Press.

Wolfbein, Seymour.

1971. *Work in American society.* Glenview, Ill.: Scott, Foresman and Co.

Woodward, Joan.

1970. *Industrial organization: Behavior and control.* London: Oxford University Press.

Wool, Harold.

1973. What's wrong with work in America? *Monthly Labor Review* 96, no. 3, pp. 38–44.

Yasui, Jiro.

1975. Rōdō no ningenka to sanka kakumei (The humanization of work and the participation revolution: A personal view of Japanese efforts). *Nihon Rōdō Kyōkai Zasshi* 17 (May):2–16.

Yoshino, M. Y.

1968. *Japan's managerial system.* Cambridge, Mass.: MIT Press.

Young, David.

1974. Stress and disease in Japan. *Asian Profile* 2:547–75.

Zald, Mayer.

1970. *Power in organizations.* Nashville, Tenn.: Vanderbilt University Press.

Zenkoku Shōken Torihikijo.

1975. *Kabushiki bumpu jōkyō chōsa, Showa 49 nendo (Survey of stock distribution, fiscal year 1974).* Tokyo: National Stock Exchange.

INDEX

Ordinance Prohibiting Changes in Place of Employment (Japan 1940), 12
Ornstein, Michael, 36, 37
Osako, Masako, 113, 240
Oyakata-kokata (master-apprentice) relations, 17, 18, 27, 249. *See also* Employees, employer-employee relations

Pakistan, 200
Palmer, Gladys, 37
Paternalism: in Japanese industry, 21, 22, 109, 110, 127, 229, 246, 252
Peace Policy Law (Japan 1900), 19
Peck, Merton, and Tamura, Shuji, 43
Perlman, Selig, 102
Permanent employment, 4, 9, 10, 12, 18, 19, 22, 31, 39, 60, 65, 88, 103, 110, 117, 120, 125, 165, 220, 241, 244, 250, 255, 263; analysis of, 22, 24, 25; benefits of, 11, 16, 19, 20, 61, 257, 259, 260, 261; and branch house system (Tokugawa), 16; consequences of, 14, 16, 62; cultural resources for, 23, 24; definition of, 11; determining, 60–63; development of, 13, 20, 21, 22, 24, 261; disadvantages of, 20; and education, 66; employer-employee relations, 14, 15, 17; and firm size, 66, 67, 78; ideology behind, 14, 15, 16, 18; and *ie* and *dozoku* systems, 16; and inter-firm job mobility, 12, 14, 39, 40, 41; and labor unions, 103, 259, 260; in large firms, 14, 22, 40; and late-development hypothesis, 29, 30; and layoffs and discharges, 62, 63, 256, 257, 258, 261; and *nenkō*, 19, 41; origins of, 11–22, 24, 33; practice of, 4, 11, 12, 15, 16, 40, 60, 62, 103, 244, 248, 256; relevance to small firms, 21; role of textile industry in, 15, 16; role of training in, 39, 41; worker acceptance of, 14, 18, 19, 20, 24, 257, 261
Perrow, Charles, 166, 209
Personnel Administration and Development Staff (General Motors), 169
Philippines, the, 95, 232
Piore, Michael, 38, 81, 105. *See also* Doeringer, Peter, and Piore, Michael
Population Census of Japan (1970), 75
Prime Minister's Office (Japan), 95
Prussia, 27

Quality control, 6, 124, 136, 164; development of, 136, 137; motivation for, 136, 141, 142, 143
Quality control circles, 6, 132, 134, 179, 180, 202, 203, 207, 212, 217, 220, 222, 225, 227, 236, 253, 254, 255; characteristics of, 137–41; definition of, 135; development of, 135, 140, 141; motivation for, 141–43. *See* Job redesign; Toyota Auto Body, quality control circles at

Quality of Employment Survey (1972–73) (United States), 226
Quinn, Robert, and Shepard, Linda, 226

Railway Ministry (Japan), 110
Rees, Albert, and Schultz, George, 3
Research Committee on the Study of Japanese National Character, 237
Reverse convergence hypothesis. *See* Dore, Ronald, and convergence hypothesis
Reynolds, Lloyd, 96
Rice Riots (Japan 1918), 20
Richardson, Eliot, 124
Rohlen, Thomas, 1, 169, 213
Rosenberg, Nathan, 197
Russia, *See* Soviet Union
Russian Revolution, 20
Russo-Japanese War, 14, 17, 19
Ryder, Norman, 35

Saab, 124, 127
Sabao, Tsuyoshi, 159
Saionji cabinet, 15
Sakurada, Mr. (chairman of *Nikkeiren*), 133
Samurai, 26, 28
Scandinavia, 127, 203
Scanlon plan, 142, 143
Schmoller, Gustav, 102
Scientific management, 103, 104, 106, 108, 110, 201, 229. *See also* Taylorism
Seniority, 2, 3, 4, 41, 82, 96, 100, 101, 105, 107, 110, 114, 241, 257. *See also* Toyota Auto Body, job-ranking system at; Wage determination
Shewhart, W. A., 135
Shiba, Shoji, 100, 200
Shimada, Haruo, 18, 95
Shokumukyū (job-based wage system), 130
Shōshūdanshuji (small-groupism), 132, 134
Shūshin kōyō, 62. *See also* Permanent employment, determining
Simmel, Georg, 102
Simon, Herbert, 103
Singapore, 200
Smith, Adam, 101
Smith, Thomas, 32
Social change: in late-development hypothesis, 5; tradition in, 4, 6
Socialist Party (Japan), 204
Social organization of work, 1, 4, 8, 10, 14, 15, 16, 17, 219; career enlargement, 8, 220, 221, 222; compared to West, 5, 8, 18; and convergence hypothesis of, 1, 8. *See also* Industrial relations practices, Japan
Social Security Administration's Continuous Work History Sample, 94
Social structure and values, 1, 8, 17, 25, 28, 110
Sohyo Federation, 217
Sony, 131
Sørenson, Aage, 34, 35

292

293